THE ROYAL NAVY AND THE NORTHWEST COAST OF NORTH AMERICA, 1810-1914:

A STUDY OF BRITISH MARITIME ASCENDANCY

The

Royal Navy

and the

Northwest Coast

of

North America,

1810-1914:

*A Study of British
Maritime Ascendancy*

Barry M. Gough

*University of British Columbia Press
Vancouver*

THE ROYAL NAVY AND THE NORTHWEST COAST OF NORTH AMERICA, 1810-1914:
A STUDY OF BRITISH MARITIME ASCENDANCY

This book has been published with the help of a grant from the Social Science Research Council of Canada, using funds provided by the Canada Council.

International Standard Book Number 0-7748-0000-3

Printed in Canada

To
P.W.B.

CONTENTS

LIST OF ILLUSTRATIONS AND MAPS

ILLUSTRATIONS

MAPS

LIST OF ABBREVIATIONS

Adm.	Admiralty Records, in the Public Record Office, London (P.R.O.)
B.C.A.	Provincial Archives, Victoria, British Columbia, Canada.
B.L.	Bodleian Library, Oxford.
B.M.	British Museum, London.
B.T.	Board of Trade Records in the P.R.O.
Cab.	Cabinet Papers in the P.R.O.
C.O.	Colonial Office Records in the P.R.O.
F.O.	Foreign Office Records in the P.R.O.
H.B.C.A.	Hudson's Bay Company Archives, London.
H.O.	Hydrographer's Office, Taunton, Somerset.
H.S.L.	Hawaii State Library, Honolulu.
M.M.B.C.	Maritime Museum of British Columbia, Victoria, British Columbia.
N.L.	Naval Library, Ministry of Defence, Earl's Court, London.
N.M.M.	National Maritime Museum, Greenwich.
P.A.C.	Public Archives of Canada, Ottawa.
R.C.S.	Royal Commonwealth Society Library, London.
W.O.	War Office Records in the P.R.O.
W.R.O.	Warwickshire Record Office, Warwick.

PREFACE

THE ACTIVITIES AND INFLUENCE of the Royal Navy on the Northwest Coast of North America during the period from 1810 to 1914, and the political implications of these developments constitute a unique chapter of history that is often neglected by historians. We begin our narrative approximately with the coming of British and Canadian fur traders overland to the Pacific and conclude about the time of the transfer of the naval base at Esquimalt, Vancouver Island, from British to Canadian authority before the outbreak of World War I. This was an era of British maritime ascendancy and imperial expansion.

The purpose of this work is to explain the way in which sea power was exercised by the Royal Navy in the development of the Northwestern Pacific coastal region of North America, particularly British Columbia.

Many years ago the late Professor J. Holland Rose of Cambridge University wrote an article entitled "Sea Power and the Winning of British Columbia," published in *The Mariner's Mirror,* VII (1921). He dealt briefly with the decisive effect of the mobilization of the British fleet, the so-called "Spanish Armament," in forcing the Spanish to acquiesce to British demands in the Nootka Sound Dispute, 1790. But the display of power on this occasion marked merely the beginning of the Royal Navy's role in protecting British commercial, political and eventually strategic interests on the Northwest Coast.

For more than a century after the Nootka crisis, British warships visited the coast, mainly on scientific missions until 1840, and as instruments of British policy thereafter. Rather than describe the varied duties of these vessels in detail, I have undertaken to pursue the argument stated by Holland Rose in relation to the period 1810-1914, namely, that the security of British interests on the Northwest Coast can be attributed mainly to British strength at sea. This security depended to a great extent on Britain's relations with other powers, especially France, Russia and the United States. Consequently, references have been made to British foreign policy and diplomatic affairs as they relate to the Northwest Coast.

Because naval history is closely related to diplomatic and political history, I have been concerned with explaining British policy generally rather than with detailing the activities of individual British warships on the coast. Descriptions of ships that visited the region for one reason or another would be pointless without explanation of the reasons for their presence and for the influence they exercised.

Although the geographical focal point of this study is the Northwest Coast, references are given, where necessary, to the Hawaiian Islands, California, the Alaskan Arctic and even the Kamchatka Peninsula off the Siberian Coast. We are just beginning to comprehend the importance, now and in the past, of the orientation of Canada and the United States toward the Pacific. It would be an error to treat the history of the Northwest Coast in isolation from developments elsewhere within the Pacific rim.

Yet this work is not meant to be all-encompassing. Captains Cook, Vancouver and Broughton have been excluded as they belong to an era of exploration in which British claims to sovereignty were extended on the basis of prior discovery. Nor is this an account of hydrographic surveying in the region. Readers will find all too little on the Royal Navy's role in policing unruly Indian tribes. I hope to write on these developments in the future. It was necessary to sacrifice attention to these matters in order to keep to the major theme. Finally, this work concentrates on an institution, the Royal Navy, rather than on personalities. Admittedly, men make history, but the British admirals and captains in the Pacific during the nineteenth century acted remarkably alike in following and interpreting the policy guidelines of the national service in which they were employed.

The documentary materials on which the study is based are extensive and scattered. Chief among these are the Admiralty papers in the Public Record Office, London. These have been supplemented by Colonial

Office and Foreign Office correspondence in the same repository, by sources in the Hudson's Bay Company Archives, also in London, and by correspondence in the Provincial Archives in Victoria, British Columbia, the Public Archives of Canada in Ottawa, and elsewhere. The appended bibliography lists these and other documents and a full enumeration of the Pacific station records is to be found in *The Journal of Pacific History*, IV (1969), 146-53, under the title "The Records of the Royal Navy's Pacific Station."

My task has been facilitated by previous research on select subjects: the pioneer work by Major F. V. Longstaff, *Esquimalt Naval Base: A History of Its Works and Its Defences* (Victoria: Victoria Book and Stationery Co., 1941), which contains brief biographies of the commanders-in-chief on the Pacific station; the writings of W. Kaye Lamb, Captain J. F. Parry, R.N., and E. C. Russell; and monographs by E. E. Rich, John S. Galbraith, Margaret Ormsby, Walter Sage, Kenneth Bourne and F. W. Howay—all cited in the bibliography. The number of scholarly articles dealing with the Northwest Coast during this period testifies to the interest shown by historians in the development of the region. Those by Willard E. Ireland, F. V. Longstaff, W. Kaye Lamb and Frederick Merk are especially useful.

My indebtedness to Professor Gerald S. Graham, formerly Rhodes Professor of Imperial History in the University of London, is extensive; I acknowledge, with thanks, his criticism, encouragement and advice over the years. Rear-Admiral P. W. Brock, C.B., D.S.O., unselfishly gave me much information and help on naval matters. Mr. Willard Ireland, Provincial Archivist and Librarian of British Columbia, Colonel J. W. D. Symons, C.D., Director of the Maritime Museum of British Columbia, and my father, John Gough, have assisted in a number of ways. So, too, have Glyndwr Williams, John S. Galbraith, John E. Caswell, C. S. Mackinnon, Hugh Wallace and E. C. Russell. Dr. J. P. S. Bach kindly lent me his important manuscript on the Royal Navy in the South Pacific.

I acknowledge the kindness of several persons who made the search less difficult: Mr. M. J. Franklin and Captain J. Ashby, R.N. (ret.), in the Public Record Office, Ashridge Repository, near Berkhamstead, Herts., England; Mr. A. W. H. Pearsall in the National Maritime Museum, Greenwich; Dr. W. Kaye Lamb in the Public Archives of Canada, Ottawa; Mr. D. Mason and Miss I. Mitchell in the Provincial Archives, Victoria, B.C.; and Commander F. Grubb in the Maritime Museum of British Columbia, Victoria, B.C. I have been aided by librarians at the Naval Library, Ministry of Defence, in Earl's Court, the Royal United Service Institution, the Royal Commonwealth Society, the Royal Geographical Society, the Institute of Historical Research, the Institute of Commonwealth Studies, the British Museum Manuscripts

Division and King's College—all in London; the Navy Hydrographer's Office, Taunton; the Bodleian Library, Oxford; Oregon Historical Society, Portland; and the Special Collections Division, University of British Columbia Library, Vancouver.

Photographs appear through the courtesy of the National Maritime Museum, the Maritime Museum of British Columbia, the Public Archives of Canada, the Provincial Archives of British Columbia, the Vancouver City Archives, the Oregon Historical Society, the Directorate of History of Canadian Forces Headquarters, the *Illustrated London News*, the Hudson's Bay Company, Miss Joy Phillips, Mr. R. A. Wadia and Rear-Admiral H. F. Pullen, R.C.N.

Finally, I am grateful for financial assistance given by the Central Research Committee of the University of London for purposes of travel and microfilming. I am indebted to the Marquess of Hertford for allowing me to quote from the papers of Admiral Sir George Seymour in the Warwickshire Record Office, to the 7th Earl of Clarendon for permission to draw from the Clarendon Deposit in the Bodleian Library, and to the Governor and Committee of the Hudson's Bay Company for access to and permission to publish from the Company Archives, where Miss A. M. Johnson, Mrs. J. Craig and Miss G. Kemp rendered friendly assistance. To all these persons, I offer my thanks.

INTRODUCTION

THE LENGTHY ARC OF LAND bordering the northeastern quarter of the Pacific Ocean was known to eighteenth-century European navigators as the Northwest Coast of North America. No more accurate geographical name exists today for the Pacific littoral which extends from Cape Mendocino on the upper California coast to about where the Aleutian Archipelago extends from southwestern Alaska. Everywhere the coast is rugged but more especially so south of Cape Flattery where good harbours are rare and, in the days of sail, the Columbia River mouth provided a hazardous entrance to the broad and fertile lands of the rich Oregon plain. At Cape Flattery, the waters of the Strait of Juan de Fuca reach inland and then south into Puget Sound and north into the Strait of Georgia and beyond, where constricted narrows divide Vancouver Island from the mainland. Above Vancouver Island and stretching to the north and west, the coast is characterized by certain large islands including the Queen Charlotte Islands and the Alexander Archipelago of the Alaska panhandle. The entrance to Cook Inlet may serve arbitrarily as the northern extremity of the Northwest Coast of North America.

Along this irregular and mountainous landscape, Captain George Vancouver and others found the coast heavily treed with conifers. They experienced heavy rains in the north and thick fogs everywhere, depend-

1

ing on the season. Fish and wildlife were abundant in numerous places along the shore such as Nootka Sound on Vancouver Island. They found Indian tribes whose distinctive cultures were based on both the land and the sea.

Situated some eighteen thousand miles from Europe by the shortest sea lane via Cape Horn, the Northwest Coast was a remote quarter of the globe in the late eighteenth century. Yet the steady expansion of European nations by sea and of the United States primarily by land were to end this isolation. In the ensuing international rivalry for the coast, the sea and sea power were to be decisive in its history.

In the development of British interests on the Northwest Coast, the Royal Navy played a paramount role that has often been neglected by historians. Beginning with the War of 1812 and for more than a century thereafter, successive British governments were remarkably consistent in pursuing policies designed to protect British commercial interests and territorial claims in what is now the Canadian province of British Columbia.

The instrument used in implementing these policies was the Royal Navy. Throughout the period 1810-1914 Britain maintained and developed an empire and seaborne trade by means of naval supremacy, carefully nurtured European alliances, skilful deployment of small military forces throughout the globe and financial strength based on foreign trade.

The Eastern Pacific, bordering the Americas on the east and northeast and stretching westward from Cape Horn to about where the International Date Line arbitrarily bisects the world, was the largest of the Royal Navy's "foreign stations." This vast precinct—"a desert of waters," according to Captain Sir Henry Byam Martin of the frigate *Grampus*— commanded a recognized priority in British naval expenditure even in times of general retrenchment in naval spending.[1] This was because the centre of British imperial interests shifted slowly but perceptibly to eastern seas after the Napoleonic Wars, as industrial developments at home fed new markets abroad and British governments reluctantly found themselves acquiring new commitments and territories as a last resort to forestall foreign aggrandizements. Yet the means at the disposal of the commander-in-chief on the Pacific station were limited to a handful of frigates, eight or nine sloops and sometimes a ship-of-the-line. The gradual introduction of steam power after mid-century increased the

---

[1]"The Pacific is a desert of waters—we seem to have sailed out of the inhabited world, & the *Grampus* to have become the Frankenstein of the Ocean. A few boatswain birds hooted us as we sailed along." Journal of the *Grampus*, 28 July 1846, Byam Martin Papers, Add. MSS. 41, 472, B.M.

effectiveness of naval units by reducing the long passages from place to place during which uncertain winds might delay for weeks a sailing ship's arrival where she was most needed. Communications were only as fast as the ships themselves. By the nature of its work, the squadron was dispersed throughout the ocean at critical points where "sloop diplomacy" was being conducted.

In these difficult circumstances, much depended on the wisdom of the admiral and his captains, and apart from Admiral Price who died ingloriously by committing suicide when he should have been preparing to engage the Russians at Petropavlovsk during the Crimean War— as described in chapter 5—they showed a high degree of professional competence and dedication. On the Northwest Coast they faced problems equally as difficult as anywhere in the Pacific or elsewhere; they proved to be dextrous consuls, trade commissioners, justices of the peace and policemen.

The period under review constituted the last phase of competition for empire in North America in which the remaining contestants seeking control of the Northwest Coast were Russia, the United States and Britain. Russia lacked a navy of any consequence; thus she lacked means of compulsion or influence. The Tsar's Ukase of 1821 was the last attempt to consolidate Alaska as a domain for the Russian America Company. Russian influence gradually waned and, after establishing close relations with the United States during the Crimean War and the American Civil War, she sold Alaska in 1867 to what had been one of her principal rivals a half-century before.

The position of the United States was somewhat similar to that of Russia. Her limited naval power until late in the nineteenth century gave Britain a distinct military and diplomatic advantage on the Northwest Coast. But the flow of settlers across the North American continent into the agricultural lands of Old Oregon near the Columbia River in the early 1840's constituted a force that not even the combined forces of the Hudson's Bay Company and the Royal Navy could withstand so long as the area remained—by Anglo-American agreement—a "no-man's land."

The North West Company and, after 1821, the Hudson's Bay Company dominated the whole Pacific cordillera until the division of the area between Britain and the United States by the Oregon Treaty in 1846. While the British lost the agricultural region near the Columbia River, the opposition manifested there by the Hudson's Bay Company to the United States probably compelled the Americans to press south to take the Mexican province of Upper California. British opposition to the United States also checked American expansion northward from the Columbia River and ports above Puget Sound, with Vancouver

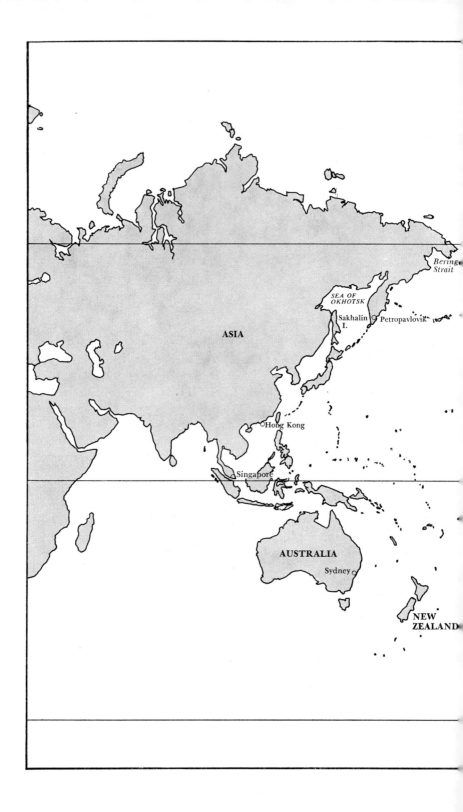

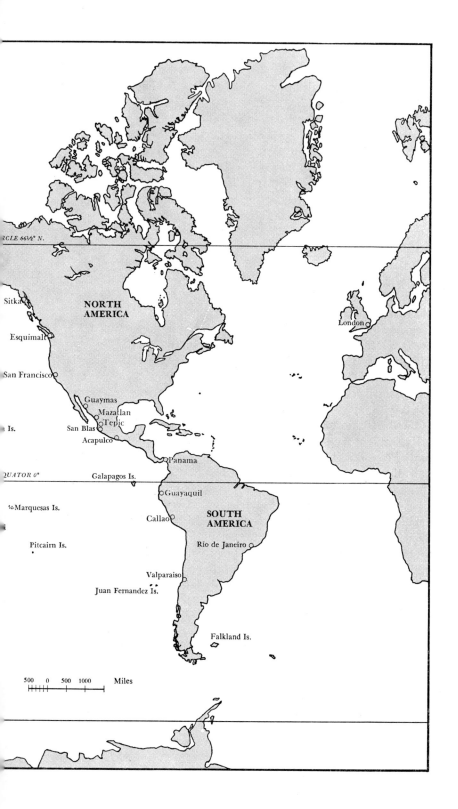

CLE 66½° N.

Sitka

NORTH
AMERICA

Esquimalt

London

San Francisco

Guaymas

Mazatlan

Is.

San Blas   Tepic

Acapulco

Panama

QUATOR 0°   Galapagos Is.

Guayaquil

Marquesas Is.

Callao

SOUTH
AMERICA

Pitcairn Is.

Rio de Janeiro

Valparaiso

Juan Fernandez Is.

Falkland Is.

500   0   500 1000   Miles

Island and the forty-ninth parallel becoming the line of last defence for British territory stretching northward to Alaska.

After 1846, Britain embarked on a policy of encouraging settlement by British subjects on Vancouver Island, using the Hudson's Bay Company as the instrument of territorial control and the Royal Navy as the means of protection. The California gold rush relieved the British position briefly by attracting Americans to San Francisco and the banks of the Sacramento. But later developments in the gold fields of the Queen Charlotte Islands, the Fraser River and the Cariboo lured the Americans back again and forced Britain to reassert her influence. These "turbulent frontiers" were incorporated into a colonial sphere in which Victoria on Vancouver Island was the regional metropolis. This further consolidation of the area as part of the British Empire was a means of defending the fledgling colony of British Columbia against internal disorders as well as against American expansion.

Meanwhile, the United States was considering ways of buttressing her newly-won empire on the Pacific Coast; eventually railways were built with this strategic objective in mind. As one American historian has explained, a Pacific railway was seen as providing "the necessary protection against Britain's sea power by enabling us to protect our western coasts without resorting to great expenditure for a navy. The shadow of the British lion lay across the path of American thinking."[2]

By the 1860's certain Canadians were thinking in terms remarkably similar to those of the advocates of railways in the United States. These Canadians had their own notion of manifest destiny which was allied and not opposed to British expansion and imperial consolidation. As a means of transporting troops, they argued, a Canadian railway to the Pacific would complement and assist British naval protection in the Pacific. It would also open up the Canadian West and British Columbia to settlement and thereby preserve an enlarged British North America from what some United States citizens thought was their natural destiny. But not until 1871 did British Columbia join the Canadian Confederation; and only in 1886 did the Canadian Pacific Railway commence its trans-continental service. In the meantime, American railroads and telegraphs had reached the Pacific, the population growth in the American far west had accelerated, and American maritime activity and aspirations in the Pacific were in the ascendant. During this era of Anglo-American antagonism, the burdens of responsibility for the defence of the British colonies on the Northwest Coast remained with the Pacific squadron.

---

[2]Leonard B. Irwin, *Pacific Railways and Nationalism in the Canadian-American Northwest, 1845-73* (reprint; New York: Greenwood Press, 1968), p. 222.

In the British North American scheme of empire then evolving, a naval base on the Northwest Coast became a necessity for the squadron, initially during the Oregon crisis and later as British commitments increased in the North Pacific—especially on Vancouver Island and in British Columbia. From the first attempts to provide a naval depot and hospital facilities at Esquimalt during the Crimean War, the value of this port increased until it became, in strategic terms, Britain's principal harbour in the Eastern Pacific. It never developed into a naval establishment of the size of Halifax, Simon's Bay or Hong Kong, but it was sufficient to serve the needs of the squadron. The proximity of Esquimalt to United States shores troubled some members of the Admiralty, who argued that the place was indefensible given its remote location and the inadequate size and scattered deployment of the Pacific fleet. Some considered it a liability rather than an asset. Yet it was never totally abandoned as certain strategic requirements had to be met, and consequently minimum standards of defence against enemy cruiser raids were maintained during the latter part of the nineteenth century. After the redistribution of the British fleets overseas in 1906, Esquimalt's importance declined further to the point where it merely served a few small armoured cruisers.

Technological changes were crucial in making sea power more effective in the latter part of the nineteenth century. Steam replaced sail as the chief motive power. Armoured steel hulls mounting revolutionary new guns superseded wooden ships with their old 32-pounders. The trans-continental railway, telegraph, wireless telegraphy, the trans-Pacific cable, a trans-Pacific steamship line, and the Panama Canal all exercised far-reaching effects on British strategy. Esquimalt, Hong Kong and Sydney were brought much closer to London.

In these new circumstances, Britain expected the Dominions to assume greater responsibility for their own local defences. But Canadian politicians and statesmen, whose national strategy was based essentially on railways, were unwilling and unable because of French Canada to support schemes for the defence of the British Empire; they created only a small army and militia and, after 1910, a diminutive navy. They were content to let the defence of Canada rest on British supremacy at sea while it lasted and on the necessary diplomatic posture of good relations with the United States.

The chapters that follow show in detail how during the era of the *Pax Britannica* the Royal Navy was protecting British interests on the Northwest Coast, beginning with British-American rivalry for the fur trade and ending roughly with the transfer of authority for Esquimalt Naval Base on Vancouver Island from Britain to Canada.

Chapter 1

THE CONTEST FOR THE COLUMBIA COUNTRY
1810-1818

IN 1776 CAPTAIN JAMES COOK of the Royal Navy sailed from England on his third and final voyage of Pacific exploration with instructions to search for the western opening of a Northwest Passage across North America. During the course of his voyage he visited the Hawaiian Islands, which he called the Sandwich Islands, and went on to the North American coast, arriving on the shores of what is now Oregon in 1778. Captain Cook's men traded with the Indians of Nootka Sound and took back with them on the homeward journey some sea-otter skins which they found they could sell for a high price to Canton merchants. After Captain Cook's death, followed in a few years by publication of the account of his voyage in 1784, international interest in the maritime fur trade increased.

Later, the trade was dominated by independent explorer-traders in a Montreal-based group that came to be known as the North West Company—the Nor'westers—although in none of the various forms in which it existed did this company ever receive a charter. They were engaged in bitter rivalry with the chartered Hudson's Bay Company and were also competing with the American fur-trading interests of John Jacob Astor.[1]

[1]Harold A. Innis, *The Fur Trade in Canada,* rev. ed. (New Haven: Yale University Press, 1962), p. 205. The relationship between fur-trading companies was extremely complex. For information on the fur traders in Canada and the United States see Innis and other works listed in the bibliography.

The way in which these groups manoeuvred for control of trade and territory is part of a much larger and extremely complicated history which is largely peripheral here. Suffice it to say that after 1793 the Americans gained increasing mastery of the fur trade on the Northwest Coast, partly because they were free of certain monopolistic restrictions that continually hampered the North West Company which lacked any charter rights. The Nor'westers could not ship sea-otter pelts to markets in China without subterfuge because other companies—notably the East India Company and, to a lesser extent, the South Sea Company—already had obtained charter rights for the China trade. The ports of Canton and Macao, the principal markets for sea-otter pelts, were essentially barred to North West Company ships while Americans could enter them freely. The Nor'westers were driven to such subterfuges as the use of merchantmen from Boston to transport their cargoes to the China ports. An additional advantage of no less importance to the Americans lay in the fact that their government was not at war at this time, while after 1793 Britain was at war with France.[2]

The Columbian Enterprise

Despite the obstacles which faced the Nor'westers, their exploration of new areas continued. In 1793 Alexander Mackenzie reached the Pacific after crossing the Rocky Mountains in the first overland crossing of the continent north of Mexico. He was followed by other Nor'westers including Simon Fraser and David Thompson, who began trading and exploring west of the Rocky Mountains.

The success of these explorations led to the birth of the so-called Columbian enterprise. This bold but difficult plan called for a transcontinental overland trading route proceeding westward from Fort William on Lake Superior. Furs would be freighted across the Rocky Mountains at Athabaska Pass and down the rivers to the Pacific where ships could unload supplies and take on furs for Asian markets. In the winter of 1807-1808, a Company servant described plans to "form a general establishment for the trade of that country on the Columbia River, which receives and conducts to the Ocean all the waters that rise West of the Mountains." He claimed that the Columbian enterprise would gen-

---

[2]Wars with France and the United States brought a rapid decline of British vessels in the maritime fur trade (primarily sea otter) , as shown by F. W. Howay, "An Outline Sketch of the Maritime Fur Trade," *Canadian Historical Association Annual Report, 1932* (Ottawa, 1932) , p. 7.

	British	American
1785-1794	25	15
1795-1804	9	50
1805-1814	3	40

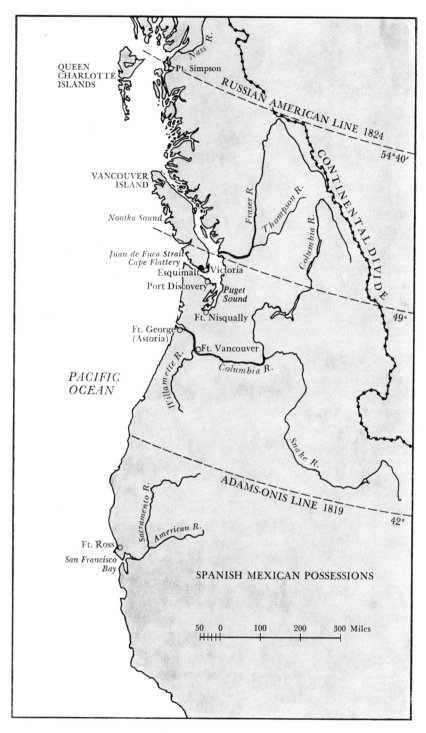

THE NORTHWEST COAST OF NORTH AMERICA, *1813-1846*

erate markets for British manufacturers but that in order to achieve this, British assistance would be necessary to control a "vast country and population made dependent on the British Empire."[3]

In the spring of 1810, shortly after the North West Company had established several posts west of the Continental Divide, the Company's Montreal agents were disturbed to hear rumours of American expeditions fitting out at New York and Boston for the Columbia River, undoubtedly financed by John Jacob Astor. If such expeditions were successful, the Americans would achieve complete control of the rich fur preserve that extended from the banks of the Columbia into the vast hinterland.

Almost immediately, the Montreal partners proposed to their London associates that the British government assist the traders in establishing, "either from the interior of the North West Country or by Sea," a permanent North West Company post on the Columbia, this to be achieved with the cooperation of the East India Company which held a monopoly of the China trade.[4] The Nor'westers accompanied their proposal with a warning that American control of the trading region, coupled with the advantage of the prior claims of the Lewis and Clark expedition—which had first charted the river's main course—could mean eventual American ownership of the Columbia territory. The appeal for help from Montreal produced no effect when it was presented on 2 April 1810 to the Secretary of State for Foreign Affairs, the Marquis of Wellesley, by the Committee of British Merchants Interested in the Trade and Fisheries of His Majesty's North American Colonies. Immediately following this appeal another was made, but it too was unsuccessful.

Simon McGillivray, an influential Nor'wester in London, was well aware of John Jacob Astor's plan to monopolize the Pacific fur trade. McGillivray already knew that Astor controlled the area to the south and west of the Great Lakes and he probably knew that since 1800 Astor had been engaged in trade from New York to the Orient, and that he had sent captains on voyages to the Northwest Coast, California, Sitka and Canton after 1809.

Evidently, McGillivray believed that the American rivals could be defeated by competition; thus the North West Company rejected an offer by Astor of a one-third interest in his trans-Pacific and trans-continental

---

[3]William McGillivray [?], "Some Account of the Trade Carried on by the North-West Company," fol. 20, R.C.S.

[4]McTavish, McGillivrays and Company to McTavish, Fraser and Company, 23 January 1810, Q/113, pp. 228-30, P.A.C.; published as "Appeal of the North West Company to the British Government to Forestall John Jacob Astor's Columbia Enterprise," *Canadian Historical Review*, XVII (September 1936), 306.

trading enterprise.[5] In June 1810, Astor decided to act alone and with-draw his offer. He formed the Pacific Fur Company as a subsidiary of the American Fur Company and organized two expeditions, one to reach Oregon by sea and the other by land. Astor's ship, the *Tonquin*, sailed around Cape Horn and arrived at the mouth of the Columbia on 22 March 1811. There her crew constructed Fort Astoria on the south bank, seven miles from the sea.

On 10 November 1810, McGillivray complained bitterly to the Secretary for War and the Colonies, the Earl of Liverpool, that since the American expedition had already sailed from New York it was almost too late to protect the "Columbia country" from falling into American hands, but he added that because the American vessel would call at various ports along the South American coast, a ship of the Royal Navy might reach the Columbia before the Americans.[6] McGillivray argued that if a British warship sailed immediately to the Northwest Coast to take formal possession and establish a settlement, British rights would be secure. He also recommended that the North West Company send an expedition overland to meet the vessel and build a post under naval protection. He contended that unless the Company gained naval support it would be unable to undertake the Columbia project, and the country and trade would fall into American hands. But for the third time the government failed to act.

As McGillivray feared, the Americans had won the race to the Columbia River Mouth. Astor's ship arrived in March 1811. David Thompson and his fellow Nor'westers reached it overland only four months later on 15 July after exploring and surveying the river and its tributaries as a possible trade route. It was unfortunate for the Nor'westers that Thompson spent so much time surveying as this probably delayed him in reaching the mouth of the Columbia before the Americans.[7]

Royal Navy Support to the Nor'westers

The war between Britain and the United States, declared in June 1812, introduced a new factor in the rivalry between the Nor'westers and the Astorians. Late in that year, North West Company agents in Montreal again urged their London partners to press the British government for

---

[5]G. C. Davidson, *The North West Company* (Berkeley: University of California Press, 1918), p. 134.
[6]S. McGillivray to Lord Liverpool, 10 November 1810, Q/113, pp. 221-23, P.A.C.
[7]See Richard Glover, ed., *David Thompson's Narrative, 1784-1812* (Toronto: Champlain Society, vol. XL, 1962), pp. 358-59; and see also Arthur S. Morton, "The North West Company's Columbian Venture and David Thompson," *Canadian Historical Review*, XVII (1936), 284-88.

convoy support for a company ship bound for the Columbia River via Cape Horn. The outbreak of war in that year ended the British Ministry's indifference to the pleas of the North West Company; the Lords Commissioners of the Admiralty discussed the proposed mission with Nor'westers Donald McTavish and John Macdonald of Garth. They then dispatched the frigate *Phoebe,* 36 guns, Captain James Hillyar, to accompany the fur-trading company vessel *Isaac Todd* to the Northwest Coast and to clear the coast of hostile vessels. The *Isaac Todd,* 20 guns, bearing letters-of-marque that would allow her to capture the enemy's merchant shipping, was the first ship of the Company's Columbian enterprise. With the North West Company partners McTavish and Macdonald on board, the *Isaac Todd* left Portsmouth with her escort, the *Phoebe,* on 25 March 1813 under secret orders to seize Fort Astoria and then to form a British settlement at the mouth of the Columbia River.[8]

An auxiliary expedition was dispatched overland from Canada. Led by the fur trader John George McTavish, one hundred Company men were to meet both ships sometime between May and August 1813. McTavish carried with him an important letter from the British government stating that the *Isaac Todd* was "accompanied by a frigate, to take and destroy everything that is American on the N.W. Coast."[9]

On 10 June 1813 at the end of a hazardous first leg of the voyage, the *Phoebe* led the *Isaac Todd* into Rio de Janeiro Harbour.[10] There, the Commander-in-Chief of the South American station, Rear-Admiral Sir Manley Dixon, learned that Hillyar had experienced great difficulty with the crew of the *Isaac Todd.* Seven of the crew deserted after arriving at Rio because of her unseaworthy condition.[11] She had proved to be a heavy sailer, probably in part because she was badly stowed, heavily rigged, and because she carried too many guns on deck. Her condition was such that Dixon concluded, "No alteration, I understand, will make her sail even tolerably."[12]

Rear-Admiral Dixon did not know the object of the mission until the

---

[8]Instructions, J. W. Croker (Secretary of the Admiralty) to Capt. J. Hillyar, 13 March 1813, Adm. 2/1380, pp. 367-79.

[9]Quoted in F. W Howay, W. N. Sage and H. F. Angus, *British Columbia and the United States* (New Haven: Yale University Press, 1942), p. 34.

[10]John Macdonald of Garth, "Journal from England to the Columbia River, North West Coast of America," MG 19, A 17, P.A.C.; printed in B. C. Payette, ed., *The Oregon Country Under the Union Jack* (Montreal; privately printed, 1961), pp. v-x. Hereinafter cited as *Macdonald Journal,* with date.

[11]Rear-Admiral Sir Manley Dixon to Croker, 21 June 1813, Adm. 1/21; in Gerald S. Graham and R. A. Humphreys, eds., *The Navy and South America, 1807-1823: Correspondence of the Commanders-in-Chief on the South American Station,* (London: Navy Records Society, vol. CIX, 1962), pp. 93-95. Hereinafter cited as *Navy and South America.*

[12]*Ibid.*

ships reached Rio; he was disgusted when McTavish and Macdonald, in ignorance or indifference, "made generally known" that the secret destination of the ships was the Northwest Coast.[13]

About this time, news reached Dixon that the American frigate *Essex*, rated by the British as a 40-gun ship, was at large, capturing British whalers and shipping in the Pacific.[14] It was felt that the *Phoebe* would not be an equal to the *Essex* should they meet in battle.

These developments caused Dixon to consider increasing the Royal Navy's protection of the Columbia mission by dispatching two sloops, the *Racoon*, 26 guns, and *Cherub*, 18 guns, for this purpose—although both had been destined for the South Pacific to protect British merchantmen, a service which could be most effectively accomplished by sinking or taking the *Essex*.[15] After considerable pondering, the Commander-in-Chief, with seamanlike precaution, ordered a squadron consisting of the *Phoebe*, *Racoon* and *Cherub* to convoy the *Isaac Todd* to the Pacific, thus providing a greater margin of safety.[16]

At Rio the crews readied the four vessels for the arduous voyage around Cape Horn. Dixon ordered the government stores in the *Isaac Todd* transferred to all three of the British men-of-war.[17] He strengthened the complements of the *Racoon* and *Cherub* by a total of sixty-five men to ensure that the naval vessels would be sufficiently strong to defeat the Americans at the mouth of the Columbia if the *Isaac Todd* fell behind.[18] Further delays followed when two officers left the *Isaac Todd*. Replacements had to be found, and discontented sailors from the same ship had to be held in custody.[19] Although every effort was made to get under way as soon as possible, the four ships did not weigh anchor until 6 July 1813.

Four days after leaving Rio for Cape Horn, Captain Hillyar opened the secret Admiralty orders conveyed to him by Dixon. "The principal object of the Service on which you are employed," the orders ran, "is to protect and render every assistance in your power to the British traders from Canada, and to destroy, and if possible totally annihilate any settlements which the Americans may have formed either on the Columbia

---

[13]*Ibid.*

[14]A. T. Mahan, *Sea Power in its Relations to the War of 1812*, 2 vols. (Boston: Little, Brown & Co., 1905), II, 248.

[15]On the early activities of the *Racoon*, see John A. Hussey, ed., *The Voyage of the 'Racoon': a "Secret" Journal of a Visit to Oregon, California and Hawaii, 1813-1814* (San Francisco; Book Club of California, 1958), pp. ix-xi.

[16]Dixon to Croker, 9 June 1813, Adm. 1/21.

[17]Reasons are given in Dixon's secret instructions to Hillyar of 1 July 1813, *ibid.*

[18]*Macdonald Journal*, 9 July 1813.

[19]Dixon to Croker, 12 March 1813, Adm. 1/21; *Navy and South America*, p. 98.

River or on the neighbouring Coasts."[20] Moreover, Hillyar was to give the Nor'westers "every assistance in the formation of any new settlement they may wish to form for carrying on their trade and in destroying any force of the Enemy which you may find in that quarter."[21]

The plan called for the *Phoebe* and the *Isaac Todd* to arrive together at the Columbia after a passage from Rio "without touching anywhere."[22] In the event that the ships were separated or encountered difficulties, they were to rendezvous at the Hawaiian Islands, the best source of supplies. It was felt that to meet there would conceal the mission better than to anchor in a port on the Pacific side of the Americas. As an alternative meeting-place, the Island of Juan Fernandez off the Chilean Coast was recommended.

Orders from Rear-Admiral Dixon required that one of the two fur-trading partners should be placed aboard the *Phoebe*. With this precaution the *Phoebe* could complete its mission even if the *Isaac Todd* arrived late at the mouth of the Columbia or failed to reach there.[23] Accordingly, Macdonald and five Company servants were transferred to the *Phoebe* and McTavish, the chief Nor'wester, remained in the *Isaac Todd*.[24] Dixon's admirable instructions reminded Captain Hillyar of the original purpose of the *Racoon* and *Cherub*—to protect British merchantmen in the South Pacific—but gave him complete discretion to retain them as long as he thought necessary to accomplish the more important mission entrusted to him by the Admiralty.[25]

No attempt was made to search for the American ship *Essex* at this time. The principal objective of the British mission was to secure the Northwest Coast at the Columbia River mouth as a field of British commerce. Moreover, it would have been virtually impossible to find the *Essex* in the vast reaches of the Eastern Pacific. Hillyar was aware that the primary responsibility of the *Phoebe* was the safe and timely arrival of the *Isaac Todd*. But both Dixon and Hillyar realized that American naval forces in the Pacific posed a threat to the Oregon venture; only the destruction of the *Essex* and any other warships that might have joined her would ensure British naval supremacy, protect British trade in the Pacific and crown the Columbia expedition with success.

Although the mission to the Northwest Coast was supposedly a secret,

---

[20]Admiralty Instructions to Hillyar, 12 March 1813, most secret, Adm. 2/1380, pp. 370-75. The instructions were to be opened 30 leagues south of Rio.
[21]*Ibid.*
[22]*Ibid.*
[23]Dixon to Croker, 21 June 1813, Adm. 1/21.
[24]*Macdonald Journal*, 10 and 12 July 1813.
[25]Dixon to Hillyar, 1 July 1813, secret, encl. in Dixon to Croker, 12 July 1813, Adm. 1/21.

news of its objective had leaked out even before the *Phoebe* and *Isaac Todd* left England on 25 March 1813. This news reached Rio de Janeiro by mid-June; from there it probably was conveyed overland immediately, and passing through informants, eventually reached the *Essex*.[26]

The *Essex* presented a formidable challenge in the Pacific. She was the first United States warship to enter the Pacific and she had already been the first beyond the Cape of Good Hope.[27] After limited success against British shipping in the South Atlantic, Captain David Porter of the *Essex* decided to venture alone into the Pacific in March 1813 (about the same time the *Phoebe* and *Isaac Todd* left Portsmouth) , and planned to survive on the prizes he could capture. After provisioning hurriedly at Valparaiso, Chile, the *Essex* sailed on 21 March for the Galapagos Islands, then the centre of whaling in the Pacific. From April to October 1813 she seized twelve of twenty British whalers in that ocean.[28] Captain Porter then fitted out one of these captured whalers as a privateer to accompany the *Essex* in her search for unarmed, or poorly armed, merchantmen; the *Essex Junior,* as the captured whaler was named, carried twenty light guns and ninety men.

Meanwhile, the British were experiencing difficulties in the passage from Rio to Cape Horn in the dead of the southern winter. During a heavy gale on 20 July 1813, the escorts almost lost sight of the slow-sailing *Isaac Todd,* and "some damage" was sustained by the *Racoon* and *Cherub* in trying to keep close to her. Two days later, the captains met on board the *Phoebe* and decided that in the event of another gale they would be compelled for reasons of safety to sail at a distance from the *Isaac Todd*.[29] Only a few days later, on 29 July, the ships were north of the Falkland Islands, when thick fog settled in and the company ship fell behind and lost contact. After weathering a heavy storm, the three men-of-war rounded Cape Horn; on 11 September they reached Juan Fernandez where they hoped to rendezvous with the *Isaac Todd,* but her whereabouts was still unknown. The squadron remained at Juan Fernandez for a week, hoping to sight the *Isaac Todd.* On 18 September the Nor'wester Macdonald and North West Company servants and stores

---

26*Ibid.* See also Bowes to Dixon, 14 September 1813, encl. in Dixon to Croker, 20 October 1813, Adm. 1/22; *Navy and South America,* p. 110; and Kenneth W. Porter, *John Jacob Astor, Business Man,* 2 vols. (Cambridge, Mass: Harvard University Press, 1931) , I, 218-19. On the leak of information, see Gabriel Franchère, *Journal of a Voyage to the North West Coast of North America During the Years 1811, 1812, 1813 and 1814,* ed. W. Kaye Lamb (Toronto: Champlain Society, vol. XLV, 1969) , pp. 20-21.
27Mahan, *War of 1812,* II, 245.
28*Ibid.,* 246.
29*Macdonald Journal,* 22 July 1813.

were again transferred, this time from the *Phoebe* to the *Racoon*.[30] The
squadron then weighed for the north, with the *Isaac Todd* apparently
lost.

Near the equator, on 2 October, Hillyar learned from a Spanish brig
that the *Essex* had taken one hundred distressed seamen to Guayaquil
on the coast of Ecuador.[31] It was thought that possibly these men were
taken from the *Isaac Todd*. On this intelligence, which must have seemed
convincing, Hillyar concluded that the *Isaac Todd* was lost. He then
decided to find the enemy if possible. The *Phoebe* and *Cherub* were sent
to the South American coast to hunt for the *Essex*, leaving the *Racoon*—
now unescorted—to continue to the Columbia River. Because the
Phoebe had been allocated by the Lords of the Admiralty as escort for a
project to which they attached importance, Hillyar's decision to leave
the *Racoon* to execute the mission without escort could be justified only
by success.[32]

When Porter of the *Essex* first learned of the strong British squadron
sailing round the Horn, he decided to prepare for battle. On 25 October,
the *Essex*, *Essex Junior* and three prizes reached the Marquesas Islands,
where a refit was carried out. Then on 14 December the *Essex* and *Essex
Junior* sailed for Valparaiso in search of the British warships.[33] They
reached what they considered to be the neutral port of Valparaiso on
3 February 1814; five days later the British ships *Phoebe* and *Cherub*
also entered the port.

A clash between the rivals seemed inevitable as soon as both forces
ventured out of the harbour. As he was stronger, Hillyar wanted to be
in a position to prevent the *Essex* and *Essex Junior* from slipping away
quietly before he was ready, so he put to sea, accompanied by the *Cherub*.
For nearly six weeks, Hillyar's force sailed close to the extreme western
point of Valparaiso harbour, a large open bay facing north. The objective was to prevent the faster American vessels from escaping between
him and the point. From his strategic position, Hillyar would have the
advantage of a chase to windward in the prevailing south-southwest
wind.[34]

Suddenly on 28 March 1814 in violent winds the *Essex* parted one
cable in the storm and began to drag another so Porter cut the cable and
made sail. He hoped to pass to the windward of the blockading British
vessels and might have done so if the main-topmast of the *Essex* had not

[30]*Ibid.*, 18 September 1813.
[31]*Ibid.*, 2 October 1813.
[32]Mahan, *War of 1812*, II, 248.
[33]*Ibid.*, 247.
[34]*Ibid.*, 248-49. See also Hillyar to Croker, 28 February 1814, copy, encl. with Dixon to
Croker, 13 May 1814, Adm. 1/22; *Navy and South America*, pp. 132-33.

snapped in a heavy squall near the outer point of the bay. This forced her to run eastward and to anchor in what has been claimed were "neutral" waters. This neutrality was debatable, since Britain did not recognize Chilean independence and Spain was an ally. Furthermore, no belligerent man-of-war could hope to take advantage of neutral waters indefinitely, as the *Essex* had done.

Hillyar ignored Porter's intent to take refuge in "neutral" waters and attacked. His object was to rake the *Essex* if possible, and if not, to reach a range at which his long guns would be effective and her carronades would not.[35] Soon the greater gun-range and manoeuvrability of the *Phoebe* proved decisive. Hillyar was able to keep his ships out of range of the *Essex*'s broadside while doing extensive damage aloft to the enemy.[36] Faced with defeat, Porter surrendered, only two and one half hours after action commenced.[37] By this single engagement, the Royal Navy gained command of the sea in the Pacific. The wisdom of Hillyar's judgement now depended on whether the *Racoon* succeeded in its mission at the Columbia River mouth.

Developments at Fort Astoria

Concurrent events at Fort Astoria were equally significant. In sharp contrast to the assistance which the Royal Navy could now give the Nor'westers, American naval support for the Astorians became impossible as the British employed their naval supremacy in an effective blockade of American ports.[38] After Astor pleaded in 1813 for a warship to protect his enterprise, the Secretary of the Navy responded by arranging for the frigate *Adams* to go to the North Pacific, but the British blockade prevented her from sailing. Astor then tried to protect the post and carry on the trade as best he could. He secretly chartered the *Forester*, a British vessel under British colours: but by the time she reached the Northwest Coast, British fur traders were already in possession of Fort

---

[35]The *Essex* mounted forty 32-pounder carronades and six 12-pounder long guns and had a minimum broadside of 676 lbs. By contrast, the *Phoebe* carried twenty-six 18-pounder long guns, four 9-pounder long guns and fourteen 32-pounder carronades, and the *Cherub* had eighteen 32-pounder carronades, six 18-pounder carronades and two 6-pounder guns, with minimum broadsides of 476 and 248 lbs. respectively. These figures explain why Hillyar kept the *Cherub* in close company to the *Phoebe* outside of Valparaiso harbour so as not to be placed at a disadvantage in a single-ship engagement with the *Essex*. They also partly explain Hillyar's tactics in defeating the *Essex*.

[36]Hillyar's description of the engagement is in his letter to Croker, 30 March 1814, copy, encl. in Dixon to Croker, 10 June 1814, Adm. 1/22; *Navy and South America*, pp. 141-42.

[37]Log of the *Essex*, 28 March 1814, in Payette, *Oregon Country*, p. 197.

[38]See Harold and Margaret Sprout, *The Rise of American Naval Power, 1776-1918* (Princeton: Princeton University Press, 1939), pp. 73-85.

Astoria. Her captain was forced to trade between California and Kamchatka on the Russian coast near the Kurile Islands.[39] In Hawaii, the commander of H.M.S. *Cherub* became suspicious of the *Forester*'s ownership and detained some of her crew on board the *Cherub*.[40]

Another of Astor's ships, the *Lark*, was allowed by British naval authorities to leave New York in 1813 on the understanding that she was bound only for Sitka with goods and supplies for the Russians.[41] But she ran aground in the Hawaiian Islands and was a total loss. Astor, as one historian observed, "was the victim of bad tactics, bad luck, and bad strategy."[42] Reverses between 1811 and 1815 dashed Astor's hopes of maintaining Fort Astoria as an essential link with the sea while at the same time the partners of the Pacific Fur Company at Astoria became increasingly aware of their insecure position.

In early October 1813 John George McTavish and his party of Nor'westers brought news overland to the Columbia that the *Isaac Todd* and a British frigate were bound for the river mouth to destroy the American post. This convinced the Astorians that their position was untenable. Additional and equally alarming news came from the Hawaiian and the Marquesas Islands: Wilson P. Hunt, Chief Agent of the Pacific Fur Company, brought word from the Hawaiian Islands of the outbreak of war between the two nations.[43] From the Marquesas on another occasion, he brought information from Captain Porter of the *Essex* that an even larger force than originally expected, consisting of a frigate, two sloops and a merchantman, was bound for the Northwest Coast to conquer Fort Astoria.[44] The disturbing news forwarded by Hunt on this second occasion was "the death warrant of unfortunate Astoria" in the words of the American author Washington Irving.[45]

The Astorians were faced with a choice of selling their establishments, guns and stocks to the Nor'westers or confronting the guns of the Royal

[39]Kenneth W. Porter, "The Cruise of the *Forester*," *Washington Historical Quarterly*, XXIII (1932), 262-69.
[40]Hillyar to Capt. Thomas T. Tucker, 14 April 1814, encl. in Dixon to Croker, 8 September 1814, Adm. 1/22; *Navy and South America*, pp. 147-48. H.M.S. *Cherub* also captured the American fur-trading vessel *Charon* and the armed cruiser *Sir Alexander Hammond* in the Sandwich Islands. Tucker to Dixon, 20 June 1814, Adm. 1/22.
[41]Howay, *British Columbia and the United States*, p. 33.
[42]Earl S. Pomeroy, *The Pacific Slope* (New York; Knopf, 1966), p. 17.
[43]Robert Greenhow, *Memoir on the North West Coast of America* (Washington: Blair & Rives, 1940), p. 159.
[44]Washington Irving, *Astoria*, 3 vols. (London; R. Bentley, 1836), III, 214.
[45]*Ibid*. See also Alexander Henry the Younger, "Journal Across the Rocky Mountains to the Pacific," 2 March 1814, Coventry Transcript, MG 19, A13, P.A.C. Published in Elliot Coues, ed., *New Light on the Early History of the Greater Northwest: the Manuscript Journals of Alexander Henry . . . and of David Thompson*, 3 vols. (London: Suckling & Co., 1897) and also printed in Payette, *Oregon Country*. Hereinafter cited as *Henry Journal*, with date.

Navy and the Company vessel *Isaac Todd.* They signed a bill of sale on 16 October 1813, nine days after the arrival of McTavish's overland party.[46] This purchase would prove to be important during negotiations for peace and even after the war.

The British take over the Fort

Meanwhile, the *Racoon* had made her way northward to the Island of Cocos, reaching it on 7 October 1813. There Captain William Black of the *Racoon* hoped to find the *Isaac Todd,* for in his instructions the island had been named as a place to take on wood and water, if needed. But after remaining two days at Cocos without sighting the North West Company vessel, the *Racoon* made sail for the Columbia.[47] During gunnery practice at sea two weeks later, a tremendous explosion of gunpowder shook the *Racoon*; of the twenty-one men who were injured six later died.[48]

By 30 November 1813, the partially disabled *Racoon* had reached the mouth of the Columbia. She anchored in Baker's Bay within Cape Disappointment. In spite of her condition and loss of men, preparations were made for "a grand attack" on Fort Astoria in the mistaken belief that the fort was still in American hands.[49] About eighty men with marines were to land from three armed boats and take the post either by surprise at daybreak or under the ship's fire. Because quite a few miles separated the *Racoon*'s anchorage from Fort Astoria, the ship's cutter was sent to find the fort's exact location and to examine the river entrance.

Ironically, the British at Fort Astoria were also expecting a military engagement. The British fur traders who now controlled the Columbia River mouth lived in continual fear of an American attack. They assumed that the *Essex* was still at large; thus, the arrival of a warship caused understandable excitement and concern on shore.

Because the colours of the *Racoon* were unrecognizable from the fort, the Nor'westers prepared to abandon the post if the ship proved to be the enemy. At one o'clock in the afternoon, a party left in a canoe to determine if the man-of-war anchored in Baker's Bay was British. When the canoe did not return four hours later, the traders on shore loaded most of their packs, arms and ammunition into canoes to search for a more secure position up the river. However, later in the evening the original investigating party returned to the fort after determining that

[46]Sale documents are in *Oregon Historical Quarterly,* XXXIII (1932) , 43-50.
[47]Hussey, ed., *Voyage of the 'Racoon',* p. xvi.
[48]Captain William Black to Dixon, 10 April 1814, from San Francisco, Adm. 1/22.
[49]A vivid description of the excitement on board the *Racoon* is given in Hussey, ed., *Voyage of the 'Racoon',* p. 4.

the unknown ship was the *Racoon*. While investigating they had gone on board and celebrated her arrival with a large quantity of Tenerife wine, which accounts for their delay in returning with the good news.[50]

The next day Captain Black of the *Racoon* examined the river mouth, using the chart made by Lieutenant W. R. Broughton in 1792 when commanding the *Chatham* brig in Captain George Vancouver's expedition. Black planned to enter by the southern channel but strong winds and tides made this impossible. Finally on 12 December Black reached shore with a small party of seamen and marines in the fur traders' coastal vessel *Dolly*.

The next morning Black is reported to have exclaimed in disgust when he saw the small stockade on a slight hill not far from the water, "Is this the fort about which I have heard so much talking? D--n me, but I'd batter it down in two hours with a four pounder!"[51]

That afternoon of 13 December 1813 a significant ceremony took place. The fort saluted Black with seven guns, and the Nor'westers raised the British flag given them by the captain. With sailors manning the guns and marines and company men parading with muskets, Black broke a bottle of wine on the flag staff, claimed the fort and country for his king, and renamed the post Fort George in honour of His Majesty.[52] Black then sent this report overland, as decyphered, to the Admiralty:

> Country and fort I have taken possession of in name and for British Majesty; latter I have named Fort George and left in possession and charge North West Company.
> Enemy's party quite broke up; they have no settlement whatever on this river or coast.
> Enemy's vessels said on coast and about islands; while provisions last, shall endeavour to destroy them. . . .[53]

The arrival of the *Racoon* and the ceremony of possession clearly confirmed British control at Fort George. Black's act formally established the North West Company's ownership of the post.

A question often posed, and still unanswered for lack of evidence, is why did the Nor'westers purchase the post from the Astorians on 16 October when the naval force was known to be on its way? According to one person on board the *Racoon*, the purchase was "diametrically

[50]*Henry Journal*, 30 November 1813, and 4 and 10 April 1814.
[51]Ross Cox, *Adventures on the Columbia River*, 2 vols. (London: H. Colburn & R. Bentley, 1831), I, 266. For other versions of what Black Said, see Coues, ed., *New Light on the Northwest*, II, 770-71, n. 36.
[52]*Henry Journal*, 13 December 1813.
[53]Black's report, 15 December 1813, decyphered, encl. in Dixon to Admiralty, 24 December 1814, Adm. 1/22. Also in *Navy and South America*, p. 149, and *Oregon Historical Quarterly*, XVII (1916), 147-48. Another copy of the report reached the Admiralty 14 October 1814 in cyphered form.

opposite to the fundamental laws of Great Britain under the head of assisting an Enemy."[54] He and others in the British warship hoped that an Admiralty Court would show that the *Racoon* had captured the fort and that the value of the seizure would be given to the ship's company. A generally held view, based on much hearsay evidence and without documentary proof, is that Captain Black thought the Nor'westers and Astorians conspired to defraud him and his crew of the prize money.[55]

The controversy had both immediate and long-term consequences. Almost certainly, animosity developed between the sailors and fur traders over the objectives and spoils of war. Furthermore, this confused beginning of British control at the Columbia River mouth tended to complicate the British diplomatic position at discussions leading to the Treaty of Ghent in 1814 and afterward.

On board the *Racoon*, the appearance of scurvy and the lack of sufficient provisions forced Black to sail from the Columbia River much earlier than the fur traders judged to be in their best interests. Wildfowl and salmon delivered to the ship by the Indians and purchased by the North West Company were welcome. But they were insufficient to offset Black's deep concern for the welfare of his ship's company, and he decided to set a course for San Francisco where he hoped to find additional provisions, after which he would sail in search of American fur-trading vessels that were known to winter in the Hawaiian Islands.

The *Racoon* departed from the Columbia on New Year's Eve, but the fur traders at Fort George remained concerned about their security; they were still under the impression that the *Essex* was at large. If they were attacked they would have to stand alone until the *Isaac Todd* arrived. And many must have doubted that she would ever appear.

At least one Nor'wester thought Black should sail directly for the Hawaiian Islands to capture "the whole nest" of wintering American vessels. It was proposed that the British fur traders buy one captured vessel for the use of the Nor'westers on the Northwest Coast. Black, however, explained that he could not sell them a prize ship unless it had been condemned by an Admiralty Court, and the nearest court was at the Cape of Good Hope.[56] He added that he intended to destroy any prizes to prevent them from being retaken by enemy warships. Black's conduct won him the praise of his Commander-in-Chief, Rear-Admiral Dixon, when the latter advised the Lords of the Admiralty: "The service on

---

[54]Hussey, ed., *Voyage of the 'Racoon'*, p. 5.
[55]See, for example, Hubert H. Bancroft, *The Northwest Coast*, 2 vols., in *History of the Pacific States of North America*, Vols. XXII and XXIII (San Francisco; A. L. Bancroft & Co., 1884) , I, 233, and see also Robert Greenhow, *The History of Oregon and California* (London: John Murray, 1844) , p. 304.
[56]Payette, *Oregon Country*, pp. xii-xiii.

which the *Racoon* has been employed has been most ably and meritoriously executed by Captain Black; he speaks highly of all his officers and ship's company in several perilous and trying situations. . . ."[57] But some Nor'westers at Fort George had a different opinion. The Nor'wester Alexander Henry the Younger, whose overall views tended toward exaggeration, had this to say of Black and his men:

> Indeed with the exception of Captain Black, the Officers of the *Raccoon* [*sic*] are not those vigilant, careful, active and fine enterprising fellows, so much talked of and admired by all the World, as the main prop of Great Britain. The Navy, were all His Majesty's Naval Officers of the same stamp as those we saw here, England would not long have it in her power to boast of her Wooden Walls.[58]

No news had been received of the *Isaac Todd* since she had separated from the squadron in late May 1813. She had not arrived at the mouth of the Columbia and many at Fort George feared that either she had fallen prey to the *Essex* as rumoured or had become a total loss. Yet they continued to hope that she would reach Oregon and alleviate the precarious position of the British, who were further threatened by warlike preparations of the Chinook Indians. Actually, the slow-sailing *Isaac Todd* was at Monterey, California, where her captain learned that the *Racoon* was in distress.

The *Racoon* had lost her false keel in crossing the bar of the Columbia River outward bound from Fort George. Somewhat miraculously, she reached San Francisco Bay with seven feet of water in her hold, greatly damaged.[59] Unfortunately, naval stores and assistance at San Francisco proved inadequate, and Black and his officers considered abandoning the *Racoon* and returning to England via Mexico. But this became unnecessary when the *Isaac Todd,* "sent as by the works of our maker," as one sailor recalled, joined the *Racoon* at San Francisco Bay with stores and help.[60] At Angel Island, the *Racoon* was careened and repairs were effected. Then the two ships parted company. The *Racoon* sailed for the Hawaiian Islands on 19 January 1814 in search of American warships and fur-trading vessels.

The *Isaac Todd* sailed for Fort George and finally reached the mouth of the Columbia on 23 April—thirteen weary months after leaving

---

[57]Dixon to Croker, 24 December 1814, Adm. 1/22.
[58]*Henry Journal,* 24 April 1814.
[59]Hussey, ed., *Voyage of the 'Racoon',* pp. 15ff.
[60]*Ibid.,* p. 20. See also Marion O'Neil, "The Maritime Activities of the North West Company, 1813-1820," *Washington Historical Quarterly,* XXI (1930), 251-52, and Vernon D. Tate, ed., "Spanish Documents Relating to the Voyage of the *Racoon* to Astoria and San Francisco," *Hispanic American Historical Review,* XVIII (May 1938), 190-91.

Portsmouth. Her arrival ensured the preservation of British interests at Fort George during wartime. Both objectives of Hillyar's bold decision were now achieved: the *Essex* had been captured and control of the Columbia River mouth was in British hands.

By the time the *Isaac Todd* reached Fort George, the North West Company had sent a second vessel, the *Columbia,* from England bound for the Northwest Coast. Again, a ship of the Royal Navy, H.M.S. *Laurel,* provided convoy support, but this time only as far as Rio de Janeiro. The *Columbia* arrived at the strongly fortified Fort George in July 1814.[61] Annually thereafter, ships brought supplies and took away furs bound for the China market. The British were thus successful in establishing the 'Columbian enterprise' even while the War of 1812 made extensive demands on the Royal Navy in various places on the high seas.

Problems of Agreement

In view of the Anglo-American rivalry to control the Columbia trade between 1810 and 1814, it seems paradoxical that the British government showed little concern for the territory west of the Rocky Mountains when peace negotiations began at Ghent. The silence of the British plenipotentiaries was later explained to the North West Company by Earl Bathurst, the Secretary for War and the Colonies, on the grounds that "requiring from the Americans any recognition or guarantee of His Majesty's rights thereto, might lead to cast doubts upon a title which was sufficiently strong and incontrovertible."[62] Such was the excuse for what was probably an oversight.

The American plenipotentiaries argued aggressively that Fort Astoria should be restored to the United States because it had been in American hands before the war. This reflected the policy of the Secretary of State, James Monroe, who instructed the delegation to insist on the restoration of the fort. With reference to the British, Monroe noted, "It is not believed that they have any claim to territory on the Pacific ocean."[63] Ultimately, the Treaty of Ghent, signed 24 December 1814, stipulated a return to the *status quo ante bellum.* Both during and after negotiations, the Nor'westers made repeated appeals to the British government for protection against the Americans. They hoped to safeguard their post

---

[61]Capt. Peter Corney of the *Columbia* described Fort George's substantial defences in his *Voyages in the North Pacific* (Honolulu; Thom. G. Thrum, 1896) , pp. 79a and 80a.
[62]"Statement relative to the Columbia River [1815]," encl. in McGillivray to Sir C. Bagot, 15 November 1817, and fur traders' demands, 7 May 1814, F.O. 5/1230.
[63]J. Monroe to Plenipotentiaries, 22 March 1814, *American State Papers, Foreign Relations,* 6 vols. (Washington, 1832-59) , III, 731.

on the Columbia, which they claimed had been acquired by purchase.[64] Nevertheless, the Treaty of Ghent failed to make specific reference to the fort at the Columbia River mouth. In fact, the Treaty's "only definite achievement," according to one authority, "was the termination of hostilities."[65] Altogether the Treaty was an unsatisfactory agreement and the cause of later disputes between Britain and the United States.

After signing the Treaty, the United States government took steps to recover the post on the Northwest Coast. In Washington, the Secretary of State, Monroe, told the British Minister in residence, Anthony St. John Baker, that inasmuch as the British force had taken possession of Fort Astoria during the war, the United States intended to reoccupy the fort without delay.[66]

When Monroe asked that a letter be addressed to the British naval commander in the North Pacific ordering the return of the fort to the Americans, Baker replied that he knew very little about the fate of Astoria although he believed that the post lay in ruins and was unoccupied.[67] Baker suggested that Sir Manley Dixon, Commander-in-Chief on the South American station and in charge of British warships in the Pacific, would possess authentic information and could communicate with any authorized American agent on the subject.

Immediately Baker wrote to Dixon to warn him of the developments in Washington. He enclosed copies of the correspondence with Monroe, and emphasized that Britain did not recognize any American possession on the Pacific Coast.[68] Although Baker did learn from the North West Company in Canada that the possession of Astoria was effected by purchase, he failed to press this advantageous position with the American Secretary of State.

It is generally believed that only the lack of naval units during 1815 and 1816 prevented the United States from sending a vessel on a mission of restitution to the Northwest Coast.[69] A suggestion in the autumn of 1815 that a naval expedition explore the Northwest Coast won support from President James Madison, but the need for economy caused the

---

[64]See Katherine B. Judson, "The British Side of the Restoration of Fort Astoria," *Oregon Historical Quarterly*, XX (1919), 243-60 and 305-306.

[65]A. L. Burt, *The United States, Great Britain and British North America from the Revolution to the Establishment of Peace after the War of 1812* (New Haven: Yale University Press, 1940), p. 371.

[66]Monroe to A. Baker, 18 July 1815, encl. in Baker to Lord Castlereagh, 19 July 1815, F.O. 5/107.

[67]Baker to Monroe, 23 July 1815, encl. in Baker to Castlereagh, 13 August 1815, *ibid*.

[68]Baker to Dixon, 24 July 1815, encl. in *ibid*. For the full diplomatic interplay, see Burt, *United States, Great Britain and British North America*, pp. 411-22.

[69]See Frederick Merk, "The Genesis of the Oregon Question," *Mississippi Valley Historical Review*, XXXVI (March 1950), 593-94.

proposal to be set aside. The U.S.S. *Congress,* which was to sail in mid-1816 for the Pacific, had to be sent to the Gulf of Mexico instead. Not until difficulties over Algiers and Florida were resolved did the United States government give attention to the Northwest Coast.

On 4 October 1817 the American sloop-of-war *Ontario,* 20 guns, Captain James Biddle, sailed from New York for the Columbia on an ill-advised secret mission to take possession of Astoria. But when Simon McGillivray of the North West Company learned of this through a breach in security, he immediately informed Sir Charles Bagot, the British chargé d'affaires in Washington.[70] John Quincy Adams, United States Secretary of State, appeared "considerably embarrassed" when Bagot asked him if the rumour were true. He admitted that the *Ontario* was sent to assert American sovereignty, but not to destroy the trade of the North West Company.[71]

Bagot was not satisfied with the response. Immediately, he notified Viscount Castlereagh, the British Foreign Secretary, that a vessel had been ordered "to the mouth of the Columbia River for the purpose of re-establishing the Settlement of which the United States was dispossessed during the late war."[72] Bagot then advised the Governor General of Canada to send an overland party to warn the Nor'westers on the Pacific Coast.[73] Optimistically, he suggested to the Foreign Secretary that a vessel from England could arrive at the Columbia before the *Ontario.*[74] But nothing was done in response to Bagot's advice.

Further information reached the Admiralty from Commodore Sir James Lucas Yeo, Commander-in-Chief on the West African Coast, that the Americans possessed a "restless and hostile spirit" toward Britain.[75] He also reported that he learned during his visit to New York that the *Ontario* was sailing for the North Pacific with commissioners on board "to obtain possession of some Island or Territory in that quarter preparatory to their establishing a very extensive commerce in those Seas."[76]

The British cabinet considered this difficult situation and sought to avert a renewal of war. The Foreign Secretary, Castlereagh, knew that the Nor'westers had actually purchased Fort Astoria. But the dilemma arose because Captain Black's report indicated that he had claimed that

[70]S. McGillivray to Sir C. Bagot, 15 November 1817, encl. in Bagot to Castlereagh, 2 December 1817, F.O. 5/123.
[71]Bagot to Castlereagh, 24 November 1817, cypher, *ibid.*
[72]*Ibid.*
[73]Bagot to Sir John Sherbrooke (Governor-in-Chief of Canada), 1 December 1817, *ibid.*
[74]Bagot to Castlereagh, 2 December 1817, *ibid.*
[75]Commodore J. Yeo to Croker, 30 August 1817, encl. in J. Barrow to Hamilton (F.O.), 3 September 1817, F.O. 5/128.
[76]*Ibid.*

territory as a conquest of war: provision in the Treaty of Ghent to return to the *status quo ante bellum* meant that Britain had to return any conquest of war. The conciliatory Foreign Secretary clearly was more interested in the stability of international relations than in additions to the British Empire. In order to give the Americans what he referred to generally as "an additional motive to cultivate the arts of peace," he decided to return the post to the Americans provided it was abundantly clear to them that this would neither recognize United States rights nor relinquish British claims to the territory.[77] To implement this generous albeit shortsighted policy, he instructed the Secretary for War and the Colonies, Earl Bathurst, to inform the fur traders of the proposed restitution of Fort George, previously Fort Astoria, to the United States. At the same time, Castlereagh instructed the Admiralty to send a warship to the Northwest Coast to restore the post officially to American commissioners.[78]

The mission was carried out by the *Blossom,* 18 guns,—a "ship-sloop" and sister to the *Racoon* and *Cherub*—previously engaged in protecting British commerce in ports on the Pacific side of South America during the war between Spain and Chile. She sailed from Valparaiso for the Columbia on 12 July 1818, carrying Colonial Office dispatches to the Nor'westers authorizing the restitution.[79] By the time she had anchored near Fort George on 1 October the American ship *Ontario* had arrived, made territorial claims for the United States and departed.[80] The British fur traders, unsure whether peace or war existed, had made preparations to defend the post.[81]

The Dispute Unresolved

In official ceremonies which followed, Captain Frederick Hickey of the *Blossom* and James Keith, a British commissioner and the factor in charge of the fort, signed the Instrument of Restoration. Then the British flag was lowered and the flag of the United States was raised. This act, which must have seemed as ridiculous to the participants as it does

[77]Sir Charles K. Webster, *The Foreign Policy of Castlereagh, 1812-1815* (London: G. Bell & Sons, 1931), p. 196. See also Gerald S. Graham, *Empire of the North Atlantic: the Maritime Struggle for North America,* 2nd ed. (Toronto: University of Toronto Press, 1958), pp. 262-64.

[78]Merk, "Genesis of the Oregon Question," pp. 603-604.

[79]F. V. Longstaff and W. Kaye Lamb, "The Royal Navy on the Northwest Coast, 1813-1850, Part I," *British Columbia Historical Quarterly,* IX (January 1945), 6; Bowles to Croker, 29 April 1818, Adm. 1/23.

[80]J. Keith to Capt. F. Hickey, 7 October 1818, encl. in Barrow to Hamilton, 10 August 1819, F.O 5/147.

[81]Hickey to Keith, 4 October 1818, encl. in Barrow to Hamilton, 10 August 1819, F.O. 5/147.

now, was intended to symbolize American "ownership" of Fort George. But it did not end the confusion. The Nor'westers continued to use the post as their headquarters on the Northwest Coast for many years. It remained the chief depot of the Hudson's Bay Company, which merged with the North West Company in 1821, until 1825 when Fort Vancouver was erected.

The territorial claims made when the American ship *Ontario* came to the Columbia in October, 1817, convinced the British ministry that differences between the United States and Britain should be resolved to maintain peace. In the negotiations which led to the Anglo-American Convention of 1818, the British proposed an international boundary along the Columbia River and joint occupancy of the land at the river mouth.[82] This, however, was unacceptable to the United States. The parties finally agreed to joint occupation of the so-called Oregon Territory, which was between Spanish-held Upper California and Russian America and lay between the Continental Divide and the Pacific Coast.

The Anglo-American Convention of 1818 postponed negotiations between Britain and the United States on territorial claims to Oregon. Failure to resolve the dispute at this time was to confuse rival traders, mariners and diplomats for many years and nearly embroil the two nations in war in 1846. By 1818, British dominance in the fur trade at the mouth of the Columbia and thus over the hinterland had been gained with the aid of the Royal Navy. In particular, convoy support given the Nor'westers by British warships during the War of 1812, the success of the *Phoebe* and *Cherub* against the *Essex,* and the completion of the missions of the *Racoon* and *Isaac Todd* ensured continuation of British fur-trading interests on the Northwest Coast. Although the contest for the Columbia country ended in Britain's favour in terms of trade, the unwillingness of the war-weary British ministry to obtain recognition from the United States in 1815 and 1818 of British territorial control led to protracted negotiations during the next three decades.

[82]Burt, *United States, Great Britain and British North America,* p. 422.

Chapter 2

GREAT BRITAIN IN THE NORTHEASTERN PACIFIC
1818-1843

AT THE CLOSE of the Napoleonic Wars in 1815, Britain stood unrivalled as a world power. This was due to her naval strength which developed during the eighteenth century in the long struggle for supremacy and empire with Spain, France and finally the United States. In the words of Admiral Sir Cyprian Bridge, British naval power was "so ubiquitous and all-pervading that, like the atmosphere, we rarely thought of it and rarely remembered its necessity or its existence."[1] British influence rested also on her industrial system then expanding into a worldwide business organization, stimulated by the increase in overseas trade.[2] Britain held virtually a monopoly of all tropical produce, and her ships—both merchant and naval—were "available for the maintenance of power on and over the seas."[3] Her marked naval superiority together with well-nurtured European alliances eliminated the threat of war for the half-century beginning with Waterloo and ending with the Crimean War.[4]

[1] Admiral Sir Cyprian Bridge, *Sea-Power and Other Studies* (London; Smith, Elder & Co., 1910), pp. 63-64.
[2] See Albert H. Imlah, *Economic Elements in the 'Pax Britannica'* (Cambridge, Mass.: Harvard University Press, 1958), p. 186.
[3] Sir Halford J. Mackinder, *Democratic Ideas and Reality* (London: Constable & Co., 1919), p. 73.
[4] See Gerald S. Graham. *The Politics of Naval Supremacy* (Cambridge: Cambridge University Press, 1965), chapter 4.

In recognition of expansion of British political influence and maritime enterprise beyond Cape Horn during this period, a separate naval station for the Pacific was created at Valparaiso in 1837. This command evolved from the old South American station and assumed its western duties.[5] The growth of British interest west of Cape Horn paralleled that east of Cape of Good Hope: the Australasian station established in 1859 and the China station founded in 1864 grew out of the old East Indies and China station. The Pacific station headquarters at Valparaiso met the two eastern stations at 170° West longitude.[6] From this new head-quarters, men-of-war protected British interests in South America and they carried treasure from ports as far north as the Gulf of California.[7]

Britain's chief rival in the Northeastern Pacific in the years 1818-1843 was the United States, which lacked all territorial advantage until American settlers began trekking into Oregon in 1842.[8] In 1818, both Britain and the United States held Oregon by agreement; both watched Russian expansion in America with suspicion; both observed Spain's declining power in California with more than casual interest; and both vied for power in the Western Hemisphere. Both countries sought to resolve several major issues including the extent to which Russian activity should be allowed to expand in North America; the question of sovereignty of the Hawaiian Islands; the possible acquisition of Upper California by one of the powers; and their dispute over Oregon.

The Russian Challenge

Russia was the first to challenge Britain's claims to the Northwest Coast which were recognized by the Nootka agreement with Spain in 1790. Alexander Baranoff, the governor of the Russian American Company in North America, had established a settlement at Sitka in the year 1799. His aim was to develop a great North Pacific empire; to this end he built Fort Ross on Bodega Bay, Upper California, in 1812 as an agricultural and fur-trading centre and a possible defence post. The Russian American Company also maintained a station on the nearby Farallones

5For the boundaries of this station, see Appendix A.
6Gerald S. Graham and R. A. Humphreys, eds., *The Navy and South America, 1807-1823: Correspondence of the Commanders-in-Chief on the South American Station* (London: Navy Records Society, vol. CIV, 1962), pp. xi-xii and xxiii-xxxiv. The genesis of the Pacific station is explained in John Bach, "The Royal Navy and the South Pacific, 1826-1876" (Ph.D. thesis; University of New South Wales, 1964), chapter 2. See also Appendix A.
7During the California gold rush, British men-of-war called at San Francisco to receive merchants' treasure for shipment to England.
8On this rivalry, see Frederick Merk, *The Oregon Question: Essays in Anglo-American Diplomacy and Politics* (Cambridge, Mass.: Belknap Press, 1967).

Islands, and it considered the Hawaiian Islands as a possible focal point of activity.

As long as the Russians did not interfere with British traders in and around Nootka Sound, the steady Russian ascendancy in Alaska received scant attention from the British government. This situation changed, however, when Tsar Nicholas I proclaimed, in his Ukase of 1821, territorial sovereignty for Russia over the lengthy arch extending from Siberia along the coasts of North America to 51° North latitude, near the northern tip of Vancouver Island, and dominion over adjacent seas 115 miles from the coast. This declaration ran counter to the claims of Great Britain and the United States, which by their Convention of 1818 had established a condominium over the Pacific Slope west of the Continental Divide from 42° North latitude, the northern border of Upper California, to an undetermined point in Alaska.

The British Admiralty knew that in 1815-1818 the Russian explorer Otto von Kotzebue had greatly extended Russian knowledge of the American continent in and around the sound which bears his name; they knew also that in 1823 the Tsar had ordered him on a "scientific mission" to Kamchatka near the Kurile Islands and to the Northwest Coast of America to protect the Russian American Company from smuggling carried on by foreign traders. Knowledge of von Kotzebue's mission and of Russian continental and maritime designs as promulgated in the Ukase of 1821 spurred British promoters of Arctic exploration on the one hand and the Hudson's Bay Company on the other to consider ways of containing their rival.

The British Foreign Office could not agree to either the territorial or maritime claims of the Tsar. The Hudson's Bay Company—with which the North West Company was now merged—as well as British whaling interests, and Sir John Barrow, the influential Admiralty secretary and promoter of Arctic exploration, all objected to the fact that the Russian intrusion, if recognized, would end free navigation on the coast.[9] Accordingly, stiff diplomatic opposition was expressed in London, plans for British exploration in the Arctic were undertaken and Hudson's Bay Company activities, in what is now the Yukon, developed apace.

John Franklin, the explorer, proposed a survey of the shores of the Polar Sea from the mouth of the Mackenzie River westward to the Northwest corner of America. The "objects to be attained," he advised Barrow on 26 November 1823 "are important at once to the Naval character and the Commercial interests of Great Britain." The particular advantage

[9]See John S. Galbraith, *The Hudson's Bay Company as an Imperial Factor, 1821-1869* (Berkeley and Los Angeles: University of California Press, 1957), p. 133 and n. 62.

would be, he felt, "the preservation of that Country, which is most rich in Animals from the encroachment of Russia and preventing the Establishment of another and at some Period perhaps a hostile Power on any Part of the Northern Continent of America."[10] The Hudson's Bay Company offered assistance to the project in order to prevent a Russian claim to the undiscovered northern coast at the expense of British interests.[11] The Admiralty immediately decided to send two ships under command of Captain William E. Parry to find the Northwest Passage via Prince Regent Inlet. Franklin was to proceed by way of the Mackenzie River and the shores of the Polar Sea as planned. Captain Frederick William Beechey, meanwhile, received instructions to sail from England to Bering Strait, extend the geographical knowledge of the northwest coast of Alaska, and, at Kotzebue Sound, meet and supply Parry and Franklin should they complete their intended travels from the east. (But of course the explorations of 1825-1827 did not result in finding the Northwest Passage.)

The Hudson's Bay Company had its own plans for checking Russian aspirations at the same time. In 1822, the Governor and Committee had already determined to expand Company interests as far north and west of the Fraser River as necessary "to keep the Russians at a distance."[12] Subsequently, Samuel Black was sent by the Company to explore the waterways parallel to and west of the Mackenzie River and Rocky Mountains with a view to drawing Indian trade in the Stikine territory away from the Russians on the coast. Thus began for the Company a successful and little-known program to stabilize and push back the northwestern frontier of its operations first on land and, after 1826, on water. So adroit was the Company in its dealings on the upper portion of the coast in the 1820's and 1830's that British warships were not required to uphold national interests.

The British were in a strong bargaining position against Russia whose maritime claims of 1821 contravened international law and whose trading aspirations could now be contained by the Hudson's Bay Company. At all odds, British trade was to be protected where British claims were legitimate. A convention was signed on 28 February 1825 in which

[10]John Franklin to John Barrow (Admiralty), 26 November 1823, copy, A. 8/1, fols. 224-29, H.B.C.A.

[11]John H. Pelly (Governor, H.B.C.) to Barrow, 29 November 1823, *ibid.*, fol. 220. Further details on British plans and strategy at this time are given in John E. Caswell, "The Sponsors of Canadian Arctic Exploration, Part III—1800 to 1839," *The Beaver,* Outfit 300 (Autumn 1969), pp. 29-30.

[12]Governor and Committee to George Simpson, 27 February 1822, A. 6/20, H.B.C.A.; printed in R. Harvey Fleming, ed., *Minutes of Council of the Northern Department of Rupert Land 1821-31* (London: Hudson's Bay Record Society, vol. III, 1940), p. 303.

Britain and Russia entered into an agreement that established the southern boundary of Russian America at 54°40′ and its eastern limits along Portland Canal to 56° North latitude and thence by the height of mountains parallel to but no nearer than ten leagues from the coast to the 141st meridian, on which line it would run to the Arctic Ocean. The Russians acknowledged British navigation rights on the coast and on rivers cutting through the Russian *lisière* or coastal strip. The British could also trade at Sitka and on the Russian coast south of Mount Saint Elias for a ten-year period.[13] These terms, essentially the same as those of a Russian-American Convention of 17 April 1824, stayed Russian progress eastward and southward while at the same time they restored British and American maritime rights.

By diplomacy and trade, therefore, the British had entrenched their own position in Northwestern North America including the coast of that area. They had done so with remarkable ease against a weaker power without resorting to the use of the Navy to make clear their position. The aim of the British was trade—not colonization. But the Monroe Doctrine, announced by the President of the United States in 1823 in an effort to end further European colonization in America, was viewed in London at the time with contempt. It has been argued that the doctrine was aimed at Britain, not Russia.[14] The Foreign Office was nonetheless prepared to uphold British interests on the Northwest Coast in the face of Russian or American rivalry, or both.[15] Foreign Office policy continued to hold that the colonization of the unoccupied portions of America would be open as before.[16]

Peaceful expansion in the face of the Russian challenge was the result of careful and successful development by the Hudson's Bay Company and the fact that differences of opinion between Britain and Russia were resolved amicably. By 1839 American and Russian competition in the fur trade of both the coast and the interior had been eliminated and the Hudson's Bay Company reigned supreme on the Northwest Coast of North America.

13Galbraith, *Hudson's Bay Company*, p. 134.
14For an attack on the thesis of H.W.V. Temperley that Russia "was extending a long arm over the Pacific," see Irby C. Nichols, Jr., "The Russian Ukase and the Monroe Doctrine: A Re-evalution," *Pacific Historical Review*, XXXVI (February 1967) , 16ff.
15G. Canning (F.O.) to R. Rush (Am. Min. in London) , January 1824, draft, F.O. 5/194, and Dexter Perkins, *The Monroe Doctrine, 1823-26* (Cambridge, Mass.: Harvard University Press, 1932) , p. 33. Russia had, in fact, sent three frigates to the Northwest coast in 1822 to exclude foreigners; Nichols, "Russian Ukase and the Monroe Doctrine," pp. 21, 24. See also Kenneth Bourne, *Britain and the Balance of Power in North America, 1815-1908* (London, Longmans, Green & Co., 1967) , pp. 64-71.
16Merk, *Oregon Question*, p. 137.

The Hawaiian Islands

In the Hawaiian Islands, international rivalry was less clearly defined and much less easily resolved. Shortly after the War of 1812, France, the United States and Britain began to display interest in the islands because of their strategic location between the potentially rich markets of the Americas and those of Asia.[17] The maritime powers considered them to be the *entrepôt* of the Pacific; their proximity to North America seemed to imply that their destiny would be determined by the nation that controlled the Pacific slope. This explains why, in 1827, the British Prime Minister, George Canning, refused to enter into an agreement with the United States in which Britain would have "foregone the advantages of an immense indirect intercourse between China and what may be, if we resolve not to yield them up, her boundless establishments on the N. W. Coast of America."[18] Knowing that the East India Company monopoly would expire in 1833, after which trans-Pacific trade would flourish, and wary of American aspirations in the Pacific, Canning would not place in jeopardy the future advantages that would accrue from a commerce linking two hemispheres. To him this represented "the trade of the world most susceptible of rapid augmentation and improvement."[19]

By 1820, Honolulu had become the principal port in the Pacific, and it remained so until San Francisco became an important maritime centre after the California gold discoveries of 1848. Consequently, the Hawaiian Islands were visited periodically by British men-of-war.

On the long cruises to Hawaii, for reasons of navigation, captains preferred to sail before the southeast trade winds from the major South American ports of Valparaiso and Callao. After reaching the Doldrums, they relied on the northeast trade winds to complete the course to Honolulu. Then, crossing the "horse latitudes," they followed the Japanese Current to the Northwest Coast, San Francisco or Monterey. Some of them took on treasure shipments at various Mexican ports for safe conveyance to England, before returning to Valparaiso and finally sailing home at the completion of a three- or four-year commission in the Pacific.

---

[17]For general accounts of American and French interest, see Harold W. Bradley, "Hawaii and the American Penetration of the Northeastern Pacific, 1800-1845," *Pacific Historical Review*, XII (1943) , 277-86; George Vern Blue, "The Policy of France toward the Hawaiian Islands from the Earliest Times to the Treaty of 1846," *The Hawaiian Islands*, Publication of the Archives of Hawaii No. 5 (Honolulu, 1930) , pp. 51-93; and Christian Schefer, "La Monarchie de Juilliet et l'Expansion Coloniale," *Revue des Deux Mondes*, 6e série, XI (1912) , 152-84.
[18]Canning to Lord Liverpool, 7 July 1826; in E. J. Stapleton, ed., *Some Official Correspondence of George Canning*, 2 vols. (London: Longmans, Green & Co., 1887) , II, 74.
[19]*Ibid.*

These treasure shipments provide a minor but interesting parenthesis to maritime history. The carrying of specie in Royal Navy ships in lawless areas had been authorized "for centuries," but was virtually confined by the nineteenth century to the Pacific Coasts of Latin America. Admiralty regulations defining to the conveyance of specie seem to have existed early in that century, though it was not until 1819 that a statute formally stated the conditions of the lucrative scheme. The statute was followed by the Proclamation of William IV dated 8 June 1831 which reduced the "freight" from one and one-half to one per cent. At the completion of the voyage, the freight was divided into four parts: two parts for the ship's commander, one part for the commander-in-chief on the station, and one part for the Greenwich Hospital for Seamen. Thus, in the case of the *Grampus* returning to England in 1848 with one of the largest treasures of the period amounting to $2,628,900 (Mexican, equivalent to about £107,000), her captain received nearly $13,145, and the commander-in-chief, Pacific, and Greenwich Hospital about $6,573 each.[20]

Returning to navigational problems in the Pacific, by the mid-1840's, "steam navigation" and the establishment of bunkering facilities were advanced enough to permit paddle-wheelers to visit the North Pacific Coast without following the usual tracks via the Hawaiian Islands. Paddle-wheelers could also reach various Pacific islands more quickly than ships dependent on wind as the sole motive power. At first steam-assisted ships did not appear in great numbers because of problems of maintenance, cost, fuel reliability and radius of action. Even as late as the mid-1850's, when the screw-propeller began to replace the paddle-wheel, the majority of warships depended entirely on the wind or were steam-assisted; thus a clockwise track of British warships was common from the coast of South America to Tahiti, Hawaii, the North Pacific Coast and then south to Valparaiso. In the Pacific the ability of a commander to get his ship under sail as quickly as possible from point to point across vast reaches of water still required great skills in navigation and seamanship.

One of the first visits of the Royal Navy to Honolulu occurred in 1824, when H.M.S. *Blonde*, 46 guns, Captain Lord George Byron, conveyed home the remains of the Hawaiian royal couple who died of measles while on a visit to England. A 46-gun frigate was sent—much larger than the sloops of 18 to 26 guns which usually patrolled the seas at this time—and this indicates the political importance Canning gave

20Admiral Sir Cyprian Bridge, *Some Recollections* (London: John Murray, 1918), pp. 127-31. 59 *Geo.* III (1819), cap. 25.

to this mission.[21] The Hawaiians had looked to Britain for security and protection ever since the visit of Captain Vancouver in 1794. The Foreign Office considered the *Blonde*'s presence especially desirable and timely since both the Russian and American governments were "known to have their eyes upon those islands which may ere long become a very important Station in the trade between the N. W. Coast of America and the China Seas."[22] Fear that the French held a superiority at sea in the Pacific was also a factor.

For these reasons—and especially to consolidate British interests in the islands—the British concluded that a naval base should be established if a suitable situation could be found. None was discovered then and Britain was obliged to rely on irregular visits of warships—which later became periodic—and the appointment of Captain Richard Charlton as consul in 1824 to guard her interests. She sought to encourage commerce, preserve the islands as a place of refreshment for ships of the Royal Navy and maintain the prevalent Hawaiian disposition "of looking to British Connection in Preference to that of any other Power."[23]

By the 1830's the Hawaiian Islands experienced the growing trade and increasing settlement which British Prime Minister Canning had prophesied earlier for the islands and for the littoral of the North Pacific. Often the Hawaiian Islands served as wintering headquarters for sea captains who sought hides and tallow on the coasts of California, whales throughout the North Pacific, and walrus teeth, sandalwood, pearl shell and other commodities among the Pacific islands.[24] Moreover, according to Captain Michael Seymour of H.M.S. *Challenger,* visiting the Hawaiian group in 1834, exotic products such as sugar cane, indigo and ginger could be grown there, as well as enough tobacco to supply all the Northwest Coast, California and Mexico.[25]

Already the islands provided a promising outlet for British manufacturers; each year £50,000 to £60,000 worth of British goods were sold there. Chief among the British trading organizations was the Hud-

---

[21]For the increase of British naval strength in the Pacific at this time, including sending a ship-of-the-line to the west coast of South America, see Liverpool to Earl Bathurst, 16 October 1823, Historical Manuscripts Commission, *Bathurst MSS.* (London, H.M.S.O., 1923), pp. 548-49, and C. J. Bartlett, *Great Britain and Sea Power, 1815-1853* (Oxford: Clarendon Press, 1963), pp. 67-69.
[22]Canning to George IV, 14 July 1824, F.O. 83/3; Jean I. Brookes, *International Rivalry in the Pacific Islands, 1800-1875* (Berkeley and Los Angeles: University of California Press, 1941), p. 50. Details of the mission are in Lord G. A. Byron, *Voyage of the "Blonde" to the Sandwich Islands, 1824-25* (London: John Murray, 1826).
[23]Board of Trade to Planta, 30 June 1825, F.O. 58/3; quoted in W. P. Morrell, *Britain in the Pacific Islands* (Oxford: Clarendon Press, 1960), p. 64.
[24]*Ibid.,* p. 66.
[25]M. Seymour, "Remarks on the Capabilities, etc. of the Sandwich Islands [1834]," Adm. 1/43.

son's Bay Company. In 1834, the Company established a commercial house in Honolulu where it sold naval stores, hardware and foodstuffs, while salmon and timber were marketed from the Northwest Coast. As in San Francisco, the Company acted also for a time as British consular agents in the Hawaiian Islands.

As Britain's political, strategic and commercial interests grew, the government watched with suspicion the increase of American maritime activity in the Hawaiian Islands. The Royal Navy intensified its vigilance over the islands, and the visit of H.M.S. *Actaeon*, 26 guns, in late 1836 helped to re-establish British influence there.[26] As was common in those days, her commander, Captain the Honourable Edward Russell, used coercion to force the Hawaiian king to remake the local laws defining alien property and to recognize the rights of Englishmen.[27]

Some indication of the degree of Anglo-American rivalry in the islands in the late 1830's is illustrated by the attitude of the British admiral in the Pacific in 1837. When the line-of-battleship U.S.S. *North Carolina*, 92 guns, entered the Pacific in that year—followed by three corvettes under the same flag—the implication seemed clear to Rear-Admiral Sir Graham Eden Hamond: "These Yankees are sly dogs," he recorded in his journal, "and I suspect they have some intention of seizing upon the Sandwich Islands."[28] His reaction was natural enough, although he certainly misjudged the Americans on this occasion. Thus by 1837, an annual visit of a British warship was considered necessary to guard national interests.[29]

During 1841, an examination of British policy for Hawaii and other areas in the Northeastern Pacific revealed that the ministry was clearly against "the formation of new and distant Colonies" all of which would involve "heavy direct and still heavier indirect expenditure, besides multiplying the liabilities of misunderstanding and collisions with Foreign Powers."[30]

This review of policy occurred when Sir George Simpson, the Gover-

[26]See Morrell, *Britain in the Pacific Islands*, pp. 70-71.
[27]Capt. E. Russell to Commodore Mason, 3 February 1837, Adm. 1/48.
[28]Rear-Admiral Sir Graham Eden Hamond, Hamond Journal, III (HAM/127), p. 31, N.M.M. His fears that the Americans were about to seize the whaling centre of the Pacific were conveyed in letters to the Admiralty, 10 December 1836 (Adm. 1/47), and 28 August 1837 (Adm. 1/48). The *North Carolina*, however, spent all her time in South American waters; Robert E. Johnson, *Thence Round Cape Horn; The Story of United States Naval Forces on Pacific Station, 1818-1923* (Annapolis, Md.: United States Naval Institute, 1963), pp. 46-53.
[29]Russell to Mason, 3 February 1837, Adm. 1/48.
[30]Views of Lord Stanley (C.O.) quoted by Lord Aberdeen (F.O.) to Richard Pakenham (Br. Minister, Mexico), 15 December 1841, F.O. 50/143; see also, Sister Magdalen Coughlin, "California Ports: A Key to Diplomacy for the West Coast, 1820-1845," *Journal of the West*, V (April 1966), 162.

nor of Hudson's Bay Company territories in North America, indicated that in the course of his travels he would be prepared to compile a secret report for the government on "the Commerce and Navigation of the North Pacific."[31] His proposal was rejected, as the Colonial Secretary, Lord John Russell explained, because Britain did not want to colonize the Hawaiian Islands, which were bound to become American anyway.[32] An earlier plea that American expansion in the Northeastern Pacific would deprive Britain of commercial and colonizing advantages had no influence on the ministry either.

The Colonial Secretary's views were shared by Sir John Barrow, a secretary of the Admiralty and usually a promoter of British interest in the North Pacific. Barrow wrote:

> Our cruizers [sic] have free access to them, and are readily supplied with anything they can afford, but even in these casual visits they frequently have to contend with the American traders and Missionaries, particularly at the Sandwich Islands; and with the French Catholic Missionaries political as well as religious, at the Society Islands.[33]

By stationing troops or ships in these islands, Barrow warned, Britain would only place herself in a "Wasp's Nest," and endless disputes with foreigners and natives would follow.[34] Barrow reasoned that Britain should also avoid a "Wasp's Nest" on the Northwest Coast, where the United States and Russia had already established themselves: he wanted to avoid a predicament based on territorial claims such as that at Nootka Sound. Barrow would admit only that a port near the Columbia River would be advantageous to British maritime enterprise.[35] The British ministry, whose views were reinforced by Barrow's recommendations, rejected the Simpson proposal on the grounds that Britain did not contemplate "any *new* acquisitions at present . . . either on the Shores, or among the Islands of the Pacific."[36]

---

[31]Sir John Pelly to Russell, 6 February 1841, C.O. 42/485. An earlier plea that American expansion in the Northeastern Pacific would deprive Britain of commercial and colonizing advantages had no influence on the ministry. Pelly to Lord Palmerston, 26 February 1840, C.O. 6/14.
[32]Russell to James Stephen, minute, 9 February 1841, C.O. 42/485.
[33]Sir John Barrow to Stephen, 11 February 1841, C.O. 42/482.
[34]*Ibid.*
[35]Barrow was not without his critics, one of whom was Sir Thomas Byam Martin: "Mr. Barrow has, in his time, greatly and mischievously misled the First Lords of the Admiralty; no public servant has done more harm for so little good." Admiral Sir R. Vesey Hamilton, ed., *Journals and Letters of Admiral of the Fleet Sir Thom. Byam Martin* (Vol. I) (London: Navy Records Society, vol. XXIV, 1903), XXIV, p. 115. For a different view, see Sir John Briggs, *Naval Administrations, 1827 to 1892* (London: Sampson Low & Co., 1897), p. 72.
[36]Stephen to Pelly, draft, 16 February 1841, C.O. 42/485.

Simpson remained unconvinced. During his travels of 1841 and 1842, he became certain that the Hawaiian Islands, California and Oregon would fall to the Americans unless the British government awakened from what he regarded as its lethargy.[37] In Honolulu and San Francisco, for example, he found British residents critical of their government for not sending enough British warships to protect them. Simpson thought the situation was alarming in view of the "very frequent" visits of American men-of-war and "increasing" calls of French men-of-war.[38] He suggested that naval vessels in the North Pacific could "run across with the Trades" to Honolulu and then back via California, thereby providing British influence in the Northeastern Pacific.[39] The Royal Navy, as has been shown, did indeed give consideration to the region at this time, and was in fact using the very passages that Simpson recommended, although less frequently than he wished.

Simpson's reports lent weight to the warnings by naval commanders on station that British influence was weakening. Admittedly, Simpson's expansionist views were inconsistent with the ministry's contention that extending sovereignty was not worth the trouble and costs of administration and protection. Undoubtedly, his dispatches relayed from the Hudson's Bay Company's London headquarters to Whitehall increased the ministry's interest in the political futures of Hawaii, California and Oregon.

Although a marked change in British policy occurred in the years 1841 and 1842, it was dictated less by the opinions of Simpson than by the circumstances of international rivalry. French imperial designs on islands in the Pacific, as well as on California, became apparent when the British Captain Jenkin Jones reached Upper California in 1841 in the *Curaçoa*, 24 guns, to investigate the semi-official mission of Duflot de Mofras, an emissary landed from the French corvette *Danaide*.[40] Jenkin Jones found that the motives of the French investigation were more than scientific, and concluded that a systematic plan of French expansion throughout the Pacific was in operation.[41] These fears, shared by the Commander-in-Chief in the Pacific, were fully realized when an expedition under the command of Rear-Admiral Du Petit-Thouars in the frigate *La Reine Blanche*, 60 guns, carrying a large military force, doubled Cape Horn in 1842 and claimed the Marquesas Islands for

[37]G. Simpson to Pelly, 10 March 1842, F.O. 5/388; in Joseph Schafer, ed., "Letters of Sir George Simpson, 1841-1843," *American Historical Review*, XIV (October 1908), 86-93.
[38]*Ibid.*
[39]*Ibid.*
[40]Rear-Admiral R. Thomas to S. Herbert (Adm.), 15 April 1842, Adm. 1/5512.
[41]*Ibid.*

France.[42] These developments exposed French imperial designs in the Pacific and showed the British position of *laissez-aller* to be obsolete.

In consequence, according to the "new Foreign Office policy" of 4 October 1842, American and French activities in the Hawaiian Islands were to be watched more closely than ever before. This decision was based on two considerations. In terms of commerce, British trade in the region showed substantial increase, exceeding that of the United States and France combined, as Captain Jenkin Jones reported.[43] In terms of strategy, the value of Hawaii as a freely accessible base for the Royal Navy justified more visits by British warships, especially since the Pacific station was to be reinforced by three men-of-war. Appropriately, the Foreign Office adopted an all-inclusive policy with political, commercial and strategic implications. It indicated the government's disinclination to establish "a paramount influence" in the Hawaiian Islands. At the same time, it stated that "no other power should exercise a greater degree of influence than that possessed by Great Britain."[44]

Complications arose when Captain Lord George Paulet of H.M.S. *Carysfort* proclaimed British dominion over the Hawaiian Islands on 25 February 1843. His action was prompted by a desire to prevent the islands from falling to a French force under Du Petit-Thouars who was thought to be sailing there from Tahiti.[45] This declaration of a British protectorate was unauthorized. Nevertheless, when news of it reached London, the Foreign Office, acting according to the new policy announced in October 1842, justified it on the grounds that the influence of the United States had exceeded that of the British.[46] To add to the confusion, the Commander-in-Chief, Pacific, Rear-Admiral Richard Thomas—who had not yet received instructions to this effect—saluted the Hawaiian ensign on reaching the Islands, 31 July 1843, thereby disavowing Paulet's action of five months earlier.

The solution to this imbroglio was the Anglo-French Treaty of 28 November 1846, signed in London. The two nations agreed, "Reciprocally to consider the Sandwich Islands as an independent State, and never

[42]Thomas to Herbert, 16 August 1842, *ibid.;* see also Morrell, *Britain in the Pacific Islands,* chapter 4.

[43]Capt. J. Jones to Rear-Admiral Ross, 6 November 1841, encl. in Thomas to Herbert, 15 April 1842, Adm. 1/5512.

[44]H. U. Addington (F.O.) to Herbert, 4 October 1842, and Admiralty Minute, 8 October 1842, Adm. 1/5525.

[45]Lord Paulet to W. A. B. Hamilton, 11 March 1843, Adm. 1/5562. Paulet's instructions from Rear-Admiral Thomas, 17 and 18 January 1842, are in Adm. 1/5531. A good account of the Paulet episode is in Ralph S. Kuykendall, *The Hawaiian Kingdom, 1778-1854* (Honolulu: University of Hawaii Press, 1938) , pp. 206-226.

[46]Foreign Office Memorandum, July 1843, F.O. 58/19; Brookes, *International Rivalry,* p. 135. On American influence, see Morrell, *British in the Pacific Islands,* p. 83.

to take possession neither directly nor under the title of Protectorate, or any other form of any part of the Territory of which they are composed."[47] But failure to include the United States in this act of self-denial meant that Britain could not act unilaterally as American pressures for annexation increased toward the end of the nineteenth century.[48]

Upper California

Like the Hawaiian Islands, Upper California was coveted by several nations. Foreign traders were active in Upper California in defiance of all Spanish laws by the beginning of the nineteenth century. Their mercantile activities continued to expand there after 1821 despite restrictions by the new authority, Mexico.

In 1805, the Russians arrived in Upper California. And in 1812 they founded the agricultural and fur-trading post, Fort Ross, near Bodega Bay, lying about 39° North latitude on the coast. They were followed by American trappers, who crossed the cordillera to the Pacific shores in 1826, and by Boston ships engaged in the hide and tallow trade. A further influx of foreigners occurred in 1829 when the Hudson's Bay Company began sending annual fur brigades to Upper California from Fort Vancouver on the Columbia, which for four years had been the hub of the Company's Pacific maritime trade. The French came to the area by sea.

Foreign interference by the United States, Great Britain, Russia, France and even Prussia, was feared by Mexico. The Mexican province, with its good ports and rich lands, promised to be a major prize for one of these powers. As for Great Britain, her presence was sustained by occasional visits from ships of the Royal Navy.

Scientific inquiry as well as international rivalry took H.M.S. *Blossom*, Captain Frederick William Beechey, to San Francisco Bay and Monterey in 1826 and 1827. The *Blossom* was one of several British ships assigned to special service in Pacific and Arctic exploration after the Napoleonic Wars, when the Navy renewed its exploration of the Pacific and its search for a Northwest Passage from the Atlantic to the Pacific via Arctic waters.[49]

---

[47]Quoted in *ibid.*, p. 85.
[48]As early as 1846, the disadvantageous British position was recognized by Captain Henry Byam Martin of H.M.S. *Grampus*. He regretted that Paulet's treaty had been cancelled because Britain would have derived great advantage from possessing these islands that lay on the high road of trans-Pacific trade and were the rendezvous of whalers. He claimed that France would not have objected. *Grampus* Journal, 15 and 24 August 1846, Byam Martin Papers, Add. MSS. 41,472, B.M.
[49]Sir John Barrow, *Autobiographical Memoir* (London: John Murray, 1847), pp. 333 and 470.

The British attached importance to these expeditions: as late as 1845 for example, Sir John Franklin's party was still seeking the passage to the west across the northern shores of North America. The Admiralty knew at that time that France and the United States had fleets in the Pacific which made discovery of a Northwest Passage strategically important, since the shortest way home for French and American men-of-war would be "through the Polar Sea"—if a sea lane could be discovered.[50] The *Blossom's* voyage to the Pacific Ocean and the Bering Sea demonstrated the Admiralty's belief that "knowledge is power." In gathering scientific information and conducting surveys, the voyage was a logical sequel to the voyages of Cook, Vancouver and Broughton.[51]

As mentioned earlier, Beechey carried orders for the *Blossom* to go to Ice Cape, Alaska, to meet and supply Captains Parry and Franklin, who were searching for a passage along the Arctic coasts. Beechey's orders were to sail from England to the Pacific by way of Cape Horn, verify the existence of some Pacific islands and reach the Bering Strait by 10 July 1826 when it was believed that Arctic waters in this region would be ice-free.[52] When the *Blossom* reached Cape Barrow, pack ice confronted her. Winter was coming, supplies were short and there was danger of being icebound. According to plan, the *Blossom* then sailed to San Francisco. Carpentry stores and medicines were unobtainable on the American side of the Pacific without going too far south; Beechey therefore set a course for Canton via Hawaii. Although he had spent an unsuccessful season in Arctic waters, he did complete extensive surveys of the North Pacific.[53]

The *Blossom* returned to the Arctic in the summer of 1827. She found no sign of Captain Franklin; Parry had returned to England. Beechey continued his surveys and then returned to San Francisco Bay for the winter. For two months he directed an extensive examination of that magnificent land-locked bay. He did not hesitate to state in his *Narrative,* published in 1831 by Admiralty authority, that the site possessed all the requirements for "a great naval establishment" and by its advantageous position in the North Pacific promised to become very important.[54] His

---

[50]Sir John Barrow, *Voyages of Discovery and Research within the Arctic Regions, from the Year 1818 to the Present Time* (London: John Murray, 1846) , pp. 16-17.
[51]*Ibid.,* p. 12.
[52]Admiralty instructions, 11 May 1825; in Capt. Frederick W. Beechey, *Narrative of a Voyage to the Pacific and Beering's Strait to Co-operate with the Polar Expeditions, 1825-28,* 2 vols. (London: H. Colburn and R. Bentley, 1831) , I, ix-xiii. Cdr. L. S. Dawson, comp., *Memoirs of Hydrography . . . 1750-1885,* 2 vols. (Eastbourne: Henry W. Keay, 1885) , I, 112.
[53]Beechey to J. W. Croker (Adm.) , 18 November 1826, Adm. 1/1574.
[54]Beechey, *Narrative of a Voyage,* II, 63-64. An interesting unpublished account of the visits to San Francisco is given in Lieutenant George Peard, Journal of H.M.S. *Blossom,* 1825-1828, Add. MSS. 35,141, B.M.

writings drew world attention to San Francisco Bay, a harbour destined to play a dominant role in United States maritime expansion in the Pacific. Beechey also examined other coastal areas, including the important Mexican port of Mazatlan.

Immediately after Beechey's account was published in 1831, the British Hydrographic Department approved plans for a more detailed inspection of the Eastern Pacific.[55] The *Beagle* went to the coast of South America as far north as Ecuador, in keeping with expanding British-South American trade. The barque *Sulphur* and her tender, the cutter *Starling,* went to sections of the Pacific Coast from Valparaiso to Alaska in 1836-1839 primarily to examine the mouth of the Columbia River and extend Beechey's earlier surveys of San Francisco Bay, especially the rivers and arms flowing into it, the Farallones Islands off the coast and the hazardous bar at its entrance.[56] They were asked also to determine the exact longitude of the North Pacific Coast, which Captain O. V. Harcourt of H.M.S. *North Star,* 28 guns, believed was about 40' incorrect in Captain Vancouver's charts.

Beechey was the obvious choice to command the mission of the *Sulphur* and *Starling.* In line with common practice, he drafted his own instructions which were approved by the Admiralty. Unfortunately, poor health prevented Beechey from directing the survey. The task was assigned first to Lieutenant Henry Kellett and finally to Captain Edward Belcher, who had been in the *Blossom* as assistant surveyor.[57]

This survey coincided with the need to examine Russian activity in Upper California. At first, British interest in Russia's Ross colony was casual: "You know they are 'interlopers,' as Master Purchas would say, and have a flourishing settlement there," Beechey informed Captain Beaufort, the Hydrographer, on 1 November 1836.[58] Nearly a year later, however, Lieutenant Andrew Hamond of the sloop *Rover,* 18 guns, was in the Mexican port of Mazatlan when he learned from visitors to Upper California of Russian expansion southward from a "grand settlement at Nootka Sound."[59] If this were true, it constituted an obvious challenge to British claims.

Hamond's report of Russian aggrandizement on the North Pacific Coast led his father, Rear-Admiral G. E. Hamond, the Commander-in-

[55]Beechey to Capt. F. Beaufort (Hydrographer), 15 August 1831, File No. Misc. 15, Folder 1, item 3, H.O.

[56]Beechey to Beaufort, 17 June 1835, *ibid.,* item 4. Beechey to Beaufort, 1 November 1836, S.L. 21, Item 4, H.O.

[57]F. V. Longstaff and W. Kaye Lamb, "The Royal Navy on the Northwest Coast, 1813-50, Part I," *British Columbia Historical Quarterly,* IX (January 1945), 10, n. 18.

[58]Beechey to Beaufort, 1 November 1836, S. L. 21, item 4, H.O.

[59]A. S. Hamond to Mason, 17 June 1837, encl. in Rear-Admiral G. E. Hamond to G. Wood (Adm.), 25 August 1837, Adm. 1/48.

Chief, to give instructions that the next ship going to Mexico in 1838 should investigate Ross colony.[60] But H.M.S. *Imogene*, 28 guns, Captain H. W. Bruce, was unable to visit the Columbia River in 1838 because of pressing matters in the Hawaiian Islands and elsewhere. Consequently, the responsibility fell to Belcher. His description of Ross in 1839, based on information gathered by a "friend," contains no political overtones. However, at the time of the examination, Belcher and the Russian governor were distrustful of each other owing to the "anticipated rupture" between their parent nations in other parts of the world over the Eastern Question.[61] Even as late as 1841 the British were suspicious of Russian intentions near San Francisco Bay and at Nootka Sound.[62]

Although the Mexicans did not challenge the Russians directly at Ross, they indicated that foreigners south of San Francisco were unwelcome. This became evident in 1840 when officials in Monterey, the capital of the Mexican province of Upper California, imprisoned forty British and American citizens for subversive activity and deported them to Tepic, in the Guadalajara province of Mexico, some fifteen hundred miles distant. Because a British man-of-war was not present, the British vice-consul there, Eustace Barron, called on the United States Navy to act for British as well as American interests.[63] Forceful diplomacy combined with the visit of the American sloop *St. Louis* resulted in release of the prisoners and brought to an end what is known as the Graham Affair.

To guard against further provocations, Barron and Sir Richard Pakenham, the British Minister in Mexico City, sent pleas to London for naval support and an increase in the strength of the Pacific squadron.[64] These pleas did not go unanswered; the *Curaçoa* was sent to the California ports to ascertain the condition of British subjects. Her commander, Captain Jenkin Jones, carried supplementary orders requiring him to object to arbitrary actions of Mexican officials against British residents and to warn them that they would be held responsible by the

[60]G. E. Hamond to Wood, 25 August 1837, *ibid.*

[61]Captain Sir Edward Belcher, *Narrative of a Voyage, Round the World in His Majesty's Ship "Sulphur" during the Years 1836-42,* 2 vols. (London: Henry Colburn, 1843), I, 313-17. No special report by Belcher on Bodega Bay and Ross Colony is to be found among the Admiralty papers in the P.R.O.

[62]See duplicate of Admiralty Board Instructions to Rear-Admiral Richard Thomas, C.-in-C., Pacific, 21 August 1841, Admiral Thomas Papers, G. 4, article 6, H.S.L.

[63]A. P. Nasatir, "International Rivalry for California and the Establishment of the British Consulate," *California Historical Society Quarterly,* XLVI (March 1967), 61-63; Johnson, *Thence Round Cape Horn,* p. 57 and n. 4.

[64]Ephraim D. Adams, "English Interest in the Annexation of California," *American Historical Review,* XIV (July 1909), 745. Professor Adams mistakenly concluded that no British naval activity followed.

British government if a repetition of the Graham incident occurred.[65]

At this stage, the Foreign Office was evidently prepared to rely on naval visits to protect British interests in Upper California. Then an overly-zealous American commodore, Thomas Ap Catesby Jones, seized Monterey prematurely in 1842 because he thought the British flagship *Dublin* had sailed from Callao to occupy California under a secret Anglo-Mexican treaty. This event prompted Britain to appoint a vice-consul for the region.[66] Thereafter, consular activities and regular calls by British warships sufficed to guard British persons and property in Upper California until war broke out between Mexico and the United States in 1846.

The Oregon Country

The fate of Oregon was of greater concern to Britain than that of California because of the strength of British claims to the area and the presence there of the Hudson's Bay Company. Since 1818 she had jointly occupied the territory with the United States. Diplomatic discussion in the mid-1820's failed to resolve the underlying Anglo-American rivalry for possession of the territory, so the *modus vivendi* was renewed in 1827 for an indefinite period. According to the terms of the agreement it could end one year after notification was given by either power.

The sovereignty of Old Oregon was still in dispute when the previously mentioned British surveying ships *Sulphur* and *Starling* reached the Northwest Coast in August of 1837 and again in the summer of 1839. They were the first British warships to call there in more than two decades and their activities were extensive.[67] Captain Belcher had several assignments to complete, one of these involving a discreet examination of Oregon, as his hydrographic instructions noted:

---

[65]Thomas to Sec. of Adm., 28 December 1841, Adm. 1/5512, and Jenkin Jones to Ross, 27 December 1841, No. 38, copy, JON/5, N.M.M.

[66]A perceptive study of this interesting episode is George M. Brooke, Jr., "The Vest Pocket War of Commodore Jones," *Pacific Historical Review*, XXXI (1962), 217-33.

[67]The details of the movements of the *Sulphur* and *Starling* in the northeastern Pacific are as follows. Leaving the Hawaiian Islands for Cook's Straits on 27 July 1837, they arrived at the Russian post of Port Etches on 26 August and took several observations. On 12 September, Belcher was at Sitka where Russian hospitality proved excellent and stores were purchased. Nootka Sound was reached on 5 October and observations again were taken. It was too late in the season to enter the mouth of the Columbia River, so Belcher repaired to San Francisco Bay where the ships were refitted and the Sacramento River was examined to "the Fork," its then navigable limit about 150 miles upstream. On 30 November, he was at Monterey and later he called at San Blas and Panama. By 1839 he was back again at Honolulu. He visited the Kodiaks and reached Sitka on 19 July of that year and the Columbia River on 28 July. Belcher to Wood, 28 December 1837, Cap B 101, Adm. 1/1586, and Belcher to Wood, 10 June 1839, Cap B 223, Adm. 1/1587.

Political circumstances have invested the Columbia river with so much importance that it will be well to devote some time to its bar and channels of approach, as well as to its inner anchorages and shores; but you must be exceedingly careful not to interfere in any manner with the subjects of the United States who live on its banks; neither admitting nor contesting their claims, respecting which there is a distinct understanding between the two Governments, and if necessary you will find some prudent pretext for desisting from the survey, rather than risk any collision or even remonstrance.[68]

Belcher's other tasks included making observations to verify the longitudes made by Captain Vancouver at Port Etches and Nootka and also visiting Sitka. These undertakings were designed to facilitate the production of new charts which were becoming essential as increased trade brought British vessels into contact with the coasts of the Americas from Chile to the Columbia.[69] No instructions of a political nature were given at this time, but presumably he was to keep an eye on Russian and American activities from Monterey north to Sitka.

Many years later, at a meeting of the Royal Geographical Society, Belcher said that he had been instructed in 1838 by the British government and the Commander-in-Chief, Pacific, to make a confidential report on Oregon.[70] If this indeed were the case, two developments probably explain why a mission was sent. First, the British government knew that William Slacum, a United States Navy lieutenant masquerading as a private individual, had visited the Columbia River in December 1836. Both Chief Factor McLoughlin at Fort Vancouver, who described Slacum as "an agent of the American government, come to see what we are doing," and the Commander-in-Chief, Pacific, were well aware that the United States was casting longing eyes on Oregon.[71] Second, in the United States Senate, a bill was introduced for the military occupation of Oregon from 42° North latitude to 54°40′ North latitude, the ending of Anglo-American condominium and the promotion of settlement.[72] Whether or not Belcher actually received instructions remains obscure. If he did, probably the Admiralty, in conjunction with the Foreign Office, must have realized that a survey of the Columbia's mouth by the

[68]Hydrographic Instructions to Captain Beechey," n.d., S.L. 21, item 6, H.O.

[69]Belcher, Narrative of a Voyage, I, xx.

[70]Proceedings of the Royal Geographical Society, IV (1859-60), 35.

[71]B.223/b/10, fol. 76d. H.B.C.A.; quoted in E. E. Rich, The Fur Trade and the Northwest to 1857 (Toronto: McClelland and Stewart, 1967), p. 278. Hamond to Wood, 28 August 1837, Adm. 1/48. Slacum's memorial to Congress is printed in Oregon Historical Quarterly, XIII (1902), 175-224.

[72]But with Palmerston at the Foreign Office, the Hudson's Bay Company could be assured that such views were unacceptable. See Rich, Fur Trade and the Northwest, p. 279.

Sulphur and *Starling* offered Belcher an opportunity to report on the state of British interests in Oregon and the influx of Americans.

The *Sulphur* and *Starling* reached the Columbia's mouth on 28 July 1839—the first British warships to appear there in more than two decades, as previously pointed out. Their examination of the intricate entrances to the river revealed a navigable channel which Hudson's Bay Company officials considered inferior to the commonly used northern one. As seemed to be the fate of most British warships that ventured into the river in those days, both vessels met with mishap: touching ground was an occupational hazard of surveying ships. In damaged condition, the *Starling* was forced to navigate one hundred miles of confined waterway to Fort Vancouver, where Belcher began his investigation and repairs were effected.[73]

Belcher ignored the Anglo-American joint occupation agreement as explained in his instructions, and assumed that the territory was British. He reported to the Commander-in-Chief in an elated manner: "The Americans do not possess an atom of land on the Columbia!"[74] Although he was received hospitably at Fort Vancouver in accordance with orders from the Company headquarters in London, Belcher was highly critical of the inability of a British "possession" to supply British warships with provisions.[75] He appears to have received the same kind of welcome and help given other travellers and settlers, but he attacked his hosts for harbouring American missionaries whom he thought to be representatives of the United States government.

The visit of the *Sulphur* and *Starling* to Oregon and Belcher's subsequent indictment of the operations of the Company brought divergent reactions from Company officials in London. On the one hand, they rejected Belcher's charges as false. On the other hand, they were grateful that the British government had awakened at last to the danger which faced the Company's interests on the Pacific slope, these interests being especially valuable because they were linked to British enterprises in other areas of the Pacific.[76]

It seems certain that Belcher criticized the Company unduly. With little knowledge of problems facing the fur trade, he evidently judged the Company mainly on patriotic grounds. Moreover, he was unaware

[73]George M. Douglas, ed., "Royal Navy Ships on the Columbia River in 1839," *The Beaver*, Outfit 285 (Autumn 1954), 39-41, based on Belcher's *Narrative of a Voyage*.
[74]Belcher to Ross, extract, 17 December 1839, C.O. 6/14.
[75]The Company was then busy meeting the demands for provisions of the Russian American Company according to a contract of 1839; Longstaff and Lamb, "Royal Navy on the Northwest Coast," pp. 14-15.
[76]Pelly to Russell, 18 May 1840, C.O. 6/14. For the Company's position, see Galbraith, *Hudson's Bay Company*, pp. 220-21.

of "the obvious course of events . . . , the passing of European Population
to the NW Coast of America and to its ultimate consequences in the
Trade of the Pacific and of China," as Lord Ellenborough, the First
Lord of the Admiralty, so aptly analysed the situation in 1846.[77] This
would account for Belcher's later explanation in 1859 that he was per-
plexed by Britain's loss of Oregon in 1846 because, during his visit in
1839, the British flag flew over old Fort Astoria while not a single
American was on the Columbia. Oregon was lost, Belcher claimed, by
the lack of "prudence" exercised by the government and the "overzeal-
ous desire" of Dr. John McLoughlin, the Director at Fort Vancouver,
in introducing American missionaries into the Willamette Valley.[78]

His official report had one lasting effect. It initiated suspicion of the
Company's role west of the Rocky Mountains, particularly regarding
the reception of American settlers at Fort Vancouver. The British government, however, was not prepared to resist American claims. In the
period between the visit of the *Sulphur* and *Starling* in 1839 and the
agreement with the Americans in 1846, the ministry surely must have
known that as long as the Hudson's Bay Company remained primarily
a commercial organization and the lack of British settlement in Oregon
continued, the westward flow of American landseekers could end the
chances of British dominion over the banks of the Columbia. The
government clearly was more concerned with trade than territory, a
fact which a close examination of the Oregon Treaty of 1846 reveals; its
terms guaranteed Hudson's Bay Company rights of trade even without
territory.

The Hardening of British Policy

British policy for the area of the Northeastern Pacific in 1818-1843 may
be summed up as fundamentally reserved and adaptive in nature. Before
1840, when international rivalry there was in its formative stages, Britain
generally regarded the moves of Russia, France and the United States
with rather casual interest. Thereafter, whether she wished to or not,
as she sought to avoid "Wasps' Nests" she found herself inextricably
drawn into contests for Oregon and Hawaii, and, to a lesser degree, for
Upper California. Behind this change in policy was the desire to reject
American dominance in the Western hemisphere, curtail Russian aggrandizement in North America, and check French imperialistic moves
in the Pacific Islands in the 1840's. Although the British government
was unwilling to support the Hudson's Bay Company's proposal of

---

[77]Ellenborough to Lord Aberdeen (F.O.) , 16 May 1846, private, Aberdeen Papers,
Add. MSS. 43,198, B.M.
[78]*Proceedings of the Royal Geographical Society,* IV (1859-1860) , 35.

1841 for British expansion to prevent competing nations from extending influence in Hawaii, Oregon and Upper California, the government did show that it would not allow any existing British commercial and strategic advantages to go unprotected, especially in the neutral Hawaiian Islands.

Of course, no rival could ignore British naval supremacy which provided the means for Britain to extend her influence in the Northeastern Pacific during the peaceful period between 1818 and 1843. The primacy of the Royal Navy also prevented threats of intervention by Russia, France or the United States as Latin American countries were winning their independence; the Royal Navy constituted the agency under which these countries could throw off the last vestiges of Spanish domination.[79] However, supremacy of the Royal Navy did not preclude possible alliances to undermine British dominance.

The actual number of visits of British men-of-war were few during this time, with perhaps only eight calling on the North Pacific Coast excluding Mexico and at least twice that number at the Hawaiian Islands.[80] But these visits sufficed to protect British political and commercial interests. At the approach of the mid-century, ships of the Royal Navy appeared with greater frequency, which indicated the growing importance of these seas to Britain.

Throughout the years 1818-1843, Britain found herself drawn into disputes as a result of political and commercial advances by Russian, French and American competitors in the Hawaiian Islands, Oregon and California. She did not seek to expand her empire with additions of questionable value, expensive to defend and troublesome to govern. But she could not isolate herself from the contest because she feared Russian, French and American aspirations and was forced to protect Hudson's Bay Company interests. After 1843, this unique interlude of peace after the Napoleonic Wars almost ended as differences sharpened between Britain and the United States over the Northwest Coast.

---

[79]In 1823, H.M.S. *Cambridge*, 80 guns, was sent from England to convey British consuls to the east and west coasts of South America. She was probably the first British ship-of-the-line to enter the Pacific after Anson's *Centurion*, 60 guns, to be followed in 1844 by the *Collingwood*, 80 guns, flagship of Rear-Admiral Sir George Seymour, Commander-in-Chief, Pacific. For the voyage of the *Cambridge*, see John Cunningham, Surgeon, "Voyage to the Pacific, 1823-4-5," JOD 21, N.M.M.
[80]The eight that called on the North Pacific Coast were H.M.S. *Blossom*, 1818; *Blossom* 1826-1827; *North Star*, 1836 (?) ; *Imogene*, 1837 (?) ; *Sulphur* and *Starling*, 1837, 1839; *Curaçoa*, 1841; *Carysfort*, 1843.

Chapter 3

THE OREGON CRISIS
1844-1846

THE ANGLO-AMERICAN CONVENTION of 1818, which was renewed in 1827, recognized the historic claims of both Britain and the United States to Oregon but did not provide for any means to settle the dispute over sovereignty by arbitration. War would be the alternative should diplomacy fail.

The diplomatic issues involved in the Oregon question are well known, even if interpretations of the outcome vary.[1] But the Royal Navy's role in the crisis has been neglected on two counts. First, it has not been explained how British naval power was largely responsible for achieving an equitable settlement for Britain and, second, the activities of British warships in supporting national political and commercial interests on the Northwest Coast at a time of frontier turbulence have not been closely examined. These pages will examine how British naval primacy influenced the course of Anglo-American relations as well as how Her Majesty's ships protected national interests and claims, pro-

---

[1]See especially, Frederick Merk, *The Oregon Question: Essays in Anglo-American Diplomacy and Politics* (Cambridge, Mass.: Belknap Press, 1967); H. C. Allen, *Great Britain and the United States: A History of Anglo-American Relations (1783-1952)* (New York: St. Martin's Press, 1955), pp. 409-14; and Charles Sellers, *James K. Polk: Continentalist, 1843-1846* (Princeton: Princeton University Press, 1966), pp. 235-58 and 357-97.

vided naval intelligence important in formulating Foreign Office policy, and made their influence felt, perhaps out of proportion to their numbers, on the Northwest Coast and in the Pacific at a time when relations with both the United States and France brought the government almost to the point of war before the Oregon crisis subsided and the area was partitioned by treaty.[2]

The territory in dispute in 1844-1846 lay west of the Continental Divide between the northern boundary of California (42°N) and the southern extremity of Russian America (54°40′N). Britain and the United States each claimed this region by virtue of exploration, discovery and trade.[3] Each nation realized that a solution to the Oregon question probably would be found in an equitable division of the country. Apart from the often exaggerated vote-getting election slogan of the Democratic Party in America—"Fifty-four Forty or Fight"—that swept James K. Polk into the presidency in 1844, each nation eventually saw the advisability of compromise. Essentially, therefore, the issue was how to divide Oregon between the two claimants. In other words, should the boundary extend along the 49th parallel from the ridge of the Rocky Mountains to the sea, as the United States insisted? Or should it follow the Columbia River from where its course intersects the 49th parallel to the Pacific, as Great Britain initially contended?

If war were to be avoided, as each party wished, it was necessary to limit the area in contention to that which extended west and north of the Columbia River to the 49th parallel, including the southern tip of Vancouver Island. Within this territory were three geographical regions of importance to fur trade, settlement and maritime development. The nucleus of British commerce on the Northwest Coast was Fort Vancouver, situated about 100 miles inland near the head of navigation on the Columbia River. Fort Vancouver was built on the north bank of the river in 1825, as officials of the Hudson's Bay Company realized that the Columbia might become the international boundary. Nearly opposite Fort Vancouver, the Willamette River joined the Columbia after draining the Willamette Valley. The Columbia River basin may have been rich in furs and lands for settlement, but it was not readily access-

[2]The influence of France on Britain's position in the Oregon crisis cannot be ignored. See George Vern Blue, "France and the Oregon Question," *Oregon Historical Quarterly*, XXXIV (1933), 39-59 and 144-63; also, John S. Galbraith, "France as a Factor in the Oregon Negotiations," *Pacific Northwest Quarterly*, XLIV (April 1953), 69-73.

[3]The full claims are given in "Correspondence Relative to the Negotiation of the Question of the Disputed Right to the Oregon Territory," *Parliamentary Papers*, 1846, LII (Cmd. 695). On the British case, see Travers Twiss, *The Oregon Question Examined, in Respect to Facts and the Law of Nations* (London: Longman, Brown, Green and Longmans, 1846) and Adam Thom, *The Claims to the Oregon Territory Considered* (London: Smith, Elder & Co., 1844).

ible to shipping owing to dangerous, shifting shoals at the river's mouth.

The second area of contention was Puget Sound, reaching southward from the Strait of Juan de Fuca. In addition to offering fine anchorages, this body of water offered possibilities of great maritime expansion for the nation that could control its shores. It also furnished, from the north, a more sheltered and safe approach to the Columbia Country than that via the Columbia's estuary. Ships could anchor near Fort Nisqually at the head of the sound and from there travellers and traders could reach Fort Vancouver by going through the Nisqually and Cowlitz river valleys.

The third district of importance, especially to the British, embraced the southern tip of Vancouver Island. This area had several fine harbours readily accessible to ships and had arable land nearby. For these reasons, the Hudson's Bay Company, whose maritime operations on the coast and in the Pacific were hindered by the difficult navigation of the Columbia River up to Fort Vancouver, built Fort Victoria in 1843. The Island was also almost certain to be in British territory after an agreement was reached with the Americans.[4] Vancouver Island was therefore the focal point of British concern and the last line of defence against American expansion in Oregon.

Throughout Oregon, the Hudson's Bay Company held a British commercial monopoly. The Company successfully destroyed competition by American and Russian traders on the Northwest Coast in the 1820's and 1830's. However, they were unable to halt the flow of American settlers who came overland by way of the Oregon Trail after 1842; settlement spelled the end of the fur trade in the Columbia River Basin in more ways than the destruction of habitat for fur-bearing animals. Although the implications of the influx of Americans received scant attention in discussions between the British and American governments in reaching a compromise over the Oregon boundary, it must be remembered that Britain could not have controlled an area populated by Americans. In retrospect, the only feasible method of permanent defence that Britain could have employed in this region was British settlement. This view is supported by reports from British naval and military officers, submitted in 1845 and 1846, which described American settlements on the south bank of the Columbia River and in the Willamette Valley. The British ministry knew that Company interests, at least south of the Columbia, would have to be sacrificed for the preservation of peaceful Anglo-American relations.

The Company understandably opposed a surrender of the Columbia

---

[4]W. Kaye Lamb, "The Founding of Fort Victoria," *British Columbia Historical Quarterly*, VII (April 1943) , 71ff.

PLATE 1.   Astoria (Fort George) in 1813, as it appeared in Gabriel Franchère's *Narrative of a Voyage to the Northwest Coast of America, 1811-1814*.

PLATE 2.   The British frigate *America*, 50 guns, a symbol of British influence on the Northwest Coast in 1845 during the Oregon Crisis. Sketch by H. F. Pullen, Assistant Clerk in the *America*.

PLATE 3. The Hudson's Bay Company post Fort Vancouver painted by Henry James Warre during the British military reconnaissance of the Oregon country in 1845.

PLATE 4. H.M.S. *Constance*, 50 guns, in Esquimalt Harbour August 1848. She was the first British warship to anchor there. Pencil sketch by Lieutenant J. T. Haverfield, R.M.

PLATE 5. The British paddle-wheel sloop *Driver* that carried Governor Richard Blanshard to the Colony of Vancouver Island in 1850.

PLATE 6. Sir James Douglas (1803-1877), who in his function as Governor of Vancouver Island (1851-1864) and British Columbia (1858-1864) opposed Manifest Destiny.

PLATE 7. The Hudson's Bay Company establishment Fort Victoria on Vancouver Island as portrayed in the *Illustrated London News* in 1848.

PLATE 8. Rear-Admiral (later Admiral of the Fleet Sir) Fairfax Moresby, Commander-in-Chief, Pacific, 1850-1853, who recommended in 1851 that the British establish a naval base at Esquimalt, Vancouver Island.

PLATE 9. Fort Nanaimo in 1859, as depicted in a watercolour by Lieutenant Edward P. Downes, R.N. H.M.S. *Tribune* lying at anchor in the harbour is probably taking on coal from the Nanaimo mines.

PLATE 10. The Allied Squadron bombarding the Russian post Petropavlovsk on the Kamchatka Peninsula in 1854.

PLATE 11. The "Crimean Huts," Esquimalt dockyard's first buildings, were built in 1855 as temporary hospital accommodation. Photo taken about 1870, by which time the buildings had served various purposes.

PLATE 12.   Panorama of Esquimalt village and naval establishment as seen from the north in 1878. This watercolour is by one of the most competent British naval artists to visit Esquimalt, Captain F. G. D. Bedford of H.M.S. *Shah*. From left to right can be seen Signal Hill; the village; the naval jetty, coal sheds and

PLATE 13.   Admiralty chart of Esquimalt Harbour dated 1847. Compiled by Lieutenant James Wood of the surveying vessel *Pandora*.

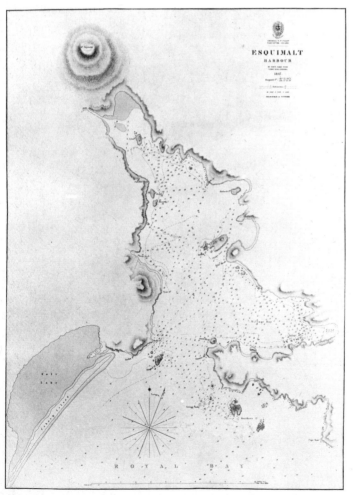

repair facilities near and on Thetis Island (the height of land in the middle of the picture); the naval storehouses and old hospital buildings on Duntze Head; and Fisgard lighthouse at the harbour entrance.

PLATE 14. A late nineteenth-century view of Wharf Street, Esquimalt, with an unidentified British warship in the harbour.

PLATE 15. Engraving from the *Illustrated London News* showing boats from H.M.S. *Plumper* surveying in Johnstone Strait, between Vancouver Island and the mainland.

PLATE 16. View of the gundeck of the screw-corvette *Satellite*, 22 guns. This ship was active in protecting British interests during the Fraser River gold rush and the San Juan boundary dispute.

PLATE 17. Flagship of Rear-Admiral Robert Lambert Baynes, the *Ganges*, mounting 84 guns, was launched at Bombay in 1821. She was the last line-of-battleship as flagship on a British foreign station.

PLATE 18. Rear-Admiral Sir Robert Lambert Baynes, K.C.B., Commander-in-Chief on the Pacific Station, 1857-1860. He was knighted for his wise course of action during the San Juan boundary dispute.

PLATE 19. The British screw-frigate *Tribune*, 31 guns, sent from Hong Kong to aid the colonial adminis tration during the Fraser River gold rush. She arrived in early 1859 and in August made a show of power at San Juan Island.

PLATE 20. The gunboat *Forward*, like her sistership *Grappler*, was sent for service in response to the Fraser River gold rush. They served in various police roles until the late 1860's.

PLATE 21. The British camp at Garrison Bay, San Juan Island, where a detachment of Royal Marines was stationed during the joint military occupation from 1860 to 1872.

PLATE 22. Admiral of the Fleet Sir Geoffrey Phipps Hornby, G.C.B. As captain of the *Tribune*, at the time of the San Juan crisis, his conduct was exemplary. He was also officer commanding the Flying Squadron which called at Esquimalt in 1871.

PLATE 23. "Maple Bank," residence of Rear-Admiral the Honourable Joseph Denman.

PLATE 24. Standing on the bridge of the steam-frigate *Sutlej* in this photograph taken in 1866 are, from left to right, a lieutenant as officer of the watch, a secretary or paymaster, Commander T. B. M. Sullivan, a lieutenant, perhaps the flag-lieutenant, Sir Lambton Loraine, Bart., Rear-Admiral the Honourable Joseph Denman, the Commander-in-Chief, Pacific, and a surgeon. Mrs. Denman is in the background

River basin and Puget Sound, and warned the Foreign Office accordingly. It felt that the British would lose a valuable field of commerce, and, more important, that the Americans would gain the upper reaches of the region giving them "the command of the North Pacific and in a certain degree that of the China Sea, objects of the greatest commercial & political importance to Gt. Britain."[5] The Company also fully realized that New England commercial and shipping interests sought these ports.[6] It appeared to Dr. John McLoughlin, Director of the Company's Western Department, that the United States Navy also hoped to develop a base on Puget Sound.[7] In view of this, the British government was caught between the appeals of the Hudson's Bay Company for support and the demands of the American government for "All Oregon."

Naval Support for the Hudson's Bay Company

While diplomatic developments ran their course the Royal Navy protected British interests on the Northwest Coast. The first mention of plans to support the British position in Oregon was contained in instructions to the Commander-in-Chief, Pacific, written in late 1842, which ordered a warship "to the coasts of the Territory of the Columbia River, the Straits of San Juan de Fuca [*sic*] and Gulf of Georgia."[8] Why no ship carried out this duty remains obscure; most likely, the demands of the station were such that no vessel was available for this service. However, the plans were fulfilled late in 1843, when the Foreign Office advised the Admiralty to instruct the British admiral in the Pacific to send a warship to the Northwest Coast, to "show the flag" at the main centres of Hudson's Bay Company trade.[9] The task fell to the sloop *Modeste,* 18 guns, Commander the Honourable Thomas Baillie.

H.M.S. *Modeste* arrived at the mouth of the Columbia River on 7 July 1844; her object was to indicate to the Americans that Britain would not tolerate interference with her trading interests and territorial claims in Oregon. Baillie rightly believed that his mission could best be achieved by taking the *Modeste* upstream to Fort Vancouver. Aided by a Company pilot, he navigated the treacherous waters as far as the post, where he learned that most of the two thousand settlers—of whom only 450 were

[5]John H. Pelly (Gov., H.B.C.) to Lord Palmerston (F.O.), 26 February 1840, copy, C.O. 6/14.
[6]See Norman Graebner, "Maritime Factors in the Oregon Compromise," *Pacific Historical Review,* XX (November 1951), 331-46.
[7]J. McLoughlin to Governor, 28 March 1845, B.223/b/33, fols. 170-72, H.B.C.A.
[8]These instructions, noted in IND. 4761, P.R.O., were received by Rear-Admiral Richard Thomas on 11 February 1843.
[9]Lord Aberdeen's instructions to the Admiralty, 23 October 1843, are in R. C. Clark, *History of the Willamette Valley, Oregon,* 2 vols. (Chicago: S. J. Clarke, 1927), I, 327-28.

British—lived south of the Columbia and that only a few lived north of the river. His report strengthened the view of the British government that only the territory south of the river should be relinquished to the United States.[10]

After a three-week stay at Fort Vancouver, Baillie sailed downstream for the river mouth, where the *Modeste* grounded on the notorious bar and narrowly escaped disaster. After repairs were made at Baker's Bay, he pointed the *Modeste* to the north and Fort Victoria. But the harbours of Vancouver Island's southern tip were as yet uncharted, and Baillie was forced to run in to Captain Vancouver's old anchorage, Port Discovery, across the Strait of Juan de Fuca from Fort Victoria. After receiving provisions from the Company off the entrance to Victoria harbour, the *Modeste* sailed for Port Simpson, the main trading centre on the north coast, near the northern extremity of British claims. There a further examination of her hull revealed more extensive damage than had been disclosed at Baker's Bay, but successful repairs eliminated the possibility that she might have to return to England.[11]

Having completed her mission, the *Modeste* sailed for the Hawaiian Islands. Her visit to the disputed district was significant in that it marked the first of a series of visits by the Royal Navy to show the Americans, and, indeed, the Hudson's Bay Company, that Britain intended to protect her interests in Oregon, notwithstanding Lord Aberdeen's conciliatory foreign policy.

This was the first use of "gunboat diplomacy" in the Oregon crisis and it coincided with the formation of plans in London to reinforce the defences of British North America. In the event of war with the United States, the critical areas of operation would be the Atlantic seaboard, the St. Lawrence River, and Lakes Ontario and Erie. In preparing for hostilities, the Admiralty and the War Office were reminded of the experiences of the War of 1812. During that war, waterways were essential to communications, and sea power on the Lakes played a decisive role. Consequently, in 1845, the Royal Navy sent Captain F. R. "Bloody" Boxer, to examine American military establishments on the Great Lakes. This officer advised the Admiralty that Britain's defence of Canada and the "exposed frontiers of Canada West" depended on maintaining "the command of the navigation of the lakes."[12] He suggested

---

[10]See "HMS *Modeste* on the Pacific Coast 1843-47: Log and Letters," *Oregon Historical Quarterly*, LXI (December 1960), 408-36, and T. Baillie to Thomas, 4 August 1844, Adm. 1/5550.

[11]F. V. Longstaff and W. Kaye Lamb, "The Royal Navy on the Northwest Coast, 1813-1850. Part I," *British Columbia Historical Quarterly*, IX (January 1945), 19.

[12]This report and those of other officers, naval and military, relating to the defences of British North America at this time, are in Adm. 7/626.

methods, which were later largely implemented, of increasing British
maritime strength on the Lakes and of conveying troops there. His
reports and those of other investigators reflected the need for increased
military preparations during the gravest foreign crisis to face Britain
since the War of 1812.

The problem of sending troops to the remote Northwest Coast would
be a major one in the event of military operations there. Soldiers would
have to be transported overland from Canada or sent by sea. As a matter
of fact, Baron Metcalfe, the Governor-General of Canada, thought that
European and native troops from India would assist the British cause.[13]
When the United States Congress passed an Oregon bill to incorporate
the territory to 54°40′ in the Union, the Prime Minister, Sir Robert
Peel, considered sending to Oregon secretly a frigate bearing Royal
Marines and a small artillery force.[14] But this remained only an idea as
the Foreign Minister, Lord Aberdeen, believed that the strength of the
Royal Navy in the Pacific was sufficient to deal with any incident.
Simultaneously, Sir George Simpson, the Governor of the Hudson's Bay
Company territories in North America, thought that the British posi-
tion could be strengthened by stationing four warships (two sail and
two steam) in the Columbia with a large body of marines and two
thousand Métis and Indians on board.[15] The ambitious proposal of the
"Little Emperor," as Simpson was called, did not bear fruit. However,
he did convince the Governor and Committee of the Company, the
Governor-General of Canada, the Duke of Wellington and the Foreign
Office that the British should have a military post near Fort Garry, Red
River, to counteract American influence in the Canadian Northwest.[16]
And finally, "in deference to the earnest entreaties of the Company," the
British government sent 346 troops of the 6th Regiment of Foot, the
Royal Warwickshires, from Cork to Lower Fort Garry by way of York
Factory in Hudson Bay.[17] These soldiers reached their destination 18
September 1846.

As an aid to this expedition, two British officers stationed in Canada

[13]Baron Metcalfe to Lord Stanley, 4 July 1846, confidential, W.O. 1/552.
[14]Sir Robert Peel to Aberdeen, 23 February 1845, Aberdeen Papers, Add. MSS. 43,064,
fols. 178-81, B.M. Peel referred to this ship as "an additional frigate"; he must have
known that the *America*, 50 guns, was then bound for Oregon.
[15]Sir G. Simpson to Pelly, 29 March 1845, copy, F.O. 5/440; on this proposal see E.
E. Rich, *The History of the Hudson's Bay Company, 1670-1870*, 2 vols. (London:
Hudson's Bay Record Society, 1958-1959), II, 724, and C. P. Stacey, "The Hudson's
Bay Company and Anglo-American Military Rivalries during the Oregon Dispute,"
Canadian Historical Review, XVIII (September 1937), 285-301.
[16]See Simpson to Lts. Warre and Vavasour, 30 May 1846, confidential, W.O. 1/552,
and Alvin C. Gluek, Jr., *Minnesota and the Manifest Destiny of the Canadian Northwest* (Toronto: University of Toronto Press, 1965), pp. 60-71.
[17]C.O. Memorandum on H.B.C. Defence, 27 November 1845, C.O. 537/96.

were sent to Fort Vancouver "as private travellers." They were to report to London and Montreal on the feasibility of sending troops overland to Oregon in the event of American encroachment on British rights there. They were also asked to gather information on American settlers, and, in cooperation with officers of the Royal Navy, to ascertain the possibilities of defending British interests on the Northwest Coast from an American attack. This hasty investigation was promoted by Simpson, who met with Peel and Aberdeen in London on 3 April 1845 and sailed for Montreal three days later with complete authority from the ministry to arrange details of the military reconnaissance of Oregon. Lieutenants Henry J. Warre and Mervin Vavasour were chosen for the undertaking and Simpson accompanied them from Montreal to Fort Garry.[18]

The first stage of the trip presented so many difficulties that these officers immediately advised the Secretary of State for War and the Colonies that a route via York Factory would be much better for any cavalry or artillery which might be dispatched to the Canadian Northwest.[19] Warre and Vavasour then began their journey on horseback across the plains and through the difficult passes of the Rockies, accompanied by their guide, Chief Factor Peter Skene Ogden, and seven Company servants. They hoped to reach the Pacific by mid-August, in advance of Lieutenant John Frémont of the United States Army, who was thought to be on a similar mission for the United States.[20]

The hazards they faced convinced Warre and Vavasour that Simpson's proposal to send British soldiers overland to Oregon was impracticable to say the least and certainly optimistic. Alternatively, they realized that Oregon could be defended best by establishing control over the strategic waterways of the area, chiefly the Columbia River and Puget Sound, in order to exclude American warships from the region. They assessed Fort Victoria as "ill-adapted either as a place of refuge for shipping or as a position of defence."[21] But not so with Fort Nisqually, which Vavasour described as having fine harbours, accessible at any season to ships of any size and therefore the most suitable place for disembarking British troops.[22]

18H. U. Addington (F.O.) to J. Stephen (C.O.), 3 April 1845, confidential, W.O. 1/553. The planned meeting with officers of the Royal Navy is mentioned in Henry J. Warre, "Travel and Sport in North America, 1839-1847," typescript, R.G. 24, F71, p. 52, P.A.C. Simpson to Pelly, 4 May 1845, D. 4/67, fols. 13-15, H.B.C.A.

19Warre and Vavasour to Sec. of State for the Colonies, No. 1, 10 June 1845, W.O. 1/552.

20Simpson to P. S. Ogden, 30 May 1845, confidential, copy, *ibid.*

21Warre and Vavasour to Sec. of State for the Colonies, No. 2, 26 October 1845, *ibid.* (Received 7 July 1846) .

22Vavasour to Col. N. W. Holloway, R.E. (Officer Commanding, Canada) , 1 March 1846, copy, F.O. 5/457.

Warre and Vavasour found Cape Disappointment to be the key position in the defence of that part of Oregon. Perhaps with some exaggeration, Simpson had emphasized that British fortification of this headland on the north bank of the Columbia would be advantageous, for enemy warships entering the river would have to "pass so close under the Cape" that shells from a battery "might be dropped almost with certainty" upon their decks.[23] On the other hand, the merit of Simpson's proposal became evident to Warre and Vavasour when they reached the river entrance. Consequently, they recommended that Chief Factor Ogden buy the land from two American settlers under the pretence that it would be used as a Hudson's Bay Company trading post.

Subsequently, Vavasour submitted plans to his commanding officer in Canada for three batteries of heavy guns at Cape Disappointment, and an additional battery of similar guns at Tongue Point on the south bank of the river.[24] With these fortifications, it was believed the British would be able to control the entrance to the hinterland from the sea. Moreover, as Warre so cogently pointed out, they could control "the whole of the country south of Puget's Sound, there being no other harbour or place of landing between the Columbia River and St. Francisco [sic], where ships of sufficient tonnage to navigate the Pacific could enter or remain at anchor in safety."[25] Nothing came of these plans, for reasons that remain obscure. Probably the British Ministry realized that the military defence of Oregon was impracticable. In any event, in a war over Oregon, the decisive theatre would not be the Northwest Coast but the Atlantic seaboard and Great Lakes region. In other words, a war over Oregon was unlikely to take place there.

Meanwhile, what Peel had referred to in September 1844 as "a good deal of preliminary bluster on the part of the Americans" continued to grow in intensity.[26] By early March 1845 the Prime Minister, although unable to persuade Aberdeen of the merits of sending a secret force from Britain to the Columbia by sea, did convince him that a British warship should appear on the Northwest Coast from time to time, and that the flagship of the Commander-in-Chief, Pacific, should also call there. Subsequently, the Foreign Office advised the Admiralty that "Rear Admiral Sir George Seymour should himself visit that Coast at an early period in the *Collingwood*, 80 guns, with a view to giving a feeling of

---

[23]Simpson to Pelly, 29 March 1845, copy, F.O. 5/440. See the sketch of the river entrance in Warre Notebook, R.G. 24, F71, P.A.C.
[24]Vavasour to Holloway, 1 March 1846, copy, F.O. 5/457.
[25]Warre, "Travel and Sport," p. 143, P.A.C.
[26]Peel to Aberdeen, 28 September 1844, no. 270, Add. MSS. 44,454, B.M. He suggested that the flagship *Collingwood*, "when she has leisure," might visit the mouth of the Columbia.

security to our own Settlers in the Country, and to let the Americans see clearly that H.M.'s Govt. are alive to their proceedings, and prepared, in case of necessity to oppose them."[27] With these words, the British ministry gave its first indication of being ready to use the Royal Navy to oppose the American "bluster."[28] The change of policy prompted Aberdeen to write to the British Minister in Washington: "At all events, whatever may be the course of the American Govt., the time is come when we must endeavour to be prepared for every contingency."[29]

Defence Preparations

The British ministry could be assured that Rear-Admiral Sir George Seymour, appointed Commander-in-Chief, Pacific, in May 1844, would employ warships to their best effect in support of British policy. Seymour was an outstanding officer whose forcefulness and ability made him the choice of Lord Haddington, the First Lord of the Admiralty, and Sir Robert Peel as Commander-in-Chief, Pacific. He knew a good deal about the Northwest Coast. Before he sailed for the Pacific on 7 September 1844, he had read Vancouver's *Voyages,* Robert Greenhow's *Memoir . . . on the North West Coast of North America,* and the Secretary of the Navy's report to Congress November 1843 on American activities in the Pacific. He had also studied the events leading to joint occupation of Oregon, examined charts of the Columbia, discussed the importance of the region with Sir John Barrow at the Admiralty, and visited Hudson's Bay House in London. He was anxious that the ships under his command should do everything within Foreign Office instructions to keep Oregon and California out of the American hands, and as many South Pacific islands as possible from falling under French control.[30]

But the Commander-in-Chief, Pacific, was acting under a handicap which had plagued his predecessors and would plague his successors until the advent of the telegraph and wireless telegraphy. Several months must elapse before a reply to his most urgent message could reach him from the Admiralty. At the time of the Oregon crisis, outwardbound dispatches were conveyed from London to Jamaica and Colon by monthly steam packet, then across the Isthmus of Panama by mule or horse, and

27Addington to Corry, 5 March 1845, secret, encl. in W. A. B. Hamilton (Adm.) to Seymour, 10 March 1845, confidential, Adm. 172/4.
28The hardening of policy was announced in the Commons. Great Britain, *Hansard's Parliamentary Debates,* 3rd series, LXXIX, 199 (4 April 1845) .
29Aberdeen to Pakenham, 2 April 1845, private, Aberdeen Papers, Add. MSS. 43,123, fol. 2476, B.M.
30Seymour, Private Diary, CR 114A/376/21, *passim,* W.R.O. On Seymour's career and the Pritchard Affair at Tahiti, see *Dictionary of National Biography,* LI (London, 1897) , 321

on to Callao, which was the port for Lima, and Valparaiso by Pacific Steam Navigation Company ships. This took 55 days, considerably shorter than the 120 days previously required on the route around Cape Horn, but still a long time. There was no certainty that a reply would reach the Admiral immediately, however, for he might be absent from port at the time. Furthermore, sending ships from point to point in the vast Eastern Pacific was time-consuming. The passage from Valparaiso to Hawaii was at least 60 days, and from Hawaii to the Northwest Coast a further 21 days under the best conditions. In view of these limitations, the responsibility placed on the flag officer as an interpreter of British diplomacy was great indeed. He had to assess the validity of old intelligence in relation to his latest instructions and make the best possible disposition of his forces under the circumstances. Similarly, captains under his command frequently were required to exercise judgement concerning their actions and movements.

Seymour was at Lima, Peru, on 6 July when he received orders to sail for Oregon. He had to decide whether to sail first for Tahiti, where he hoped to forestall the French who were planning to establish a protectorate, or to sail directly for the North Pacific. He decided to wait at Lima for news of events in London and Washington. On 14 July he read a Liverpool paper reporting that no action on the Oregon issue could occur for some time, no matter how arrogant President Polk might be.[31] He therefore decided to sail for Tahiti and then for Honolulu, where he could obtain further intelligence on the state of the Oregon question.

Seymour knew, in setting a course for Tahiti, that the British frigate *America*, 50 guns, Captain the Honourable John Gordon, was bound directly from England to the North Pacific because of the Oregon crisis and would soon be in the Strait of Juan de Fuca.[32] Seymour realized that the *America* could not cross the bar of the Columbia, because she drew more than fifteen feet of water. Therefore, she would have to take up her station in the less hazardous, albeit less influential, position at Port Discovery, near the entrance to Puget Sound. From there a party could go by water and land to Fort Vancouver. Seymour believed that this would suffice to show the British in Oregon that their government was "well inclined to afford them protection."[33]

When Chief Factor John McLoughlin at Fort Vancouver received news that the *America* was on the way, he complained to the Governor of

---

[31]Seymour, Private Diary, CR 114A/374/22, 14 July 1845, W.R.O.
[32]For a more detailed account of this mission, see Barry M. Gough, "H.M.S. *America* on the North Pacific Coast," *Oregon Historical Quarterly*, LXX (December 1969), 292-311.
[33]Seymour to Corry, 14 July 1845, Seymour Order Book I, CR 114A/414/1, W.R.O. A copy of Seymour's instructions to Gordon, 13 February 1845, are in *ibid*.

the Hudson's Bay Company in London that a frigate would be absolutely no use to the Company in Oregon; instead a smaller vessel which could ascend the river to Fort Vancouver was required.[34] McLoughlin's complaint was legitimate, but he did not know that Seymour intended to send the sloop *Modeste* back to the coast of Oregon and to Fort Vancouver, if necessary, to strengthen the British position.

The *America* did not reach the Strait of Juan de Fuca until 28 August 1845 because of calms and contrary winds. Captain Gordon of the *America* was the brother of the Earl of Aberdeen, the Foreign Secretary, and one of his officers was Lieutenant William Peel, son of the Prime Minister and an able officer in his own right.[35] The presence in the ship of two persons with such prominent connections caused at least one official, Thomas Larkin, the United States Consul in Monterey, Upper California, to ponder the purpose of the *America*'s visit to the Pacific Northwest.[36]

From the *America*'s anchorage in Port Discovery, Lieutenant Peel went by launch to Fort Victoria. He had two purposes. His first was to deliver a letter given to Gordon in England and addressed to the Officer-in-Charge of the Fort explaining that the principal object of the *America*'s visit was to assure Company authorities that the British government would oppose American encroachments in the Columbia River basin. The second purpose was to request the use in Puget Sound of the Company steamer *Beaver*.[37] The *Beaver* was away on a trading cruise so the request could not be granted; consequently, Peel and his party were forced to take the frigate's launch to the head of the sound and then travel overland to Fort Vancouver.[38]

Peel had been ordered by Captain Gordon—and may even have been selected by Seymour—to report on the settlements on the banks of the Columbia and Willamette Rivers.[39] His two reports are well known and reveal the judgement that distinguished him as an officer. In the first,

[34]McLoughlin to Governor, 28 March 1845, B. 223/b/33, fols. 170-72, H.B.C.A.
[35]On Peel, see Capt. J. Gordon to Seymour, 22 October 1845, Adm. 1/5564; *Dictionary of National Biography*, XLIV (London, 1895), 224; and Admiral Sir Albert H. Markham, *The Life of Sir Clements R. Markham* (London: John Murray, 1917), pp. 39-41. Markham thought Peel "the perfect model of what a British naval officer ought to be."
[36]T. Larkin to Dr. John Marsh, 19 August 1845, Marsh Collection, California State Library, Sacramento; in John A. Hawgood, ed., *First and Last Consul* (San Marino, Calif.; Huntington Library, 1962), p. 33.
[37]Gordon to Officer-in-Charge, Fort Victoria, 31 August 1845, Port Discovery, B. 226/b/1, fols. 35-36d, H.B.C.A.
[38]Lt. Thomas Dawes, "Journal of HMS 'America' . . .," JOD/42, MS 57/055, p. 85, N.M.M.
[39]Gordon to Lt. Wm. Peel, 2 September 1845, encl. in Corry to Addington, 13 February 1846, F.O. 5/459.

addressed to his captain, he gave details on the territory investigated.[40] In the second letter, to Richard Pakenham, the British Minister in Washington conducting talks with the United States government on Oregon, he expressed agreement with Gordon's belief that Vancouver Island must be retained by Britain if the 49th parallel became the demarcation line. Gordon's contention was based on the fact that the northern channel around Vancouver Island was unnavigable for sailing ships, and thus Britain would lack access to the inland passages from the Strait of Juan de Fuca to latitude 51°N.[41] Peel noted that the Island commanded the Strait of Juan de Fuca, possessed a good harbour and had been selected by the Hudson's Bay Company as the eventual hub of trading activities on the Northwest Coast. In his description of growing settlements between the Willamette and Sacramento Valleys, he foretold the inevitable American control of the port of San Francisco which would give the United States a decided maritime superiority in the Pacific.[42]

Peel reached the Admiralty with vital dispatches from Gordon and McLoughlin on 10 February 1846. On the same day, copies were sent to the Foreign Office. It is not known if this intelligence had any influence on the British ministry or the discussions then taking place in Washington. Undoubtedly it did add greatly to British information on the Oregon country at a critical stage in negotiations with the United States.

Before the *America* sailed from Fort Victoria for Honolulu on 1 October 1845 Captain Gordon and other officers enjoyed the hospitality of Roderick Finlayson, Officer-in-Charge of Fort Victoria.[43] According to Finlayson's account of Gordon's visit to Fort Victoria, Gordon claimed he would not exchange "one acre of the barren hills of Scotland for all he saw around him."[44] What especially disgusted Gordon was that the salmon were caught by baits or nets, and not by the fly as in his beloved Scotland. "What a country," he is reported to have exclaimed, "where the salmon will not take to the fly."[45] His negative reactions were not shared by all the naval officers on the coast, and Finlayson stated that

---

[40]Wm. Peel to Gordon, 27 September 1845, encl. in Hamilton to Addington, 10 February 1846, F.O. 5/459. Inscribed on the back, probably in Aberdeen's hand, is "a very good report."

[41]Gordon to Admiralty, 19 October 1845, Adm. 1/5564.

[42]Peel to R. Pakenham, 2 January 1846, F.O. 5/459.

[43]R. Finlayson to McLoughlin, 24 September 1845, Fort Victoria, B. 226/b/1, fol. 37d, H.B.C.A.

[44][Roderick Finlayson], *Biography* [of Roderick Finlayson] (Victoria, 1891), p. 15; see also, his "History of Vancouver Island and the Northwest Coast," typescript, 34, B.C.A.

[45]From Finlayson's Journal, B.C.A., quoted in John T. Walbran, British Columbia Coast Names (Ottawa, 1909), p. 210. See also, Leigh Burpee Robinson, *Esquimalt: "Place of Shoaling Waters"* (Victoria, B.C.: Quality Press, 1947), pp. 29-30.

several who visited Fort Victoria earnestly desired to be sent on a mission of conquest, claiming "that they could take the whole of the Columbia country in 24 hours."[46] Gordon's apathy in regard to British and Company interests in Oregon was also noticed by James Douglas, then Chief Factor at Fort Vancouver, who now had good reason to wonder to what degree the promised naval protection would be made available should circumstances require it.[47] Gordon evidently saw no reason to extend his visit to the Strait of Juan de Fuca or visit Nootka Sound and by 1 October the *America* had cleared Cape Flattery bound for Honolulu and the ports on the west coast of Mexico.

About a week later, the *Modeste,* Commander Baillie, returned to the Strait of Juan de Fuca to continue protection of the Hudson's Bay Company.[48] The obvious reason for her reappearance lay in the fact that she was more manoeuvrable and had a more shallow draft than the *America.* She therefore could enter the Columbia to support the British position, if required. Rear-Admiral Seymour knew that the Hudson's Bay Company would require assistance to maintain law and order, especially in view of the great tide of immigration then flowing into Oregon. He had already informed the Admiralty that he was willing to stop the Americans if circumstances required drastic action, despite his inability to send even small ships such as the *Modeste* into the Columbia without some degree of hazard.[49]

At Fort Nisqually, Commander Baillie found Hudson's Bay Company officials most anxious for him to take his ship into the Columbia. James Douglas, for one, told him of McLoughlin's warning to Gordon that unless the government took "active measures" they would lose Oregon.[50] Under these pressures, Baillie sailed for the river mouth and eventually brought the *Modeste* to anchor off Fort Vancouver on 30 November 1845, the passage having taken almost a month owing to difficult winds and currents in the river.

What were the reactions at Fort Vancouver to the reappearance of the British sloop? Warre and Vavasour considered the arrival of a British warship extremely timely as it encouraged British subjects to support their rights. Moreover, it discouraged Americans from taking the law into their own hands; and it gave protection to Hudson's Bay Company

---

[46]Finlayson, "History of Vancouver Island," p. 35, B.C.A.

[47]James Douglas to Simpson, 20 March 1846, private, D. 5/16, H.B.C.A.; Douglas was indeed correct in his views on Gordon, for the latter thought Oregon of little importance, especially in contrast to California. See Gordon to Sec. of Adm., 19 October 1845, Adm. 1/5564.

[48]Baillie's instructions from Seymour, 12 August 1845, are in Adm. 1/5561.

[49]Seymour to Corry, 14 July 1845, Y 158, Adm. 1/5550.

[50]Douglas to Baillie, 8 October 1845, copy, B. 223/b/33, fols. 107-107d, H.B.C.A.

property.[51] In other words, they believed that the presence of the *Modeste* achieved the desired effect: American immigrants who had arrived recently were acting peaceably. A similar view was held by McLoughlin, who wrote that the ship's presence "has both a moral and political effect and shows that our government is ready to protect us."[52] The importance of stationing a British warship at Fort Vancouver is best revealed by the fact that the *Modeste* remained until May 1847. She was indeed indispensable to British authority in the Lower Columbia.

The Oregon crisis was on Seymour's mind continually while he attended to affairs in Tahiti. On 19 August 1845 he instructed Captain John Duntze of the frigate *Fisgard*, 42 guns, to prepare to sail with the steamer *Cormorant*, 6 guns, to Puget Sound during the spring of 1846 if the United States and Great Britain did not soon come to an agreement. With this possibility in mind Seymour also considered a plan "to push our Steamers" into the Columbia. There they would be beyond any gun batteries that the Americans might have built on Cape Disappointment.[53] The *Cormorant* and *Salamander*, 6 guns, both paddle-wheel sloops, were the only steamers then available to Seymour. There seems to have been not more than two steamers on the station until about 1857 when some screw-frigates and corvettes became available.

His fears were somewhat allayed when the *Collingwood* reached Hawaii in September 1845. He believed that news of the British flagship's presence at Honolulu would eventually reach Oregon and convince Americans there that Britain attached great importance to her interests on the Northwest Coast.[54] At Honolulu, he met his American counterpart, Commodore John F. Sloat. Naturally, each was suspicious of the other, but each also expressed hope that the two nations could reach a peaceful agreement on the definition of the Oregon boundary. Seymour was especially concerned for the fate of Upper California after his conversation with Sloat.[55] At this time, Sloat told him that if the Oregon question were not settled it would be entirely the fault of the American government.[56]

When Seymour returned to Valparaiso on 15 February 1846 he learned

[51]Report of Lts. Warre and Vavasour to Sec. of State for the Colonies, 8 December 1845, in Joseph Schafer, ed., "Documents relative to Warre and Vavasour's Military Reconnoissance [sic] in Oregon, 1845-46," *Oregon Historical Quarterly*, X (1909), 64.
[52]McLoughlin to Governor, 20 November 1845, in E. E. Rich, ed., *The Letters of John McLoughlin from Fort Vancouver to the Governor and Committee, Third Series, 1844-46* (London: Hudson's Bay Record Society, vol. VII, 1944), p. 48.
[53]Seymour to Gordon, 12 August 1845, private, Tahiti, CR 114A/418/1, W.R.O.
[54]Seymour to Corry, 3 October 1845, Honolulu, Y7, Adm. 1/5561.
[55]*Ibid.*
[56]Seymour, Private Diary, CR 114A/374/22, Appendix, W.R.O.

that Sloat's squadron was being reinforced from the East Indies station by the ship-of-the-line *Columbus* and the frigate *Constitution*. This information substantiated his fears that the United States Navy was soon to act against either the British in Oregon or the Mexicans in Upper California—or perhaps even both. Therefore, he immediately sailed north to Callao with the brig *Spy*, 6 guns, to await news and dispatches from London and New York. There he learned of President Polk's "arrogant declaration" of 2 December 1845 to the United States Congress.[57] Polk had reasserted the Monroe Doctrine, called for an end to the joint occupation of Oregon and proposed that Federal jurisdiction be extended to that territory. Such expansionist views hardly could fail to provoke a war, Seymour believed.[58] "To provide for war taking place," he sent the *Cormorant* north, along with a supply of coal in the chartered merchant ship *Rosalind*, made arrangements for the provisioning and deployment of the squadron in case of war, and issued instructions for part of the squadron expected at Valparaiso—particularly the frigate *Grampus*, 50 guns, on her way from England.[59]

Before the *Collingwood* left Callao for the North Pacific to meet the growing crisis, Seymour penned a lengthy report to the Admiralty informing their Lordships of the situation and appealing for additional naval support. In essence, he expressed concern over the inadequacy of his squadron for guarding British interests in the vast Pacific. At a time when the possibility of war with the United States and France was so great, he had only fifteen ships under his command: one ship-of-the-line, two frigates, ten sloops, one brig and one storeship.[60] The inferiority of the squadron was substantiated in his "Account of Foreign Naval Force at present employed in the Pacific" which accompanied his letter to the Admiralty. This listed the French naval vessels at sixteen (two frigates, nine sloops and five smaller ships) and the American vessels at eleven (one ship-of-the-line, two frigates, five sloops, and two schooners, with an additional frigate, the *Congress*, expected). Clearly, the British would be at a disadvantage in the Pacific if France and the United States joined forces in a war.

To counteract the growth of rival sea power in the Pacific, especially American influence in Oregon, Seymour made a bold appeal to the Admiralty to assign two more ships-of-the-line for duty in Puget Sound. He also requested an arsenal or port for his squadron, as well as a naval-stores depot somewhere between the Northwest Coast and New Zealand.

---

[57]Seymour, Private Diary, CR 114A/374/23, 26 February 1846, W.R.O.
[58]*Ibid.*
[59]*Ibid.*, 7 March 1846.
[60]Seymour to Sec. of Admiralty, 6 March 1846, Adm. 1/5568.

Seymour realized, however, that enlarging his squadron would not overcome the limits of the role that the Royal Navy could play in supporting
the British position in the Pacific Northwest. As he admitted to the
Admiralty, the rapid increase of American settlers would suffice to give
them control of the Lower Columbia without the aid of the United
States government. Unless a British military force opposed them—and
Seymour was reluctant to send naval brigades a great distance from their
ships—the Royal Navy could do very little beyond the areas accessible
to ships.[61] This was a fact the Americans knew very well.[62]

Nevertheless, he sought to strengthen his case for an increase in the
number of British men-of-war in the Pacific by sending a private letter
to his friend, the Earl of Ellenborough, the First Lord of the Admiralty.
Seymour could not ignore the deteriorating situation in Oregon, even
though some of his acquaintances at the Admiralty considered Polk's
address to Congress "mere blustering." It was essential, as he explained
to Ellenborough, that "a force commensurate with the superiority of our
Navy over that of all other Nations should be sent to these seas. . . ."[63]

These words achieved their desired effect. The Admiralty supported
Seymour's urgent demands and informed the Foreign Secretary on 6 June
1846 that it was necessary to increase the Pacific squadron to give it "a
decided preponderance" over that of the United States.[64]

The decision was made with some reluctance. Their Lordships feared
that strengthening the force in the Pacific would weaken the Royal Navy
in home waters, for the French had sixteen or seventeen ships-of-the-
line in commission.[65] Fear of French intentions arose two years earlier,
in 1844, when the Prince de Joinville published his famous *Note sur
l'état des forces navales de la France,* in which he contended that French
steam-power could transport thirty thousand French troops across the
English Channel at night. This pamphlet touched off a stormy debate
in England on national defence, in which alarmists such as Palmerston had warned that steam had "bridged the channel."[66] Thereafter the
Admiralty kept a sharp eye on the strength of the French at sea.

These developments prompted the Lords of the Admiralty to explain
to the Foreign Office that the Royal Navy was placed in an awkward

61*Ibid.*
62See, for example, Report of William Wilkins (Secretary of War) , 30 November
1844, *Senate Documents,* 28th Cong., 2nd Sess., vol. I, pp. 113ff.
63Seymour to Lord Ellenborough, 7 March 1846, **Ellenborough Papers, PRO**
30/12/4/20, P.R.O.
64Corry to Smythe, Under-Secretary of State for Foreign Affairs, 6 June 1846, F.O.
5/461.
65*Ibid.*
66For a critical evaluation of the crisis, see C. J. Bartlett, *Great Britain and Sea
Power 1815-1853* (Oxford: Clarendon Press, 1963) , pp. 148-74.

position by the possibility of a French invasion of England and a war with the United States over Oregon. Henry Corry, the Secretary of the Admiralty, explained the gravity of the situation in these words:

> My Lords consider that it would be inconsistent with the character this country has hitherto borne as a Predominant Naval Power, and with that degree of prudent precaution which under the most flattering circumstances of amity with France we ought still to observe, were we to exhibit our Naval Force at home as inferior to that of France, and this too at a period when there are unsettled differences with America, which may unfortunately terminate in war.[67]

But if an increase in force for the Pacific were authorized by the Foreign Office, more ships would have to be commissioned for protection at home, a difficult matter owing to the shortage of seamen.[68]

The reply of the Foreign Secretary, Lord Aberdeen, to the recommendations of the Admiralty indicated that war with the United States seemed then to be unlikely. He disagreed with Seymour's proposal for strengthening the Pacific squadron on the "supposed probability of war with the United States or with France, or with both countries."[69] Although Aberdeen could see the wisdom in a small increase in the force for the Mexican Coast to protect British merchants and trade—especially as war between the United States and Mexico appeared imminent—in his opinion the Oregon question provided no threat to British interests. In fact, owing to diplomatic developments, Seymour's fears were now believed to be unfounded.[70]

Aberdeen's confident answer regarding the state of Anglo-American relations can be explained by the fact that Britain gained the upper hand in her diplomatic dealings with the United States by June 1846. In these negotiations she was able to use her supremacy at sea as a threat. The British Cabinet, like Seymour, was outraged by Polk's statement, mentioned earlier, to the United States Congress on 2 December 1845. Certainly Peel decided that the time had come for action when on 6 January 1846 he informed a friend, "We shall not reciprocate blustering with Polk but shall quietly make an increase in Naval and Military and Ordnance Estimates."[71]

From January to June, Ellenborough at the Admiralty repeatedly urged the Prime Minister to further increase the estimates to prevent

[67]Corry to Smythe, 6 June 1846, F.O. 5/461.
[68]*Ibid.*
[69]Addington to Corry, 19 June 1846, confidential, Adm. 1/5568.
[70]*Ibid.*
[71]Peel to Lord Egerton, 6 January 1846, Peel Papers, B.M.; quoted in Wilbur D. Jones and J. Chal Vinson, "British Preparedness and the Oregon Settlement," *Pacific Historical Review,* XX (November 1953), 360.

the Royal Navy in the Pacific and elsewhere from becoming inferior to the American force.[72] Concessions were made to Ellenborough in this regard but finally Peel was forced to state categorically that he could not sanction further demands on the Treasury in time of peace. He concluded his sharp rejoinder to the First Lord by declaring that Britain was far in advance of her American rival in actual preparedness for war.[73] Peel assured his colleague that the United States knew this, and would see the advantage of signing a treaty ending the dispute over the Oregon boundary. Nevertheless, Ellenborough, the most belligerent member of the cabinet, remained unconvinced. Eventually, in July 1846, he resigned in objection to the unwillingness of his "timorous Colleagues" to be ready for war.[74]

The Treaty of 1846

The strength of the Royal Navy may well have been inadequate in Ellenborough's view. It is now clear, however, that Britain's superior strength at sea was the decisive factor in precipitating an agreement between the two powers over Oregon. On 6 January 1846 Louis McLane, the American chargé d'affaires in London, met with Aberdeen to discuss the points of dispute. His report of this meeting to officials in Washington warned that the British planned to commission immediately some thirty ships-of-the-line in addition to steamers and other vessels held in reserve.[75] In all likelihood, this alarming news induced the Americans to adopt a less belligerent attitude.[76]

Meanwhile, at the Foreign Office, plans were underway for a carefully calculated diplomatic manoeuvre. The intent was to draw from the American delegate to the negotiations in Washington a proposal that the boundary west of the Rocky Mountains should be the 49th parallel to

[72]Ellenborough to Peel, 5 March 1846, Peel Papers, Add. MSS. 40,473, fols. 78-78b, B.M.
[73]Peel to Ellenborough, 17 March 1846, secret, Peel Papers, ADD. MSS. 40,473, fols. 120-23, B.M. The naval estimates of 1846 were 12 per cent higher than those of the previous year because of developments in steam engineering, fear of war with France, and, according to Peel, "relations with the United States." Julius W. Pratt, "James K. Polk and John Bull," *Canadian Historical Review*, XXIV (1943), 346.
[74]Ellenborough to Seymour, 28 June 1846, Ellenborough Papers, PRO 30/12/4/20, P.R.O. On Ellenborough at the Admiralty, see Albert H. Imlah, *Lord Ellenborough: A Biography*, Harvard Historical Studies, vol. XLIII (Cambridge, Mass.: 1939) 236-38. and Bartlett, *Great Britain and Sea Power*, p. 182.
[75]See Hunter Miller, ed., *Treaties and Other International Acts of America*, V (Washington: U.S. Gov't. Printing Office, 1936) , 58, and Merk, *Oregon Question*, pp. 341-42.
[76]On this point, see the convincing article by Jones and Chal Vinson, "British Preparedness and the Oregon Settlement," pp. 361-64. Merk *Oregon Question*, pp. 362-63, in discounting the importance of sea power in this crisis, makes no reference to the above-mentioned work.

the middle of the Strait of Georgia, and then the middle of the channel leading to the Pacific, thereby leaving Britain in full possession of Vancouver Island. Under the threat of British sea power, the Americans accepted these terms, which formed the basis of the Oregon Treaty signed on 15 June 1846. The final partitioning of the continent between Britain and the United States therefore was achieved by an adroit combination of British diplomacy and naval primacy.

Throughout the period when the ministry was reaching an accord with the United States government, Rear-Admiral Seymour possessed sufficient strength on the Northwest Coast to protect British interests in the region. After the *Congress,* 54 guns, flagship of Commodore Robert F. Stockton, arrived in the Pacific, Seymour concluded that the Americans were about to take action against the British in Oregon.[77] Consequently, he had carried out his plan, discussed above, of sending the *Fisgard* and the steamer *Cormorant* to join the *Modeste* in those waters. He was confident that they would reach the Strait of Juan de Fuca before the *Congress,* thus forestalling an American occupation of Oregon.[78]

The difficulty of sending ships into the river mouth handicapped the Navy in supporting the Hudson's Bay Company at Fort Vancouver. Ships that drew more than fifteen feet could rarely pass over the bar, and most ships at Seymour's disposal had a draught in excess of this. Because of this, the *Fisgard* on 30 April 1846 was forced to take up a station at Fort Nisqually at the very head of Puget Sound, after reaching the Strait of Juan de Fuca and receiving supplies at Fort Victoria. Her captain, John Duntze, had instructions that emphasized that he was to send the *Cormorant* and even, if circumstances warranted, the *Fisgard* into the Columbia in order to "afford British subjects due security."[79] However, the matter continued to disturb Seymour, who noted in his diary on 19 July that his sleep would improve if, somehow, he could put the *Fisgard* into the Columbia River without danger.[80]

By this time, other ships had been sent north to check American influence in Oregon and Upper California.[81] The *Grampus,* 50 guns, was to join the *Talbot,* 26 guns, at Honolulu; the *Juno,* 26 guns, *Frolic,* 16 guns, the *Collingwood* and *Spy* were in Californian and Mexican waters.

Seymour also expected the *America* to be in the Northeastern Pacific. To his surprise and disgust, he learned that she had sailed for England

---

[77]Seymour to Corry, 7 April 1846, San Blas, Y 63, Adm. 1/5561.
[78]*Ibid.*
[79]Seymour to Capt. J. Duntze, 14 January 1846, copy, Adm. 1/5561.
[80]Seymour, Private Diary, 19 July 1846, CR 114A/374/22, W.R.O.
[81]On Seymour's policy for California, see Ephraim D. Adams, "English Interest in the Annexation of California," *American Historical Review,* XIV (1909) , 756-61. Seymour to Corry, 7 April 1846, San Blas, Adm. 1/5561.

"without orders, with money."[82] In this, Captain Gordon had acceded to the pressure of British merchants on the Mexican coast. They feared a Mexican-American war and thought their funds would be endangered if sent in H.M.S. *Daphne,* 18 guns, to England. Gordon evidently thought this was the best means of protecting British interests. The *America* reached the English port of Spithead on 19 August 1846. According to Seymour, Captain Gordon had made an "ill judged decision which might have turned the fate of war with the U.S. against us by taking off the station the only strong ship except the *Collingwood* when he was aware I considered war most probable."[83]

When the *America* reached Portsmouth, a court martial was assembled, "and after due deliberation to the pros and cons," as a junior officer recalled somewhat sarcastically, "our worthy old Chief was doomed to be reprimanded, as indeed if a war with the United States had been brought on, he would have deserved to have been shot. Fortunately for him Polk and Aberdeen made it up somehow."[84] The charge of "leaving his station contrary to orders of his Admiral" was "fully proved" and Gordon was "severely reprimanded."[85] At the court martial, pecuniary gain from the freight monies he received for conveying funds to England was ruled out as a motive. Gordon retained command of the *America* for a brief time and then returned to take advantage of a newly-instituted retirement scheme.

As for Seymour, his anxieties ended on 23 August when he learned that Britain and the United States had resolved the Oregon question. With obvious relief that there would be no further need to send warships over the bar of the Columbia, he wrote to the senior naval officer on the Northwest Coast to inform him of the Treaty. His frustration with the whole crisis was revealed when he added, ". . . the terms are what I understand our Government were ready to give two years ago without all the bluster which has since occurred."[86]

The Treaty effectually signified the end of the Hudson's Bay Company's territorial—but not commercial—domination in Old Oregon. Important provisions in the agreement allowed them to retain full navigation rights south of the 49th parallel and to enjoy access to the har-

---

[82]Seymour, Private Diary, 14 August 1846, CR 114A/374/23, W.R.O.
[83]*Ibid.,* Appendix, p. 129. Seymour expressed his displeasure on this subject to Capt. H. Byam Martin, C.B., of the *Grampus,* and the latter knew that "with so great a probability of an American war" Gordon would be "called to account." *Grampus* Journal, Byam Martin Papers, Add. MSS. 41,472, B.M.
[84]Dawes, "Journal of HMS 'America' . . .," p. 107, N.M.M.
[85]Courts Martial Books, Adm. 13/103 and 104 for 26 August 1846.
[86]Seymour to Senior Naval Officer of H.M. Ships in Oregon, 3 October 1846, Honolulu, CR 114A/481/2, W.R.O.

bours of Puget Sound.[87] Although it could be argued that the Treaty did not limit the Company's enterprise, the interests of the Hudson's Bay Company in Oregon declined understandably after 1846.[88] The new depot at Fort Victoria soon began to flourish as it took the place of Fort Vancouver, which was outliving its usefulness as the hub of Company trade in the Pacific. Indeed, Fort Victoria constituted a more suitable port than Fort Vancouver for an organization whose interests west of the Rockies were becoming increasingly involved in coastal shipping, trade with the Hawaiian Islands and commerce with London by way of the sea lanes round Cape Horn.

Success of Naval Diplomacy

The Royal Navy continued to safeguard the property rights of the Company in Oregon for three years after the signing of the Treaty. Because the terms were variously interpreted in Oregon, the *Modeste* remained at Fort Vancouver until 3 May 1847; she left only after Captain Baillie received information that cleared up all confusion.[89]

Thereafter, Seymour pursued a policy based on the conviction that the security of Company interests in what had become American territory could not depend on the continued presence of one of Her Majesty's ships in the Columbia River. He recommended to his successor that a ship should "show the flag" in Puget Sound in the summer of 1848 as an alternative to a Hudson's Bay Company request for a small force to replace the *Modeste*.[90]

In recognition of the continuing presence of the British at Fort Vancouver, Seymour also advised that the Royal Navy make occasional visits to the settlements on the Columbia.[91] British warships were on the Northwest Coast in 1847, 1848 and 1849, but none ventured into the Columbia; the gradual extension of American authority in Oregon Territory coincided with the withdrawal of the Hudson's Bay Company. At no time during this transfer of influence were British interests endangered.

---

[87]These became points of dispute later. John S. Galbraith, *The Hudson's Bay Company as an Imperial Factor, 1821-1869* (Berkeley and Los Angeles: University of California Press, 1957) , pp. 253-55, 260-61 and 271.

[88]Frank E. Ross, "The Retreat of the Hudson's Bay Company in the Pacific Northwest," *Canadian Historical Review*, XVIII (September 1937) , 262-80.

[89]Company agents at Honolulu had advised Seymour of the great necessity "to leave one of HM Ships at the River until everything was finally settled." Reported in Pelly and Allan to Gov., H.B.C., 1 October 1846, A, 11/62, fols. 139-139d, H.B.C.A.

[90]Seymour to Ward, 27 September 1847, Y 174, Adm. 1/5578.

[91]This advice was forwarded to the next Commander-in-Chief, Pacific. W. A. B. Hamilton to Rear-Admiral T. Phipps Hornby, 10 December 1847, instructions, PHI/3/5, N.M.M.

The Royal Navy played a dual role throughout the Oregon crisis. In the first place, ships on the Northwest Coast acted in various capacities—upholding the interests of the Hudson's Bay Company, maintaining law and order, and acting as deterrents to any possible American filibuster. According to Company officials at Fort Vancouver, the *Modeste*'s presence helped prevent a "collision between the inhabitants of British origin, that would have led to most serious difficulties with the parent states."[92] Six ships were stationed on the coast during 1845-1846 and others were ready to act in support of British interests if needed. Hudson's Bay Company officials were accordingly grateful for such overwhelming protection. As Chief Factor James Douglas remarked, the British government had indeed shown "an extraordinary degree of solicitude and taken most active measures for the protection of British rights in this Country."[93]

In the second aspect of its dual role, the very fact of the Royal Navy's predominance in the world—if not always in the Pacific as Seymour and Ellenborough knew—proved instrumental in keeping the peace.[94] There is little reason to doubt that the Oregon compromise, as two notable scholars of American sea power have shown, "saved the United States from a repetition of disasters" characteristic of the War of 1812.[95] The overall fact of British supremacy at sea, the operations of British warships at points of stress such as Oregon, and artful British diplomacy in European and American affairs enabled Great Britain to accomplish its objectives—to protect colonial territories of her worldwide empire and to provide security for the homeland and for growing seaborne trade. As a result of this strength Polk's "bluster" proved to be exactly that.

[92]Directors of H.B.C. at Ft. Vancouver to Capt. T. Baillie, 1 May 1847, extract, in Seymour to Ward, 27 September 1847, Y 174, Adm. 1/5578.
[93]Douglas to Governor and Committee, Hudson's Bay Company, 28 July 1846, extract, encl. in Pelly to Earl Grey, 11 December 1846, C.O. 305/1 (copy in B. 223/b/34, fol. 34, H.B.C.A.).
[94]Statistics on the relative strength of British, American, and French warships, both sail and steam, are given in Merk, *Oregon Question*, p. 348.
[95]Harold and Margaret Sprout, *The Rise of American Naval Power, 1776-1918* (Princeton: Princeton University Press, 1939), p. 132.

Chapter 4

THE COLONY OF VANCOUVER ISLAND
1846-1853

THE OREGON TREATY of 1846 gave Britain title to Vancouver Island and to the continental territory north of the 49th parallel sometimes known as New Caledonia. The Treaty underscored a conflict of interest between settlement and fur trade: Americans received the arable lands of the Columbia Basin and the British the less-fertile territories of the northern fur-trading domain. The boundary, therefore, was in a very real sense an extension of the interests of the two nations: the United States inherited agricultural lands suitable for settlement, and Britain retained a fur-trading area with a distinct maritime character.

Arable lands were scarce on Vancouver Island except near Fort Victoria; hence settlement did not displace the fur trade as quickly as in Oregon. But a trade in such staples as fish, lumber and coal developed as the fur trade declined. Throughout the formative years of "the seaboard colony" of Vancouver Island, the Royal Navy played a fundamental role.

Colonizing Vancouver Island

In 1846 the British government, which had learned an important lesson from the Oregon dispute, began systematic agricultural colonization of Vancouver Island to consolidate its control of the remnant of the Oregon Territory left to it by the Oregon Treaty, and thereby halt the advancing tide of American settlement on the frontier. James Stephen, the forceful

Permanent Under-Secretary of State for the Colonies, argued that Vancouver Island should be colonized because of its good harbours, at least
one of which would be suitable for a station for the Royal Navy in the
Pacific. On strategic grounds, he knew that a British naval base at Vancouver Island would serve as a counterpoise to the American port of San
Francisco and thus limit the rise of a rival maritime power in that ocean.[1]

The question was who should undertake the task of taming this
wilderness where farmland was at a premium? Certainly not the government itself because any further drain on the Imperial purse would be
unacceptable to Parliament.[2] The Hudson's Bay Company had not
forgotten the ill-success of its Red River Colony, and believed settlement
of the land was incompatible with the fur trade. On the other hand, the
Governor of the Company, Sir John Pelly, determined that to protect
the fur trade no other organization but the Company should conduct
the colonization of Vancouver Island.[3]

Earl Grey, the Secretary of State for War and the Colonies, was well
disposed toward the Hudson's Bay Company. When he accepted the
position in Lord John Russell's Whig ministry in July 1846, the question
of the future of Vancouver Island was of minor importance in comparison to the challenges that faced the Colonial Office in other parts of the
Empire—New Zealand, Australia, the Cape, the Maritimes and Canada.

Grey was committed both to reform in colonial policy and to a belief
in empire.[4] As a master of compromise, he surmounted objections of
"Little Englanders" by replacing "economic restraint" with "political
freedom." This fundamental principle, as Professor E. E. Rich has explained, was to "rest upon a common heritage of laws, institutions and
experience—in effect upon emigration from Great Britain."[5] Like his
fellow Colonial Reformer, Edward Gibbon Wakefield, Grey believed
that privileged land companies could be used to populate waste areas
and relieve over-population at home. The Hudson's Bay Company was
a staple-trading rather than a land company, but Grey maintained that

[1]Paul Knaplund, "James Stephen on Granting Vancouver Island to the Hudson's Bay
Company, 1846-1848," British Columbia Historical Quarterly, IX (October 1945),
264.
[2]One estimate of the capital needed for the enterprise is £50,000. A. S. Morton, A
History of the Canadian West to 1870-71 (London: T. Nelson & Sons, [1939]), p. 751.
[3]For an account of Hudson's Bay Company motives at this time, see John S. Galbraith,
The Hudson's Bay Company as an Imperial Factor, 1821-1869 (Berkeley and Los
Angeles: University of California Press, 1957), pp. 284-92, esp. 287 and 307.
[4]The intention of his policy is given in Earl Grey, The Colonial Policy of Lord John
Russell's Administration 2 vols. (London: R. Bentley, 1853), I, 1-49. A brief account
of his Vancouver Island policy is in W. P. Morrell, Colonial Policy in the Age of
Peel and Russell (Oxford: Clarendon Press, 1930), pp. 444-46.
[5]E. E. Rich, The History of the Hudson's Bay Company, 1670-1870, 2 vols. (London:
Hudson's Bay Record Society, 1958-1959), II, 750.

its large financial resources and experience in governing the Indians in western America made it the best-qualified agency for colonizing Vancouver Island.[6]

While discussions between the Colonial Office and the Company proceeded, Lieutenant Adam Dundas, R.N., cautioned the British government against entrusting the responsibility to the Hudson's Bay Company. Dundas, who returned to England after service in H.M.S. *Modeste* during her lengthy Columbia River visits, discussed the problem with his brother, George, a Member of Parliament who shared his interest in colonization of Vancouver Island by Scottish emigrants.[7] At a meeting with Benjamin Hawes, Parliamentary Under-Secretary at the Colonial Office, Lieutenant Dundas described from first-hand knowledge the disadvantages of placing the Island under Company superintendence. These remarks greatly influenced Under-Secretary Hawes, who asked Dundas to compose a memorandum on the subject for the Colonial Office.[8] In his memorandum, Dundas stressed that the Company was dominated by a spirit "wholly and totally inapplicable to the nursing of a young Colony," and that the role which the Company would play as the colonizing agency at Vancouver Island would be "repugnant" to colonists, who would consequently leave.[9]

Neither these words nor parliamentary opposition led by Gladstone affected Grey, who was predisposed to support the Hudson's Bay Company.[10] A proposal by the Dundas brothers for colonizing Vancouver Island with Scottish emigrants was rejected. So, too, were schemes proposed by Mormons from Utah, by British whaling interests, by a joint-stock company of settlers and by a coal mining and colonization corporation.

In lengthy discussions lasting through 1847 and ending in May 1848, the Colonial Office and the Hudson's Bay Company agreed to terms of the Charter of Grant.[11] Under these terms the Company agreed to bring British settlers to Vancouver Island: the government made it clear that

[6]Minute of Earl Grey, 16 September 1846, on Sir J. H. Pelly to Grey, 7 September 1846, C.O. 305/1.

[7]Paul Knaplund, "Letters from James Edward Fitzgerald to W. E. Gladstone concerning Vancouver Island and the Hudson's Bay Company, 1848-1850," *British Columbia Historical Quarterly*, XIII (January 1949), 12, n. 26. Minutes of B. Hawes and Grey, 7 June 1848, C.O. 305/1.

[8]Adam Dundas to Grey, 30 May 1848, *ibid.*; printed in *Report of the Provincial Archives Department of British Columbia . . . 1913* (Victoria, B.C., 1914), p. V49.

[9]*Ibid.*

[10]See Great Britain, *Hansard's Parliamentary Debates*, 3rd Series, vol. CI, 263 ff.; Knaplund, "Letters from James Edward Fitzgerald to W. E. Gladstone," 1-21; and John S. Galbraith, "Fitzgerald versus the Hudson's Bay Company: the Founding of Vancouver Island," *British Columbia Historical Quarterly*, XVI (1952), 191-207.

[11]Draft grant, encl. in Order-in-Council, 4 September 1848, B.T. 1/470/2506.

the Company could gain no "pecuniary profit" and was to apply all proceeds from land and mineral sales to "the colonization and improvement of the Island."[12] The success of the undertaking, according to the Colonial Office, now depended on the Company's ability to inspire sufficient confidence to attract settlers to Vancouver Island.[13]

To provide for naval services, the Charter stipulated that the Company should reserve lands for which the government would pay a "reasonable price."[14] By this means, the Hudson's Bay Company was also to defray all costs of defence, "except, nevertheless, during the time of hostilities between Great Britain and any foreign European or American power,"[15] a clause which became important during the Crimean War.

Behind all these provisions lay a carefully calculated intention of the British government to establish a colony for settlement, and not to prolong the fur trade.[16] For this reason the government made provisions for the political management of the colony. Local government, independent of Company interests, was invested first in a governor and, eventually, an elected assembly was established. In July 1849, the Colonial Office appointed Richard Blanshard, an English barrister with some colonial experience, to the office of Governor of Vancouver Island.[17] Blanshard was chosen because he was not a servant of the Company and thus could function independently of the colonizing agency, or so the Colonial Office hoped.

The government's intentions were certainly excellent in making this appointment, but the Colonial Office did not understand how the Company dominated the frontier. Blanshard was virtually powerless where the fur traders ruled. If the Colonial Office had listened to the opponents of monopoly such as Lieutenant Dundas and James Stephen, an alernative agent of the Crown at Vancouver Island might have been found.[18]

It will be recalled that in 1843 the Hudson's Bay Company had decided to transfer its general headquarters in the northeastern Pacific from Fort Vancouver on the Columbia River to the southern tip of Vancouver Island. Although the Company planned to withdraw from Oregon after the Oregon Boundary Treaty, they considered it necessary to maintain

---

[12]H. Merivale (C.O.) to Pelly, 13 March 1848, encl. in Merivale to Le Marchant, 8 September 1848, *ibid.*
[13]*Ibid.*
[14]Draft grant, encl. in Order-in-Council, 4 September 1848, *ibid.*
[15]*Ibid.*
[16]Rich, *Hudson's Bay Company*, II, 755-56.
[17]On Blanshard, see Morton, *History of the Canadian West*, p. 753; Willard E. Ireland, "The Appointment of Governor Blanshard," *British Columbia Historical Quarterly*, VIII (July 1944), 213-26; and W. Kaye Lamb, "The Governorship of Richard Blanshard," *ibid*, XIV (April 1950), 1-40.
[18]Knaplund, "James Stephen," p. 268.

law and order there until the United States assumed its rightful duty.[19]

To Company officials it appeared that the Royal Navy would be needed to keep law and order as it had during the Oregon crisis. Indeed, the famous massacre at the Whitman mission near Walla Walla in 1847 seemed proof to the Company that a British warship should be stationed in the Columbia. But Rear-Admiral Phipps Hornby, the Commander-in-Chief on the Pacific station, argued with much merit that supporting Company interests in American territory did not come within his jurisdiction.[20] He was content to rely on the presence of the frigate *Constance*, 50 guns, in the waters of the Pacific Northwest in 1848 to maintain order in the "Columbia Country."[21]

The arguments of Hornby were supported by Captain Courtenay of the *Constance*. After his visit to the Northwest Coast, he wrote in trenchant fashion of the anomalous position of a British commercial concern acting as an overlord on American soil. He believed that the sooner the Hudson's Bay Company gave up their posts and farms in Oregon and retired within British territory, the sooner an end would come to "their bickerings with the Americans. . . ."[22] The commercial advantages of remaining in Oregon would keep the Company there as long as possible and, in his words would induce it, "to cry Wolf," as long as the government listened.[23] His objections were met in 1849 when the western headquarters of the Company were at last transferred to Fort Victoria.

The Commander-in-Chief did not guard the Company's property in Oregon by placing a ship in the Columbia River, but on the other hand he did not ignore the need of protecting the Vancouver Island settlements.[24]

The visit of the *Constance* in 1848 was followed by that of the frigate *Inconstant*, 36 guns, in 1849. The *Inconstant* came to aid and protect

---

[19]This argument was made as late as October 1848; J. Douglas to Capt. G. W. C. Courtenay, 10 October 1848, copy B. 223/b/37, fols. 39-41, H.B.C.A.
[20]Rear-Admiral Phipps Hornby to H. G. Ward (Adm.), 23 August 1848, Adm. 1/5589.
[21]*Ibid.*
[22]Courtenay to William Miller (Br. Consul, Honolulu), 12 September 1848, extract, in Miller to Addington (F.O.), 23 October 1848, in *Report of the Provincial Archives . . . 1913*, p. V77.
[23]*Ibid.*
[24]Until the visit of the *Constance* in 1848, Company officials complained that the British Admiral in the Pacific was unconcerned about "the only British territorial possession in these seas: a circumstance which we exceedingly regret, and to which the attention of the British Government ought to be forcibly drawn." Ogden and Douglas to Simpson, 16 March 1848, B.223/b/37, fol. 6d, H.B.C.A. Soon these same officials maintained that a warship should be permanently stationed to guard Fort Victoria, which was "peculiarly exposed to be attacked and plundered by predatory vessels." Ogden and Douglas to Simpson, 23 February 1849, B.223/b/38, fol. 72, H.B.C.A.

Fort Victoria, which was menaced by an Indian uprising.[25] The long-standing dispute between the Company and several war-like bands of Haida and Tsimshian Indians—who came to Victoria annually to trade pelts for guns, ammunition, liquor and other items of trade—had reached alarming proportions by then. The officer-in-charge of the post, Roderick Finlayson, urged Captain John Shepherd of the *Inconstant* to refrain from issuing any ammunition while the ship lay in port in order to prevent further military stores from getting into Indian hands.[26] The previous year, at the time of the visit of the *Constance,* 250 sailors and Royal Marines paraded outside the stockade in a display of arms as a warning to nearly one thousand Indians.[27] But Finlayson was unwilling to ask the captain of the *Inconstant* to act against the natives because an Indian war would be "extremely impolitic" at the time when British emigrants were expected to settle on Vancouver Island.[28]

Fears of an Indian attack were well founded according to Captain Shepherd, who believed and reported that the colony could not survive for long unless a detachment of troops came out from England.[29] When this suggestion reached London, and eventually Hudson's Bay House, the Company opposed undertaking the costs of defence, arguing that one object of the Company was to civilize the Indians, which could be achieved best by conciliatory measures without the use of troops.[30] Admittedly, however, the Company realized that periodic calls by British warships would assist in keeping Indians and Americans alike in awe of British sovereignty on Vancouver Island.[31] The Company thanked the Admiralty for directing the Commander-in-Chief, Pacific, to send ships to the Northwest Coast.[32] The government failed to press its demands for reimbursement on the Company, and the matter of defence languished until another crisis arose.

Blanshard Arrives as First Governor

The next warship sent to Vancouver Island was the paddle-wheel sloop *Driver,* 6 guns. Besides guarding the Company's interests during the withdrawal from Oregon, she had the special responsibility of transport-

---

25Capt. J. Shepherd to Officer-in-Charge, Fort Victoria, 12 May 1849, B. 226/b/2, fols. 18d-19, H.B.C.A.

26R. Finlayson to Shepherd, 13 May 1849, *ibid.,* fols. 19d-20. Finlayson to Douglas, 23 May 1849, *ibid.,* fols. 21d-22.

27F. V. Longstaff and W. Kaye Lamb, "The Royal Navy on the Northwest Coast, 1813-1850, Part II," *British Columbia Historical Quarterly,* IX (April 1945) , 123-24.

28Finlayson to Douglas, 23 May 1849, B. 226/b/2, fol. 21d, H.B.C.A.

29Hornby to J. Parker (Adm.) , 29 August 1849, PHI/2/1, N.M.M.; in *Report of the Provincial Archives . . . 1913,* p. V74.

30Pelly to B. Hawes (C.O.) , 22 November 1849, A.8/6, fols. 14-15, H.B.C.A.

31*Ibid.*

32A. Barclay to Sec. of Adm., 22 November 1849, A.8/17, fol. 46, H.B.C.A.

ing the first Governor of the Crown Colony of Vancouver Island to his official seat at Fort Victoria. On 10 March 1850 the *Driver* arrived at Fort Victoria. Blanshard went ashore the following day to read his commission, little realizing that he had commenced an uneasy, short governorship.

During his brief tenure, Blanshard undertook to solve several problems. Soon after his arrival and at his request, the *Driver* transferred 86 cattle and 830 sheep from Fort Nisqually to Fort Victoria, which was then in need of food supplies.[33] To meet the defence needs of the colony, he advised the Colonial Secretary that a garrison of regular troops, preferably marines, would be sufficient.[34] Blanshard differed from Company officials, who did not believe a garrison was necessary, even though they realized that American encroachments on British territory were possible.[35] His proposal was therefore dismissed summarily by the Company as fallacious. Because the government again failed to take a stand on the matter, British warships on the coast remained the only means of coercion at the Governor's disposal.

The next concern of Blanshard was the Indian menace, which had reached serious proportions by 1850. Near Fort Rupert, a coal mining community on the northeast coast of Vancouver Island, some Indians of the Newitty tribe murdered three British sailors who deserted from the merchantship *Norman Morison,* which was trading in the area. With Governor Blanshard on board the corvette *Daedalus,* 19 guns, Captain George Wellesley, reached the scene of the murder in October 1850, and her boats were sent ashore to arrest the criminals.[36] After an exchange of rifle fire in which an officer and several sailors were wounded, the population of the Indian village fled into the hinterland. As punishment, naval parties set fire to the deserted cedar houses, demonstrating that brutality was not peculiar to Indians. The British on the Northwest Coast employed harsh measures to maintain their dominant position: this was "forest diplomacy."[37]

---

[33]Cdr. Johnson to Hornby, 21 June 1850, Valparaiso, PHI/3/5, N.M.M.
[34]R. Blanshard to Grey, 18 September 1850, C.O. 305/2. See also, Willard E. Ireland, "Pre-Confederation Defence Problems of the Pacific Colonies," *Canadian Historical Association Annual Report, 1941* (Toronto, 1941) , p. 44.
[35]*Ibid.,* n13.
[36]R. E. Gosnell, "Pacific Province: Colonial History, 1849-1871," *Canada and its Provinces,* 23 vols. (Toronto: Glasgow, Brook & Co., 1914) , XXI, 94-95.
[37]James Douglas, who won the respect of the Indians, was a master of "forest diplomacy." See the account of the Company-Navy expedition to Cowichan Bay and Nanaimo in 1853 to secure two murderers of a company shepherd in John Moresby, *Two Admirals* rev. ed. (London: Methuen & Co., 1913) , pp. 109-110. Some 130 men from H.M.S. *Thetis* were employed in this operation; see W. Kaye Lamb, ed., "Four Letters relating to the Cruise of the "Thetis," 1852-1853," *British Columbia Historical Quarterly,* VI (July 1942) , 155-57.

In 1850, no Royal Navy ship had as yet been authorized to remain on the Northwest Coast. It was not until 1858-1859, at the time of the Fraser River gold rush, that two gunboats were sent to Vancouver Island as a permanent measure. Thus, when the *Daedalus* left Vancouver Island for San Francisco in search of provisions, the Governor was alarmed that the murderers of the British seamen could not be seized without some force, naval or otherwise.[38] Simultaneously, he decried the fact that ships of the Royal Navy which called only "at rare intervals, and for short calls" were the colony's sole safeguard.[39] According to Blanshard, a possible solution would be to send two companies of regular troops to Vancouver Island, as proposed by Captain Walter Colquhoun Grant, formerly in the Scots Greys and the colony's first independent settler.[40] Once again the important question of defence had been raised.

But again the Company skilfully evaded the issue of defence, this time in a carefully-constructed piece of literary legerdemain sent to Earl Grey. The Company could see no merit in Blanshard's belief that only the presence of an overwhelming force, either in the form of a warship permanently stationed at Vancouver Island or of sufficient troops, could enforce the authority of the Crown.[41] Yet it admitted that a British warship could help Company officials deal with the Indian problem. Like Blanshard, the Governor of the Company urged Grey to request that warships pay longer and more frequent visits to the Colony. But as for the Colonial Office suggestion that the Company undertake permanent measures of defence instead of relying on occasional visits by ships of the Royal Navy, the Company explained that its posts were adequately defended by Métis in its employ, a view which shows that the Company was little interested in encouraging settlement at a distance from its forts.[42] A conflict existed: according to Blanshard, protection for colonists was inadequate; according to the Company, it was sufficient.

Under these circumstances, the Colonial Office could do nothing. The Company could not be forced to pay for a garrison; the British government was unwilling to assume the expensive task of maintaining troops on Vancouver Island. In consequence, the full responsibility for colonial defence beyond the Company stockades rested with the Navy. It is small wonder that settlement did not prosper.

Meanwhile, under the guidance of Chief Factor James Douglas, the

---

[38]Blanshard to Grey, 18 August 1850, encl. in Hawes to Pelly, 30 November 1850, A. 8/6 fol. 140, H.B.C.A.
[39]Blanshard to Grey, 18 September 1850, encl. in Grey to Pelly, 25 February 1851, *ibid.*, fols. 149-51.
[40]*Ibid.*
[41]Pelly to Grey, 2 December 1850, *ibid.*, fol. 143.
[42]A. Colvile to Grey, 18 December 1850, *ibid.*, fols. 146-47. Pelly to Grey 28 February 1851, *ibid.*, fols. 152-53.

Company sought a reconciliation with the Newitty tribe. Douglas considered Blanshard's desire to hold the whole tribe responsible for the murders "as unpolitick as unjust" and a policy that might possibly lead to an Indian war of disastrous proportions.[43] When the Commander-in-Chief, Rear-Admiral Fairfax Moresby, learned from Captain Wellesley of the *Daedalus* that the Indians evidently had flouted British authority, he determined to put an end to the problem by taking the matter out of the hands of the Company.[44] Hence he decided to visit Vancouver Island in his flagship, the frigate *Portland*, 50 guns, accompanied by the sloop *Daphne*.

After conferring with Blanshard and Douglas at Fort Victoria, Rear-Admiral Moresby dispatched the *Daphne*, bearing the Governor, to Fort Rupert to exact rigorous justice. Moresby's policy was that the whole tribe was to be punished unless the guilty few surrendered. The murderers were not given up by the tribe, and the *Daphne* "stormed and burned" the camp, forcing the tribe to seek refuge in the forest and to settle on the west coast of Vancouver Island.[45] In this action two Indians were killed and some sailors wounded. The use of "forest diplomacy" by the Navy did not bring the murderers to justice, but a pathetic event followed: the attack on the village so terrified the tribe that the Indians executed the guilty themselves to bring peace, and then they delivered the corpses to Fort Rupert.

The brutal but effective discipline carried out by the *Daphne*, and other acts of subjugation which followed, were part of the larger movement occurring in North America and elsewhere establishing European supremacy over various groups of native peoples. Fortunately, actions like those of the *Daphne* were few in number on the Northwest Coast and policy guidelines in such instances were soon established for naval officers.

In 1853, the Law Officers of the Crown advised the Foreign Office of the extent to which ships' commanders could exact redress from natives "in cases where the wrongs done by them to British Subjects extend to the loss of life by unprovoked and deliberate murder". If naval commanders should *"actually witness"* murder of British subjects, redress could be exacted from the chief of the tribe to which the offender belonged. Without witness, extreme forebearance was to be used before resorting to force.[46] Ships of the Royal Navy were dispatched on missions against

---

43Douglas to J. Blenkinsop, 27 October 1850, B.226/b/3, fol. 14d, H.B.C.A.
44Rear-Admiral Moresby to Blanshard, 27 August 1851, F. 1217, B.C.A.
45Douglas to P. S. Ogden, 6 August 1851, B. 226/b/3, fols. 116-17, and Douglas to Grey, 31 October 1851, A.8/6, fol. 244, H.B.C.A
46Law Officers of the Crown to Lord Clarendon (F.O.), 28 July 1853, encl. in Osborne to Rear-Admiral Price, 9 August 1853, Adm. 172/3, No. 6.

the Indians until the 1880's when civil authorities took up the task of controlling and aiding native peoples.

Douglas Becomes Governor

The Indian threat diminished after 1851 partly because of the appointment that year of Chief Factor James Douglas to succeed Blanshard as Governor of Vancouver Island.[47] Blanshard had found his position untenable in a colony where Company interests were dominant and problems of island settlement were largely ignored. Without regret he sailed from Fort Victoria in H.M.S. *Daphne* 1 September 1851 upon learning that the Colonial Office had accepted his resignation. His successor, characterized by a commanding presence and bold policies, was able to keep the war-like natives in awe. He could now maintain order on the coast through the combined influence of the Company and the Navy. Douglas was already the Agent of the Hudson's Bay Company in the new colony. Now he added to his duties, at the age of forty-eight, what he later described as a "responsible and disagreeable office," solely to please the Governor and Committee of the Hudson's Bay Company.[48] According to Professor Rich, Douglas's interests at this stage were "unmistakably those of the Company, of the fur trade, and of Victoria as a port and depot, rather than the broader aspects of settling the whole island".[49] It must be added, however, that Douglas—in both aspects of his role, as Colonial Governor and as Company Official,—remained dedicated to strengthening British interests on the Northwest Coast.[50] In this regard, his outlook coincided with that of Earl Grey.

Rear-Admiral Moresby had no quarrel with Douglas, whose experience, intelligence and vigour had earned him rapid promotion in the Company. But he did object to the unwillingness of the Company to encourage the lamentably small growth of colonization.[51] He found during his visit in 1851 that the difficulties that the Company placed on colonists in obtaining land, for example, were "incompatible with the free and liberal reception of an Emigrant Community."[52] This charge, as well as others, reinforced those of Blanshard. The Commander-in-Chief's report on the state of the colony proved to be only one of several

[47]On Douglas and Vancouver Island, see Walter N. Sage, *Sir James Douglas and British Columbia* (Toronto: University of Toronto Press, 1930), chapter 6.
[48]Douglas to Gov. and Comm., 15 November 1853, B.226/b/14, fol. 11, H.B.C.A.
[49]Rich, *Hudson's Bay Company*, II, 762.
[50]Douglas enjoyed the prestige of double office. "It is to the credit of the man that he was, on the whole, true to both offices and betrayed neither trust." Morton, *History of the Canadian West*, p. 762.
[51]Moresby to Sec. of Adm., 7 July 1851, encl. in Peel to Pelly, 20 December 1851, A.8/6, fols. 203-211, H.B.C.A.
[52]*Ibid.*

that exposed the domination of the Company and its unwillingness to encourage colonization.[53]

These charges did not go unanswered by the Company, which asserted that everything was being done "for the colonization and improvement of the Island, which it is no less their interest than their duty to promote."[54] It is evident, however, that the Company was unwilling to invest in an unproductive colony. The California gold rush drained labour from the Pacific Northwest, the fur trade was in decline and the colony lacked colonists. "God's will be done," Douglas wrote despairingly to Sir George Simpson, the Governor of the Company in North America, in March 1854, "I have done everything in my power to give it an existence in defiance of the adverse circumstances of the times, which have caused me so much trouble and anxiety."[55]

Nor did the future look any brighter; continental expansion by the Americans since 1845 threatened to absorb British possessions on the Northwest Coast.[56] Douglas, especially, was well aware of the threats to the colony from the United States, which assumed a military form in 1859 with the occupation of the disputed San Juan Island. Unlike Blanshard, who thought that the Hudson's Bay Company was reneging on its obligations as a colonizing agency, Governor Douglas blamed the British government for the ill-success of the colony. The Government was apathetic, Douglas noted, about Vancouver Island, "the only British possession of the west coast of America and a most favourable point commercially and politically for counterbalancing the rapidly growing influence of the United States in this part of the world. . . ." Unless the British government ended its indifference, Douglas believed, all the efforts of the Company to develop settlements and check American peaceful penetration were doomed.[57]

One method of countering any attempted filibuster from the American shore, Douglas contended, was not to station troops which would be

---

[53]*Ibid.* Moresby had complained about the price of provisions; Galbraith, *Hudson's Bay Company*, pp. 294-96.

[54]Pelly to Grey, 14 January 1852, A.8/6, fol. 219, H.B.C.A.

[55]Douglas to Simpson, 20 March 1854, B. 226/b/11, fols. 38-38d, H.B.C.A. The Company agent at Fort Vancouver believed that the Colony of Vancouver Island, as conceived, was "injurious to the concern and ruinous to the Colonists." John Ballenden to Douglas and Work, 2 November 1852, B. 223/b/40, fol. 38, H.B.C.A.

[56]Several projects and plans were put forward during this period to extend American communications, trade and empire to the Pacific, even to Asia. See Charles Vevier, "American Continentalism: An Idea of Expansionism, 1845-1910," *American Historical Review*, LXV (January 1960), pp. 326-30. One British writer, probably Lt. Adam Dundas, R.N., had warned against such American continental growth and expansion into the Pacific Northwest in 1848; "Oregon and Vancouver Island," *Nautical Magazine*, XVII (October 1848), 517-23.

[57]Douglas to Pelly, 13 April 1852, B.226/b/6, fols. 60-61, H.B.C.A.

difficult to transport to the decisive quarter, but rather an armed government or naval steamer. Such a vessel could sail with ease through intricate, tide-bound waters to the place of need.[58] In Douglas's contention lies the origin of a proposal implemented at Vancouver Island during the Crimean War.

Douglas was not alone in recognizing American aspirations for continental dominion at a time when British interests in the whole of the Western Hemisphere were endangered. The British Minister in Washington, Sir John Crampton, complained in early 1853 to the Foreign Minister, Lord Clarendon, that the Monroe Doctrine appeared to be developing into a United States law for the Americas, made without the due consent of nations.[59] Indeed, Britain's awareness of American power in the New World changed her statecraft toward the United States in 1853.[60] British policy was committed to Vancouver Island, as Douglas in his ignorance did not realize. Similar concern was felt for the endangered position of Britain's other North American possessions, as well as her sphere of influence in the Caribbean, and her communications across the Isthmus of Panama. The latter were endangered by American desires to dominate the route from the Atlantic seaboard to California.

In short, at mid-century United States pretensions to continental dominion alarmed the British government. Continued reassertions of the Monroe Doctrine ended what Douglas believed to be indifference on the part of the British ministry.[61] The revised policy aimed at the peaceful containment of American expansion; it met with success in British North America in general and in Vancouver Island in particular.

This change of attitude around 1853 marked a turning point in the history of Britain's interest in the Northwest Coast. After this time Britain relied largely on the Royal Navy to prevent American expansion on the Northwest Coast.

The Royal Navy and the Island Resources

From the beginning of regular operations in the North Pacific, in the 1830's, British warships faced two major handicaps. First, they depended on strategic commodities such as spars, timbers and coal which came invariably from distant Europe. Second, they did not have an adequate

[58]*Ibid.*
[59]Sir J. Crampton to Clarendon, 7 February 1853, in Richard W. Van Alstyne, ed., "Anglo-American Relations, 1853-57," *American Historical Review*, XLII (April 1937), 494-95.
[60]See Kenneth Bourne, *Britain and the Balance of Power in North America, 1815-1908* (London: Longmans, Green & Co., 1967), pp. 170-85.
[61]See *ibid.*, pp. 184-205.

naval base anywhere in the Pacific, although storeships were positioned on the South American coast at Valparaiso in 1843 and at Callao in 1847. Gradually, it became apparent to naval officers that the natural resources of Vancouver Island offered solutions to their problems, provided that the Admiralty and the Hudson's Bay Company could agree to their use.

During the sailing-ship era, timbers for shipbuilding ranked high in strategic value. With insufficient forests at home, the search for this essential staple continued; sources were found in the Baltic and North America. John Meares, the first to profit in the spar trade of the Northwest Coast, wrote with little exaggeration in 1791 that the fine stands of timber on the Northwest Coast would be sufficient for the needs of "all the navies of Europe."[62] The Hudson's Bay Company entered this trade in the 1830's and sold timber suitable for a variety of purposes—masts, spars, piles and deals—in various Pacific ports, notably Honolulu.[63]

But the Royal Navy did not fully recognize the value of Pacific Northwest timber until the Oregon crisis brought British warships frequently to the region. In 1845, the captain of H.M.S. *America* was instructed to report on timbers "fit for the Navy".[64] He procured at Port Discovery, which was the actual centre of Douglas fir distribution, as many spars as the shored-up decks of the *America* could carry. The Commander-in-Chief, Pacific, Rear-Admiral Sir George Seymour, who was an expert on naval stores,[65] preferred the spars that the *America* brought from the Northwest Coast to those cut from a softer species of wood near Monterey, California. The former were fashioned for the masts of the flagship *Collingwood*.[66] Seymour was so impressed by the quality of

[62]John Meares, *Voyages Made in the Years 1788 and 1789, from China to the North West Coast of America* (London, 1790), p. 224; quoted in W. Kaye Lamb, "Early Lumbering on Vancouver Island," *British Columbia Historical Quarterly*, II (January 1938), 32.

[63]Frederick Merk, ed., *Fur Trade and Empire: George Simpson's Journal*, rev. ed., (Cambridge, Mass.: Belknap Press, 1968), pp. 122 and 298. Simpson's 1829 Report, D.4/93, fol. 57d, H.B.C.A., quoted by W. Kaye Lamb in *The Letters of John McLoughlin from Fort Vancouver to the Governor and Committee; First Series, 1825-38* (London: Hudson's Bay Record Society, vol. IV, 1941) p. xcii. John A. Hussey, *The History of Fort Vancouver* (Tacoma: Washington Historical Society, 1957), p. 64.

[64]Rear-Admiral Seymour to J. Gordon, 13 February 1845, Seymour Order Book I, CR 114A/414/1, W.R.O.

[65]As Third Lord of the Admiralty, 1841-1844, his knowledge of these matters grew. See his Adm. Notebook, CR 114A/409, pp. 1-89, W.R.O.

[66]Seymour, Private Diary, CR 114A/373/23, p. 138, W.R.O. H.M.S. *Blossom's* crew had cut Monterey pines (*Pinus taxifolia*) near the San Rafael mission in 1826; Lt. Geo. Peard, Journal of H.M.S. *Blossom*, 1825-1828, Add. MSS. 35, 141, fols. 99, B.M. The firs from the Pacific Northwest which Seymour preferred were probably Douglas fir or Douglas spruce (*Pseudotsuga taxifolia*), a wood valued for construction but which is not a true fir or spruce.

these timbers that he ordered a shipment of spars sent from Vancouver Island to Portsmouth dockyard for testing.[67] The tests showed that the fir of Vancouver Island was superior to that from Riga in the Baltic, then considered by the Admiralty to make the best spars in the world.[68] As a result of Seymour's initiative, the Admiralty had gained a new source of spars.

Although the value of this resource was unquestioned, the problem remained of how to transport these bulky, heavy materials some eighteen thousand miles by way of Cape Horn to England, at a price competitive with spars from the Baltic and the Maritimes. The example of Captain E. Swinton of London shows the difficulties involved. He proposed in 1844 to supply the Admiralty with spars from the Northwest Coast suitable for topmasts. Three years after his proposal their Lordships agreed to receive some eighty spars for trial.[69] Swinton then sent the merchant ship *Albion* to the Strait of Juan de Fuca to fill the contract. But Captain William Brotchie, her supercargo, foolishly chose to cut spars near New Dungeness on the American side of the strait. There, in April 1850 the ship was seized by United States customs officials for cutting spars on United States soil without permission.[70]

Undeterred, Brotchie next sailed in H.M.S. *Daedalus* for the north end of Vancouver Island, reported to be another suitable source of spars.[71] He was plagued by financial problems resulting from the confiscation of the *Albion* and unable to convince the Hudson's Bay Company to enter into the spar trade with him. Brotchie never made the venture a success, although he did send several shipments of spars to England after 1852.[72]

Not until 1855, when the Crimean War led to a great increase in construction of ships and dockyard facilities did the Admiralty turn to

[67]Lamb, "Early Lumbering," pp. 32-33.
[68]Report of 27 December 1847, encl. in J. Meek to Seymour, 10 January 1848, Adm. Corr. I, B.C.A. Robert G. Albion, *Forests and Sea Power: the Timber Problem of the Royal Navy, 1852-1862* (Cambridge, Mass.: Harvard University Press, 1926), p. 141.
[69]Lamb, "Early Lumbering," p. 33. R. Dundas (Storekeeper Gen., Adm.) to Barclay, 7 July 1847, A.8/14, fol. 234, H.B.C.A.
[70]Lamb, "Early Lumbering," pp. 33-34; F. W. Howay, W. N. Sage and H. F. Angus, *British Columbia and the United States* (New Haven: Yale University Press, 1942), p. 134; and Ogden to Sir G. Simpson, 14 June 1850, private, B.223/b/39, fol. 42, H.B.C.A.
[71]Douglas to Blenkinsop, 30 September 1850, B.226/b/3, fols. 15-15d, H.B.C.A.
[72]Brotchie to Governor and Committee, 21 March 1851, B.226/b 5b, fols. 1-1d and enclosures; Douglas to Brotchie. 16 February 1852, B.226/b/4, fols. 46-46d; Douglas to Barclay, 7 December 1852, B.226/b/6, fol. 151; Douglas to Simpson, 17 March 1853, *ibid.*, fols. 195-96, H.B.C.A. Prevost to Moresby, 7 June and 23 July 1853, Adm. 1/5630; Lamb, "Early Lumbering," pp. 34-38.

the Northwest Coast as a source of supply for spars.[73] But it should not be forgotten that during the preceding and following decades, many warships sailed from Vancouver Island bearing new spars of sturdy quality, sometimes stowing them for the use of other ships on the Pacific station. Generally speaking, the timber problem had been solved for British warships employed in this vast ocean, at a time when sail was the chief means of motive power.

The Importance of Coal

Even more important to a navy increasingly dependent on steam was the necessity of finding a ready and cheap source of coal.[74] The Admiralty was generally opposed to the introduction of steam in the late 1820's and 1830's. In 1836, the Senior Naval Officer in the Pacific pressed the Admiralty to attach a steamer to the Pacific squadron. He argued that such a vessel would be invaluable in those seas where, because of calms and trade winds, passages were "more precarious, and uncertain" than in any other quarter of the world.[75] Alexander Forbes, a promoter of British expansion in California and the Pacific, also believed that the Pacific squadron, supplemented by one or more steamers, would be better able to protect British interests and encourage British trade in Pacific America.[76]

By the 1840's, their Lordships came to recognize the strategic advantages of ships being able to manoeuvre independently of the wind. In 1846, steamers played only an auxiliary role to sailing ships, as indicated by the fact that the paddle-wheel sloop *Cormorant*, Captain George T. Gordon, went to the Northwest Coast during the Oregon crisis partly to tow sailing vessels in the straits. In the confined waters separating Vancouver Island from the mainland, where strong tides are prevalent, the great advantages of steam propulsion was clear.[77]

[73]Bruce Journal, 14 June, 14 July, 14 September 1855, Adm. 50/308; Bruce to Osborne, 11 September 1855, Adm. 1/5656.

[74]Technological advances during the mid-nineteenth century have been considered in Appendix E. See also Gerald S. Graham, "The Transition from Paddle-wheel to Screw Propeller," *Mariner's Mirror*, XLIV (1958), 35-48; and Geoffrey Penn, *"Up Funnel, Down Screw!" The Story of the Naval Engineer* (London: Hollis & Carter, 1955).

[75]Commodore Mason to Rear-Admiral Hamond, 29 November 1836, Callao, Adm. 1/48.

[76]Alexander Forbes, *California: A History of Upper and Lower California* (London: Smith, Elder & Co., 1839), pp. 332-42.

[77]Gordon's *"Cormorant* Remark Book from 1 January to 31 December 1846" was kept by the Hydrographer's Office for reference purposes. File No. Misc. 16, Folder 1, item 3, H.O. In this document, Gordon referred to Esquimalt harbour as "Fisgard Harbour."

Eventually, the success of the screw-propeller removed the objection to the paddle-wheelers with their limited broadsides. At the same time, the gradual introduction of engines of higher pressure increased the efficiency of auxiliary power. As a result of this revolutionary technological advance, by the mid-1850's almost all new ships were equipped with steam power of some sort. British naval operations during the Crimean War—especially at Petropavlovsk in the Northwestern Pacific—revealed the full advantages of steam for all warships. Although sail was employed in the Pacific on some warships until just before World War I, steam became increasingly prevalent after 1843, when the Admiralty ordered the first steamer, the paddle-wheel sloop *Salamander,* to the Pacific.

A steam vessel was "endowed with a constant and voracious appetite for coal."[78] Hence the commander of the *Salamander* was under strict instructions to economize on the use of this costly commodity.[79] Some idea of the expense involved in supplying a steamer is shown in the case of the transport *Rosalind,* chartered at £250 per month to deliver coal to Fort Victoria for the use of the steamer *Cormorant* during the Oregon crisis. If a local supply could be delivered to the Navy at a price competitive with English coal, the fuel problem would be solved.

The rapid growth of steam navigation in the Pacific after 1840 led the Hudson's Bay Company to develop mines off the northeast coast of Vancouver Island: one important consumer of Company coal was the Pacific Mail Steamship Company, which began a service between Panama and the coast of Oregon in 1848 with three paddle-wheel steamers of one thousand tons burthen.[80]

At the time of the Oregon crisis, the Hudson's Bay Company began a serious investigation of surface outcroppings of coal reported by Indians in 1835 at Beaver Harbour.[81] These were already being used by the Company steamer *Beaver,* but the Company investigated and hoped to develop the mine commercially by supplying the Pacific squadron and other users of coal on a regular basis. The efforts of the Company to promote this trade coincided with investigations and trials by ships of the Royal Navy to determine if the Vancouver Island coal deposits

---

[78]W. S. Jevons, *The Coal Question,* 3rd ed., rev. (London: Macmillan & Co., 1906), p. 133.

[79]Rear-Admiral Thomas to Cdr. A. S. Hamond, 23 May 1843, extract, encl. in Thomas to S. Herbert (Adm.), 26 October 1843, Adm. 1/5538. See also, John Bach, "The Royal Navy and the South Pacific, 1826-1876" (Ph.D. thesis; Sydney: University of New South Wales, 1964), pp. 53-54.

[80]John H. Kemble, "Coal from the Northwest Coast, 1848-1850," *British Columbia Historical Quarterly,* II (April 1938), 123-30.

[81]Douglas to Capt. J. Duntze, 7 September 1846, C.O. 305/1.

would meet the needs of the squadron.[82] An examination in 1846 of the *Cormorant* by Commander George T. Gordon—whom Rear-Admiral Seymour considered one of the best steam officers in the Navy—revealed abundant quantities at Beaver Harbour of a quality "at least equal to the best Scotch coal."[83] The significance of this was clear to Seymour. The deposits, he informed the Admiralty, would add greatly to "the future value of the British Possessions on the North West Coast and contribute the means to extend their commerce, and to facilitate their defence, as California and the Neighbouring Countries become of more consequence, and acquire additional Population."[84] Very wisely, he recommended that these mines be reserved for the public interest, or, in other words, that the Crown should regulate the exploitation of the coal deposits.

As with spars sent from Vancouver Island, samples of coal were tested in England. The Museum of Practical Geology in London reported to the Admiralty that the coal was suitable for steam propulsion.[85] In fact, the samples were so promising that at one stage the Admiralty planned to send a steamship and sloop from England with a scientific officer and equipment to test the fuel more fully.[86] This expensive plan was not carried out, probably because subsequent reports by naval officers proved sufficient to convince the Admiralty of the quality of Vancouver Island coal.

Before the Hudson's Bay Company received the Royal Grant of Vancouver Island, word of extensive coal deposits on the island increased the British government's conviction that the island should be in proper hands for the development of this resource.[87] Samuel Cunard, a well-known and important pioneer of trans-Atlantic steam navigation, urged the Admiralty in 1848 to reserve the mines for the Crown.[88] Such a measure would prevent private interests from staking claims and prohibit American steamship interests in the Pacific from entering into contracts with the Hudson's Bay Company for the coal. The Admiralty

---

[82]In 1845 and 1846, Rear-Admiral Seymour sent instructions to captains to report on coals fit for the Navy. Seymour to J. Gordon, 13 February 1845, Seymour Order Book I, CR 114A/414/1, W.R.O., and Seymour to Duntze, 14 January 1846, Adm. 1/5561.

[83]Reported in G. Gordon to Duntze, 7 October 1846, copy, C.O. 305/1.

[84]Seymour to Ward, 8 February 1847, Official Letter Book II, CR 114A/416/2, W.R.O.

[85]Sir Henry De la Beche to Hamilton, 30 January 1848, A.8/17, fols. 28, 30, H.B.C.A.

[86]Hamilton (Adm.) to Hawes, 19 October 1848, and Merivale to Hamilton, 2 November 1848, "Papers re: Vancouver's Island," Great Britain, *Parliamentary Papers*, 1849, XXXV (103), p. 12.

[87]Minute to Earl Grey, 9 February 1848, C.O. 305/1.

[88]S. Cunard to Ward, 3 January 1848, encl. in Ward to Seymour, 5 February 1848, *Parliamentary Papers*, 1849, XXXV (103), p. 11.

accepted this recommendation and advised the Colonial Office accordingly.[89]

The coal deposits became an important consideration in discussions between the Colonial Office and the Hudson's Bay Company on the terms of the charter-grant. To ensure that coal mining would aid the public welfare at Vancouver Island, the Colonial Office asked the Company to modify and to accept an agreement similar to that already concluded between the government and Henry Wise, a proprietor on the Island of Labuan, a British naval outpost in the South China Sea. Under this agreement Wise paid a lease and royalties and agreed to supply coal to the Royal Navy at the pit's mouth for eleven shillings per ton.[90] The Hudson's Bay Company explained glibly that it did not seek financial gain in colonizing Vancouver Island, and that all profits from coal mining would be spent in promoting the good of the colony. It refused to accept revised terms such as those relating to Labuan Island.[91] The statement of good intent evidently satisfied the British government. Ultimately the two parties agreed to a royalty of two shillings and six pence per ton, of which the Company would get ten per cent, the rest going to the development of the colony. Unfortunately for the Navy, the fuel remained expensive and this often prohibited its use.

Meanwhile, Captain George W. C. Courtenay of H.M.S. *Constance* had been dispatched to the Northwest Coast to report on the state of British interests there and to assess the coal deposits at Beaver Harbour. When the *Constance* reached Esquimalt on 25 July 1848, Courtenay sent to Hudson's Bay Company officials at Fort Vancouver and Fort Victoria copies of Cunard's recommendation to the Admiralty, along with a request for information on prices of Vancouver Island coal delivered both on the spot and at South American ports.[92]

After making local enquiries, which substantiated rumours about the high quality of Vancouver Island coal, Captain Courtenay tried by various means to strengthen British claims to the resources. First, he urged James Douglas to instruct subordinate Hudson's Bay Company officials to "keep a vigilant lookout" over the coalfields and to evict any

[89]Acknowledged in Merivale to Adm., 18 February 1848, *ibid.*, p. 12.
[90]"Memorandum of an Agreement for 30 years' Lease . . . ," in 'Labuan Papers,' *Parliamentary Papers*, 1847-1848, LXII, (460) , p. 8. On Wise and Labuan, see Gerald S. Graham, *Great Britain in the Indian Ocean: A Study of Maritime Enterprise, 1810-1850* (Oxford: Clarendon Press, 1967) , pp. 395-98.
[91]Pelly to Grey, 4 March 1848, C.O. 305/1.
[92]See "Principal Services required from the Squadron in 1848," by Rear-Admiral Seymour, PHI, 3/16, N.M.M. Courtenay sent letters to the officer-in-charge of Fort Victoria and to Chief Factor Douglas at Fort Vancouver. Both, dated 25 July 1848, from Esquimalt, are in B.223/b/37, fols. 31-33, H.B.C.A.

persons found settling near the mines.[93] Second, he erected a hut on the site of the deposit to constitute a "claim," as was customary, and posted a proclamation in the Queen's name to warn intruders against mining or settlement.[94] Courtenay's gesture had no legal basis, or so Douglas and Rear-Admiral Hornby thought.[95] Erection of the hut was more a symbolic act than anything else. It merely reinforced locally what the British government was emphasizing in its dealings with the Company, that is, that the coal was to benefit British public interests such as the colony and the Navy rather than private interests.

By mid-1849, the mines at Beaver Harbour were operating and Fort Rupert had been built nearby to protect the settlement from Indian attack.[96] Gradually the coal trade developed, as steam navigation in the Pacific increased. When the paddle-wheeler *Driver* visited the area of the mines in 1850, her commander reported no less than twelve hundred tons of coal lying on the beach, collected by Indians. He found an establishment of forty Company servants, including eight Scottish miners.[97] British naval commanders sometimes complained of finding shale in the coal, but the Company gradually found means of quality control. In 1852, the Company began work on promising outcroppings at Nanaimo, closer to Fort Victoria.[98] This coal proved superior to that from the mines at Beaver Harbour, which were abandoned subsequently. Bituminous coal from Nanaimo was adequate for low-pressure boilers but gave way to Welsh anthracite when high-pressure steam engines were introduced after the 1860's.

Paradoxically, although good coal was available at Vancouver Island, the Royal Navy in the Pacific was forced to rely heavily on coal from Britain purchased on the Chilean coast, and shipped as ballast on the outward passage in vessels making the return voyage laden with the potent fertilizer guano, coal was cheap at Valparaiso and other ports.[99] In any case, it was less expensive than that from the Northwest Coast. Thus Rear-Admiral Hornby advised his successor in 1851:

[93]Courtenay to Douglas, 29 July 1848, *ibid.*, fol. 33d.
[94]Courtenay to Douglas, 17 August 1848, copy, *ibid.*, fols. 37-38.
[95]Douglas and J. Work to Governor and Committee, 5 December 1848, B. 223/b/38, fol. 63d, H.B.C.A.; and Hornby to Ward, 28 November 1848, Adm. 1/5589.
[96]Men were brought from the Stikine and Columbia basins for this task.
[97]Johnson to Hornby, 21 June 1850, Valparaiso, PHI/3/5, N.M.M.
[98]On the growth of Company interest in coal, see Walter N. Sage, *Sir James Douglas and British Columbia* (Toronto: University of Toronto Press, 1930), pp. 172-76 and James Audain, *From Coalmine to Castle: The Story of the Dunsmuirs of British Columbia* (New York: Pageant Press, 1955), pp. 8-23. On Nanaimo specifically, see B. A. McKelvie, "The Founding of Nanaimo," *British Columbia Historical Quarterly*, VIII (July 1944), 169-88.
[99]Gerald S. Graham, *The Politics of Naval Supremacy* (Cambridge: Cambridge University Press, 1965), pp. 102-103.

Eventually Vancouver Island promises a plentiful supply but owing to the difficulty and uncertainty of working the Mines, and the exorbitant price of 50s per Ton demanded by the Hudson's Bay Company, it is not desirable to look to that quarter at present.[100]

From time to time, however, Her Majesty's ships did purchase coal from the Company, as in the case of the paddle-wheel sloop *Virago,* 6 guns, in 1853, and to a greater degree during the Crimean War. Although this coal was exorbitant in price, its availability made any steamer visiting the remote Northwest Coast virtually independent of supplies from other parts of the Pacific station or England.[101] As for the Company, their coal trade represented one encouraging element in an otherwise depressed economy at Vancouver Island.

The possibility that the island might satisfy the Navy's requirements of certain naval stores increased in 1850 with a report that the Hudson's Bay Company had discovered the nettle hemp plant growing in profusion.[102] Specimens of rope made from this fibre were sent to London and were found to bear strains in excess of Admiralty standards. It was argued in 1851 that the discovery of hemp might have almost as great an effect on the prosperity of the colony as the coal mines.[103] But the Admiralty did not enter into a contract with the Company to receive a supply of hemp, as far as can be determined. Nor did the Company develop the industry on a commercial basis. As with spars and coals, the promising hemp resource was not exploited by the Admiralty, whose supplies were adequate from other quarters.

Esquimalt as a Future Naval Base

During the Oregon crisis the need for a naval station on the North Pacific Coast became apparent to the Commander-in-Chief, Pacific, Rear-Admiral Seymour and to the First Lord of the Admiralty, the Earl of Ellenborough, who advocated that Britain should seize San Francisco Bay for that purpose. No action took place because Ellenborough's suggestion was inconsistent with British policy.[104]

It was necessary to meet the requirements of the squadron for a base,

---

[100]Hornby to Moresby, 12 February 1851, PHI/2/2, N.M.M.
[101]Price and not quality of Vancouver Island coal determined its use by the Royal Navy at this time. Rear-Admiral Fairfax Moresby to Sec. of Adm., 13 October 1853, Adm. 1/5630.
[102]See note in *Nautical Magazine,* XX (January 1851), 56.
[103]*Ibid.* The fact that Joseph Kaye Henry's *Flora of Southern British Columbia and Vancouver Island* (Toronto: W. J. Gage, [c. 1915]), the standard botanical reference, makes no mention of hemp as being native to the region casts doubt on this matter. Incidentally, the Indians of the area made rope from shredded cedar.
[104]See chapter 8.

and commanders-in-chief received instructions to keep on the watch for a suitable situation, especially an island off the coast of Central America, preferably on a possible inter-oceanic route in view of the projected Panama Canal. British warships examined several potential positions, notably the Galapagos Islands. They found their answer at Esquimalt, an easily accessible and safe harbour adjacent to Victoria on Vancouver Island. It was, as Governor Blanshard advised Earl Grey in 1850, "the only Harbour in the Southern part of the Island worthy of notice, as it is of large extent, has good anchorage, is easy of access at all times, and in all weather is well watered and in many places the water is of sufficient depth to allow ships anchoring along the shore."[105] True, it was far from any possible site for a trans-isthmian canal. But it had strategic value because it could halt American enroachment on British soil on the Northwest Coast.

The interest of the Royal Navy in Esquimalt Harbour resulted from the Oregon crisis. The possibility that many British warships would be sent to the Strait of Juan de Fuca in 1846, in the event of war with the United States over Oregon, led Rear-Admiral Seymour to dispatch the barque *Herald*, 26 guns, and the brig *Pandora*, 6 guns, to inspect the intricate island waterways from Cape Flattery to Puget Sound and Haro Strait. The southern tip of Vancouver Island, which had not been surveyed in the days of Vancouver and Broughton, was of particular interest because of the increase in shipping and expansion of Hudson's Bay Company trade. Captain Henry Kellett of the *Herald* directed the examination of Victoria, Sooke, and other harbours. Lieutenant James Wood of the *Pandora* surveyed Esquimalt Harbour aided by naval instructor Robert Inskip and midshipmen from the frigate *Fisgard*.[106] The findings of these and other surveys were published in 1847-1849 in Admiralty charts.[107] This information constituted a valuable addition to the Navy's knowledge of Vancouver Island, for it permitted commanders to enter the straits without undue fear of obstacles to navigation. It was now

[105]Blanshard to Grey, 15 June 1850, encl. in Hawes to Pelly, 21 September 1850, A. 8/6, fol. 110, H.B.C.A.
[106]See Leigh Burpee Robinson, *Esquimalt: "Place of Shoaling Waters"* (Victoria, B.C.: Quality Press, 1948) , pp. 39-42.
[107]In 1846, the *Herald* and *Pandora* also charted Hood Canal, Puget Sound, and Haro Strait. The *Pandora* returned to the region from Central America for the period 7 August to 19 September 1846 to examine the Gulf of Georgia. Cdr. Wood to Sec. of Adm., 19 September 1848, Adm. 1/5596. PHI/1, 15 November 1848 and 25 February 1849, N.M.M. Detailed reports on the Indians of the Strait of Juan de Fuca were also sent to London; see enclosures in Wood to Sec. of Adm., 11 November 1848, Adm. 1/5596. The *Herald* meanwhile was bound with H.M. Discovery Ship *Plover* for the western Arctic in search of the Arctic expedition of Sir John Franklin. See Flora Hamilton Burns, "H.M.S. *Herald* in Search of Franklin," *The Beaver*, Outfit 294 (Autumn 1963) , pp. 3-13.

certain that ships-of-the-line could enter Esquimalt with ease.[108]

By mid-century, the assets of Esquimalt and Vancouver Island had been recognized by naval commanders and Company officials alike. Among the former was Commander James Wood of the *Pandora,* who saw in Vancouver Island, with its colony and naval base, a place to restore British prestige in the North Pacific.[109] Rear-Admiral Moresby, the first Commander-in-Chief to visit the Northwest Coast, also appreciated the possibilities of developing a naval depot at Esquimalt when he called there in 1851. Consequently, he recommended that the colonial government reserve the harbour and its shores for the Crown, because it was the only place where an establishment meeting the essential criteria for a depot for Her Majesty's ships could be formed.[110]

Similar views were expressed by Hudson's Bay Company officials. The Company agent at San Francisco, for example, had political reasons for writing to his superiors in London in 1849 that the sooner the British government established a naval depot on the island the better.[111] He reasoned that such a base—together with one in the Hawaiian Islands—would counterbalance the great influence Americans were exercising in the Pacific through possession of California and its ports.[112] James Douglas also knew that the Royal Navy could provide protection against American expansionists who acquired the banks of the Columbia in 1846 and who would undoubtedly turn their attention to Vancouver Island—the only part of "British Oregon" he believed that could be colonized.[113]

With this in mind, Douglas wrote to Hudson's Bay Company headquarters that the harbours of the southern tip of the Island offered several splendid sites for a secure naval base where ships of the Royal Navy could provision and refit. Not only did Vancouver Island contain ports preferable to any in Pacific America, but it possessed coal deposits of which ships could take advantage as well as "the finest spars in the world for the trouble of dragging them from the forests."[114] In a concluding remark that reveals Douglas as a man with considerable foresight, he noted: "The colony and naval depot would be a material benefit to

[108]Seymour to Ward, 26 February 1847, Adm. 1/5577; printed in R. M. Martin, *The Hudson's Bay Territories and Vancouver's Island* (London: T. Brettell, 1849) , p. 44.
[109]Commander J. Wood, "Vancouver Island, British Columbia," *Nautical Magazine,* XXVII (December 1858), 664.
[110]Moresby to Sec. of Adm., 3 July 1851; in W. Kaye Lamb, ed., "Correspondence Relating to the Establishment of a Naval Base at Esquimalt, 1851-57," *British Columbia Historical Quarterly,* VI (October 1942) , 280.
[111]Geo. Allan to Barclay, 7 April 1849, A.11/64, fol. 27d, H.B.C.A.
[112]*Ibid.*
[113]Douglas to Barclay, 23 November 1848, Ft. Victoria, B.223/b/38, fol. 69, H.B.C.A.
[114]*Ibid.*

each other, the one producing and the other consuming the products of the land."[115]

Clearly, Esquimalt with its accessibility to spars and coal, water and provisions would be an asset to the Royal Navy in the entire Pacific as a base and also as a position of strategic importance to British interests in the North Pacific. How these qualities caused Esquimalt to evolve into a naval station during the 1850's and 1860's will be discussed later.[116]

Changing Status of Vancouver Island

Developments at Vancouver Island in the seven years following the resolution of the Oregon boundary question in 1846 were not at first encouraging for several reasons. First attempts at colonization did not meet with success. The plans of the British government for settlement failed because the Colonial Office selected for a colonizing agency a staple-trading rather than a land company. It should be added, however, that the Hudson's Bay Company was only partly to blame for this state of affairs; it might have fulfilled its obligation better if arable lands at low prices had been abundant.

Earl Grey's faith in the Company's ability to colonize the land proved ill-founded. The faltering progress of the Colony of Vancouver Island showed, in large measure, that frontier communities of settlement do not grow quickly, if at all, under the dominance of monopolies. Thus by 1852 only 300 persons lived at Fort Victoria and 150 at Fort Nanaimo— and most of these were Company servants. In fact, only 435 emigrants had been sent out by this time; 11 had purchased land, and another 19 had applied for land.[117] In short, the prospects of the colony appeared bleak because settlement had not been effectively promoted by the Hudson's Bay Company.

More auspicious was the growing association of the Royal Navy with Vancouver Island during the period between 1846 and 1852 when commanders-in-chief, Pacific, assigned at least one ship annually to visit the Northwest Coast in support of British interests. These ships undertook a variety of tasks encouraging to the eventual settlement and economic development of the island. They transported foodstuffs for the Company to aid settlers, punished unruly Indians and kept Americans in awe of British power during this unsettled period in Anglo-American relations.

---

[115]*Ibid.*
[116]See chapters 5 and 8.
[117]A. Colville to Pakington, 24 November 1852, A.8/7, H.B.C.A.

When warships came to Vancouver Island for these purposes, spars, coals and hemp were tested to determine their suitability for naval requirements. A safe harbour, Esquimalt, was found. Adjacent waters were charted to facilitate the coastal trade upon which the life and progress of the colony mainly depended. Thus, as Douglas had predicted, the Royal Navy and Vancouver Island experienced mutual benefits.

By 1853, there were indications of an approaching end to the combined efforts of the Hudson's Bay Company and the Royal Navy at Vancouver Island. The climax came in 1858 when the royal grant held by the Company was not renewed.

The informal partnership of fur traders and sailors on the Northwest Coast, which began with the expedition of the Royal Navy's *Racoon* to the mouth of the Columbia River in 1813 in support of the North West Company, lasted throughout the Oregon crisis and the early years of the colony of Vancouver Island. After that, the Royal Navy was chiefly responsible for protection of the seaboard colony which was moving towards self-government and provincial status in Canada.

Chapter 5

WAR WITH RUSSIA IN THE PACIFIC
1854-1856

IN MARCH 1854, Britain and France entered the Crimean War to protect
the British corridor to India and the Far East and French spheres of
influence in the Near East.[1] Subsequently, the allied navies clashed with
the Russian enemy in four regions—the Black Sea where the Crimea
became the major battleground, the Baltic Sea, the White Sea and the
North Pacific Ocean. The North Pacific was far from being the decisive
theatre of action, naval or otherwise, but the activities of the Royal Navy
there resulted in the development of a naval depot and hospital at Esquimalt on Vancouver Island and preserved British interests along the
Pacific Coast of North America from the dangers of a threatened Russian-American alliance. The chief operations of the Pacific squadron
consisted of an attack which failed ignominiously on the Russian outpost
of Petropavlovsk, on the Kamchatka Peninsula; a brief occupation of the
by-then deserted post the following year; a search for elusive Russian warships on Asian and American shores which demonstrated the weakness of
the Russian navy's position in the Pacific; and visits by the Royal Navy
to Esquimalt for coal, medical aid, repairs, provisions and naval stores.

[1]See W. F. Reddaway, "The Crimean War and the French Alliance, 1853-1858,"
Cambridge History of British Foreign Policy, 3 vols. (Cambridge: Cambridge Uni-
versity Press, 1923) , II, 357ff., and H. W. V. Temperley, *England and the Near East:
The Crimea* (London: Longmans, Green & Co., 1936) , chapters 8 and 9.

Owing to its remoteness from the European theatre where the final outcome of the conflict was decided, the North Pacific has been overlooked as an area of the Crimean War.[2] The failure of the Allies against the Russians in battle at Petropavlovsk in 1854 was not well reported at the time and the fiasco resulted in little more than a demonstration of why an assault force should not land in the face of superior enemy numbers defending a strong position. Little has been written on the Petropavlovsk affair in the Pacific theatre of the war, and no previously published account has been based upon Admiralty sources.[3]

The Deepening Crisis

As Russia expanded her interests in Siberia and the North Pacific during the mid-nineteenth century, she sought to foster settlements and trading posts on her eastern shores.[4] By fortifying centres such as Ayan on the Sea of Okhotsk and Petropavlovsk on the Kamchatka Peninsula, which lay only a few miles from the Kurile Islands, she hoped to strengthen her fur trade in North America, exploit the rich whaling grounds of the North Pacific, and enter into commerce with China and Japan.

Immediately before the Crimean War, Russia had gained *de facto* control of the Amur River, an important waterway leading eastwards from Siberia to the Sea of Japan. The river mouth was held by the Chinese supposedly, but Russian naval explorations from 1849 to 1855 revealed that Chinese gunboats did not defend the Amur, as one mistaken Russian admiral maintained.[5] Consequently, Russia was able to extend her influence down that river to its mouth and along the adjacent shores of Eastern Asia with impunity.

---

[2] Three volumes published by the Navy Records Society have dealt with European aspects of the war: D. Bonner-Smith and Capt. A. C. Dewar, eds., *Russian War, 1854, Baltic and Black Sea: Official Correspondence*, vol. LXXXIII (London, 1943); D. Bonner-Smith, ed., *Russian War, 1855, Baltic: Official Correspondence*, vol. LXXXIV (London, 1944), and Capt. A. C. Dewar, ed., *Russian War, 1855, Black Sea: Official Correspondence*, vol. LXXXV (London, 1945). No volume has yet appeared on operations in the Pacific.

[3] Previous accounts include C. D. Yonge, *The History of the British Navy*, 3 vols. (London: R. Bentley, 1866), III, 323-25; W. Laird Clowes et al., *The Royal Navy: A History*, 7 vols. (London: Sampson Low & Co., 1897-1913), VI, 429-32; Capt. J. F. Parry, *Sketch of the History of the Naval Establishments at Esquimalt* (typescript of a paper read before the Natural History Society of British Columbia, 19 February 1906; reprinted from *Victoria Daily Times*, 20 and 21 February 1906); and Michael Lewis, "An Eye-Witness at Petropaulovski, 1854," *Mariner's Mirror*, XLIX (November 1963), 265-72.

[4] For a brief account, see A. S. Morton, *A History of the Canadian West to 1870-71* (London: T. Nelson & Sons, [1939]), pp. 367-68.

[5] Hector Chevigny, *Russian America: the Great Alaskan Venture, 1741-1867* (New York: Viking Press, 1965), p. 214. See also, Commodore C. Elliot to Rear-Admiral Sir James Stirling (Commander-in-Chief, China), 25 November 1855, S22, Adm. 1/5672.

From their explorations and surveys near Sakhalin, the Russians learned that the Amur could be entered from the sea by two passages, either from the north or from the south entrance to the Gulf of Amur (or Tartary). However, the allied commanders were under the impression from the findings of La Pérouse and Broughton that it was impossible to enter the river's shallow mouth.[6]

Subsequent events revealed that British naval officers, much to their embarrassment, were ill-informed about the mouth of the Amur.[7] The matter was no longer of academic interest; it was of strategic importance.

A dominant motive for Russian eastward expansion at this time was fear of British aggrandizement in the North Pacific, especially along Asian shores.[8] Although Britain had no such plan, the Governor-General of Eastern Siberia, General Nikolai Muraviev, was suspicious of English intentions. He believed that Britain wanted to become the dominant power in that ocean and favoured a Russian-American alliance to check British maritime ascendancy.[9]

Moreover, Muraviev knew that Russian ports on Sakhalin and the Kurile Islands would be easy prey to hostile British warships; Russian naval vessels depended on these islands for supplies. Through Muraviev's initiative, a thousand men, chiefly infantry and field artillery, were sent down the Amur from the Transbaikal Provinces, along with stores for Russian warships.[10] By the spring of 1854, a third of the force and General Muraviev himself joined the fifty-man garrison at Petropavlovsk. There, unbeknown to the British or French, they completed extensive preparations to defend the post, which had become the Russian bastion of the North Pacific, against a possible allied naval attack.

The situation was markedly different on the Northwest Coast of North America, where British and Russian fur-trading organizations understood each other's problems and even did business with one another while the parent nations fought. Indeed, an agreement was entered into in 1839 between the British and Russian companies.[11] This agreement formed the basis of an understanding which lasted until Russia sold

---

[6]The best compendium used by mariners at this time was A. G. Findlay, *Directory for Navigation of the Pacific*, 2 pts. (London: R. H. Laurie, 1851). For Petropavlovsk, see pt. II, pp. 594-604.

[7]See, for instance, Stirling to Sec. of Adm., 13 February 1856, S64, Adm. 1/5672.

[8]Frank A. Golder, *Russian Expansion in the Pacific, 1641-1850* (Cleveland: Arthur H. Clark Co., 1914), pp. 263-64.

[9]*Ibid.*

[10]E. G. Ravenstein, *Russians on the Amur: Its Discovery, Conquest and Colonization* (London: Trübner & Co., 1861), pp. 116-25.

[11]The text of the agreement is printed in full in E. H. Oliver, ed., *The Canadian North-West: Early Development and Legislative Records*, 2 vols. (Ottawa: Government Printing Bureau, 1914-1915), II, 791-97.

Alaska to the United States in 1867.[12] The terms of the 1839 agreement assigned to the Hudson's Bay Company almost total control of the maritime fur trade as far north as Cape Spencer, increased the Company's influence in the Stikine Territory behind the *lisière* or coastal strip and gave the Company other commercial advantages. For the Russians it guaranteed a steady supply of land-otter skins and foodstuffs from the British traders. Finally—because war between the respective nations seemed possible in 1839—the agreement specified that in the event of such a conflict, the Russian American Company would guarantee the peaceful removal of their British counterparts from the *lisière* for up to three months after learning of war.[13]

The threat of war in early 1854 impelled officials of the Russian American Company to seek a further agreement with the Hudson's Bay Company to provide for proclamation of neutrality over the whole Northwest Coast in time of war.[14] When the matter was referred to the Foreign Office, the British government consented to the proposal because territorial acquisitions had been renounced as a war aim. In keeping with this policy, instructions were sent at once to commanders of British warships in the Pacific advising that hostile acts were not to be committed in the Tsar's American dominions.[15] But the fine point of distinction consisted in the fact that neutrality was to be "territorial only."[16] During war, Russian warships and merchantmen on the high seas were liable to capture, and the coasts and posts of Russian America were subject to blockade.

This "quarantine" of the area in time of war was unquestionably beneficial to the commercial interests of both nations. But in excluding Russian America as an object of war, the British government may have acted too hastily. By August 1854 the possibility of a Russian-American alliance had led Palmerston at the Home Office to suggest to the Earl of Clarendon, the Foreign Secretary, that the "nominal possession" of the area might "forestall the Bargain between Nicholas and the Yankees."[17]

---

[12]See Donald C. Davidson, "Relations of the Hudson's Bay Company with the Russian American Company on the Northwest Coast, 1829-1867," *British Columbia Historical Quarterly*, V (January 1941) , 33-51.

[13]John S. Galbraith, *The Hudson's Bay Company as an Imperial Factor, 1821-1869* (Berkeley and Los Angeles: University of California Press, 1957) , pp. 154, 163.

[14]W. Politkowiski and others to H.B.C., 2/4 February 1854, encl. in A. Colvile (Gov., H.B.C.) to Clarendon (F.O.), 28 February 1854, A. 8/19, fols. 23-24, H.B.C.A.; Galbraith, *Hudson's Bay Company*, pp. 165-69; and S. B. Okun, *The Russian-American Company*, trans. C. Ginsburg (Cambridge, Mass.: Harvard University Press, 1951) , pp. 235-43.

[15]H. U. Addington (F.O.) to Colvile, 22 March 1854, A. 8/19, fols. 24-25, H.B.C.A.

[16]*Ibid.*

[17]Lord Palmerston (Home Office) to Lord Clarendon, (F.O.) , 29 August 1854, Clarendon dep., c. 15, fol. 172, B.L.

Moreover, at least one imperially-minded Canadian favoured seizing the territory as an addition to British North America of strategic and commercial importance.[18] In any event, the Anglo-Russian pact on neutrality of the Northwest Coast did not help Russia overcome her major disadvantage in the North Pacific as elsewhere during the Crimean War— that is, her inferiority to the Allies at sea. The British squadron in the Pacific could have damaged Sitka and other Russian settlements. But the British government did not seek to upset trading relations between the Russian American Company and the Hudson's Bay Company. Neither did it seek territorial expansion in an area of questionable value. For these reasons, the government adopted essentially a passive policy for the Northeastern Pacific.[19]

On 24 February 1854, nearly a month before the Allies declared war on Russia, the Admiralty acted on the advice of the Foreign Office and instructed commanders-in-chief on the foreign stations to cooperate with their French counterparts against Russia in the event of war.[20] So inevitable did hostilities seem that their Lordships also sent orders to the Commander-in-Chief on the China station to plan operations against Russia.[21] And British and French admirals in the Pacific needed to know only that war had been declared before moving against the enemy.[22] The paddle-wheel sloop *Virago* was sent to Panama to await such news from England.

Outbreak of War

On 7 May 1854 the *Virago* brought to Callao dispatches for Rear-Admiral David Price, the Commander-in-Chief, Pacific, informing him that Britain and France had joined forces against Russia on 28 March. Price, however, did not act with any apparent haste. Two days after receiving this news along with certain instructions, he issued a general memorandum to his squadron indicating the part it should play in the conflict:

---

[18]A. R. Roche, *A View of Russian America in Connection with the Present War* (Montreal, 1885) ; see also, W. L. Morton, *The Critical Years: The Union of British North America, 1857-1873* (Toronto: McClelland and Stewart, 1964) , p. 26.
[19]Galbraith, *Hudson's Bay Company*, pp. 165-66.
[20]Adm. Circular, 24 February 1854, Adm. 116/857.
[21]Stirling to Sec. of Adm., 6 March 1854, S64, Adm. 1/5629, acknowledging receipt of these instructions.
[22]Initially, Sir James Graham, the First Lord of the Admiralty, was cognizant of the need to give the Commander-in-Chief, Pacific, some warning of the critical state of European affairs, especially as it was intended to send a frigate for the protection of Vancouver Island. J. Graham to Clarendon, 25 January 1854, private, Clarendon dep., c. 14, fol. 150, B.L. The signing of the Anglo-Russian neutrality agreement for the Northwest Coast removed the need for sending this ship.

In carrying out these instructions the Rear Admiral desires to record his opinion that there will be much to be done upon this Station by the Squadron under his Orders, and that Great Britain has a right to expect from it a proper account of the Russian Frigates that are known to be on the Station as well as the numerous Privateers that it is known will be [there].

To these words, Price added his hope that men on the station would show such bravery in action as to "render them not only superior to their Enemy but inferior to none in the World."[23]

Price's primary aim was to clear the seas of Russian shipping. He knew that the enemy frigates would avoid their stronger opponents and probably seek refuge in harbours on the coast of Siberia. So he proceeded, rather slowly, to gather his force at successive points—Callao, Nuku Hiva, the French Pacific naval headquarters in the Marquesas Islands, and Honolulu—before sailing for the Northwestern Pacific.[24] By the time the combined squadron reached the Hawaiian Islands on 17 July, it consisted of the *President*, 50 guns, *Amphitrite*, 24 guns, and *Virago*, 6 guns, and the *Forte*, 60 guns, *Artemise*, 30 guns, *Eurydice*, 22 guns, and *Obligado*, 18 guns, the last four of these belonging to France.

The arrival of the allied squadron did much to strengthen British and French influence in the Hawaiian Islands, although this was not the purpose of the call. Since 1846 the two governments had upheld a policy of independence for the Hawaiian kingdom. On this occasion Rear-Admiral Price and his counterpart, Rear-Admiral Fevrier-Despointes, stressed to Kamehameha III that Hawaiian sovereignty was of utmost importance in view of American pressures to annex the islands.[25] The growing Russian-American *rapprochement* increased the strategic importance of the islands. If Sakhalin remained in Russian hands and Hawaii were under American control, British and French power in the North Pacific would be reduced correspondingly.[26] The auspicious appearance of eight warships,[27] the largest squadron yet seen there, certainly added

---

[23]General Memo No. 11, 9 May 1854; in "Journal kept by Alexander V. Maccall, Clerk's Assistant, 1854-1856, in H.M.S. *Victory, Pique* and *Amphitrite*," LOG/N/P/1, MS 9397, N.M.M. Hereafter cited as *Maccall Journal* (unpaginated).
[24]W. P. Morrell, *Great Britain in the Pacific Islands* (Oxford: Clarendon Press, 1960), p. 194.
[25]Rear-Admiral Price to R. Osborne (Sec. of Adm.), 25 July 1854, Y136, Adm. 1/5630. On British and French consular pressure, see Merze Tate, "Hawaii: A Symbol of Anglo-American Rapprochement," *Political Science Quarterly*, LXXIX (December 1964), 555-56. See also, Richard W. Van Alstyne, "Great Britain, the United States, and Hawaiian Independence, 1850-1855," *Pacific Historical Review*, IV (1935), 15-24.
[26]Jean I. Brookes, *International Rivalry in the Pacific Islands, 1800-1875* (Berkeley and Los Angeles: University of California Press, 1941), p. 208.
[27]The British ship *Pique*, 40 guns, joined the others at Honolulu, 22 July 1854.

weight to the concerted pressure of the French and British admirals.[28] This display of naval power, reinforced by simultaneous diplomatic activity in Washington by Britain and France, delayed—if but for a few decades—the American annexation of Hawaii.

At Honolulu, a further indication that Russia and the United States might be acting in concert reached Price in the form of news that San Francisco merchants were fitting out American privateers to aid the Russians in the Pacific. He decided therefore to dispatch the *Amphitrite* and *Artemise* to the California coast to protect allied trade; in order to keep this mission secret, the two vessels remained with the squadron until three days after its departure from the Hawaiian Islands.

The Allies at Petropavlovsk

Rear-Admiral Price learned also at Honolulu from a Hudson's Bay Company agent that two Russian vessels—later discovered to be the *Aurora*, 44 guns, and *Dvina*, 12 guns—were bound for Petropavlovsk on the Kamchatka Peninsula.[29] He had known earlier of the existence of these ships, for the *Aurora* arrived at Callao in mid-April to find four British and French warships awaiting news of the declaration of war.[30] Yet Price did not sail from Callao to pursue the Russian ships until ten days after receiving this information. Probably he was reluctant to engage the enemy, a view that is substantiated by strange events preceding the attack on Petropavlovsk.

In point of fact, Price had little to fear from his enemy at sea; the ships of the Russian Imperial Navy certainly were not the equal of the British and French in the Pacific, from the point of view of numbers, condition or armament. The only Russian ships of note in the Pacific were the frigate *Diana*, 50 guns, and the *Aurora*, the few others being corvettes and brigs. Russian commanders realized their inferiority, as shown by the fact that Russian vessels sought the protection of the mouth of the Amur River and of harbours on the Asian coast such as Ayan, Petropavlovsk and De Castries Bay.[31]

Even though the Allies acquired command of the sea in the Pacific at

[28]Price to Osborne, 25 July 1854, Y136, Adm. 1/5630.
[29]The Hudson's Bay Company agent at Honolulu reported that the *Aurora* left there 28 May 1854 for Kamchatka and the Northwest Coast on a surveying expedition. R. Clouston to A. Barclay (Sec. H.B.C.) , 3 June 1854, A. 11/63, fol. 64, H.B.C.A. H.M.S. *Trincomalee,* with supplies for British Arctic expeditions, left the following day. She did not pursue the Russian warship because news of war had not yet reached the islands.
[30]Ravenstein, *Russians on the Amur,* pp. 120-21.
[31]De Castries Bay, south of the Amur's mouth, is on the mainland facing across to Sakhalin. There the Russians planned to establish "a Naval Station of some magnitude"; Lt. Dent (H.M.S. *Sybille*) to Cdr. Forsythe, 29 May 1855, S109, Adm. 1/5657.

the very outset of the war, they were unable to engage the enemy at sea. As will be shown, success eluded them because the superior geographical knowledge possessed by Russian captains enabled them to evade allied warships, which searched the North Pacific in vain.[32]

The two Russian warships *Aurora* and *Dvina* found safety in the most important of the Russian havens, Petropavlovsk. The town lay seven miles inland from the entrance to, and on the eastern shore of, Avatcha Bay on the Pacific side of the Kamchatka Peninsula.[33] A long, narrow mountainous peninsula pointing southward guarded the town on the west; between this and the shore was "a clear and deep narrow entrance" leading to an inner harbour at the head of which was the town.[34] Close behind a sand spit, which extended west-northwest from the mainland toward the peninsula, lay the *Aurora* and *Dvina*—protected in this position from being hulled near the water-line.

On arrival, 29 August 1854 the Allies considered the defences of Petropavlovsk stronger than expected, but not particularly formidable.[35] The outer defences of primary importance consisted of three batteries: a 5-gun battery at the extremity of the peninsula, an 11-gun battery on the opposite shore, and a 3-gun battery farther out on the same side.[36] The broadsides of the Russian ships also faced the harbour entrance and approaches. According to one estimate, a total of eight hundred Russians and fifty-two guns defended the town.[37]

But events were to show that outward appearances were deceiving. These words of Commander F. W. Beechey, written after his visit there in 1827, were prophetic:

> Should the North Pacific ever be the scene of active naval operations, Petropaulovski must doubtless become of immense importance. At present it may be said to be unfortified, but a very few guns judiciously placed would effectually protect its entrance.[38]

[32]On this point generally, see A. T. Mahan, *The Influence of Sea Power Upon History, 1660-1783* (London: Sampson Low & Co., 1890) , p. 14.

[33]*Avatska* and *Awatska* are common spellings, but *Avatcha* is used in Admiralty charts and Pilot.

[34]Captain Fenton Aylmer, ed., *A Cruise in the Pacific from the Log of a Naval Officer,* 2 vols. (London: Hurst and Blackett, 1860) , II, 59.

[35]Rear-Admiral P. W. Brock, H.M.S. *President* dossier, MS, p. 9, M.M.B.C.

[36]Capt. Nicolson to Commodore Frederick, 19 September 1854, Cap N52, Adm. 1/5631.

[37]Ravenstein, *Russians on the Amur,* p. 124. There were four Paixhans guns. The rest were mainly 36- and 24-pounders. See the plan of Petropavlovsk in *Illustrated London News,* 16 December 1854, p. 622.

[38]Quoted by Capt. J. C. R. Colomb, "Russian Development and Our Naval and Military Position in the North Pacific," *Royal United Service Institution Journal,* XXI (1877) , 665. Throughout the late nineteenth century, the importance of Petropavlovsk to Russia increased, which led to much debate among strategists in London. The expert Ravenstein, whose work is frequently referred to here, was often in attendance at meetings at the Royal United Service Institution.

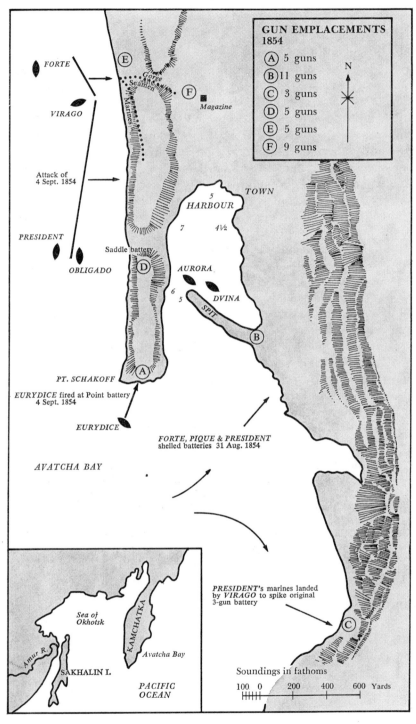

GUN EMPLACEMENTS
1854

Ⓐ 5 guns
Ⓑ 11 guns
Ⓒ 3 guns
Ⓓ 5 guns
Ⓔ 5 guns
Ⓕ 9 guns

N

FORTE

VIRAGO

Ⓔ

Gorse
Seamen

Ⓕ

Magazine

Attack of
4 Sept. 1854

TOWN

5

HARBOUR

PRESIDENT

7

4½

Saddle battery

OBLIGADO

Ⓓ

AURORA

6

5

DVINA

SPIT

Ⓑ

PT. SCHAKOFF

Ⓐ

EURYDICE fired at Point battery
4 Sept. 1854

EURYDICE

FORTE, PIQUE & PRESIDENT
shelled batteries 31 Aug. 1854

AVATCHA BAY

PRESIDENT's marines landed
by VIRAGO to spike original
3-gun battery

Ⓒ

Sea of
Okhotsk

KAMCHATKA

Amur R.

Avatcha Bay

SAKHALIN I.

PACIFIC
OCEAN

Soundings in fathoms

100 0   200   400   600 Yards

ALLIED ATTACK ON PETROPAVLOVSK, 1854

Debacle at Petropavlovsk

The strength of the squadron assembled seemed to indicate that the Allies could make themselves masters of Petropavlovsk with little trouble: there were three frigates (the British flagship *President,* Captain Richard Burridge; the *Pique,* 40 guns, Captain Sir Frederick W. Nicolson, Bart.; and the *Forte,* flagship of Rear-Admiral Fevrier-Despointes) plus a corvette (the *Eurydice*) and a brig (the *Obligado*). The squadron's handicap was that it possessed but one steamer, the *Virago.* Although she was weak in armament, she proved invaluable in the operations because her 120-horsepower engines gave her the manoeuvrability that the other vessels lacked in those confined waters during the lengthy calms that prevailed. In total, six vessels were assembled, painted black on the exterior of their gun decks to conceal their armament, mounting 190 guns, and carrying some two thousand men. Despite the strength of this force, it was evident throughout the engagement that followed that the lack of steam-power in five of the ships placed them at a distinct disadvantage in exchanges with shore batteries. Indeed, manoeuvrability proved to be as important as armament, a development which underlined the potentialities of steam as a motive power.[39]

During the afternoon of 29 August 1854 Rear-Admiral Price reconnoitered Avatcha Bay in the *Virago* to determine the strength of the Russian fortifications; he concluded that the outer defences, already mentioned, were of no great strength. Some shelling followed of the saddle battery by the *Virago,* and perhaps by others, but there was no general engagement. Later, on board the *President,* plans were made for an attack the next morning.[40]

Now a strange turn of events overtook the squadron. Just as the *Virago* was towing the *Forte, Pique* and *President* into position on 30 August, Price shot himself through the lungs and died three hours later. Captain Burridge in the flagship at first thought this was an accident, but later concluded that the act was a result of "intense mental anxiety."[41] Undoubtedly, at the climax of his professional life, Price was unprepared for war and unequal to the task.[42] The best available evidence in sup-

[39]See Bernard Brodie, *Sea Power in the Machine Age* (Princeton: Princeton University Press, 1941), chapter 5.

[40]The extent of these plans is not known. However, one source claims, perhaps in excess, that none were made: "no decided opinion was given as to the strength or size of it (Petropavlovsk) or even the capability of attacking it, consequently, no plan for the morrow was made . . ." *Maccall Journal,* unpaginated N.M.M.

[41]Capt. R. Burridge to Nicolson, 30 August 1854, Cap N52, Adm. 1/5631.

[42]Lewis, "Eye-Witness at Petropaulovski," pp. 267, 269-70. Also Michael Lewis, *The Navy in Transition, 1814-1864: A Social History* (London: George Allen & Unwin, 1965), pp. 79, 81, 124. Cf. J K. Laughton's biography of Price in *The Dictionary of National Biography,* XLVI (London, 1896), 326.

port of this view is given in a comment by the Clerk's assistant in the *Pique*:

> Throughout the whole voyage [from Callao] he had evidently shown great weakness in allowing everybody to sway him as they willed; consequently when he was expected to show forth in the purest and truest light, his nerves gave way under the responsibility . . . and by this act of his . . . threw the Squadron into a state such as is unparalleled in English naval history.[43]

The responsibility for implementing the plan against the batteries now devolved upon Fevrier-Despointes.

During the early-morning calms of the following day, the *Virago*—her engines barely equal to the task—placed the *President, Forte,* and *Pique* before the batteries near the harbour mouth. In order to take the 3-gun battery on the east, which "from its raking position, was expected to give some annoyance," a party of marines and seamen were landed from the *Virago*; they captured and spiked the guns.[44] But when a body of Russians disembarked from the *Aurora* to counterattack—their number being two hundred according to one claim[45]—the allied party re-embarked under cover of fire from the *Virago*.

At this juncture in this trial-and-error campaign it became clear that a battery near the landward end of the spit on the eastern shore would have to be silenced, as it was directly in line with the allied ships, the Russian ships behind the spit, and the town. Then the Allies could get their vessels closer to shore and bring their guns closer to the Russian ships and the town. Fresh afternoon breezes permitted the *President* and the *Forte* to move near the battery, whereupon all four allied ships fired at and silenced the emplacement. Then for the night they withdrew out of range from other batteries—suffering some damage during the process.[46] This brought to a conclusion what might be called a prelude to defeat.

Three days of correspondence and discussion followed in the allied ships. The French admiral, worried by the damage the *Forte* had sustained, showed reluctance to press the attack, contending that it was impossible for the Allies to make themselves masters of Petropavlovsk without great loss of life, defended as it was by such apparently formidable batteries.[47] He advocated, as a better alternative, that the squadron

---

[43]*Maccall Journal*, unpaginated, N.M.M.

[44]Nicolson to Frederick, 19 September 1854, Cap N52, Adm. 1/5631. This was the official report, written sometime after the action. It is carefully worded, to protect all concerned. Despite this, it is the best extant account of those strange, confusing events.

[45]Laird Clowes, *Royal Navy*, VI, 430.

[46]Nicolson to Frederick, 19 September 1854, Cap N52, Adm. 1/5631.

[47]Fevrier-Despointes to Nicolson, 2 September 1854, *ibid*.

should cruise to intercept a Russian squadron consisting of the frigate *Diana* and two consorts. In his view, this was preferable to making a landing, which would risk weakening the allied force and rendering it inferior to Russian warships at sea. Like Fevrier-Despointes, Captain Nicolson, the senior British officer, was mentally unprepared for the responsibilities thrust upon him by Price's death.[48] In his reply to his superior, he did not fully reveal his anxieties, but stated simply that he hoped the Allies would meet the Russian squadron somewhere in the North Pacific.[49]

Subsequent questions from Fevrier-Despointes, demanding categorical answers, forced Nicolson to oppose the views of the French admiral. Nicolson knew and admitted that casualties were unavoidable, but he had reason to believe that if the batteries were attacked from the rear, as some Americans there had advised him, success would be certain.[50] The fall of the batteries, capture of the Russian ships, and the destruction of the defences would make the place unfit as a retreat for the expected Russian frigates. His most conclusive remark emphasized that unless further attempts were made, the national honours of England and France would be compromised.[51] It seems certain that if Nicolson had not exerted pressure on Fevrier-Despointes in this fashion, the allied ships would have withdrawn, bringing the encounter to an early, albeit unsuccessful, conclusion.

But after receiving additional intelligence respecting some batteries not visible from the allied warships and after further consultations with Nicolson and other officers, both French and British, the French admiral agreed to simultaneous attacks on the saddle battery and the round fort near the gorge—the latter being the most northerly position of Russian defence along the shore. In short, the frontal attack was abandoned for one from the rear.

On 4 September 350 men from each nation were in readiness in the *Virago*. On one side of the steamer lay the *Forte*; on the other, the boats for the disembarkation. The *President* was in tow.[52] As the ships drew near the northern half of the peninsula, intense firing from the shore damaged the riggings of the *Forte* and *President*. The *President* engaged the saddle battery at six hundred yards before silencing it, while the *Forte* put the round fort out of action, thereby allowing marines and seamen

[48]See *Maccall Journal;* unpaginated, N.M.M.
[49]Nicolson to Fevrier-Despointes, 2 September 1854, Cap N52, Adm. 1/5631.
[50]Nicolson to Fevrier-Despointes, 3 September 1854, *ibid.* The Americans, deserters from a whaler, proposed that they were prepared to guide a landing party in the attack in return for a passage to Hawaii; Brock, *President* dossier, p. 12, M.M.B.C. An agreement was made and adhered to: eleven Americans were taken to Honolulu.
[51]Nicolson to Fevrier-Despointes, 3 September 1854, Cap N52, Adm. 1/5631.
[52]Nicolson to Frederick, 19 September 1854, *ibid.*

to land. The assault plan called for marines, assisted by seamen from the *Forte* and *Eurydice,* to ascend the steep hill which guarded the town on the west.[53] Simultaneously, seamen from the *Pique, President* and *Virago* were to move by the road to the left of the hill, clear the gorge and thereby open the way for a direct advance on the town.

This overall plan was doomed from the outset, largely because the landing party had neither special training nor opportunity to rehearse the operation. On the left, the seamen met with little success against the Russian battery firing grape-shot down the gorge. On the right, the marines suffered heavy losses in consequence of enemy fire from superior positions along the ridge and on both sides of the saddle. Captain C. R. Parker, R.M., was killed; his subalterns were wounded; the men fell back; and when all attempts to rally them failed, they fled in utter disorder to boats on the beach, several being killed by musketry during the embarkation. The guns of the *Forte, Obligado* and *Virago* covered the retreating force as best they could, and when all the men were on board, the ships moved out into the bay.[54] The Allies had been repulsed decisively.

The attack from the rear thus was as much a failure as the frontal assault. Because the Russian ships in the harbour were the most important object, the attempt to take the town seems to have been inconsistent with the original plan.[55] This is borne out in the views of Rear-Admiral H. W. Bruce, Price's successor, who consulted with British, Russian and American witnesses in 1855 and concluded that the marines and seamen were evidently "landed to *spare the ships*; where had the party been at their guns, and in the proper place . . . their enemy was prepared to yield."[56]

The Allies paid a heavy toll for poor reconnaissance, faulty planning and bad execution. Of the 700 landed, there were 209 casualties: 26 French and 26 British killed or missing, 78 French and 79 British wounded.[57] Nevertheless, the Chaplain of the *President*, the Reverend Thomas Holme, overstated the case when he described the battle as "a

[53]Burridge to Nicolson, 5 September 1854, encl. in Nicolson to Frederick, 19 September 1854, *ibid.*
[54]*Ibid.*
[55]Brock, *President dossier,* p. 13, M.M.B.C.
[56]Rear-Admiral H. W. Bruce to Sir Charles Wood (First Lord of the Admiralty), 24 February 1856, confidential, Halifax Papers, Add. MSS. 49, 549, B.M. In a second letter on this subject, dated 1 April 1856, Bruce informed Wood, ". . . as far as I have heard the land attack was a badly managed business . . . not only was the attack wrongly made but badly executed." 1 April 1856, *ibid.*
[57]According to the final tally, the *Virago,* lost 5 men; the *Pique,* 17; and the *President,* 11. Frederick to Osborne, 15 November 1854, Y1, Adm. 1/5656.

most bloody defeat" and "a tragedy perhaps more horrible than has ever happened in the British Navy."[58] Holme probably had never before witnessed a battle. The confusion of the whole train of events plus the heavy casualties led him to an exaggerated conclusion. The recent publication of Holme's account has done little to dispel the generally held views of terrible carnage. Admittedly, the events at Petropavlovsk were a fiasco; but there was no wholesale slaughter as in the Charge of the Light Brigade.[59]

Nonetheless, news of the repulse was not well received in London, and inaccurate reports found their way into the British press. When the official account reached the Admiralty, their Lordships voiced their displeasure in a dispatch sent to Captain Nicolson. This informed him that the defeat was

> of a nature which ought to impress upon the officers of H.M. Ships that the utmost discretion is necessary in undertaking expeditions on shore and detaching Seamen and Marines from their ships in the neighbourhood of fortified positions of the Enemy, with imperfect knowledge of the Nature of the Country and the force expected to be encountered.[60]

The reprimand failed to recognize that the shortage of steam-assisted vessels in the Pacific prohibited the Allies from "wheeling around in small circles" and delivering successive broadsides against the shore batteries, as in the successful operations at Odessa in the Black Sea.[61]

Owing to the number of wounded and the lateness of the season, it was necessary to postpone further assault on Petropavlovsk until the following spring when the harbour ice had broken up. The squadron sailed 7 September. Outside of Avatcha Bay, they sighted two sails in the distance.

The *President* and *Virago* gave chase and captured the *Anadis*, a Russian government schooner, and the *Sitka*, 10 guns, a Russian American Company vessel bound for Petropavlovsk with army officers, gunpowder and provisions. The Russian prisoners told Nicolson—and he had every reason to believe them—that the enemy at Petropavlovsk was indeed stronger than the Allies had been led to expect.[62] After this, the warships and the prize *Sitka* sailed for the Northwest Coast of America, some three thousand miles away.[63]

---

[58]Quoted in Lewis, "Eye-Witness," p. 268.
[59]See, for example, *ibid.*, p. 271.
[60]Admiralty Minute, 6 December 1854, Cap N52, Adm. 1/5631.
[61]Brodie, *Sea Power*, p. 71.
[62]Nicolson to Frederick, 19 September 1854, Cap N52, Adm. 1/5631.
[63]The *Anadis*, given over to the French, was evidently destroyed. The *Sitka*, a new vessel of 800 tons, was a valuable prize. See below, n.70.

The British ships *President, Pique* and *Virago* reached Esquimalt on 3 October. Their crews repaired sails and running gear, blacked down rigging, painted hulls and cut and stowed spars and firewood. The ships received a large, but insufficient, quantity of provisions from farms close to Esquimalt. Coal was brought from nearby Nanaimo and water from adjacent lakes and streams. Although much needed hospital facilities were not available, the value of Esquimalt as a place of repair and refreshment clearly was evident.

War Scare at Vancouver Island

The arrival of the squadron eliminated the danger of a Russian attack from Sitka or Petropavlovsk. This had worried Victoria residents, especially James Douglas, the Governor of Vancouver Island. Even before unofficial news of war reached Victoria in mid-June, the gravity of the situation led him to draft hurried plans for defence.[64] As wise as these plans were, they won little support either in London or the colony. His proposal for a regular military force of five hundred men, along with pieces of ordnance, brought a terse rejoinder from the War Office that the Commander-in-Chief, Pacific, had received instructions to send warships frequently to the colony.[65] Nor did Douglas get much support from the Legislative Council of Vancouver Island. This body rejected a militia scheme proposed by the Governor,[66] although arrangements were made to charter and arm the Hudson's Bay Company steamer *Otter* at the expense of the Imperial government to serve as a guardship until Britain made adequate provisions against an attack by Russian warships or privateers.[67]

Douglas had been especially alarmed by rumours that a Russian frigate had sailed from San Francisco to shell Victoria. But Commodore Charles

[64]James Douglas to the Duke of Newcastle (Sec. of State for War and the Colonies), 16 May 1854, W.O. 1/551, fols. 143-47. See also, Donald C. Davidson, "The War Scare of 1854: The Pacific Coast and the Crimean War," *British Columbia Historical Quarterly*, V (October 1941), 243-54; Walter N. Sage, *Sir James Douglas and British Columbia* (Toronto: University of Toronto Press, 1930), pp. 180-82. On the defence of the colony, see Willard E. Ireland, "Pre-Confederation Defence Problems of the Pacific Colonies," *Canadian Historical Association Annual Report, 1941* (Toronto, 1941) pp. 45-46.

[65]G. C. Manby (War Dept.) to J. Sheperd (Dep. Gov., H.B.C.), 31 August 1854, A. 8/7, fol. 139, H.B.C.A.

[66]Douglas planned to conscript men of the colony, including Indians. But the Council felt that there were too few whites to be of any use, and that armed Indians might turn on the colonists. *Minutes of the Council of Vancouver Island. 1851-1861*, British Columbia Archives Memoir No. 2 (Victoria, B.C., 1918), pp. 24-25.

[67]*Ibid.* According to the charter-grant of Vancouver Island (1849), the Hudson's Bay Company was to defray costs of defence "except nevertheless during time of Hostilities between Great Britain and any Foreign European or American Power"; Draft of Grant, encl. in Order-in-Council, 4 September 1848, B.T. 1/470/2506.

Frederick in H.M.S. *Amphitrite* at San Francisco, advised the Admiralty on 13 November 1854 that no such vessel had been sighted at either place. Because Vancouver Island was considered neutral territory, he was certain that the Governor's fears were unfounded.[68].

Still, British possessions on the coast were liable to blockade by Russian vessels, and on this basis Douglas's apprehension was justified; the neutrality agreement in no way guaranteed the protection of Vancouver Island from blockade or from interception of supply ships from England by the Russian warships and privateers thought to be at large in the Pacific.[69] Only the presence of British men-of-war could allay the fears of the colonists.

Naval Searches and Blockades

After remaining thirteen days at Esquimalt, the squadron sailed on 16 October for San Francisco Bay, evidently in search of hospital facilities and more provisions. Within this bay, the British vessels anchored at the favourite watering place Sausilito, where they found Her Majesty's Discovery Ship *Plover* from the Arctic.[70] The *Amphitrite*, flagship of Commodore Frederick, arrived from Hawaii to join the other British vessels. Frederick then transferred his broad pendant to the *President* and sailed in her for Valparaiso to meet the new Commander-in-Chief, Rear-Admiral Bruce.[71]

As soon as Bruce reached Valparaiso by packet from Panama on 5 February 1855 he began deploying ships under his command to fulfill his object: defeat of the Russians at Petropavlovsk. Vast sailing distances in the Pacific made supplying the squadron a difficult matter, so the *Rattlesnake* was used as a store-ship at Honolulu.[72] Warships received provisions and naval stores from her before making the final leg of the voyage to Petropavlovsk. Bruce planned for the squadron to sail to Esquimalt after the attack on the Russian post. He knew that hospital facili-

---

[68]Frederick to Osborne, 13 November 1854, Y15, Adm. 1/5656.

[69]Rumours of these vessels caused great excitement, see J. Parker (Adm.) to Clarendon (F.O.), 28 September 1855, Adm. 116/857, and Bruce to Osborne, 11 July 1856, Y106, Adm. 1/5672.

[70]The *Plover* had been with the *Herald* in the Arctic, 1849-1850. She was sold in San Francisco, and her officers and men sailed the prize *Sitka* to England. See Rochfort Maguire, "Journal kept on bd. H.M.S. Plover," 2 vols. (Dublin: National Library), II, entries for October and November 1854. See also, Maguire to Sec. of Adm., 8 April 1855, Cap M 103, Adm. 1/5658.

[71]The *Amphitrite*, Capt. Matthew Connolly now in command, returned to Honolulu Roads to find the *Trincomalee, Pique, Alceste, Eurydice* and *Artemise. Amphitrite's* log, Adm. 53/5018, 11 December 1854. These ships were there to prevent an American seizure of the Hawaiian Islands; Graham to Clarendon, 7 December 1854, Clarendon dep., c. 14, fols. 535-36, B.L.

[72]Bruce Journal, Adm. 50/308, 13, 14 and 25 February 1855.

ties, coal, and fresh meats and vegetables would probably be needed, so he sent a request to Governor Douglas asking that these be ready for the following July.[73]

The Governor, who was also the agent for the western department of the Hudson's Bay Company, had always shown a willingness to do business with the Royal Navy for the two-fold reason that the warships brought business for the Company and gave the colony protection during their calls. Thus, he lost little time in informing Bruce that a thousand tons of coal had been ordered from the Nanaimo mines, and that two thousand sheep and as many head of cattle as possible would be purchased from the Puget's Sound Agricultural Company post, Fort Nisqually. But in order to ensure that supplies would always be on hand for British warships, Douglas advised Bruce that he considered it a "proper and necessary step" to appoint a commissary for the squadron.[74] Finally, he explained that hospital buildings would be available to receive the sick and wounded of the fleet. In this way the Governor—at once businessman and public servant—prepared to meet the squadron's needs after what was expected to be another assault of major proportions at Petropavlovsk.[75]

Prior to the 1854 fiasco, the Admiralty thought the British force of seven vessels "unnecessarily large" and, in consequence, Price had assigned four of the seven ships intended for use against the enemy to other duties on the station.[76] But in 1855 the Admiralty strengthened the Pacific squadron. A ship-of-the-line, the *Monarch*, 84 guns, was ordered to the Pacific because of fears of a Russian-American alliance and a possible American seizure of the Hawaiian Islands; the frigate *President* remained on the station; and the screw-corvette *Brisk*, 16 guns, was sent to replace the smaller paddle-wheel sloop *Virago*.[77] In addition, the Admiralty ordered two vessels from the China station—the screw-corvette *Encounter*, 14 guns, and the paddle-wheel sloop *Barracouta*, 6 guns, to rendezvous with ships from the Pacific station prior to the at-

[73]Bruce to Douglas, 14 February 1855, extract in Bruce to Osborne, 14 September 1855, Y116, Adm. 1/5656. Original in B.C.A.; published in W. Kaye Lamb, ed. "Correspondence Relating to the Establishment of a Naval Base at Esquimalt, 1851-57," *British Columbia Historical Quarterly*, VI (October 1942) , 281-82.
[74]Douglas to Bruce, 8 May 1855, Adm. Corr. I, B.C.A.
[75]Hudson's Bay Company officials in London were also soliciting the Navy's business. See Sheperd to T. Phinn (Adm.) , 24 July 1855, enclosing Douglas to Barclay, 19 May 1855, Y116, Adm. 1/5656.
[76]Parry, *Sketch of the History of the Naval Establishments at Esquimalt*, p. 2. The four ships were the *Dido, Amphitrite, Trincomalee* and *Cockatrice*.
[77]Graham to Clarendon, 25 September 1854, Clarendon dep., c. 14, fol. 443, B.L. The *Monarch* did not reach Petropavlovsk until 23 June 1855.

tempt on Petropavlovsk.[78] They were intended to supply more steam propulsion to the Pacific squadron and thus overcome the disadvantage from which the Allies suffered in 1854. The *Encounter* and *Barracouta* arrived at the rendezvous on 14 April 1855 "full of coal and with a large supply of ammunition."[79]

The formidable squadron of twelve British and French vessels approached the coast of Kamchatka on 30 May 1855 with every expectation of finding the Russians firmly entrenched at Petropavlovsk.[80] But when the fog cleared two days later, Bruce reconnoitered Avatcha Bay in the steamer *Barracouta* and found to his amazement that the Russians had completely disappeared.[81] It was reported that one of the few American traders, who were now the sole inhabitants of the post, said to Bruce: "I guess ye're rather late, Admiral."[82]

An explanation for the Russian evacuation was given by Captain Martinov, the aide-de-camp to the Governor-General of Eastern Siberia, who appeared from the hinterland to exchange prisoners with the Allies.[83] Evidently officials in St. Petersburg believed that Petropavlovsk could not withstand another attack by allied warships unless the frigate *Diana*, 50 guns, arrived to strengthen the position. Accordingly, orders were sent to the effect that, should the Russian ship not appear, Petropavlovsk was to be abandoned and an escape made in the *Aurora, Dvina* and other available vessels. In fact, the *Diana* was wrecked off Japan in January 1855. Thus the Russians, some 470 in number, cut their way through the ice in the harbour, sailed from Petropavlovsk, and hurried to safety in De Castries Bay and subsequently in the Amur River.[84]

All Bruce could do was conduct a thorough examination of Avatcha Bay: only a deserted and dismantled bark was found in a nearby harbour.

---

[78]The position was 50°N, 160°E. J. M. Tronson, *Personal Narrative of a Voyage . . . in H.M.S. Barracouta* (London, 1859) , pp. 85-90.

[79]Rear-Admiral Sir James Stirling to Sec. of Adm., 15 April and 1 October 1855, S76, Adm. 1/5657.

[80]At a second rendezvous, 20 miles southeast of Avatcha Bay, the following assembled: the *President*, 50 guns, *Pique*, 40 guns, *Trincomalee*, 24 guns, *Amphitrite*, 24 guns, *Dido*, 18 guns, and *Brisk*, 14 guns, from the Pacific squadron; the *Encounter*, 14 guns, and *Barracouta*, 6 guns, from the China squadron; and the *Forte*, 60 guns, *Alceste*, 54 guns, *Eurydice*, 32 guns, and *Obligado*, 8 guns, from the French Navy. Clowes, *Royal Navy*, VI, 475n. For the *Brisk's* voyage, see Admiral Sir Cyprian Bridge, *Some Recollections* (London: John Murray, 1918) , pp. 117-19.

[81]Reported in Stirling to Sec. of Adm., 1 October 1855, S141, Adm. 1/5657.

[82]Tronson, *Personal Narrative*, p. 94.

[83]Bruce to Osborne, 17 July 1855, Sitka, Y83, Adm. 1/5656. See also Major F. V. Longstaff, *Esquimalt Naval Base: A History of Its Work and Defences* (Victoria, B.C.: Victoria Book and Stationery Co., 1941) , p. 16.

[84]Commodore C. Elliot to Stirling, 7 June 1855, S109, Adm. 1/5657.

He then ordered the destruction of the gun emplacements and garrison buildings at Petropavlovsk.[85]

There was, then, no engagement with the enemy: taking the post without a shot being fired was the direct result of allied supremacy at sea. The capture of the Russian post demonstrated the inadequacy of Russian naval power, a decided advantage to Britain and France throughout the war in other seas as well.

Bruce was determined to seek out the Russians on Asian shores, so he now sent ships to several points: the *Encounter* to the mouth of the Amur, before returning to the China station; and the *Barracouta* and *Pique*, and later the *Amphitrite*, to scrutinize the north entrance to Tartar Strait and the port of Ayan. These vessels discovered that the enemy had withdrawn from Ayan, removed the guns and levelled the batteries.[86] The British destroyed a half-built Russian American Company vessel there, then left to search for the north entrance to the Amur. But heavy weather and strong currents made this impossible.

At this juncture, a squadron of British and French ships from the China Seas under the command of Commodore Charles Elliot assumed the duty of finding the Russian vessels on the Asian coast. This allowed the *Pique* and *Barracouta* to sail for Hong Kong, and the *Amphitrite* for the Northwest Coast of America. In his search for the Russian ships, Elliot was at first successful, finding them in De Castries Bay. In the belief that he would need reinforcements, he withdrew and returned with more ships only to find that the Russians had again escaped, this time into the mouth of the Amur.[87] The increasingly frustrated Lords of the Admiralty vented their disappointment on Elliot and his Commander-in-Chief.[88] Once more the Russians, as a result of their superior geographical knowledge, had made British naval commanders look foolish.

In the meantime, the Commander-in-Chief, Pacific, believed that he might find the elusive Russian vessels at Sitka, the major depot of the Russian American Company on the eastern shores of the Pacific. He sailed thence on 30 June in the flagship *President*, leaving behind the *Amphitrite* and *Trincomalee*, the latter to exchange prisoners with the Russians and to await the *Monarch*, before sailing with her to Sitka to join the *President*, *Brisk* and *Dido*. Eventually, the French vessels *Forte*,

[85]Bruce found emplacements for 72 guns. See his report to Osborne, 15 June 1855, enclosing map of defences, Y95, Adm. 1/5656.
[86]Remark Book of Capt. C. Frederick, No. 7, Adm. 172/2.
[87]Golder, *Russian Expansion*, pp. 265-66, and P. B. Whittingham, *Notes on the Late Expedition against the Russian Settlements in Eastern Siberia* (London: Longman, Brown, Green & Longmans, 1850) , pp. 94-99.
[88]See Admiralty Minutes of 9 October 1855 (S109) and 8 December 1855 (S141), Adm. 1/5657.

the flagship of Rear-Admiral Fourichon,[89] and the *Obligado, Alceste,* and *Eurydice* joined the British off Cape Edgecumbe, Krusov Island, on the west side of Sitka Sound.

The search on North American shores proved as unrewarding as that on the Asian coast, for neither in the harbour of Sitka, which was visited 13 July, nor in nearby channels and inlets, were Russian warships found.[90] With completion of their duties on the coast of Russian America, the allied ships dispersed on 17 July, after the arrival of the *Monarch* and *Trincomalee* from Petropavlovsk. The French vessels sailed for San Francisco, while the British made for Esquimalt or San Francisco.[91]

Why all the ships in the British squadron did not go directly to Vancouver Island seems clear. San Francisco, a centre of maritime interests in the Pacific, was a frequent port of call for Russian ships. It was a place to be watched for American naval and privateering activity in view of rumours of an alliance between Russia and the United States.[92] Consequently, the British and French warships periodically exchanged the duty of keeping under close surveillance Russian merchant ships, which dared not set to sea from this port for fear of capture; they also watched American shipping. Occasionally, Rear-Admiral Bruce received unsubstantiated accounts of Russian warships and American privateers at large in the Pacific. This confirmed his decision to assign allied warships to watch Sitka as well as San Francisco during the final phase of the conflict.[93]

---

[89]Fevrier-Despointes, like his unfortunate counterpart Price, died in the Pacific, but of natural causes. His successor, Fourichon, reached Petropavlovsk in the *Forte.* Bruce Journal, Adm. 50/308, 8 June 1855.

[90]*Ibid.,* 13 July 1855. See also, Capt. Voevodsky to Tsar, 18 August 1855 (O.S.) ; extract in Report of Russian American Company, 16 November 1855, *Alaska Boundary Tribunal, Counter Case of the United States. Appendix II* (Washington, 1903) , 20; and Longstaff, *Esquimalt Naval Base,* 17. No British account of the meeting with Russian officials exists.

[91]The *Brisk* to Vancouver Island, San Francisco, Mexico; the *Trincomalee,* expected from Petropavlovsk, to await the *Amphitrite* at Sitka until 20 August before sailing to Esquimalt, San Francisco, Honolulu; the *Dido* to watch the coast of Russian America and await the *Trincomalee* near Sitka, then proceed to San Francisco. Bruce Journal, Adm. 50/308, 13 July 1855.

[92]See Sir James Graham to Clarendon, 25 October 1854, in Richard W. Van Alstyne, ed., "Anglo-American Relations, 1853-1857," *American Historical Review,* XLII (Apr. 1937) , 498. Also Frank A. Golder, "Russian American Relations during the Crimean War," *ibid.,* XXX (April 1926) , 462-76, and Kenneth Bourne, *Britain and the Balance of Power in North America, 1815, 1908* (London: Longmans Green & Co., 1967) , pp. 179-83.

[93]Bruce Journal, Adm. 50/308, particularly 18 September 1855. This information came from Capt. Frederick of the *Amphitrite,* off Cape Edgecumbe, 8 August. The British Minister in Washington had reason to believe that American privateers might be operating out of Sitka. See Sir John Crampton to Clarendon, 12 March 1855, Clarendon dep., c. 43, fols. 121-22, B.L.

The Crimean War was brought to a conclusion by the Treaty of Paris, 30 March 1856. The Treaty terms were largely consistent with the recognized objects of the entry of the Allies into the war. The life of the Ottoman Empire was prolonged, and Russian aspirations in the Near East were curtailed.[94] The Treaty contained no reference to Russian expansion in the Pacific, which caused the British government to watch her former enemy with growing suspicion in the postwar period. In fact, British warships were dispatched to the Northwestern Pacific in 1857 and 1858 to investigate Russian activities and trade at the mouth of the Amur River—which China recognized in 1858 as a Russian possession. Subsequently, reports to the Admiralty indicated that the Russian presence on Asian shores was permanent.[95]

Lessons of the War

In drawing conclusions about the naval aspects of the war with Russia in the Pacific, it should be noted first, that nothing approaching a general fleet action occurred, not even a notable duel, because the Russian force was no match for the allied navies and it sought safety in waters largely unknown to the Allies. Second—on the technical side—the war witnessed the introduction on a modest scale of steam propulsion for fighting ships and the use of shell as a general ship weapon. The effectiveness of shell fire revealed itself in engagements with shore defences, and the first experiments with armour were made.[96] Third—on the human side—the debacle at Petropavlovsk, like operations in the Baltic and Black Seas, revealed the need for younger senior officers as well as for greater thoroughness in preparing for war. Fourth, as a result of exaggerating the importance of coastal operations, the Admiralty decided to construct large numbers of gunboats and shallow-draught vessels.

From the point of view of naval strategy in the Pacific, perhaps the most important lesson revealed at Petropavlovsk was the value of steam power over sail. Accordingly, the transition from sail to steam was accelerated. Sir Charles Wood, the First Lord, in comparing the British with the French Navy in 1857 remarked that in the future sailing vessels ought

---

[94]See Agatha Ramm, "The Crimean War," in *The Zenith of European Power, 1830-1870, The New Cambridge Modern History* (Cambridge: Cambridge University Press, 1967), X, 487-92.

[95]Reports by commanders of H.M.S. *Calypso* and *Havannah* are in Adm. Pac. St. Rec., R.G. 8, IIIB, vol. 34, P.A.C. See also, *Nautical Magazine*, XXVI (February 1858), 96-98.

[96]The introduction of shell spelled the end of wooden warships; see J. P. Baxter, *The Introduction of the Ironclad Warship* (Cambridge, Mass: Harvard University Press, 1933), *passim*, esp. pp. 17 and 69.

to be almost "left out of consideration."[97] In the following year, he went even further when he said: "Sailing vessels, though useful in time of peace, would never be employed again during war."[98] However, neither the current financial resources nor the engineering capacity of Britain permitted a complete and immediate turnover. Nor could sails be dispensed with entirely on the Pacific station where long voyages were common.[99]

The Crimean conflict also revealed, as Sir Julian Corbett noted generally, "how impotent [sea power] is of itself to decide a war against great continental states, how tedious is the pressure of naval action unless it be nicely coordinated with military and diplomatic pressure."[100] But there were explanations for the disappointing performance of the Royal Navy including "the inefficient condition of the fleet, its indifferent leadership, and the antiquated state of its supply organization."[101] Quick successes were impossible under these circumstances.

The outmoded system of supplying the Royal Navy was improved after the Crimean War. In the course of this conflict, as we have seen, the first concentration of British warships occurred in the North Pacific. Five warships, including the first line-of-battleship to visit the place, the *Monarch*, called at Esquimalt in 1855 for refit and refreshment. Although the value of Esquimalt became increasingly apparent during the war—particularly as a point of supply for the Pacific squadron—it was not until the British Columbia gold rush of 1858 and the Anglo-American dispute over the San Juan boundary in 1859 that the presence of British warships led to establishing a provisional and eventually permanent stores depot there.

On the other hand, as an immediate result of this war, the Navy did possess at Esquimalt the beginnings of a store establishment in three buildings known locally as "the Crimea Huts."[102] It will be recalled that in February 1855 Rear-Admiral Bruce requested Governor Douglas to build a hospital to receive casualties expected from a second attack on Petropavlovsk. But Bruce failed to give exact instructions as to what was

[97]Great Britain, *Hansard's Parliamentary Debates*, 3rd. Series, CXLV, col. 426; Brodie, *Sea Power*, p. 73.
[98]Great Britain, *Hansard's Parliamentary Debates*, 3rd. Series, CXLIX, col. 915; Brodie, *Sea Power*, p. 73.
[99]Even as late as 1893, the Constructor for the Admiralty, Sir William White, was insisting that sail power in cruisers was still a necessity. *Transactions of the Institution of Naval Architects*, Vol. XXXIV, p. 33; see also, Brodie, *Sea Power*, p. 76.
[100]Quoted in Captain S. W. Roskill, *The Strategy of Sea Power: Its Development and Application* (London: Collins, 1962), p. 91.
[101]*Ibid*.
[102]Madge Wolfenden, "Esquimalt Dockyard's First Buildings," *British Columbia Historical Quarterly*, X (July 1946), 235-40.

required, and so the Governor proceeded, through no fault of his own, to erect what he thought would be adequate structures. When the matter of reimbursement arose, the Admiralty owed nearly £1,000 to the Colony of Vancouver Island. Bruce was justifiably distressed that a "temporary" structure should cost so much, because it was no longer of use as a hospital.[103]

Bruce, an advocate of a naval base at Esquimalt, was prepared to recommend the retention of the buildings for hospital purposes if a store and provisions depot were formed there.[104] For his part, Douglas was anxious to have the hospital off his hands, and urged the Colonial Office to press the Admiralty for the amount outstanding.[105] The dispute continued into 1857 when the Admiralty paid not only the cost of the Crimea Huts but considerable interest and maintenance charges.

Thus, the Pacific squadron found itself with a shore establishment at Esquimalt, the first of its kind in the Eastern Pacific, in a curious fashion perhaps typical of the calamities and unexpected occurrences that the squadron experienced during the Crimean War. The Navy's operations were less than satisfactory in all the theatres of war. Yet allied superiority at sea contributed substantially to the final result which was the defeat of Russia.

[103]Bruce to Osborne, 14 September 1855, Y 116, Adm. 1/5656.
[104]*Ibid.*
[105]Douglas to Smith (C.O.), 10 October 1855, encl. in Smith to Sec. of Adm., 22 December 1855, *ibid.*

Chapter 6

GOLD RUSH CRISES
1850-1868

THE BRITISH EMPIRE expanded chiefly as the incidental result of activities carried on by British soldiers, sailors, traders, merchants and colonial governors rather than from conscious government policy to acquire and consolidate territory beyond Britain's shores. Except for Vancouver Island—proclaimed a Crown colony in 1849—this was certainly true of British territory on the Northwest Coast of North America at the middle of the nineteenth century. The region was a remote, fur-bearing wilderness of little interest to anyone but the Hudson's Bay Company. Settlers were few in number. Successive gold discoveries in the 1850's and 1860's, each followed by a flood of adventurous and turbulent miners, transformed this peaceful scene. Officials in Whitehall, colonial authorities in the wilderness, and naval officers on the coast were forced to protect British soil from being seized by thousands of Americans coming from California and Oregon.

During these turbulent years, the Royal Navy supported the colonial government's actions to enforce law and order, and implemented decisions of the British government designed to guard against American encroachment. The commanders-in-chief on the Pacific station and senior naval officers at Esquimalt employed such force as was required or available to protect territorial claims, uphold law and report on developments in the gold fields. In short, throughout this era, the Navy was a major instrument of British policy for colonial territory on the Northwest Coast, a region whose primary attraction had evolved from furs to settlement, and then to gold. Without naval support, local civil authorities would have been powerless.

The Queen Charlotte Islands

Early in August of the year 1850, Governor Blanshard of Vancouver Island advised his superiors in London that Indians had discovered gold on the little known Queen Charlotte Islands.[1] He also advised them that the Hudson's Bay Company planned to send an expedition to barter with the Indians for the precious metal.[2] Blanshard's successor, James Douglas—together with fellow Hudson's Bay Company officials—urged the British government in 1851 to exclude American ships from the islands. But these efforts under the guise of protecting British sovereignty were clearly designed to make the Company masters of the gold fields and keep interlopers from Company domains. The Secretary of State for War and the Colonies, Earl Grey, who was dissatisfied with the Company's efforts to colonize Vancouver Island, would not agree to extend its charter-grant to the Queen Charlotte Islands.[3]

In early 1852, Governor Douglas was alarmed by word that four vessels carrying some 550 adventurers plus their crews had sailed for Gold (Mitchell) Harbour. He believed that the history of American expansion in the previous two decades supported amply his contention that the lawless "floating population of California" would operate virtually with a free hand in the gold fields unless the authority of the Crown were strengthened by a show of British power. He thus made two requests for aid: one to the Commander-in-Chief on the Pacific Station, Rear-Admiral Fairfax Moresby;[4] the other to the Colonial Office.[5]

After the Oregon Treaty of 1846, the British government pursued policies designed to protect "British Oregon" from irregular settlement by Americans. When the governor's alarming statement reached London—pointing out that Americans intended to colonize and establish an independent government in the Queen Charlotte Islands "until by

---

[1]This gold rush and subsequent naval exploration revealed the existence of more than one island. For convenience, the term Queen Charlotte Islands will be used here.
[2]General considerations relative to the rush are given in F. W. Howay and E. O. S. Scholefield, *British Columbia, From the Earliest Times to the Present*, 4 vols. (Vancouver: S. J. Clarke, 1918), II, 1-9, and Corday McKay, Queen Charlotte Islands (Victoria, B.C.: Province of British Columbia, Department of Education, 1953), pp. 39 and 45.
[3]W. P. Morrell, *British Colonial Policy in the Age of Peel and Russell* (Oxford, 1930), p. 445.
[4]J. Douglas to Rear-Admiral Moresby, 29 January 1852, Adm. Corr. I, B.C.A.
[5]Douglas to Earl Grey, Sec. of State for the Colonies, 29 January 1852, C.O. 305/3.

force or fraud they become annexed to the United States,"—the government acted quickly.[6] Douglas was appointed Lieutenant-Governor of the islands; the Foreign Office instructed the Admiralty to have Rear-Admiral Moresby station a vessel there permanently to protect British territory against "Marauders without title"; and the British Minister in Washington was directed to ask the United States government to restrain its expansive citizens.[7] In this three-fold action, the British government showed a clear determination to check anything resembling an American filibuster. The Queen Charlotte Islands were not to fall to Manifest Destiny.

By the time Admiralty instructions reached Moresby he had already dispatched the frigate *Thetis,* 38 guns, Captain Augustus L. Kuper, from Callao to the Northwest Coast.[8] This, in fact, was an interim measure, for in response to the Governor's request for a steam vessel—of more use in the numerous bays and confined waters of the Queen Charlotte Islands than a sailing ship such as the *Thetis*—Moresby intended to send the paddle-wheel sloop *Virago,* 6 guns, Commander James C. Prevost, after her refit at Valparaiso.[9] The flagship *Portland* was also available if required for service on the Northwest Coast. And Kuper possessed instructions to request the use of the Hudson's Bay Company steamer *Beaver,* if needed.[10] The Commander-in-Chief was confident that these measures would be adequate to deal with the Americans. He was right. The *Thetis* and *Virago* sufficed to meet the emergency.

These vessels were almost the sole symbols of British authority in the Queen Charlotte Islands. Throughout the summer of 1852 Captain Kuper issued declarations of British sovereignty but he did not prohibit about a dozen American merchantmen from visiting mining districts, as Douglas wished him to do.[11] Because of the presence of the *Thetis,* of her replacement after January 1853, the *Virago,* and still later H.M.S. *Trincomalee,* 26 guns, no attempts were made to overthrow British authority.[12] The zealous Commander Prevost further deterred lawlessness by posting a notice warning Americans against selling goods or visiting the islands for mining without licence.[13] This warning was necessary only

[6]*Ibid.*
[7]Lord Malmesbury (F.O.) to Sec. of Adm., 13 May 1852, copy, Adm. Corr. I, B.C.A.
[8]Rear-Admiral Moresby to Sec. of Adm., 30 August 1852, encl. in Stafford to Merivale, 22 October 1852, A. 8/7, fol. 22, H.B.C.A.
[9]*Ibid.*
[10]*Ibid.*
[11]Douglas to A. Barclay (Sec., H.B.C.), 12 July 1852, B.226/b/6, fol. 97, H.B.C.A.
[12]In the main, reports of the quantity of gold found were highly exaggerated. Nonetheless, there were some large findings. See A. Kuper to Moresby, 20 July 1852, San Francisco, in W. Kaye Lamb, ed., "Four Letters Relating to the Cruise of the "Thetis," 1852-53," *British Columbia Historical Quarterly,* VI (July 1942), 192-99.
[13]Cdr. J. C. Prevost to Moresby, 7 June 1853, Y 73, Adm. 1/5630.

briefly as the rich output of the Queen Charlottes dwindled within a few months. Before long, the miners transferred their attentions to new Eldorados on the mainland.[14]

Fraser River Gold Strikes

In late 1857 and early 1858, news of fabulous gold strikes on the Fraser spread quickly around the world. No statements are more exaggerated than those of gold miners, as the Senior Naval Officer at Esquimalt, Captain Prevost—now in the screw-corvette *Satellite,* 22 guns—was well aware.[15] He knew that many reports from the diggings were of doubtful credibility, but he informed the Commander-in-Chief on the Pacific station, Rear-Admiral Robert Lambert Baynes, that the existence of a great abundance of gold on the Fraser River was beyond doubt.[16] To prove his point he sent a sample of gold to the Admiralty. He foresaw that lawlessness, misery and bloodshed would be the consequences of the impending mass movement of prospectors into an area that lacked all means of subsistence.[17]

The dangers inherent in an avalanche of alien miners into an unsettled area which was controlled by the Hudson's Bay Company were also abundantly clear to James Douglas both as the Governor of Vancouver Island and as an official of the Company. Douglas, who was long an opponent of American expansion in the Pacific Northwest, could see that British authority would be confronted with an American challenge based on numbers. Hence in late December 1857, he used provisional regulations to establish Crown control over mining rights in the Fraser and Thompson districts of New Caledonia, an area that he did not actually govern.[18] The promulgation of laws by a central figure appears to have been the opposite of what happened on the California mining frontier, where miners made their own laws and exacted their own justice. By asserting the power of the Crown, Douglas sought to restrain the influx of foreigners into British territory and in this, gen-

---

[14]At this time there was no warship permanently stationed on the Northwest Coast. But the Admiralty advised that it was "highly desirable" that a warship "frequently" visit Vancouver Island. R. Osborne (Adm.) to Moresby, 2 March 1852, Adm. Corr. I, B.C.A.

[15]Prevost to Rear-Admiral Baynes, 7 May 1858, encl. in Prevost to Sec. of Adm., 7 May 1858, Y108, Adm. 1/5694.

[16]*Ibid.*

[17]*Ibid.*

[18]As communications between Whitehall and many colonial governors were so slow before the advent of the telegraph, the governor was required to assume authority often in direct violation of his instructions. The Provisional Regulations of Governor Douglas, 29 December 1857, are printed in *Report of the Provincial Archives . . . 1913* (Victoria, B.C., 1914) , p. vl12.

erally, he had the support of his superiors in London.

From the outset it was his intention to stabilize the frontier. To strengthen his position, Douglas requested that the British government place a naval or military force at his disposal.[19] He then stressed to the Commander-in-Chief on the Pacific station that the only solution to the impending crisis of unrestricted entry of twenty to thirty thousand foreigners into the unpoliced gold districts lay in maintaining the governor's authority with sufficient naval force.[20] Douglas knew that the two British warships then on the coast—the *Satellite* and the screw surveying vessel *Plumper,* 12 guns,—would assist if required; but he was anxious that nothing should interfere with their survey of the disputed San Juan Archipelago for the Boundary Commission. Nevertheless, he soon had to request the *Satellite* to take up a station in the south arm of the Fraser River to enforce his Proclamation forbidding mining on the mainland by unlicensed persons.[21] This was a crafty move on the Governor's part, for there the corvette would strengthen the hand of the Chief of Customs against American vessels openly violating "the British frontier."[22]

The Navy now came to the Governor's aid in upholding civil authority in this unorganized territory. Captain Prevost, in the *Satellite,* chose to meet Douglas at Point Roberts—the nearest American encampment to the mouth of the Fraser River—as a show of British power. Next he sent a launch with a guard of six Royal Marines to aid customs authorities at Fort Langley, thirty miles up the river.[23] Finally, he positioned the *Satellite* at the mouth of the Fraser, where she remained for most of the summer. By this time it was patently clear that Prevost himself would require support, especially since the boundary in nearby waters was an issue of contention between the British and American governments.

At the conclusion of an inspection tour of the gold fields with Douglas on 7 June 1858, Prevost again advised Baynes, this time in more emphatic terms, that a naval force was necessary to maintain British rights, law and authority, and to support the Governor in his difficult position.[24] Although most miners were law-abiding, Prevost warned that this might not continue when twenty thousand persons known to be en route from San Francisco arrived. Already at Hill's Bar, a miner's profit averaged

[19]Douglas to H. Labouchère (C.O.) , 8 May 1858, C.O.60/1.
[20]Douglas to Baynes, 12 May 1858, encl. in Baynes to Sec. of Adm., 25 June 1858, Y 132, Adm. 1/5694.
[21]Douglas to Lord Stanley (Sec. of State for the Colonies) , 19 May 1858, "Papers Relative to the Affairs of British Columbia, I," *Parliamentary Papers,* 1859, XVII (Cmd. 2476) , p. 11.
[22]Douglas to Prevost, 21 May 1858, Cap P 102, Adm. 1/5696.
[23]Lt. T. S. Gooch, R.M., and 5 marines. An Indian was hired as pilot.
[24]Prevost to Baynes, 7 June 1858, *ibid.*

sixty dollars a day; when the river fell during the summer further discoveries and increased yields were likely. The bustle on the river banks
seemed to indicate that "the whole country" was "rich in gold," richer
even than California.[25] Lesser men than Prevost and Douglas might have
given up their responsibilities and joined the throng.

To reach these gold fields, two routes were common. One was from
Whatcom (Bellingham) in the adjoining Territory of Washington overland to the Fraser. Many Americans went this way to avoid licensing
officials at the British port of Victoria and in the river mouth. This trail
was hazardous. Generally speaking, adventurers "found that geographic
conditions are stronger than patriotic leanings, and a navigable river is
a better highway than a rude mountain trail."[26] For this reason many
turned back to try the easier route by sternwheeler, boat, raft or canoe up
the Fraser River as far as possible and the rest of the way on foot.

For most miners who came from California by sea, Victoria was the
half-way house, the stepping-stone to the Fraser. Overnight a tent-city
grew up around the Hudson's Bay Company post. The population rose
from 500—before the *Commodore*, the first vessel from San Francisco,
arrived with 450 miners on 25 April 1858—to some 6,000 by late July.
People arrived in swarms, in all kinds of crafts. They brought their own
money, printing presses, businesses, mining methods and squabbles. But
the mere presence of the Royal Navy in the harbours of Victoria and
Esquimalt constituted a psychological force sufficient to quell lawlessness
and disorder ashore.[27] The rush of miners and merchants into Esquimalt—the Navy's principal anchorage in the North Pacific—especially
concerned the Senior Naval Officer there. Speculation meant that the
Admiralty would be forced to purchase properties for any future naval
establishment at astronomical prices.[28]

Maintaining Order

The problems of maintaining authority at Vancouver Island were minor
in comparison to those on the banks of the Fraser. The Governor's
method of controlling the population was by issuing licences, a disagreeable matter for all concerned. In addition to paying for the costs of
administration and police, the licences enabled the government to check
on the numbers in the gold fields and established the supremacy of the

[25]*Ibid.*
[26]F. W. Howay, W. N. Sage, and H. F. Angus, *British Columbia and the United
States* (New Haven: Yale University Press, 1942), p. 147.
[27]Richard Mayne, *Four Years in British Columbia and Vancouver Island* (London:
John Murray, 1862), p. 53 and Margaret A. Ormsby, *British Columbia: A History*
(Toronto: Macmillan, 1958), p. 159.
[28]Prevost to Baynes, 7 June 1858, Cap P 102, Adm. 1/5696.

Crown from the time the miners entered the Fraser. The licences were $5 a year, without regard to the nationality of the licensee. Thus any American claims of discrimination on grounds of citizenship were unfounded.

Because the river had many entrances, the job of the Navy was difficult. Off the mouth of the south arm, officers and men of the *Satellite* boarded vessels to preserve territorial rights by issuing licences to the miners.[29] On one typical occasion a launch, cutter and gig—all well-manned and armed—halted the American sternwheeler *Surprise* and compelled miners on board to buy licences. Many American vessels, however, navigated other channels unnoticed. To minimize this practice Prevost recommended that the Governor's Proclamation be posted on all steamers carrying passengers from Victoria to the Fraser River and that all passengers sailing in those vessels should have mining licences.[30] Moreover—in order to stop evaders of the regulations—he proposed that a small vessel should be stationed below Annacis Island, where the north arm enters the main stream of the river. If this proved insufficient, a mud battery mounted on the south bank of the river would halt river boats that failed to heed warnings of British revenue agents or, as they were later called, Gold Commissioners.[31]

Other measures designed to eliminate the illegal entry of miners into the mining districts were added. The Company steamer *Otter* kept watch on the route of passenger ships between Victoria and the river mouth. Then in early August, when the river was at its lowest and the rush was at its peak, the *Plumper* joined the force in the river. To check illegal entries via the overland route from Whatcom, the *Satellite*'s launch and later the colonial government guardship *Recovery,* under Prevost's orders, were stationed at Fort Langley, some thirty miles from the river mouth. In all, four tax-collecting vessels were operating in addition to auxiliary boats enforcing regulations as miners moved up the Fraser River to the gold fields beyond Fort Hope.

While the two naval vessels were busy on the coast, the British government, in late June 1858, gave serious attention to the growing crisis on the mainland. If British authority were to be upheld, an adequate "show of force" would be required. For this reason, Rear-Admiral Baynes at Valparaiso received instructions, dated 28 June 1858, to proceed in the *Ganges,* or send a senior officer, to Vancouver Island to determine the adequacy of the naval force.[32] Apparently Baynes had no

[29]Prevost to Douglas, 28 June 1858, Adm. 1/5713.
[30]*Ibid.*
[31]*Ibid.*
[32]Admiralty instructions to Baynes, 28 June 1857, Adm. Corr. II, B.C.A.

knowledge of the degree of gold excitement when he wrote to Governor Douglas on 25 June 1858 that because of the pressing needs of the station and the shortage of vessels, only the *Satellite* and *Plumper* were available for guarding the river and Victoria. When further alarms reached London from Douglas, the Admiralty instructed Baynes in concise terms that upholding British sovereignty during the Fraser River gold rush was the most pressing duty of ships on the Pacific station and that it was essential for the Commander-in-Chief to give the Governor of Vancouver Island all the support he required.[33]

However, help for Douglas was not yet in sight. The arrival of the corvette *Calypso,* 18 guns, Captain Frederick Montresor, at Esquimalt in mid-August left Baynes unable to meet Douglas's plea for more warships.[34] The *Calypso* lacked steam-power; she was thus useless for service in the intricate mouth of the Fraser.[35]

When Douglas asked Montresor to send a marine detachment in support of his intended excursion to the gold fields, Montresor was still unable to help. His instructions did not give him discretionary powers; Montresor felt compelled to leave Esquimalt on 25 August having completed his mission of supplying the *Satellie* and *Plumper.* The *Calypso's* orders left little leeway. She was required to reach Hawaii by early October, remain there during the period the whaling vessels called and keep watch that Mormons rumoured to be coming from Utah did not try to seize Hawaii.[36] The Governor's appeal to Montresor was not unanswered, however; Captain Prevost of the *Satellite* was able to send a substitute force instead.

Prevost correctly predicted a mass inrush from California. Up to 15 June 1858, more than ten thousand adventurers started out from San

---

[33]On this matter, see Baynes to Sec. of Adm., 25 June, 1858, Y 132, Adm. 1/5694. See also, W. G. Romaine (Adm.) to Baynes, 16 August 1858, "Papers relative to the Affairs of British Columbia, I," p. 52, and related correspondence.

[34]By the time Douglas's alarm of 1 July 1858 (C.O. 60/1) reached London, the Admiralty had already informed the Colonial Office of the intended visit of Baynes to Vancouver Island. Minute of N. Irving, 10 October 1858, *ibid.*

[35]The fact that the *Calypso* lacked auxiliary power could have had two effects: (1) she might be compelled to lie farther out from the river entrance than a steam ship, and (2) the size of landing parties might be small because of the need to retain sufficient hands to man the sails in an emergency. Some of the difficulties of entering the river at this time were described by Captain George H. Richards in *Vancouver Island Pilot, Part 1* (1st ed., London: Hydrographic Office, Admiralty, 1861), pp. 97-101.

[36]Baynes to Sec. of Adm., 26 June 1858, Y 135, and Baynes to Sec. of Adm., 22 July 1858, Y 156; both in Adm. 1/5694.

Francisco.[37] During the six-week period ending 1 July, for example, some nineteen steamers, nine sailing vessels, and fourteen deck-boats carried six thousand hopeful argonauts into British territory.[38] Moreover, the "tide of immigration" continued to roll on with no promise of ending,[39] which led one contemporary to remark, "Never, perhaps, was there so large an immigration in so short a space of time into so small a place."[40] Small wonder that Douglas and Prevost feared lawlessness in the face of this overwhelming migration of toughened diggers.

Under these pressures, Prevost abandoned the boundary survey to give full attention to safeguarding British interests on the mainland. In late August, he sent a bodyguard for the Governor during the latter's investigation of the mining camps. But he was handicapped by desertions. The *Satellite* had a complement of 260 men. By the end of August 1858, at least twenty men had fled to the gold fields and thirty were patrolling the river mouth in small vessels.[41] Therefore, he was able to supply a force only of sufficient size to afford the Governor security on his second mission to the Fraser. This contingent consisted of Lieutenant Howard S. Jones, R.M., twenty marines with Lieutenant-Colonel J. S. Hawkins, R.E., and fifteen sappers and miners.[42] By the time they reached Fort Hope, the dispute between some miners and incensed Indians had been settled.[43]

The fracas revealed that a large number of regular military rather than naval troops should be stationed in the region for the preservation of life, order and British prestige.[44] On 26 September 1858, Douglas and

---

[37]Douglas to Stanley, 1 July 1858, C.O. 60/1. According to the report in the *Nautical Magazine*, XXVII (December 1858), p. 687: "Some idea of the extent of the trade and travel created by the Fraser River mania, may be gathered from the fact that in the 'Alta California' of July 14th, besides the six large steamships running into Puget Sound, there were advertised, six clipper ships, (including one of 2,200 tons,) three barques, five brigs, and seven schooners—in all twenty-seven vessels on the berth." See also, E. W. Wright, ed., *Lewis and Dryden's Marine History of the Pacific North-West* (Portland, Ore.: Lewis and Dryden Printing Co., 1895), p. 69.
[38]Douglas to Stanley, 1 July 1858, C.O. 60/1.
[39]*Ibid.*
[40]Alfred Waddington, *The Fraser Mines Vindicated* (Victoria, V.I.: Printed by P. de Garro, 1858), pp. 16-17; quoted in Walter N. Sage, *Sir James Douglas and British Columbia* (Toronto: University of Toronto Press, 1930), p. 204.
[41]Prevost to Douglas, 26 August 1858, Cap P 141, Adm., 1/5696.
[42]The 65-man detachment of Royal Engineers had arrived in H.M.S. *Havannah*, 18 guns, Captain Thomas Harvey, on 12 July 1858. They were originally sent from England via Panama for Boundary Commission duty. The *Plumper* carried them to the Fraser.
[43]Douglas to Sir E. Bulwer Lytton, Sec. of State for the Colonies, 29 September 1858, C.O. 60/1; Douglas to Lytton, 12 October 1858, encl. in H. Merivale to Sec. of Adm., 26 January 1859, Adm. 1/5621. Sage, *Sir James Douglas*, p. 227.
[44]Prevost to Baynes, 31 August 1858, Cap P 141, Adm. 1/5696.

his marine guard, now two less because of desertions, returned to Victoria.

But this was not the last naval sortie into a wilderness which naval officers justifiably contended was becoming more and more the responsibility of the War Office. As already mentioned, the *Satellite* and *Plumper* were under instructions since early July to maintain order among "adventurers resorting to the gold fields."[45] If the need arose, Governor Douglas planned to make further calls on the Royal Navy to reinforce his declared policy that "all claims and interests" would be "rendered subordinate to the great object of peopling and opening up the new country, and consolidating it as an integral part of the British Empire."[46]

Meanwhile, the Admiralty ordered reinforcements for the Pacific station to meet the emergency. Initially, Sir John Pakington, the First Lord, ordered the sending of the *Argus,* a paddle-wheel sloop of six guns. But at the insistence of Sir Edward Bulwer Lytton, the Secretary of State for the Colonies, he was forced to dispatch a larger vessel, a steam-frigate. Pakington firmly believed that Baynes would reach Vancouver Island before *"any* fresh ship" could do so, but he succumbed to Lytton's pressure and sent Captain Geoffrey Phipps Hornby from London across Asia to Hong Kong to assume command of the screw-frigate *Tribune,* 31 guns.[47] Pakington also issued instructions that the Commander-in-Chief on the China and East Indies station was to dispatch the *Tribune* to Esquimalt "with as many supernumerary Marines as she can carry and he can spare."[48] The corvettes, the *Pylades,* 21 guns, and the *Amethyst,* 26 guns, were to follow as soon as their services in the Far East were no longer required.

Transferring these ships from China waters to the Northwest Coast constituted the quickest method of reinforcement that the Admiralty could adopt.[49] But in these days before the advent of the telegraph and fast cruisers, sending orders across Asia to dispatch ships across four thousand miles of the North Pacific was a matter of three or four months. Another mode of reinforcement took even longer. The two gunboats *Forward* and *Grappler,* specially fitted out for service in the new colony of British Columbia, sailed from England in August 1859 escorted by the

45Douglas to Lytton, 29 September 1858, C.O. 60/1. Douglas was obliged to Prevost and Richards for their "cordial and unflinching support in every emergency."
46*Ibid.* Lytton shared these views. See his Minute No. 2 to Douglas, n.d., and the resulting Lytton to Douglas, 16 October 1858, *ibid.*
47Sir J. Pakington to Vice-Admiral Martin, 24 August 1858, Martin Papers, Add. MSS. 41,409, fols. 45-48, B.M.
48*Ibid.*
49This was the opinion of Sir John Pakington, First Lord of the Admiralty, as reported in Lytton to Douglas, 16 October 1858, draft, C.O. 60/1.

screw-frigate *Termagant,* 25 guns; they did not reach Esquimalt until 12 July 1860, almost a year later.[50] Thus while Douglas's requisitions continued to reach Whitehall, the Secretary of State for the Colonies could only issue reassuring reports to the anxious Governor that more ships were on their way.[51]

Of the many warships dispatched, the first to come to the support of Prevost and Douglas was the flagship *Ganges,* 84 guns, with Rear-Admiral Baynes on board.[52] Baynes had intended to sail from Callao in the paddle-wheel sloop *Vixen,* 6 guns, a more useful vessel under the circumstances than the line-of-battle ship *Ganges,* but a defect in her hull prevented her use. Upon arrival at Esquimalt on 17 October 1858, Baynes immediately offered his cooperation to the delighted Douglas. The fact that Admiralty instructions to Baynes emphasized the great importance of securing the newly-established colony of British Columbia—that "no part of his station was more important than B.C."—reveals the British government's anxiety for their endangered territory.[53] Douglas was understandably pleased that more resources for maintaining law and order were now at his disposal.

Ironically, by the time Baynes and the *Ganges* reached the Strait of Juan de Fuca, the miners had begun their exodus to California. They preferred the more comfortable climate of San Francisco to a bleak winter in flimsy tents on the Fraser's frozen banks. The miners were followed by merchants who left their makeshift shanties in Victoria as business declined.[54] This development prompted Baynes to report to the Admiralty that although he had been sent to the scene as a result of pressures exerted on the British government by the Governor of Vancouver Island, everything was now peaceful.[55] Indeed, the gold rush continued to decline.

Creation of British Columbia as a Colony

At the same time that the Admiralty dispatched additional ships and men to the Northwest Coast, the Colonial Office and Parliament consolidated the British hold on New Caledonia—that vast area west of the Rockies which Queen Victoria significantly now named "British Colum-

---

[50]These economical and useful gunboats were ordered by the Admiralty on 13 February 1859. Minute of A. Blackwood (Adm.) , 17 June 1859, C.O. 60/6.

[51]Douglas to Stanley, 27 August 1858, and Lytton (who had replaced Stanley in May 1858) to Douglas, 16 October 1858, draft, C.O. 60/1.

[52]Baynes to Sec. of Adm., 20 October 1858, Adm. 1/5713.

[53]Quoted in Minute No. 1, Lytton to Douglas, n.d. (early October 1858) , and Minute No. 2, Lytton to Douglas, n.d. (probably 14 October 1858) , C.O. 60/1.

[54]Prevost to Baynes, 11 October 1858, Cap P 163, Adm. 1/5696.

[55]Baynes to Sec. of Adm., 16 November 1858, copy, C.O. 60/5.

bia." By an Act of Parliament, dated 2 August 1858, the colony on the Pacific came into being.[56] Lytton as Secretary of State for the Colonies thought it would be strange indeed if the Imperial government were obliged to contribute to the upkeep of the colony, "which has been actually forced into existence through the sample supplies of gold afforded by the country it occupies."[57] British Columbia, he believed, was unique in the Empire: in its gold, it yielded an immediate source of prosperity which many of the early colonial settlements lacked.[58] He was adamant therefore that the colony should pay its own way, for the free-trade principle on which mid-Victorian Imperial policy was based left scant room for additional levies on the British taxpayer. But the Mother Country was to continue to contribute the "protection of her navy, and in time of emergency, of her troops."[59] The action of Parliament creating the colony took the control of British Columbia out of Hudson's Bay Company hands immediately, as Lytton intended; Douglas was appointed Governor providing he sever his company connections. The gold rush thus led to creating a new colony in which British free-trade practices would have further scope.

The first governor of Britain's newest colony was installed in office at Fort Langley, a place chosen as the seat of government because of its strategic position on the lower Fraser between the sea and the gold region. Douglas proceeded to Fort Langley via Point Roberts in the *Satellite*, which the Commander-in-Chief provided so that His Excellency could disembark near the river mouth with "the customary honors, salutes, etc." Baynes believed this display would be beneficial to the Governor's authority in the infant colony.[60] The Governor, accompanied by Rear-Admiral Baynes and both civic officials and naval officers, transferred to the *Otter* at Point Roberts for passage to Fort Langley. There Douglas assumed the office of Governor of British Columbia, 19 November 1858.[61] This was a crowning moment for him. But he remained concerned about the problem of adequate naval and military power to enforce his government.

The matter of sufficient force to meet the expected rush during the spring of 1859 arose before the departure of the *Ganges* for duties on other parts of the station. On 22 December 1858 Baynes informed Douglas of his reluctance to leave Esquimalt unless he were assured first,

[56]An Act to Provide for the Government of British Columbia, 21 and 22 *Vic.*, c. 99.
[57]Quoted in A. S. Morton, *History of the Canadian West to 1870-71* (London: T. Nelson and Sons, [1939]) , p. 772.
[58]*Ibid.*, p. 773.
[59]*Ibid.*
[60]Baynes to Sec. of Adm., 16 November 1858, copy, C.O. 60/5.
[61]See Ormsby, *British Columbia*, p. 162, and Sage, *Sir James Douglas*, pp. 232-34.

that the Governor did not fear an outbreak of violence; second, that Douglas believed the *Satellite* and the *Plumper,* which were at his disposal, were sufficient to meet any emergency and third, that he did not consider the Admiral's presence necessary for "the preservation of that good order" that Douglas had "so happily established in both colonies."[62] Obviously Baynes did not wish to be chastened by the Admiralty a second time for ignoring British interests on the Northwest Coast. Initially Douglas thought that the *Tribune* and *Pylades,* expected from China, would be adequate for assisting the colonial government. But Baynes disagreed, claiming that even more warships should be on hand during the spring when a great influx of gold-seekers would arrive.[63] He himself promised to return in the *Ganges* when circumstances permitted; and he was clearly willing to provide additional ships should conditions warrant. As a result of Baynes's advice, Douglas recognized the importance of having a "respectable" naval force to face the large immigration expected in the spring.[64]

In January 1859, an incident occurred at Hill's Bar, a camp on the Fraser's icy banks near Yale where rowdy California miners had chosen to winter. Douglas received reports that the notorious vagabond Ned McGowan had broken prison at Yale and was conspiring to overthrow British authority. Quickly he called on the Senior Naval Officer at Esquimalt for support. Prevost then sent the *Plumper* to the lower Fraser River with all the marines and seamen available from the *Satellite*—a total of forty-seven men together with a 12-pounder (Light) Brass Howitzer field-piece.[65]

For other than shallow-draught stern-wheelers, navigation of the Fraser in winter was next to impossible and the *Plumper* could not move farther up the river than Langley, just below MacMillan Island.[66] From there her commander, Captain George H. Richards—an important figure in the maritime history of British Columbia in his own right—was forced to dispatch Lieutenant Richard Mayne by canoe to communicate

[62]Baynes to Douglas, 7 December 1858, "Papers relative to the Affairs of British Columbia, II, "*Parliamentary Papers,* 1859 (Session II), XXII (Cmd. 2578), p. 49.
[63]Baynes to Douglas, 14 December 1858, Ships' letters, F 1212a, B.C.A.
[64]Douglas to Lytton, 27 December 1858, "Papers relative to the Affairs of British Columbia, II," p. 47.
[65]Prevost to Baynes, 10 January 1859, copy, C.O. 60/5. When the Admiralty received a copy of this letter, they advised the Colonial Office that a *military,* not a *naval,* force should aid the civil power because the use of seamen and marines on shore made Her Majesty's ships "inefficient for the general Service of the Station." H. Corry to Merivale, 21 March 1859, *ibid.*
[66]C. Brew (Inspector of Police) to Douglas, 12 January 1859, in F. W. Howay, ed., *The Early History of the Fraser River Mines,* British Columbia Archives Memoir, No. 3 (Victoria, B.C., 1926), p. 68 and notes.

with officials at Fort Yale.[67] Because of the transportation problems of the expedition Mayne's objective was to find the acting Lieutenant-Governor, Colonel Richard C. Moody, R.E., and explain that reinforcements would have to wait in the *Plumper* until the stern-wheeler *Enterprise* returned to Fort Langley to convey the force to the critical area.[68] Shortly after the two men met, Moody anxiously directed Mayne to carry secret instructions to Fort Hope, twenty miles downstream, to order up twenty-five Royal Engineers. Next, Mayne continued sixty-five miles downstream in the *Enterprise* to bring up the force waiting in the *Plumper* at Fort Langley.[69] Then the stern-wheeler returned to the head of navigation bearing twenty-one small-arms men and seven marines from the *Plumper*, plus the marines and field-piece party from the *Satellite*—seventy-seven men in all.[70] When he reached Hope, Mayne found instructions from Colonel Moody to advance with the seven marines and to leave the blue-jackets at Hope. Ironically, by the time the force arrived at Yale, the situation was under control; McGowan and other desperados had been arrested by the local constabulary.

The "Ned McGowan War" was a true farce, but the resolute manner in which the threat was faced and extinguished showed that Douglas would not tolerate lawlessness in the new colony. Timely supporting action by the Navy brought about full restoration of order and patently demonstrated the Douglas rule that "laws cannot be disregarded with impunity, & that while the intention exists to maintain them, the power to carry out that intention is not wanting."[71]

By mid-February 1859, the *Tribune* and *Pylades* finally reached Esquimalt from the Far East, and the *Satellite* and *Plumper* could now resume their duties with the Boundary Commission.[72] Although the *Tribune*

---

[67]Richards was outstanding as a surveyor. He completed 36 principal charts of the Northwest Coast and compiled the *Vancouver Island Pilot* during his service in the North Pacific, 1856-1864. When Richards returned to England to succeed Admiral Washington as Admiralty Hydrographer in 1864, Assistant Surveyor Daniel Pender was left in charge of the survey of the North Coast, which he largely completed in the hired vessel *Beaver*. G. H. Richards to Prevost, 12 January 1859, copy, C.O. 60/5.

[68]The *Plumper* had gone farther up the river than most had expected. See Dorothy Blakey Smith, ed., "The Journal of Arthur Thomas Bushby, 1858-1859," *British Columbia Historical Quarterly*, XXI (January-October, 1957-1958), 126-27.

[69]Merivale to Sec. of Adm., 11 April 1859, Adm. 1/5721; Prevost to Baynes, 29 January 1859, C.O. 60/5; and Mayne, *Four Years in British Columbia*, pp. 66-73.

[70]Log of H.M.S. *Plumper*, 17 January 1859, Adm. 53/6854.

[71]Prevost to Baynes, 10 January 1859, copy, C.O. 60/5.

[72]The *Tribune* arrived from Hong Kong 13 February 1858; the *Pylades* from Singapore three days later. Baynes to Sec. of Adm., 30 April 1859, Y 84, Adm. 1/5713. See Mrs. Fred (Mary Augusta) Egerton, *Admiral of the Fleet Sir Geoffrey Phipps Hornby, G.C.B., A Biography* (Edinburgh: Wm. Blackwood and Sons, 1896), pp. 55-61, and Commander Francis M. Norman, *"Martello Tower" in China and the Pacific in H.M.S. "Tribune," 1856-60* (London: George Allen, 1902), pp. 229, 246.

and *Pylades* came from the China and East Indies station to strengthen the hand of the Royal Navy during the Fraser River gold rush, their presence on the Northwest Coast actually proved to be more advantageous during the San Juan crisis of July and August 1859.[73]

The *Tribune* brought 164 supernumerary Royal Marines from China to aid the civil power in British Columbia.[74] Of these, 139 officers and men were employed clearing the site of the new colonial capital, New Westminster. Douglas thought these men would receive double pay and a free grant of land after six years' service. Previously the ships' companies of the *Satellite* and *Plumper* received three months' double pay, and Douglas assumed that the new men would receive double pay as well. Baynes and the Admiralty opposed this, however, even though it could prevent desertions to the gold fields, for they feared that it would set a precedent for all ships visiting the new colony.[75] Much to Douglas's embarrassment, double pay was not awarded. On the recommendation of the Colonial and War Offices, the Admiralty ordered the marines—in short supply in other parts of the Empire—to withdraw from work which had little to do with protecting British interests.[76]

The spring of 1859 failed to bring the great swarm of prospectors expected by civil and naval authorities.[77] Doubtless, gold yields were insufficient to attract miners, but perhaps also the restrictive practices of the Governor—as enforced by the Gold Commissioners and supported by the Navy and the military forces—proved too stifling. The British adventurer Radcliffe Quine, for example, claimed that fifteen thousand persons "left for a freer and better government."[78] Admittedly, this first period of British Columbia's colonial history was not marked by democratic government. But in view of the transplanted American population numbering in the thousands, the autocratic power exercised by Governor Douglas in 1858 and 1859 proved wise. He was supported by the "hanging judge," Matthew Begbie, who was said to have "trained an unruly public into habitual reverence for the law."[79]

[73]See chapter 7.
[74]Baynes to Sec. of Adm., 30 April 1859, Y 84, Adm. 1/5713; Baynes to Sec. of Adm., 9 September 1860, Y 169, Adm. I/5736; Vice-Admiral Seymour to Sec. of Adm., 27 November 1858, extract, C.O. 60/5; and Willard E. Ireland, "Pre-Confederation Defence Problems of the Pacific Colonies," *Canadian Historical Association Annual Report, 1941* (Toronto, 1941), p. 48.
[75]Baynes to Sec. of Adm., 20 October and 9 November 1858, and Admiralty Minutes thereon, Adm. 1/5713.
[76]Irving to Under-Secretary of State, War Office, 3 October 1859, C.O. 60/5; Lugard (W.O.) to Merivale, 16 June 1859, minute of Blackwood, 17 June 1859, and H. Corry to Under-Secretary, War Office, 9 June 1859, C.O. 60/6.
[77]M. de Courcy to Baynes, 24 February 1859, copy, C.O. 60/5.
[78]R. Quine to his brother and sister, 22 April 1861, Manx Museum, Isle of Man; transcripts in London School of Economics Library.
[79]Morton, *History of the Canadian West*, p. 774.

The majority of miners returned to the Mother Lode country of California; others were drawn from the Fraser by reports of new findings in Idaho and Montana. But the remote British territory on the North Pacific still continued to attract some gold-seekers and in August 1859, for the second time in the decade, the Queen Charlotte Islands became a centre of attention. Again, Douglas requested that a British warship visit the mining camp of a prospecting expedition,[80] all the while hoping that the *Forward* and *Grappler,* the two gunboats sent specifically to aid the colonial government, would soon reach Vancouver Island and be available for service.[81] Actually, the *Pylades* was at hand to assist the Governor, but there was no need for this vessel to go to the islands because the miners returned to Victoria empty-handed and sooner than expected.[82]

Gold-seekers were disappointed in the Cariboo Country, where large nuggets were unearthed in the summer of 1860. Among those who hurried into the upper reaches of the Fraser, especially along the Quesnel, were sailors from Her Majesty's ships at Esquimalt and marines from the guard at San Juan Island. They left their posts for what they thought would be more lucrative occupation. Hopes of higher wages and of striking it rich certainly added to the seamen's innate desire for a change, which Nelson said would induce them to desert from heaven to hell.[83]

Events in the Stikine Territory

Subsequent discoveries of gold in the far northern Stikine region during the years 1861 and 1862 involved the Navy directly. Access to the gold fields was mainly by the Stikine River which coursed through the Russian-American panhandle at about 57° North.[84] But both Russian and British officials on the coast remained confused as to the terms of the 1825 Anglo-Russian convention which, in fact, allowed British subjects free navigation through the Russian-American panhandle to the British hinterland.[85]

---

[80]Report of Douglas on the State of the Colony, 23 August 1859, C.O. 60/5.
[81]See note 50 of this chapter.
[82]Baynes to Sec. of Adm., 13 September 1859, Adm. 1/5713.
[83]Rear-Admiral Sir T. Maitland to Sec. of Adm., 24 May 1861, Y 164, Adm. 1/5761. The British merchantman *New Briton* in Esquimalt lost all her crew to the Cariboo gold fields. Maitland to Sec. of Adm., 30 September 1861, Y 292, *ibid.* Rear-Admiral P. W. Brock, Dossier of H.M.S. *President*, p. 19, M.M.B.C.
[84]Territorial and trading matters are considered in John S. Galbraith, *The Hudson's Bay Company as an Imperial Factor, 1821-1869,* (Berkeley and Los Angeles: University of Californifla Press, 1957) , pp. 169-74; and in C. Ian Jackson, "The Stikine Territory Lease and Its Relevance to the Alaska Purchase," *Pacific Historical Review,* XXXVI (August 1967) , 289-306, and "A Territory of Little Value: The Wind of Change on the Northwest Coast, 1861-67," *The Beaver,* Outfit 298 (Summer 1967) , pp. 40-45.
[85]See Maitland to Sec. of Adm., 12 July 1862, Y 124, Adm. 1/5790. Copies of this and other reports relative to the Stikine Rush are in R.G. 8, IIIB, Vol. 34, P.A.C.

In order to prevent any misunderstanding with Russia concerning British rights to navigate the Stikine to the British hinterland, the Commander-in-Chief, Rear-Admiral Sir Thomas Maitland, dispatched the paddle-wheel sloop *Devastation*, 6 guns, Commander John W. Pike, to Sitka so that her captain could discuss the matter with Russian authorities.[86] Pike found the Governor of the Russian American Company grateful for the concern shown by the Royal Navy.[87] Evidently the Russians planned to station at least one vessel at the mouth of the river to supply food and clothing at "moderate" prices to distressed miners as they retreated from the gold fields with the beginning of winter.[88]

The *Devastation* then steamed from Sitka to the mouth of the Stikine River where Pike received requests from numerous persons for protection. At one settlement, Port Highfield, he found that Europeans were saved from outraged Indians by reports that a British warship would "surely visit Stikeen during the season."[89] When the Russian American Company steamer *Alexander* arrived with provisions and clothing for the destitute miners, Pike, who was uncertain of British rights of navigation in the Stikine Territory, relinquished control over the Indians to the Russian naval officer in command of the *Alexander*. Then the *Devastation* sailed for Vancouver Island carrying forty-four refugees from a wilderness soon to be transferred to the administration of the Governor of British Columbia.[90]

By 1863, this new maritime frontier was included within the boundaries of British Columbia. For the Navy, the most important consequence of the Stikine rush was that it increased by seven hundred miles the extent of coast to be protected by the Royal Navy and necessitated the presence of yet another vessel in the waters of Britain's Northwest Coast.[91] This vessel was the screw-sloop *Cameleon*, 17 guns, Commander Edward Hardinge, sent by Rear-Admiral Maitland in the spring of 1863

[86]Maitland to Sec. of Adm., 12 July 1862, Y 214, Adm. 1/5790.

[87]J. Pike to Maitland, 6 October 1862, encl. in Maitland to Sec. of Adm., 2 December 1862, Y 306, *ibid*.

[88]J. Furuhjelm (Governor of Russian Colonies in America) to Maitland, 25/6 September 1862, R.G. 8, IIIB, Vol. 34, P.A.C.

[89]James Cooper (Harbour Master, B.C.) to Colonial Sec., 17 October 1862, in Ships' letters, F 1210, 3, B.C.A.

[90]Order-in-Council, 19 July 1862; Howay and Scholefield, *British Columbia*, II, 84. By July 1863, the greater part of the Stikine Territory was included in British Columbia.

[91]Maitland to Sec. of Adm., 3 September 1862, Y 246, Adm. 1/5790. Herein Maitland also explained that he had suggested to the Governor that proclamations be issued warning British subjects against travelling in canoes from Victoria to the Stikine River unless accompanied by armed coasting vessels or steamers. While the *Devastation* patrolled the North Coast, the paddle-sloop *Hecate*, Captain George Henry Richards, was to survey the northern part of Vancouver Island and "keep the Indians in awe." The *Grappler* and *Forward* guarded Nanaimo and Victoria.

to protect British subjects expected on the North Coast during the mining season.[92] Here, as in the Queen Charlotte Islands and Fraser River gold rush, the Royal Navy was the instrument of British authority.

Use of Naval Personnel Inland

During the 1850's and 1860's, officials utilized naval personnel at inland points as well as on the coast. The Fraser River gold rush revealed the necessity of this. This was in fact, an issue not confined to this period or to the Pacific station. It became a lively issue in 1867 and 1868 when a dispute arose over the use of sailors on shore at a distance from their ships. At Grouse Creek in the Cariboo, the presence of Governor Frederick Seymour—the successor to Douglas—and two naval captains was sufficient to halt a quarrel between rival gold-mining companies. But no sooner did the party leave the district than the wrangle began again.

The Governor then asked the Commander-in-Chief, Rear-Admiral the Honourable George F. Hastings, what aid would be available in the event of a rebellion, explaining that he doubted "whether Her Majesty's Possessions on this Coast are to expect more than the moral support of Her Majesty's Forces in case of difficulty, internal trouble and possible rebellion. Such I believe is not the case on the other side of the Rocky Mountains."[93] Seymour seemed to ignore the fact that seamen might have to be dispatched some seven hundred miles inland, which was contrary to Admiralty instructions that officers and men were not to be employed at a distance from their ships. Thus Hastings rightly could promise cooperation only if vessels or their boats could be deployed.[94]

The need for a force never arose, but the issue reached London. On the one hand, the Secretary of State for the Colonies, the Duke of Buckingham and Chandos, held that in "event of riot threatening life and property" available forces should be sent, providing the safety of the ships could be maintained.[95] On the other hand, the Lords of the Admiralty—who had the final say in this case—were willing to supply what they termed "local aid." They would not sanction sending officers and men at a distance from their vessels for fear of "rendering the ships inefficient."[96] This was a stern defence of the Pacific station standing

[92]Maitland to Sec. of Adm., 7 February 1863, Y 30, Adm. 1/5826.
[93]Governor Seymour to Rear-Admiral Honourable G. F. Hastings, 29 August 1867, encl. in F. Rogers (C.O.) to Sec. of Adm., 11 November 1867, Adm. 1/6026.
[94]These were defined in Admiralty instructions to Rear-Admiral J. Denman, 16 July 1864, copy, C.O. 60/30.
[95]Rogers to Sec. of Adm., 19 December 1867, Adm. 1/6026.
[96]Minute of Blackwood, 31 December 1867, *ibid.* The Admiralty informed the Colonial Office that the Commander-in-Chief, Pacific, was correct. See Lennox to Elliot, 28 October 1867, Y 12, Adm. 1/6056.

order of 1865 that stipulated that the Navy would act where ships could sail.[97]

The Navy was an effective instrument of Britain's policy for upholding British sovereignty on the Northwest Coast during the turbulent gold-rush years in the Queen Charlotte Islands, lower Fraser River country and the Stikine territory. During each successive rush of adventurers into these three unorganized frontiers, British warships were on hand to enforce law and order.

Undoubtedly, Governor Douglas played a significant role during these years. His importance should neither be ignored, nor should it be over-estimated. Without the various means at his disposal to enforce the authority of the Crown—for example, the Royal Engineers, the Gold Commissioners, a very stern judge, and the men and ships of the Royal Navy—he would have been virtually powerless and without doubt historians would have given him considerably less attention.[98] Douglas was resourceful, but essentially it was the assistance that the Imperial government was able to provide that proved decisive in maintaining British presence on the Northwest Coast during the gold-rush years. In particular, the Navy reached the scene of each crisis before the establishment of colonial jurisdiction in that region.[99] In each case, the Commander-in-Chief or the captains of warships took action that strengthened British control over territories which became integral parts of what was known after 1866 as the Crown Colony of British Columbia.

[97]*General Orders for Her Majesty's Squadron on the Pacific Station, 1865* (printed Valparaiso 1865) , p. 13; copy in Adm. 13/184/13.
[98]See, for example, Morton, *History of the Canadian West.* p. 787. Also the somewhat less laudatory view by Walter N. Sage, "The Gold Colony of British Columbia," *Canadian Historical Review,* II (1921) , 340-59.
[99]The development of colonial jurisdiction on the Northwest Coast has been eluci-dated by Willard E. Ireland in "The Evolution of the Boundaries of British Colum-bia," *British Columbia Historical Quarterly,* III (October 1939) , 263-82.

Chapter 7

DISPUTE OVER THE SAN JUAN ISLANDS
1854-1872

SAN JUAN ISLAND, which dominates the channel between the southern tip of Vancouver Island and the mainland, lay on the route of the adventurers bound from Victoria to the Fraser River gold fields. As the surgeon of the British warship *Plumper* wrote in October 1859, it was "the *Military Key* to *British Columbia*." He noted somewhat acidly that while the British were "*diplomatizing*, the Yankees landed 600 soldiers & took possession of it: had the councils of Govr. Douglas prevailed we should have turned them out of it for we have enough force here just now to have eaten them."[1]

Evidently, San Juan was strategically important to the British.[2] Furthermore, the Royal Navy predominated in nearby waters. One wonders now—as the angry inhabitants of Victoria did then—why forces were not embarked from British warships to oust the Americans? The answer is that British policy in the mid-Victorian years was characterized by restraint. Britain was secure at home and abroad. She sought no self-

[1]Charles Wood to Alfred Martin, 31 October 1859, EB W851, B.C.A.
[2]Another British naval officer thought the Island only important for its strategic value; Richard C. Mayne, *Four Years in British Columbia and Vancouver Island* (London: John Murray, 1862) , p. 42. Some even have referred to it as the "Cronstadt of the Pacific" as in note 3 of this chapter.

aggrandizement. Naval commanders on foreign stations during this period frequently served as interpreters of the policy of "minimum intervention." They had to decide how and when to employ force in guarding British commercial and territorial interests. Sometimes, as in the San Juan crisis, British citizens at the scene of contention considered these officers overly cautious. But their actions conformed to their government's foreign policy. No officer dared to intervene where powerful nations had claims to the same territory unless British rights were in grave danger; if he did so without cause, he would face the censorship of Parliament, the Foreign Office, the Admiralty and the British public.

In the San Juan crisis, it is to the credit of Rear-Admiral Robert Lambert Baynes and Captain Geoffrey Phipps Hornby that their sound judgement and patience prevailed, and that an Anglo-American war was averted. The same cannot be said either of Brigadier-General W. S. Harney, the Commander-in-Chief of the United States Army in the Oregon Territory, or of James Douglas, the Governor of Vancouver Island and British Columbia. Douglas advocated strongly that the American filibuster contrived by Harney should be met with a like measure, a tactic which would have brought a clash of arms. Fortunately, no local incident occurred that was explosive enough to embroil Britain and the United States in a war over a few islands of little value.[3]

Background to the Dispute

The dispute over San Juan Island's sovereignty arose from a vague definition of the boundary separating Vancouver Island from the mainland, as specified in the hastily formulated Oregon Treaty of 1846. That agreement called for a demarcation between territories of Britain and the United States west of the Rocky Mountains along "the forty-ninth parallel of north latitude to the middle of the channel which separates the continent from Vancouver's Island; and thence southerly through the middle of the said channel, and of Fuca's Straits to the Pacific Ocean. . . ." There was no difficulty in determining the land boundary: but what constituted "the middle of the channel?"

[3]The best accounts of the dispute are James O. McCabe, *The San Juan Water Boundary Question* (Toronto: University of Toronto Press, 1964); Keith A. Murray, *The Pig War* (Tacoma: Washington State Historical Society, 1968); and Hunter Miller, *San Juan Archipelago* (Bellows Falls, Vt.: Printed at the Wyndham Press, 1943). See also Vol. VIII, Hunter Miller's *Treaties and Other International Acts of the United States of America*, 8 vols. (Washington, D.C.: U.S. Gov't. Printing Office, 1931-1948). Of lesser value are Viscount Milton, *History of the San Juan Boundary Question* (London: Cassell, Petter and Galpin, 1869); John W. Long, Jr., "The Origin and Development of the San Juan Island Boundary Controversy," *Pacific Northwest Quarterly*, XLIII (1952), 187-213; and Archie W. Shiels, *San Juan Islands; the Cronstadt of the Pacific* (Juneau: Empire Printing Co., 1938).

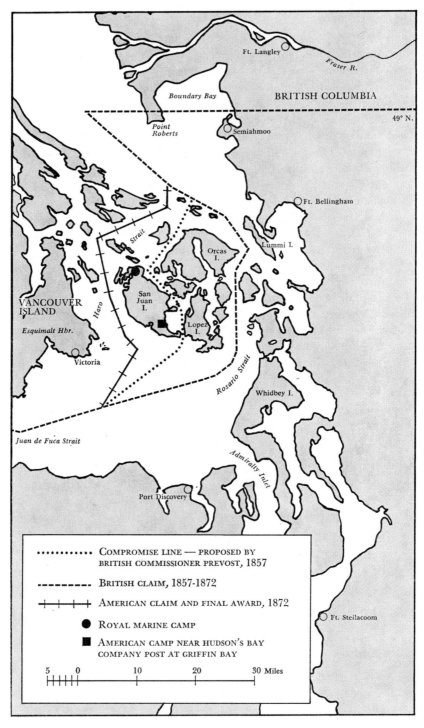

············ COMPROMISE LINE — PROPOSED BY BRITISH COMMISSIONER PREVOST, 1857

– – – – – – – BRITISH CLAIM, 1857-1872

+–+–+–+–+ AMERICAN CLAIM AND FINAL AWARD, 1872

● ROYAL MARINE CAMP

■ AMERICAN CAMP NEAR HUDSON'S BAY COMPANY POST AT GRIFFIN BAY

5   0   10   20   30 Miles

SAN JUAN BOUNDARY DISPUTE

Signatories to the Treaty did not know that there was more than one principal channel leading southward into the Strait of Juan de Fuca. In fact, there were two channels. The first and most easterly channel, called Rosario or Vancouver Strait, had been explored in 1792 when Captain George Vancouver visited the Northwest Coast. On that occasion he sent Lieutenant Broughton in the *Chatham* to make a cursory survey of the myriad of islands that bar an easy passage from the Strait of Juan de Fuca to the Strait of Georgia.[4] The second and most westerly passage ran through the eight-mile wide Canal de Haro, now termed Haro Strait, dividing San Juan Island from Vancouver Island. Haro Strait provided the most direct route for Hudson's Bay Company steamers bound from Fort Victoria to the coal mines at Nanaimo in the 1850's. But this passage had been relatively unknown when the Oregon Treaty of 1846 was signed.

After 1846, Royal Navy ships such as the *Cormorant* and *Driver* followed the eastern channel as shown on Captain Vancouver's charts. Indeed, when it became clear by 1852 that a dispute existed as to what formed "the middle of the channel," British naval commanders continued to take the eastern channel through Rosario Strait, hoping that this would give added weight to the importance Captain Vancouver had attached to that waterway.[5]

Between Haro Strait and Rosario Strait lay three main islands—San Juan, Orcas and Lopez. Only the westernmost, San Juan, need be of concern here. On that island the Hudson's Bay Company established a fishing station in 1850 and a sheep farm three years later. Their reasons were both political and commercial but principally the Company wanted to settle the island to strengthen British claims.[6] In 1854, the Americans countered by including San Juan and adjacent islands within Whatcom County, Washington Territory, an act which led the Foreign Office to advise the Admiralty to send a naval force to "show the flag" in the disputed straits.[7]

After Rear-Admiral H. W. Bruce visited the Northwest Coast in 1855, he reported "a serious difficulty" developing over the ownership of San Juan "owing to the grasping spirit and habits of the neighbouring Amer-

---

[4]J. Neilson Barry, ed., "Broughton's Log of a Reconnaissance of the San Juan Islands in 1792," *Washington Historical Quarterly*, XXI (1930), 55-60. Edmund S. Meany, *Vancouver's Discovery of Puget Sound* (Portland, Ore.: Binfords-Mort, 1942), chapters 8 and 9.
[5]Capt. Prevost to Rear-Admiral Fairfax Moresby, 7 June 1853, Y73, Adm. 1/5630.
[6]Miller, Treaties, VIII, 307-309.
[7]Reported in J. Douglas to A. Barclay (Sec., H.B.C.), 19 December 1854, B 226/b/11, fol. 92, H.B.C.A.

icans. . . ."[8] But he was confident that the frigate *President,* due at
Vancouver Island late that same year, would strengthen the hand of
Governor James Douglas, "a man of clear views, ability and decision
of character."[9] Bruce was cautioned by the First Lord of the Admiralty
to avoid an incident with the Americans, especially in view of the great
anxiety in England over the possibility of war with the United States,
partly due to American support to Russia in the Crimean War.[10] He
was also advised on 16 February 1856 to draw all his ships north to
Central America and Vancouver Island as a show of security to British
interests in the face of American filibusters.[11]

The year 1856 passed without incident; a crisis in Anglo-American
relations was avoided by the establishment of a mixed commission of
two to rectify the ill-defined boundary. In response to Foreign Office
suggestions that a naval officer be appointed British Boundary Commissioner and that a ship—a steamer if possible—be stationed at Vancouver Island to "give weight" to the British case, the Admiralty selected
Captain James C. Prevost, familiar with those waters from his service
in the *Virago,* and they assigned to him the *Satellite* for the task at
Vancouver Island. Prevost reached Esquimalt in June 1857.[12] He was
joined later by the Chief Surveyor and Astronomer on the British side,
Captain George H. Richards, in H.M.S. *Plumper.*

From June to October 1857, discussions between Prevost and his
American counterpart, Archibald Campbell, revealed differences of
opinion as to a matter of procedure. The British wanted merely to
establish the water boundary, but the Americans intended to define
the entire boundary between British and American lands west of the
Rockies.[13] It was finally agreed that the land boundary should be surveyed, and sixty-five Royal Engineers were sent from England in the
summer of 1858 for the purpose.[14] Meanwhile, the *Satellite* and *Plumper*
continued to survey the waterways.

On the maritime-boundary question, the views of the two commissioners were irreconcilable: Prevost, acting on instruction from the
Foreign Office, contended that the line should run through Rosario

[8]Rear-Admiral H. W. Bruce to Sir Charles Wood (First Lord of the Admiralty), 18
September 1855, Halifax Papers, Add. MSS. 49,549, B.M.
[9]*Ibid.*
[10]Wood to Bruce, 16 November 1855, Halifax Papers, Add. MSS 49,565, fol. 33, B.M.
[11]Wood to Bruce, 16 February 1856, *ibid.*
[12]E. Hammond (Permanent Under-secretary, F.O.), to Sec. of Adm., 16 September
1856, Adm. 1/5678.
[13]Prevost to Lord Clarendon (F.O.), 12 August 1857, Cap P, 60, Adm. 1/5684.
[14]The Engineers were transported from Panama to Vancouver Island in H.M.S.
Havannah. Admiralty Minute of 30 October 1857, Prevost to Sec. of Adm., 14 August
1857, *ibid.;* Admiralty Minute of 11 November 1857, Adm. 1/5687.

Strait; Campbell argued in favour of Haro Strait.[15] The British Commissioner's argument rested on considerations of navigation and trade. As he explained in a letter to the Admiralty, Rosario Strait provided the best passage for sailing ships, and control of it was essential to the rapidly growing trade in Nanaimo coal, which was carried almost exclusively in sailing vessels. With Rosario Strait in American hands, however, ships would coal at Bellingham Bay on the American mainland rather than sail through the difficult Haro Strait to Nanaimo.[16]

These points reveal Prevost's ignorance of a clause in the Oregon Treaty which guaranteed to both parties freedom of navigation in the straits south of the 49th parallel. But even if he had been aware of this clause, Prevost might not have emphasized it. He rested his case on "natural law rather than artificial legislation," an argument made popular by the Swiss jurist, Vattel.[17]

Prevost did recognize that Britain's main outposts on the North Pacific, namely Victoria and Esquimalt, would be imperilled with San Juan in American hands because of the island's proximity to the southern tip of Vancouver Island. Later this danger caused admirals on the Pacific station considerable anxiety. Prevost stated the danger clearly to the Foreign Office when he wrote: ". . . as the value of Vancouver's Island to us as a Naval Station and perhaps a terminus of a great railroad scheme becomes generally known, the [British] possession of San Juan as a wall of defence to its peaceful occupation will be equally appreciated."[18]

In other words, the defence of Esquimalt would be facilitated by British ownership of San Juan Island. The Americans seemed equally aware of San Juan Island's strategic value. The United States Board of Engineers concluded: "By establishing a military and naval station at Griffin Bay, on the southeastern shore of San Juan Island, we shall be able to overlook those inner waters equally with Great Britain from Esquimalt harbour, and thus counterbalance the preponderance she is seeking to establish."[19]

The Admiralty, however, generally did not support Prevost's appeals

[15]F. Napier (Br. Minister, Washington) to Clarendon, 9 January 1858, encl. in F.O. to Adm., 4 February 1858, Adm. 1/5699. Prevost had instructions from the Foreign Office stipulating that Rosario Strait fitted the description given in the Oregon Treaty. See McCabe, San Juan, pp. 20-21.

[16]Prevost to Sec. of Adm., 17 December 1857, Adm. 1/5699.

[17]See Prevost to Sec. of Adm., 7 December 1847, ibid. The Foreign Office was satisfied with the position taken by Prevost; Malmesbury (F.O.) to Prevost, 14 May 1858, ibid.

[18]Prevost to Hammond, 13 April 1858, F.O. 5/810; quoted in McCabe, San Juan, p. 26.

[19]Series 1393, U.S. Senate Ex. Doc. 8, 41st Cong., 1869, I, Engineer's Report, 2; quoted in McCabe, San Juan, p. 32.

to check the steady but peaceful American penetration of San Juan.[20] Their Lordships' primary concern was free navigation of the straits, although they acknowledged that ownership of San Juan Island would be advantageous.[21] A year later, when British policy and claims came under review, the Admiralty did not deviate from this stand.[22]

By December 1858, the survey of the maze of waterways had been completed by the *Plumper* with the *Satellite* acting in an auxiliary capacity. A report submitted by Captain Richards of the *Plumper* gave added weight to the Foreign Office opinion that Britain's claims to San Juan were just.[23] Nevertheless, the Foreign Office was anxious for compromise with the Americans and did not insist that the International Boundary should be drawn down the middle of Rosario Strait.[24] Essentially the question became one of deciding on which side of San Juan Island the boundary should run. But within a few months the dispute entered a more hazardous stage.

"The Pig War"

How war nearly erupted between Britain and the United States over the shooting of a Hudson's Bay Company pig on San Juan is a colourful and often exaggerated tale.[25] According to the British view, the guilty party was Lyman A. Cutler, an American "squatter" on the company's land. Evidently the "provocative pig" made several profitable forays into Cutler's potato patch. The last occurred on 15 June 1859, when the irritated farmer shot the pig. Immediately Cutler realized his blunder and offered compensation to Hudson's Bay Company officials.

The shooting heightened attention over which nation possessed sovereignty. Already American officials had attempted to collect taxes from the Company for landing thirteen hundred sheep without observing United States revenue laws; but this attempt was thwarted by Douglas.[26] To many American settlers, however, the killing of the "British"

---

[20]Sir John Pakington, the First Lord of the Admiralty, thought the advantages of possessing the island questionable. See Minute of Sir J. Pakington, 11 March 1858, Adm. 1/5699. His views were the opposite of his predecessor. See Sir C. Wood to Clarendon, 17 February 1858, Clar. dep., c. 82, fols. 150-151, B.L.

[21]Adm. to F.O., 6 April 1858, draft, *ibid.* (Sent 8 April 1858) .

[22]Admiralty Board Minute, 2 March 1859, on Hammond to Sec. of Adm., 5 February 1859, Adm. 1/5719.

[23]Encl. in Prevost to Malmesbury, 30 November 1858, copy sent in Hammond to Sec. of Adm., 5 February 1859, *ibid.* Richards noted that charts by Vancouver (1792) and Kellett (1847) were still valuable.

[24]Memorandum of Hammond, 20 April 1858, F.O. 5/813; McCabe, *San Juan*, p. 30.

[25]An indication of the interest in this subject is registered in the mass of writing on it. See note 3 of this chapter for the principal works.

[26]Hubert H. Bancroft, *British Columbia, 1792-1887* in *History of the Pacific States of North America*, XXVII (San Francisco: History Company, 1867) , pp. 607-608.

pig appeared to be a justifiable retaliation. In the mistaken belief that Cutler had been mistreated by British authorities, the incensed settlers petitioned military authorities in Oregon for assistance.[27]

As a result, on 18 July 1859, Brigadier-General W. S. Harney at Fort Vancouver ordered a sixty-man infantry detachment to proceed from Fort Bellingham to protect Americans on San Juan. The American soldiers took up positions on the island with instructions to oppose any interference by colonial officials of Vancouver Island.[28]

Harney's action was based on two erroneous assumptions. First, he believed that the Royal Navy was implicated in the insult by the use of a British naval vessel to transmit a Hudson's Bay Company official to the island to seize Cutler.[29] On this, Harney was misinformed. As Baynes later stated to the Admiralty, no ship of the Royal Navy was in the region at the time of the incident.[30] In reality, the vessel was the *Beaver*, and it was "purely accidental" that A. G. Dallas, the President of the Board of Management of the Company's Western Department, was on San Juan.[31] Secondly, Harney assumed that San Juan Island was "as important to the Pacific States as Cuba is to those of the Atlantic."[32] The second assumption was probably decisive for Harney. Very likely he intended to gain San Juan for an American naval base which he believed would provide a counterpoise to Britain's base at Esquimalt.[33] Whatever the pretext, Harney's unwarranted and unauthorized conduct, resulting as it did from anti-British and expansionist tendencies,[34] brought embarrassment to the American government and caused his recall.[35]

It is ironic that prior to the so-called "pig battle" and Harney's rash acts, the British government had informed Washington of its hope that "local collisions" could be avoided.[36] But the British government erred in making no attempt to rescind or modify instructions relayed to Governor Douglas by the Colonial Office.[37] These instructions gave Douglas a formal sanction for his own view that the Americans were intruders

[27]See McCabe, *San Juan,* pp. 37-39.

[28]Walter N. Sage, *Sir James Douglas and British Columbia* (Toronto: University of Toronto Press, 1930) , p. 266.

[29]General W. S. Harney to Douglas; 6 August 1859, C.O. 305/12.

[30]Rear Admiral R. L. Baynes to Sec. of Adm., 12 August 1859, Adm. 1/5713.

[31]Dallas to Harney, 10 May 1860, B.226/b/19, fol. 127, H.B.C.A.

[32]Quoted in Richard W. Van Alystyne, *The Rising American Empire* (Oxford: Blackwells, 1960) , p. 118.

[33]McCabe, *San Juan,* p. 39.

[34]For a close examination of Harney, see Murray, *Pig War,* pp. 15-22.

[35]See his biography in *The Dictionary of American Biography,* VIII (New York, 1932) , pp. 280-81.

[36]Lord Lyons to General Lewis Cass (U.S. Secretary of State) , 12 May 1859, copy, C.O. 305/30.

[37]Hammond to H. Merivale (C.O.) , 27 April 1859, C.O. 305/12.

on San Juan, which he always considered a dependency of the Colony of Vancouver Island. Further, Douglas found encouragement in his instructions for believing that Americans should be warned against claiming sovereignty. The Governor's conduct in this crisis has been questioned by his most eminent biographer.[38] In Douglas's defence, it must be stated that his policy was in keeping with Foreign Office instructions to maintain British rights on San Juan. Douglas, who dealt firmly with Americans earlier during the Fraser River gold rush, intended to do much the same on the disputed island.

Well within the terms of his Foreign Office instructions, the Governor sent a magistrate and justice of the peace, Major John de Courcy, to enforce law and order on "the British island." On 27 July 1859, after arriving from Victoria in the *Satellite,* de Courcy read his commission under a British flag at Griffin Bay.[39] At this stage both the Americans and the British realized the dangers of the situation and acted with due caution.

To support the magistrate with force, Douglas, who had no soldiers at his disposal, turned to the Royal Navy; for once, the Governor did not have to wait for warships to arrive. His pleas for British warships during the British Columbia gold rush in 1858 had resulted in the arrival of the frigate *Tribune* and the corvette *Pylades* from the China and East Indies station. The flagship *Ganges* was expected at Vancouver Island during early August 1859 to protect British interests at the height of the gold-rush season. Consequently, the question of assuring sufficient ships to deal with the San Juan emergency never arose as it did in other crises on the Northwest Coast.

By sending the *Tribune* to Griffin Bay, where the Americans had made camp, Douglas planned to prevent further American landings on the British "dependency."[40] It was his intention, at this stage, to use the *Tribune* against the American soldiers on shore only if they were erecting fortifications or making further landings.[41] At the same time, he intended to have the British magistrate accomplish the eviction of the Americans on shore. In short, Douglas anticipated that the Americans would withdraw when faced with British law backed up by the *Tribune.*[42]

---

[38]Sage, *Sir James Douglas,* p. 39.

[39]M. de Courcy to Baynes, 5 August 1859, and A. G. Young (Col. Sec., Vancouver Island) to J. de Courcy, 23 July 1859, encl. in Baynes to Sec. of Adm., 8 August 1859, Y 146, Adm. 1/5713.

[40]Douglas to M. de Courcy, 29 July 1859, encl. in Baynes to Sec. of Adm.. 8 August 1859, *ibid.*

[41]Douglas to Prevost, 29 July 1859, encl. in Baynes to Sec. of Adm., 8 August 1859, *ibid.*

[42]*Ibid.*

But when the Governor learned that the Americans (now some 100 to 150 in number) were making preparations to oppose the British with arms, he requested that another warship be sent to the scene from Esquimalt. As a result, Captain Michael de Courcy, the Senior Officer at Esquimalt and cousin of the British magistrate, dispatched the *Satellite* to join the *Tribune* and, on 1 August, the *Satellite,* hitherto engaged in the Boundary Commission, was placed under orders of Captain Hornby of the *Tribune.*[43] Such overwhelming superiority of naval force at San Juan, Douglas thought, surely would prevent the Americans from resisting the British magistrate by arms or otherwise.[44]

Because the crisis seemed certain now to intensify, the Legislative Council of Vancouver Island met the same day, 1 August, and decided that Colonel J. S. Hawkins, R.E., should be sent to London with information for the British Cabinet on the state of affairs. In the hope that a ship could reach San Francisco by 5 August, when the packet for Panama was scheduled to leave, the *Pylades* left Victoria with Hawkins aboard. Head winds outside Cape Flattery proved too strong for her steam engines, capable of 350 horsepower, and her commander concluded that she would be unable to reach her destination in time. Therefore he turned back toward Vancouver Island, where he thought his ship might be more useful in protecting the colony if the erratic Americans attacked.[45] Hawkins reached London by other means.

At the same meeting on 1 August, the Legislative Council resolved to withdraw the British magistrate from San Juan and reverse the decision to land troops, as it was clear that a joint occupation could only result in bloodshed.[46] These wise policies can be attributed to Captain Michael de Courcy, the Senior Naval Officer, who overruled the more bellicose Douglas.[47] Despite the prudence of the Council, Douglas maintained firmly the belief that force should be met with force. His convictions were based on his long awareness of American advancement into the Pacific Northwest prior to the Oregon Treaty and his belief that Britain and the Hudson's Bay Company were about to lose further domains.[48]

At San Juan, meanwhile, the presence of the Royal Navy did not

[43]M. de Courcy to Prevost, 1 August 1859, *ibid.*
[44]Douglas to M. de Courcy, 30 July 1859, *ibid.*
[45]M. de Courcy to Baynes, 5 August 1859, encl. in Baynes to Sec. of Adm., 8 August 1859, *ibid.*
[46]Reported in *ibid.*
[47]Douglas to Capt. G. Phipps Hornby, 2 August 1859; in Sage, *Sir James Douglas,* p. 270.
[48]See, for example, Douglas to M. de Courcy, two letters of 29 July 1859, and Douglas to Baynes, 17 August 1859, in *ibid.,* pp. 266, 267, 272-73.

result in an American withdrawal.[49] On 2 August, the *Plumper* brought forty-six Royal Marines and fifteen Royal Engineers from the Fraser River to increase the military force available if a landing proved necessary.[50] As long as the British remained in their ships and the Americans occupied San Juan, American *de facto* control of the island was ensured. Nevertheless Captain George Pickett, who was in charge of the American detachment, was alarmed justifiably when he saw the *Tribune, Satellite* and *Plumper* lying in Griffin Bay in "a menacing attitude"; he reported that the British warships were of such overwhelming strength that his troops would be a mere "mouthful for them. . . ."[51] This led Brigadier-General Harney, who was still in command, to write immediately to San Francisco, the headquarters of the United States Pacific squadron for naval support.

Naval Restraint in the San Juan Crisis

The preservation of peace in this tense situation can be attributed largely to the actions of Captain Geoffrey Phipps Hornby, of the *Tribune,* son of Admiral Phipps Hornby, who was Commander-in-Chief on the Pacific station, 1847-1850. Captain Hornby was one of the most respected sailors in the Royal Navy. His discretion during the San Juan crisis won him the praise of his commander-in-chief and of the Admiralty. He believed that neither British nor American troops should occupy the island, and he rightly held that the British could afford to be forbearing in view of their superior naval strength. Thus his objective was to place on the Americans the responsibility for any rupture that might occur in the already endangered Anglo-American relations. Because Pickett refused to withdraw his force at Hornby's demand, Hornby told him that the American government would be responsible for subsequent developments, and that British marines and engineers would be landed if "the honor or the interests of England" were in jeopardy.[52]

Pickett's force was strengthened greatly on 1 August by the arrival of 120 United States troops in the armed transport *Massachusetts.*[53] At this difficult moment, Hornby and Prevost were on the island searching

---

[49]Hornby to Baynes, 5 August 1859, Adm. 1/5713.
[50]*Ibid.*
[51]G. Pickett to Harney, 3 August 1859; Miller, *Treaties,* VIII, 358.
[52]In the *Tribune* were 69 Royal Marines and 15 Royal Engineers. Hornby to Baynes, 5 August 1859, Y 146, Adm. 1/5713. Mrs. Fred (Mary A.) Egerton, *Admiral of the Fleet Sir Geoffrey Phipps Hornby, G.C.B., A Biography,* (Edinburgh: Wm. Blackwood & Sons, 1896) , p. 66.
[53]The disembarkation of 120 Americans constituted "a most unprecedented and unjustifiable act of aggression." Prevost to Malmesbury, 3 August 1859, C.O. 305/12.

for Pickett to discuss joint occupation.[54] David Boyle, the First Lieutenant, was left in charge of the *Tribune*. He had been in command for
an hour when the *Massachusetts* anchored near the *Tribune* and prepared to disembark soldiers. Boyle informed the captain of the troopship
that the British intended to prevent troop landings. The Americans
ignored this warning, ordered the boats to be lowered and proceeded
with the disembarkation. Just as Boyle was about to beat to quarters,
the *Plumper* brought instructions cancelling the Governor's orders to
prevent any more landings of American troops.[55] An incident that
might have led to war was avoided by only a few minutes.

Four days later, on 5 August the *Ganges*, the flagship of Rear-Admiral
Baynes, the Commander-in-Chief, Pacific, reached Esquimalt. Baynes,
who had no previous knowledge of the crisis, in fact, had arrived to
check on the state of British interests at the height of the gold-rush season. Upon learning of the "pig war" and of the Governor's warlike plans,
he is reported—perhaps with some exaggeration—to have said, "Tut,
tut, no, no, the damned fools."[56] At once, he realized that a collision of
forces had been avoided only through the sound judgement and restraint
of Hornby, for the implementation of the Governor's original policy
would have resulted in war.[57] Although Douglas evidently was ignorant
of a larger consequence of his policy—war between rival maritime
powers—Baynes saw the crisis in its true perspective, and his reaction
was justified.

The Admiral had two reasons for rejecting the Governor's plans.
First, the orders to Hornby of 2 August would have meant a clash of
arms in which the British would have been forced to evict the Americans
from the island and hold it against attack.[58] Second, the landing of
British forces was not required, for British claims to the island were in
no way invalidated by the absence of British troops there, nor were
British citizens in any way endangered.[59] Baynes's logic testifies to his

---

[54]Commander Norman claimed that Pickett tricked the naval officers by inviting
them to a picnic, a "preconcerted device for denuding the British frigate of most of
her officers in anticipation of what had been planned to come off." Commander
Francis M. Norman, *"Martello Tower" in China and the Pacific in H.M.S. Tribune,
1850-60* (London: George Allen, 1902), p. 269.

[55]*Ibid*, p. 271. The earlier orders were "to prevent the landing of United States Troops
and the erection of military works by the detachment occupying San Juan." Douglas
to Hornby, 2 August 1859; in Sage, *Sir James Douglas*, p. 270.

[56]F. W. Howay and others, eds., "Angus McDonald: A Few Items of the West," *Washington Historical Quarterly*, VIII (July 1917), 196. According to McDonald, Chief
factor at Fort Colville, Baynes told Douglas he would refuse an order from the
Governor to attack the American camp on San Juan. *Ibid.*, p. 195.

[57]Baynes to Adm., 12 August 1859, Adm. 1/5713; Egerton, *Admiral Hornby*, p. 68.

[58]Baynes to Douglas, 13 August 1859, confidential, Ships' letters, F 1213, B.C.A.

[59]*Ibid.*

admirable ability to view the petty squabble in perspective, for at stake here was the preservation of peaceful Anglo-American relations.

But Douglas tried to cast aside the Admiral's criticism by turning on Hornby and blaming him for inactivity. Douglas believed that if Hornby had disembarked troops, further American landings and fortifications would have been prevented. Indeed, although Douglas claimed that he had been forced to agree with what he termed derisively a "passive and retrograde" policy as urged by the naval officers at the meeting of the Legislative Council—he had ordered Hornby to participate in a joint-occupation.[60] Surely this indicates the Governor's failure to foresee the consequence of the action he expected Hornby to pursue. In general, Douglas's point of view won little, if any, support from naval or army officers, including Colonel R. C. Moody, Officer Commanding the Royal Engineers in British Columbia. Moody praised Hornby for not following orders given in Douglas's "very clever letter," which would have placed the responsibilities for the landing of troops squarely on Hornby's shoulders.[61]

While Baynes pursued his policy of forbearance, the Americans continued to land troops to the increasing disadvantage of the British. Within a week of the Admiral's arrival, between 200 and 300 were in possession of San Juan—further proof to Baynes that the *Ganges* should not return to England as expected but remain instead to strengthen the British position.[62] Another week saw the balance of power shift to the Americans in terms of actual soldiers available. The Americans had 400 men, 6 field pieces, and 100 to 150 civilians on the island, plus 400 artillery men at Fort Steilacoom on Puget Sound. By comparison, circumstances were unfavourable to the British because of insufficient military force, isolation of Vancouver Island from other parts of the Empire, dependence of the colony on American routes for mail and supplies, and numerical predominance of Americans in the colonies of Vancouver Island and British Columbia. All of these factors, as Baynes perceived, were certain indications of the folly of going to war.[63] But war would have been equally foolish for the Americans. As the Secretary of State for the Colonies, the Duke of Newcastle, later explained to Governor Douglas, the superiority of British sea power on the Northwest Coast at the same time made clear to the Americans the wisdom of Britain

---

[60]Douglas to Baynes, 17 August 1859, Vancouver Island Misc. Letter-Book, No. 2, 216-20, B.C.A.; in Sage, *Sir James Douglas*, pp. 272-73.
[61]Col. R. C. Moody, R.E. to Sir John T. Burgoyne (Inspector-General of Fortifications), 8 August 1859; Egerton, *Admiral Hornby*, pp. 66-67. Moody's plans for the defence of British Columbia, mainly by the Royal Navy, are given in this letter.
[62]Baynes to Sec. of Adm., 12 August 1859, Adm. 1/5713.
[63]Baynes to Sec. of Adm., 19 August 1859, *ibid.*

taking "the moderate course of remonstrance instead of violent measures."[64]

As a result of the crisis, the British government made speedy preparations to reinforce the Pacific station. Stationing a garrison of several hundred soldiers at Vancouver Island would not have appealed either to Parliament or the British public at a time when colonial garrisons were being reduced, so the more popular and less permanent measure of dispatching ships-of-war was taken. On the suggestion of the Foreign Secretary, Lord John Russell, the first-class screw-frigate *Topaze*, 51 guns, and the screw-corvette *Clio*, 22 guns, were sent to join the five warships already on the Northwest Coast.[65] The Foreign Office further recommended, in instructions dated 3 October 1859, that the *Ganges* should remain at Vancouver Island until ordered to return to England.[66]

Sending additional ships to foreign stations such as the Pacific in time of need prevented the reductions in Treasury estimates sought by the Chancellor of the Exchequer, Gladstone. During this crisis, the First Lord of the Admiralty, the Duke of Somerset, bemoaned the fact that the introduction of steampower had not resulted in the anticipated reduction of vessels on distant stations: "At present time there is an unusual, and I hope, never to be repeated demand upon our naval force; from Vancouver's isle to the river Plate from the West Indies to China the Admiralty is called upon by Secretaries of State to send ships of war."[67] A few days later he wrote to Gladstone on the same subject:

> If there were any certainty as to the demands which would be made on the Admiralty for naval force, we should be relieved of much embarrassment, but the calls are always sudden & unforseen. The other day for instance two vessels, a frigate & corvette were directed to be sent to Vancouver's isle and an eighty gun ship, which we had ordered home was detained there by the Admiral (very properly under the circumstances). This however makes a difference of above 1000 men: and I do not see how the Admiralty can be prepared for such contingencies. The undeniable fact is that we are doing or endeavouring to do much more than our force is sufficient for.[68]

[64]Duke of Newcastle to Douglas, 21 October 1859, G/336, pp. 114-16, P.A.C.; in Sage, *Sir James Douglas*, p. 277.

[65]Hammond to Sec. of Adm., 2 October 1859, and W. G. Romaine to Hammond, 11 October 1859, C.O. 305/12.

[66]Adm. to Baynes, 3 October 1859, encl. in F.O. papers, Adm. 1/5720 (received 2 December 1859). Baynes did not leave Vancouver Island for England until 10 September 1860, leaving Captain J. W. S. Spencer of H.M.S. *Topaze*, 51 guns, as Senior Officer, Vancouver Island.

[67]The Duke of Somerset to W. E. Gladstone, 12 October 1859, Gladstone Papers, Add. MS. 44, 304, fols. 13-14, B.M.

[68]Somerset to Gladstone, 15 October 1859, *ibid.*, fols. 17-18.

It is little wonder that the First Lord of the Admiralty felt pleased that the world was not larger, for there seemed to be no "limit to the service of the fleets."[69]

The Pacific squadron was then composed of thirteen ships (one ship-of-the-line, three frigates, eight corvettes, and one paddle-wheel sloop).[70] But during the period from 1845 to 1865, the number of ships varied from nine to sixteen, according to the needs of the day and the units available to the Admiralty. Extra ships were sent to the Pacific as needed to deal with crises on the Northwest Coast, especially the Oregon dispute, the Fraser River gold rush, and the San Juan problem. While the British government sought no additions to its mid-Victorian Empire, at the same time it was reluctant to allow any possession or territory to which it had claims to pass to a rival nation. The best means of enforcing this policy was to send ships of the Royal Navy, although the drain on the Treasury often proved to be an embarrassment to a ministry which preached economy.[71]

Another outcome of the San Juan incident was that the American Secretary of State assured the British Minister in Washington, Lord Lyons, of the peaceful intentions of the United States government. The intemperate Harney was recalled and General Winfield Scott was sent to the Pacific Northwest by the War Department in the prestigious capacity of Commander-in-Chief of the United States Army. Scott possessed instructions to effect a joint military occupation until the nations agreed on a definite boundary; when he reached Puget Sound, he proposed such an occupation by a force of one hundred men from each nation. This proposal was agreeable to Douglas but not to Baynes, who favoured a joint civil occupation, thereby "placing matters exactly as they were previous to General Harney's unjustifiable act."[72] Ultimately, the American proposal was accepted by the British government as it did not compromise rights and it prevented war.[73]

A further dispute between Baynes and Douglas developed when the Governor received Colonial Office instructions to requisition from Baynes a Royal Marine detachment for the military occupation of the portion of San Juan Island assigned to the British by Anglo-American agreement. Baynes, who clearly lacked confidence in Douglas, asked

---

[69]Ibid.

[70]Navy Estimates, Ships and Men, 1860-1, printed for the Cabinet, confid., ibid., fol. 52.

[71]See C. J. Bartlett, "The Mid-Victorian Reappraisal of Naval Policy," in K. Bourne and D. C. Watt, eds., Studies in International History: Essays Presented to W. Norton Medlicott (London: Longmans Green & Co., 1967), pp. 189-208.

[72]Baynes to Sec. of Adm., 26 October 1859, Adm. 1/5713, and Baynes to Sec. of Adm., 9 November 1859, Y 1, Adm. 1/5736.

[73]Hammond to Sec. of Adm., 21 October 1859, encl. in F.O. papers, Adm. 1/5720.

for a copy of the document, evidently to verify the request from the British government. Affronted, Douglas refused on the grounds that because he was the Queen's representative, his instructions could not be delegated.[74] In this situation of mutual distrust, the British government sided with Baynes.[75] The petty squabble ended when the Commander-in-Chief received instructions from the Admiralty and Foreign Office to send a captain and one hundred marines to the island to participate in the joint occupation while the sovereignty of San Juan remained undetermined.[76]

Subsequently, Baynes ordered Captain George Bazalgette, R.M.L.I., in charge of the marines, to set up camp at Garrison Bay near Roche Harbour on the island's north end, and on 21 March 1860, the detachment landed from the *Satellite*.[77] For twelve years, the marines maintained their vigil at "English Camp," Garrison Bay, some ten miles northwest of the "American Camp" at Griffin Bay. Throughout this period, British warships visited San Juan occasionally; but after the *Pylades* returned to Esquimalt on 7 December 1859, the use of warships as a "show of force" at the island was suspended.

In retrospect, Baynes's policy of non-intervention appears to have been the correct one. At the time, however, not only Douglas, but the colonial legislature and the Victoria press thought otherwise. On 17 August 1859, for example, the *British Colonist* carried an editorial asking "Why were not troops landed at San Juan?" Five days earlier, the Speaker of the Legislature asked the same question: "Why all this expense and show, if for a parade? . . . Instead of fighting, Her Majesty's Captains take to diplomacy. . . ."[78]

Admiral Baynes and Captain Hornby were well aware of the reasons for not intervening. Throughout the crisis, the Navy remained "perfectly passive" and "forbearing" to a degree to which Baynes feared the Admiralty might not approve.[79] But he justified his policy on the "almost certainty" of a clash of arms in a very remote quarter of the world. In his opinion, providing the British flag was not compromised, the interests of Britain and the Pacific colonies were served best by reducing the chances of war.

The Commander-in-Chief's successful strategy won the wholehearted

[74]Baynes to Sec. of Adm., 25 January 1860, Y 30, *ibid.*
[75]Admiralty Minute, 19 March 1860, on Baynes to Sec. of Adm., 25 January 1860, Y 30, *ibid.*
[76]Hammond to Sec. of Adm., 22 December 1859, in F.O. Papers, Adm. 1/5720.
[77]Baynes to Capt. G. Bazalgette, R.M.L.I., Memo of 20 March 1860, encl. in Baynes to Sec. of Adm., 28 March 1860, Y 71, Adm. 1/5736.
[78]*British Colonist* (Victoria, B.C.) , 17 August 1859.
[79]Baynes to Sec. of Adm., 9 November 1859, Y 1, Adm. 1/5736.

approval of the Admiralty. In fact, the First Lord of the Admiralty, the Duke of Somerset, commended Baynes in glowing terms. He informed him that the members of the British Ministry often talked of the "good sense and prudence" that Baynes displayed during the crisis caused by the "intemperate proceedings" of General Harney, which would have resulted in serious complications if Baynes had not "met them by calm remonstrance and dignified but conciliatory language."[80] Shortly thereafter, Baynes was knighted for his outstanding services to Great Britain.[81]

Treaty of Washington, 1871

The Treaty of Washington of 1871, finally resolved many long-standing Anglo-American difficulties.[82] In discussions leading to the Treaty, the Americans rejected compromise, for in such a solution Great Britain probably would have received San Juan Island. Negotiators for the United States, therefore, insisted that the arbitrator, Kaiser Wilhelm I, Emperor of Germany, should decide which channel—Haro or Rosario— was most in accordance with the terms of the 1846 agreement. American insistence upon this point ended any British hope for an equitable division of the archipelago, and the issue thus rested upon the strength of the claims of the rival nations.

Of the two cases presented to the Kaiser, the British was obviously the weaker for two reasons.[83] In the first place, hydrographic data showed that Haro Strait was the main channel. In the second place, historical evidence revealed that in discussions preceding the Oregon Treaty, Lord Aberdeen, the Foreign Secretary, had merely wanted to preserve for Britain Vancouver Island, and not the adjacent islands.[84] Not surprisingly, therefore, the Kaiser in his award of 21 October 1872 named Haro Strait as "most in accordance with the true interpretation of the Treaty."[85] The entire San Juan archipelago thus became American territory; accordingly, the Foreign Office quickly instructed the Senior Naval Officer at Esquimalt to withdraw the British garrison. This was accomplished by the British warships *Scout* and *Peterel* on 25

80Somerset to Baynes, 31 March 1860, BAY/2, N.M.M.
81Somerset to Baynes, 17 May 1860, 36 MS 1061, N.M.M. Baynes received a K.C.B. the following day.
82See H. C. Allen, *Great Britain and the United States: A History of Anglo-American Relations (1783-1952)* (New York: St. Martin's Press, 1955), pp. 511-17.
83Prevost prepared the British case with the aid of F. S. Reilly of the Foreign Office and, before him, Sir Travers Twiss, famed international jurist, Professor of Law in King's College, London, and author of *The Oregon Question Examined* (London: Longman, Brown, Green and Longmans, 1846).
84McCabe, *San Juan*, pp. 114-17.
85In *Supplement to the London Gazette*, 30 October 1872.

November 1872, an event which brought to an end the twelve-year joint occupation of the island.

The termination of the controversy meant that for the first time in Anglo-American relations no North American boundary dispute existed. But to citizens of the new Canadian province of British Columbia and, indeed, to many Canadians on the eastern side of the Rockies, the Kaiser's award appeared as a betrayal of Canadian interests on the Northwest Coast much like the Oregon Treaty.[86] In London, *The Times* contained a leading article often described as "cut the painter" advice which advised Canada to assume responsibility for her own affairs, the days of apprenticeship being over.[87]

The United States gained a strategic advantage from the possession of San Juan Island, for if batteries were mounted to command Haro Strait the passage of British warships through that channel could be prevented. Sir John A. Macdonald, as Prime Minister of Canada and a member of the British delegation at discussions leading up to the Treaty of Washington, believed that even if the island were awarded to the Americans, as long as England remained "mistress of the seas," she could still "seize upon the island and hold it against all comers," should war break out. But he noted with dismay, "Whenever she ceases to have the naval supremacy the whole coast will be at the mercy of the American fleet. . . ."[88] Macdonald was quite correct in his view that British Columbia was dependent on the British squadron in the Pacific for protection. Moreover, he had touched on a matter that was assuming greater significance in view of the growth of American hemispheric interests: the security of Canada depended in large measure on peaceful Anglo-American relations.

Britain lost San Juan Island, but she did not lose the peace. The overall security of her worldly interests demanded forbearance in certain instances. Self-assertion and interference were not her objectives. Certainly, she possessed naval power at Vancouver Island sufficient "to have eaten" the American soldiers on San Juan, as the surgeon of the *Plumper* remarked, but a belligerent course of action was inconsistent with her policy.

---

[86]The theme was repeated in the Alaska Boundary Tribunal Award (1903), with more repercussions in Canada.

[87]The *Times*, 30 October 1872. Viscount Milton, who had written a history of the dispute (see note 3 of this chapter), thought it "unjust and impolitic on the part of the Mother Country to virtually sacrifice the independence and power of her colonies at the same time that she is urging self-reliance and independence upon them." Milton to Clarendon, 22 December 1869, Clar. dep., c. 510 (fol. 1), B.L.

[88]Sir John A. Macdonald to Charles Tupper, n.d. [1871?], Macdonald Papers, Macdonald-Tupper Correspondence, II, 165ff., P.A.C.; in Goldwin Smith, "Notes on the Problems of San Juan," *Pacific Northwest Quarterly*, XXXI (1940), 185.

The protracted quarrel over San Juan Island revealed again the necessity of maintaining a large British naval force in the Pacific. Thus during the period from 1859 to 1866, no fewer than twelve, and sometimes as many as sixteen, warships were on the Pacific station.[89] As a result of gold-rush crises, problems with hostile Indians, growth of trade, and the San Juan dispute, the Commander-in-Chief, Pacific, was forced increasingly to spend more time in northern waters. As the Civil War years were to reveal, British maritime interests in the North Pacific and on the Northwest Coast were in the ascendant. And the two British colonies on the Northwest Coast were to be made more secure within the Empire by the establishment of Esquimalt as the Pacific station headquarters in 1862 and by the union of Vancouver Island with British Columbia in 1866.

[89]See Appendices B and C for the number of ships on the Station.

Chapter 8

THE EVOLUTION OF ESQUIMALT NAVAL BASE
1846-1869

EVER SINCE THE ADMIRALTY had sent warships to the west coast of South America and the Pacific islands during the first decade of the nineteenth century, problems of supplying and repairing vessels and of providing hospital facilities had been manifest. Storeships moored at Valparaiso after 1843 and at Callao after 1847 proved inadequate. A good base of operations was sorely needed. Consequently British warships investigated locations such as the Galapagos Islands, Panama and islands off the coasts of Mexico and California as possible sites. As Admiralty interest in the Northwest Coast and its fine harbours grew after 1845, Esquimalt, on the southeastern tip of Vancouver Island, developed as a suitable place for refreshment and repair for ships of the Royal Navy. Esquimalt had two major disadvantages: its nearness to the western United States, an attraction for deserting seamen, and its remoteness from the South Pacific where the Pacific squadron had heavy patrol duties. Still, with its sheltered harbour, healthy climate, timber and provisions, and proximity to ample supplies of coal, it afforded the best available situation in the eastern Pacific for a naval base.[1]

Heretofore, historians have generally thought that Esquimalt did not become a depot until 1865, when an official Order-in-Council authorized

[1]Alexander Rattray, M.D., an assistant surgeon in H.M.S. *Topaze,* showed statistically that Esquimalt had a more healthy climate than England. A. Rattray, *Vancouver Island and British Columbia* (London: Smith, Elder & Co., 1862), pp. 54, 148.

"A small establishment . . . for the custody, etc., of stores and provisions for Her Majesty's Ships in the North Pacific."[2] Actually, as will be shown, a more significant development occurred three years before, when Esquimalt had become the Pacific station headquarters. In fact, the development of this port as a naval base began even earlier—in the late 1840's and 1850's—although the exact date of the creation of an establishment defies definition.

The Navy began to search for a site for a base in the North Pacific during the 1840's, a period of international rivalry and naval operations in the Society Islands and along the North Pacific Coast. The Earl of Ellenborough, the First Lord of the Admiralty, contended in 1846 that a base at Pago Pago, Samoa, would help check French expansion in the South Pacific; and that another on the North Pacific Coast, preferably San Francisco Bay, would control American aggrandizement in California and Oregon.[3] However, Lord Aberdeen at the Foreign Office would act on neither suggestion because to incorporate further territories within the Empire would involve "heavy direct and still heavier indirect expenditure, besides multiplying the liabilities of misunderstanding and collisions with Foreign Powers."[4]

Palmerston, who entered the Foreign Office as part of Lord John Russell's administration in July 1846, was more amenable to Ellenborough's suggestions; in 1847 and 1848 the Admiralty considered several locations including the Galapagos Islands, owned by Ecuador, and Panama, where the Navy had a coal depot. But both had unhealthy climates. Sites on the Mexican coast were similarly undesirable, though the islands of Cedros and Guadalupe off Baja California were classified as possibilities. In point of fact, however, neither Palmerston nor the Admiralty thought it expedient to acquire either of these as such a move would appear to the United States to be a clandestine operation on the part of Britain.[5]

---

[2]Order-in-Council, 29 June 1865, copy, Adm. 1/5961; printed in Admiralty, *Orders-in-Council*, Vol. III (London, 1873), pp. 79-80. See also, Major F. V. Longstaff, *Esquimalt Naval Base: A History of its Work and its Defences* (Victoria, B.C.; Victoria Book and Stationery Co., 1941), p. 21.

[3]Lord Ellenborough to Lord Aberdeen, 16 May 1846, private, Aberdeen Papers, Add. MSS 43, 198, B.M. The Revillagigedo Islands off the west coast of Mexico were an alternative of lesser promise.

[4]Aberdeen to R. Pakenham (Br. minister, Mexico), 15 December 1841, F.O. 50/143. See also, E. D. Adams, "English Interest in the Annexation of California," *American Historical Review*, XIV (July 1909), 747.

[5]H. G. Ward (Adm.) to Rear-Admiral Phipps Hornby, 17 March 1848, PHI/3/15, N.M.M. Kenneth Bourne, *Britain and the Balance of Power in North America, 1815-1908* (London: Longmans Green & Co., 1967), pp. 176-77 and notes. For a good description of what a naval base should afford, see Gilbert N. Tucker, *The Naval Service of Canada: Its Official History*, 2 vols. (Ottawa, 1952), I, 45-46.

PLATE 25.   H.M.S. *Satellite*, the second of her name to call at Esquimalt, showing her gun deck.

PLATE 26.   Gun deck of H.M.S. *Sutlej*, about 1860.

PLATE 27. The first British ironclad in the Pacific, H.M.S. *Zealous,* flagship of the Commander-in-Chief, Pacific, 1867-1872.

PLATE 28. Rear-Admiral the Honourable George Fowler Hastings, C.B., Commander-in-Chief on the Pacific Station, 1867-1869. Much to the disappointment of the Admiralty, he kept the *Zealous* at Esquimalt for most of that time to guard against any possible Fenian attack.

PLATE 29. Part of the Flying Squadron at Esquimalt in 1871. The ships are, from left to right: the *Liver-pool* (in front), *Endymion* (behind), *Liffey*, *Zealous* (flagship, Pacific station), *Phoebe* and *Charybdis*.

PLATE 30. Rear-Admiral Arthur Farquhar, Commander-in-Chief, Pacific, 1869-1872. He was greatly interested in the potential of Vancouver Island coal.

PLATE 31. H.M.S. *Sparrowhawk*, a screw-gun vessel of the first class on the Pacific station 1865-1872. Of graceful design, she was built during the Crimean War when a need existed for ships of modest size and light draft suitable for coastal operations.

PLATE 32. At the time of the Russian "bombardment bogie" of 1885, *Torpedo Boat 39* (the *Swift*) was one of two such vessels purchased from Chile to guard against Russian cruiser raids on Esquimalt.

PLATE 33. The screw-sloop *Alert* on the Northwest Coast periodically during the 1860's.

PLATE 34. The iron screw-sailing ship *Triumph*, flagship of Rear-Admiral Sir Michael Culme-Seymour, on the left and the protected cruiser *Caroline* with a merchant ship on the right in Burrard Inlet, 1887.

PLATE 35. Rear-Admiral Sir Michael Culme-Seymour, Bart., Commander-in-Chief, Pacific, 1885-1888. He realized the strategic implications of the cession of Pearl Harbour to the United States in 1887.

PLATE 36. H.M.S. *Cormorant* was the first British warship to use the Esquimalt graving dock, in 1887. The flagship *Triumph* can be seen in the distance.

PLATE 37. The *Amphion,* a protected cruiser of the second class, in dry dock at Esquimalt.

PLATE 38. The armoured cruiser *Warspite*, flagship of the Commander-in-Chief, Pacific, 1890-1893 and 1899-1902. This photo was taken 1 July 1892 when she was decorated for Dominion Day celebrations in Vancouver.

PLATE 39. H.M.S. *Grafton*, a protected cruiser first class, passing Fisgard Lighthouse outward bound from Esquimalt. She was the flagship on Pacific Station 1902-1904.

PLATE 40.   A portion of the Pacific squadron ready in Esquimalt Harbour at the time of the Bering Sea dispute, 1891.

PLATE 41.   H.M.S. *Amphion* leaving Esquimalt Harbour about 1889.

PLATE 42. Lowering of the flag during the handing over of H.M. Dockyard at Esquimalt to Canada 9 November 1910.

PLATE 43. Present at the transfer were, from left to right, Rear-Admiral C. E. Kingsmill, Director of the Naval Service of Canada, Commander G. W. Vivian, R.N., of H.M.S. *Shearwater*, Commander-in-Charge for Station Duties on the West Coast of America, Commander J. D. D. Stewart, R.N., of H.M.C.S. *Rainbow*, Mr. S. J. Desbarats, Deputy Minister of Defence, Mr. George Phillips, Admiralty Agent, and Commander C. D. Roper, R.N., Canadian Chief-of-Staff.

PLATE 44. H.M.C.S. *Rainbow,* a light cruiser, was purchased by Canada from the Admiralty for £50,000 in 1910. She was a training ship and the first Canadian warship in the Pacific. Her career ended in 1920.

PLATE 45. The Canadian submarines *CC1* and *CC2* with their tender, H.M.S. *Shearwater,* one of two Royal Navy sloops stationed on the West Coast of North America in 1914.

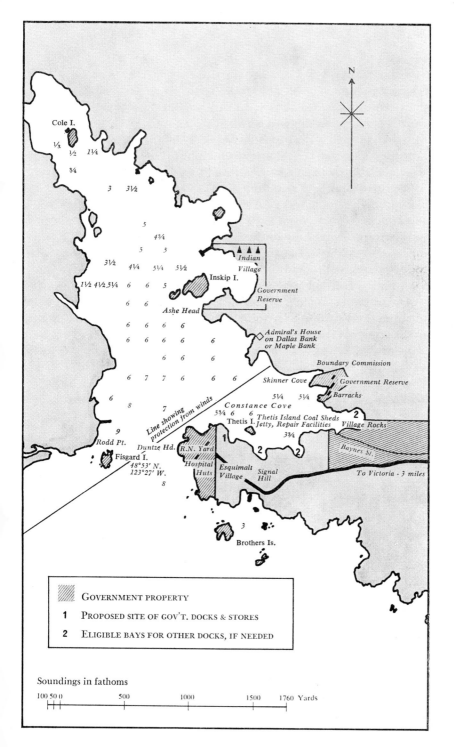

ESQUIMALT NAVAL BASE, EARLY 1860's

However, in 1846 when Britain gained uncontested title to lands bordering on the North Pacific, it was possible to establish a naval base somewhere on the British portion without fear of an international incident. The Oregon crisis had revealed that Vancouver Island could furnish many supplies to British warships. The Hudson's Bay Company's Fort Victoria usually could supply provisions. Timbers suitable for spars were available there, as was water. And coal deposits near the north end of the island appeared promising.[6]

Esquimalt, three miles to the west of Fort Victoria, provided easy access to sailing vessels, as it was large and virtually land-locked. Its upper or northern reaches entirely justified the Indian name "Esquimalt," meaning "a place gradually shoaling." Along the harbour's southern and more rocky shores stood pines and firs. By contrast to ports-of-call in the South Seas, however, Esquimalt was decidedly not exotic. It lacked swaying palms, tropical sun and Polynesian hospitality. But sailors found some solace in the English society of nearby Victoria, in hunting and fishing in the area, in a change of climate, and, for a few, in the chance to desert to nearby gold fields. Accordingly, Esquimalt was not entirely detested by seamen.

First Stages of Development

An observer who happened to be on Duntze Head on the east side of the entrance to Esquimalt harbour on 25 July 1848 would have seen the approach of the first of Her Majesty's ships to anchor there: the frigate *Constance*. On that day, she left the open waters of the Pacific by entering the Strait of Juan de Fuca at Cape Flattery, and made her way up the 15-mile wide strait until clear of Race Rocks. Then she came into view, her sails white against the Olympic Mountains on the American shore, and turned northward to run into Esquimalt Harbour, taking Fisgard Island on her port and Duntze Head on her starboard beam. She came to anchor, protected from the prevailing winds, in the cove in the southeast corner of Esquimalt Harbour which was to bear the ship's name. The *Constance* was later followed by over one hundred British warships that made Constance Cove their usual haven on the Northwest Coast.

Gradually the Navy occupied lands to the east and south of Constance Cove. One was Thetis Island, first used as a refitting spot by the *Thetis* in 1852, on which crews of various ships built primitive sawpits, coal sheds, and blacksmith and carpenter shops. In the course of the land speculation accompanying the Fraser River gold rush, James Douglas and John

6See chapter 4.

Work as supposed "Trustees for the Fur Trade" sold the island to one Jeremiah Nagle for £ 1. This appeared to rob the Navy of the only land they used in the harbour. The Commander-in-Chief, Pacific, Rear-Admiral Bruce, was alarmed when he heard of the transaction. He pointed out that possession was nine-tenths of the law, and advised the Secretary of the Admiralty that Thetis Island doubtless was naval property by virtue of its occupancy by the Navy for at least fifteen years.[7]

In subsequent discussions involving the Admiralty, the Colonial Office, and the Hudson's Bay Company, which owned most of the land around the harbour, the Company acknowledged Admiralty title to Thetis Island.[8] This constituted a reservation of land for naval purposes, the first of its kind at Esquimalt, and it conformed to the provisions stipulated in the charter-grant of 1849 whereby the Company obtained colonizing powers at Vancouver Island. The value of Thetis Island was enhanced in 1860 when the Admiralty approved construction of a depot there to hold 1,300 to 1,400 tons of coal. This project was designed to eliminate the necessity for all ships needing coal to go to the pit-heads at Nanaimo, some eighty miles by sea to the north.[9]

At the harbour entrance on Fisgard Island, a lighthouse was constructed in 1860 as an aid to navigation. This lighthouse, visible to mariners for ten miles in clear weather, was complemented by another built at Race Rocks at the same time. The two lighthouses, which enabled ships to enter Esquimalt Harbour by day or night in good weather are still in use, although captains now also employ more sophisticated electronic devices for navigation.

The southern shore of the harbour adjacent to Thetis Island provided several good bays and on these auxiliary services were developed, which provided the foundations for a small dockyard complex which was constructed later. At the western extremity of this southern shore was Duntze Head, known locally as "Old Hospital Point," where hospital huts had been erected in 1855 during the Crimean War.[10] These buildings were put in efficient condition in 1858, and their grounds generally were considered as government property. Nearby stood Esquimalt Village, a cluster of ship-chandleries, dwellings, public houses and brothels. To the east lay Signal Hill, its strategic position commanding the rocky peninsula which enclosed Esquimalt Harbour on the south, and along which rough roads led to Victoria on the east.

[7]Rear-Admiral H. W. Bruce to R. B. Osborne (Sec., Adm.), 21 January 1858, and enclosures, Adm. 1/5694. Bruce was incorrect: the earliest claim of the Navy to Esquimalt was the visit of the *Constance* in 1848, and the *Thetis*, after which the island was named, was there in 1852-1853. The first survey of the harbour was in 1846.
[8]Rear-Admiral R. L. Baynes to Governor J. Douglas, 26 October 1858, Adm. 1/5713.
[9]Baynes to Sec. of Adm., 10 January 1860, Adm. 1/5969.
[10]See above, chapter 5.

On the northeastern side of Constance Cove, barracks, which were constructed for the Royal Engineers engaged in the Boundary Commission survey of 1859-1862, were destined to become naval property— simply to keep them from falling into private hands. Further north on this same shore stood "Dallas Bank," later known as "Maple Bank," where the Commander-in-Chief resided after 1864. In the upper reaches of Esquimalt Harbour lay Cole Island, chosen by naval and military officers as a site for a munitions depot in 1860, one year after the Admiralty decided to establish a powder magazine to supply Her Majesty's ships in the North Pacific.

Such a facility seemed especially necessary because the international tension between Britain and the United States appeared likely to develop into war. In the words of Rear-Admiral Sir Thomas Maitland:

> A powder magazine must be built as soon as possible as there is at present no secure place for ammunition, and in case of War, it would be many months before a supply could be sent out from England. The ammunition at Valparaiso would be quite out of the way from that part of the station, and if it became a Neutral Port, the Chilian Government [sic] might possibly object to its being kept there.[11]

By the end of 1862 the magazine had been constructed at last and a marine guard posted for its protection. No longer were powder and shell sent to the storeships at Valparaiso and Callao. The Admiralty decision to erect a munitions depot at Esquimalt Harbour was consistent with its realization that the headquarters of the Pacific squadron would be transferred from Valparaiso to Esquimalt.[12]

Esquimalt becomes Pacific Station Headquarters

The decision of 1862 to transfer the station headquarters from Valparaiso was dictated mainly by political influences. Admittedly, the need for a depot to hold provisions and naval stores at Esquimalt had become evident as early as 1851, when Rear-Admiral Fairfax Moresby, Commander-in-Chief, Pacific, recommended that the harbour be reserved for naval purposes.[13] A similar suggestion came four years later from Rear-

11Rear-Admiral Sir T. Maitland to Sec. of Adm., 1 February 1862, Adm. 1/5790. The problems of keeping stores at Valparaiso have been considered in John Bach, "The Maintenance of Royal Navy Vessels in the Pacific Ocean, 1825-1875," *Mariner's Mirror*, LVI (August 1970) , 262-64.
12Minute of Admiral Milne, 6 June 1859, on Baynes to Sec. of Adm. 28 March 1859, Adm. 1/5713.
13Rear-Admiral F. Moresby to Sec. of Adm., 3 July 1851; in W. Kaye Lamb, ed., "Correspondence Relating to the Establishment of a Naval Base at Esquimalt, 1851-57," *British Columbia Historical Quarterly*, VI (October 1942) , 280.

Admiral Bruce.[14] But as we have seen, the Admiralty and Foreign Office neglected to give more than casual thought to the problem of a satisfactory base for the Pacific squadron until the Crimean War. At that time, the rise of Russian naval power in the Pacific and the suspected clandestine cooperation of the United States with Russia in 1856 alarmed Sir Charles Wood, the First Lord of the Admiralty. Wood knew that increasing the number of British warships in the Pacific would be expensive, though not difficult; but—as he advised the Earl of Clarendon, the Foreign Secretary—"the want of any good place for repairs and refitting is serious."[15] Hopefully, a remedy could be found; accordingly, instructions were sent to Bruce to report on the suitability of Esquimalt and other sites on Vancouver Island as a naval base.[16] No other locations were under consideration.

After his visit to Vancouver Island in the summer of 1856, Bruce advocated that a base be located at Esquimalt. In his opinion, this would strengthen the British colony of Vancouver Island, "sandwiched" as it was between territories of two expanding powers, Russia and the United States.[17] But in the postwar period, in keeping with the Ministry's concern for British interests in Central America that were threatened by American filibusters, the Admiralty considered Taboga Island off Panama as a possible base.[18] There the Pacific Steam Navigation Company maintained a storehouse and hospital and the Navy, as already mentioned, possessed a coal depot. Esquimalt was momentarily forgotten.

However, the northward shift of the centre of the station duties in 1858 and 1859 constituted one important reason for rejecting Taboga Island. The Northwest Coast was where most ships on station were needed, and to a degree which required more than the periodic attention of the Commander-in-Chief. Captain James Prevost, the Senior Naval Officer at Vancouver Island, touched on this fact when he wrote to the Secretary of the Admiralty in 1858 that the value of Vancouver Island to

---

[14]Bruce Journal, 11 September 1855, Adm. 50/308. He thought the storeship *Naiad* should be moved from Callao to Esquimalt.

[15]Sir Charles Wood to Lord Clarendon, 2 January 1856, Halifax Papers, Add. MSS. 49, 565, B.M.

[16]Wood to Bruce, 16 February 1856, *ibid.* In these instructions, the First Lord noted of Esquimalt: "It is so far from us, and the access to it overland is so difficult that it would be impossible to succour it in time to preserve it from an unforseen assault. On the other hand, there is coal, wood and supplies of various kinds of which it might be well to avail ourselves in a good climate."

[17]Bruce to Wood, 22 September 1856, *ibid.*

[18]Minutes of A. Blackwood (Adm.) , 20 February 1858, on H. Vansittart (F.O.) to Sec. of Adm., 17 November 1857, Adm. 1/5696. Neither Baynes nor Maitland favoured a permanent naval depot at Panama, but merely sought the use of the Pacific Steam Navigation Company's facilities. Maitland to Sec. of Adm., 22 February 1861, Adm. 1/5761.

Britain increased with the rapid growth of American interests in the Territories of Oregon and Washington. With more ships-of-war calling at Esquimalt, even a temporary establishment for coal and provisions would be useful.[19]

The lack of a base of operations in the North Pacific became even more noticeable during the Fraser River gold rush and the San Juan boundary dispute. The flagship *Ganges,* for example, was unable to proceed to the storeships at Callao and Valparaiso for nearly two years; and she encountered delay in returning to England because she could not carry out a quick refit at Esquimalt.[20] It is not surprising that Rear-Admiral Baynes recommended establishing a supply depot at Esquimalt.[21]

The Admiralty wanted to find a solution and lost no time in reviewing the question of the best location for the Pacific station headquarters. The higher cost of sending supplies to Esquimalt compared to Panama caused some concern.[22] Nevertheless, by 1859 it had become apparent at the Admiralty that in Vancouver Island Britain possessed a colony "offering all the advantages we can desire."[23] By frequenting this territory, the Navy would protect its trade, increase its commerce and develop its resources. Britain could expect freight rates to decline with the growth of trade. Above all, increased strategic advantages would arise from having a base in the North Pacific.[24] This convincing argument shifted Admiralty policy in favour of Esquimalt.

The supporting views of Vice-Admiral W. F. ("Fly") Martin, the Senior Naval Lord, were also influential. Martin realized that the duties of the squadron were shifting gradually from southern to northern latitudes, and that the centre of British interests in the Eastern Pacific was in actuality the British portion of the Northwest Coast of America. This judgement was accurate. Without reservation, he advocated that a harbour on Vancouver Island should become the station headquarters— not necessarily Esquimalt but certainly the best one available. And he wrote:

> The sooner this is done, the sooner we shall be able to commence arrangements indispensable for operations in the Pacific in the event of a war with the United States or Russia. If these powers have dockyards & resources in the North Pacific and we have not, for every shilling spent by either of them, in that sea, in a war with us,

[19]Prevost to Sec. of Adm., 7 June 1858, Adm. 1/5696.
[20]Baynes to Sec. of Adm., 18 December 1860, Adm. 1/5761.
[21]Baynes to Sec. of Adm., 1 December 1859, Adm. 1/5969.
[22]Minute of Rear-Admiral Sir Richard Milne, 10 Feb. 1859, *ibid.* Panama would be the main depot with a subsidiary storeship kept at Esquimalt, according to Milne.
[23]Minute of Vice-Admiral Sir Richard Dundas, 11 February 1859, *ibid.*
[24]*Ibid.*

we should spend a Guinea. Indeed, without some basis of operations in Vancouver island, we should have to abandon those seas
in an American War. The duties of the station can be as well conducted from Vancouver's island as from Valparaiso or the Bay of
Panama whilst the frequent visits of our ships will be of infinite
importance to the colony.[25]

The Lords of the Admiralty were now in general agreement that a
change from Valparaiso to Vancouver Island was desirable, but they
deferred the decision until Rear-Admiral Baynes could report on matters
of supply, depot ships, communications, sites for a naval yard and
hospital, and notably the benefits that the presence of the Navy would
confer on the colonies of Vancouver Island and British Columbia.[26] In
connection with the last of these objectives, instructions subsequently
sent to Baynes stated clearly that the proposed transfer to northern
waters would not affect operations in the Pacific islands, and added that
"while in a political point of view and in connection with Kamschatka
[sic] and with China, the position of British Columbia may present
important advantages which should be fully considered in your report."[27]

Baynes's reply testifies both to the shift of British interests to the North
Pacific and to the superiority of Esquimalt over Panama as the Pacific
naval station headquarters. Only on two counts did Baynes question
the suitability of Esquimalt. He was concerned about the ease with
which sailors could desert from there to the gold fields of Pacific America,
and the ease with which enemy warships could shell the harbour.[28] In
view of Esquimalt's military vulnerability, he was reluctant to recommend it as station headquarters until after Captain George H. Richards
of H.M.S. *Plumper* completed surveys of the island's harbours and of an
alternative site at Burrard Inlet, a commodious haven on the mainland
shore near the mouth of the Fraser River.[29]

[25]Minute of Vice-Admiral W. F. Martin, 17 February 1859, *ibid.*
[26]Minute of Sir John Pakington (First Lord of the Admiralty), 19 February 1859,
ibid.
[27]Admiralty instructions to Baynes, 10 March 1859, draft, *ibid.*
[28]Baynes to Sec. of Adm., 12 May 1859, *ibid.*
[29]In 1859, a public debate began as to whether Esquimalt or Burrard Inlet should
become the headquarters. See the *Times* (London), 15 March and 22 June 1860;
Matthew MacFie, *Vancouver Island and British Columbia* (London: Longman,
Green, Longman, Roberts & Green, 1865), p. 127; and J. D. Pemberton, *Facts and
Figures Relating to Vancouver Island and British Columbia* (London: Longman,
Green, Longman & Roberts, 1860), p. 12. Actually, lands on Burrard Inlet did not go
unnoticed, for in 1860 some were reserved "for naval purposes." See Douglas
to the Duke of Newcastle (C.O.), 23 December 1859, and enclosures, C.O. 60/5; Plan
of Sections reserved for Naval Department, item 16, Adm. Corr. II, B.C.A.; File Misc.
4 (Parry Papers I), Item 8, H.O., For sailing ships, access to Burrard Inlet was
"entirely unsuitable"; Rear-Admiral the Honourable George Hastings to Sec. of Adm.,
18 October 1867, Adm. 1/6008.

To Baynes, the obvious disadvantages of Esquimalt were of no consequence in comparison to its principal advantage—providing a base from which British warships could support the infant colony. Baynes firmly believed that the British possessions on the Northwest Coast promised to become "of immense importance," for their healthy climate and secure harbours would foster commercial development and population growth.[30] Their proximity to Russian America on the north and the United States on the south were proof to him that at all times they deserved as much care as the British government and the Commander-in-Chief, Pacific, could give them. This meant that a harbour on Vancouver Island should be designated as the Pacific station headquarters.

The surveys of Captain Richards showed not only that Esquimalt unquestionably was the most suitable harbour on the British portion of the Northwest Coast but that it could be properly defended.[31] This was all that Baynes required to press the Admiralty for the transfer of the headquarters.[32] Probably his recommendation would have been acted on at once if a change had not occurred in the Admiralty's membership when a new cabinet was formed in June 1859. Panic over the rapid construction of armoured ships by France, notably *La Gloire*, also caused the much less critical issue of the Pacific station headquarters to receive little if any attention until the following March. Even then, their Lordships seemed reluctant to follow the policy of their immediate predecessors. They instructed Rear-Admiral Sir Thomas Maitland, the new Commander-in-Chief, to report on the suitability of Esquimalt as station headquarters. This caused additional delay in resolving what the Comptroller of Victualling considered to be a most critical question.[33]

Maitland's recommendations were remarkably similar to those of Baynes and therefore need little comment here.[34] In the main, the Admiralty policy of 1862 on the change of station headquarters from Valparaiso to Esquimalt was based on these recommendations.[35] On

[30]Baynes to Sec. of Adm., 12 May 1859, Adm. 1/5969.

[31]Report of Captain George H. Richards on the Harbours of Vancouver's Island and British Columbia, encl. in Richards to Douglas, 23 October 1859, "Papers re: British Columbia, Pt. II," *Parliamentary Papers*, 1859 (Session II), XXII (2578), with charts and maps. See also Admiral J. Washington, Hydrographer, Memorandum of 5 May 1859, encl. in H. Merivale (C.O.) to Sec. of Adm., 26 June 1859, Adm. 1/5721.

[32]Baynes to Sec. of Adm., 14 November 1859, Adm. 1/5969. He also thought that the War Office should consider the matter of shore batteries.

[33]Victualling Dept. to Sec. of Adm., 13 March 1860, and minute of Eden, 19 March 1860, Adm. 1/5761.

[34]See his three reports to the Secretary of the Admiralty for 25 January 1861 (Adm. 1/5761), 27 August 1861 (Adm. 1/5969), and 10 January 1862 (Adm. 1/5790).

[35]Instructions to Rear-Admiral Kingcome, 2 December 1862, Adm. 13/5. See also, John Bach, "The Royal Navy and the South Pacific, 1826-1876" (Ph.D. thesis; University of New South Wales, 1964). A commodore at Valparaiso was in charge of the Southern Division (south of the Equator).

only one matter was there a difference of opinion. Maitland recommended that an old frigate be used as a storeship at Esquimalt until storehouses were built. However, the Admiralty decided to construct storehouses immediately and allocated £1,000 for that purpose. This proved to be a hasty decision, for the Admiralty soon learned to their chagrin—as naval commanders had warned—that the Navy held no clear title to suitable land in Esquimalt Harbour other than Thetis Island, which by this time was almost entirely covered with coal sheds.[36] Consequently, the construction of the storehouses had to be deferred to a later date.[37]

The Admiralty's decision to transfer the station headquarters to Esquimalt represented a significant step in the growth of British commercial and political interests on the Northwest Coast.[38] This development, especially auspicious for the colonies of Vancouver Island and British Columbia, resulted in an expansion of naval base facilities in 1863 and 1864. A guard house was built on Duntze Head and the hospital was removed to buildings vacated by the Royal Engineers on the northeastern side of Constance Cove.[39] The hospital now became a permanent facility, as opposed to a temporary one, in keeping with the importance Esquimalt had assumed as station headquarters.[40] In view of this expansion, the Colonial administration at Vancouver Island refused permission to private individuals wishing to build wharves in Esquimalt Harbour until such time as the Admiralty formulated its plans for the naval establishment.[41] All this indicated a growing importance—albeit small in comparison to other parts of the world—of British interests in the Pacific.

A fur trader who later became a collector of customs summed-up Esquimalt's importance to the British in 1863 as follows:

> Apart from its immense advantages of access for the larger class of vessels in a mercantile point of view, it [Esquimalt] has been selected as the rallying point for the squadrons commissioned to protect in the North Pacific the interests of Great Britain. Here in a land-

[36]Maitland to Sec. of Adm., 8 August 1861, Adm. 1/5761.
[37]Maitland, Colonel R. C. Moody, R.E., and Capt. Richards recommended that two sites would be suitable for a naval establishment of docks and storehouses. One, adjacent to Thetis Island (finally selected), was most convenient for ships, yet would be exposed to enemy bombardment. The second was at the head of Constance Cove. Maitland to Sec. of Adm., 24 April 1861, Adm. 1/5969.
[38]Instructions to Kingcome, 2 December 1862, Adm. 13/5.
[39]Elevations and plans of these buildings are in File No. Misc. 18, Item 2, H.O.
[40]See Kingcome to Sec. of Adm., 23 November 1863, and Minute of Richards (now Hydrographer of the Admiralty), 14 January 1864, ibid.
[41]Maitland to Douglas, 26 June and 2 September 1862, F 1206, 28 and 34, Ships' letters, B.C.A.

locked harbour wherein large fleets may be safely moored with a thriving colony of British subjects around, and with a sister colony (that of British Columbia) teeming with mineral wealth, and within a few hours sail, commanding, too, as it does in the hands of Britain, should future difficulty arise, the whole commerce of the N. Pacific, from California to Siberia, from Siberia to Japan, Esquimalt it would seem, is destined to become a point of extreme importance on the Western Coast of America for the furtherance and protection of British interests and commerce.[42]

Changes at Esquimalt after 1862

Although Esquimalt had become the chief haven of the Navy in the Pacific and the focal point of its operations in 1862, no proper depot for provisions, clothing or stores had been constructed. It was still necessary for ships to go to Valparaiso for replenishing stores and for some refitting purposes. The limited facilities which Esquimalt did possess for storage—two small storehouses built on Duntze Head in 1862—were of wood, which made them a fire hazard. What is more, they had been built unwisely in a position exposed to possible enemy bombardment. When Rear-Admiral John Kingcome reviewed the matter in 1863, he came to the conclusion that the storehouses should be moved to a more protected site within the harbour. In this, he knew he had the support of the War Office, which had objected to buildings being constructed on Duntze Head, for this strategic position commanded the narrow harbour entrance and provided a likely site for future gun emplacements.[43] Henceforth, future structures were built of brick and in more secure positions.

By the close of 1863, Kingcome had realized some of his aims. A small staff consisting of an assistant paymaster, clerk, ship's steward, storeman and cooper, came from England to take charge of the storehouses.[44] Ammunition was stored on Cole Island and on Thetis Island, all "in sight of and under the immediate care of the Senior Officer at Esquimalt" and visited nightly by a guard boat.[45] Valparaiso's role as a supply centre declined. Stores were transferred from Valparaiso to Esquimalt and provisions were sent directly from England to Esquimalt along with machinery required for maintaining a navy then undergoing a technological transformation.[46]

---

[42]A. C. Anderson, "History of the Northwest Coast" 1878; typescript in B.C.A. from the original in the Academy of Pacific Coast History, University of California at Berkeley, pp. 106-107. Anderson was not alone in his enthusiasm, as the works of Mayne, Pemberton, MacFie and Rattnay cited in this chapter will attest.

[43]Kingcome to Sec. of Adm., 14 July 1863, Esq. Nav. Estab. Rec., I, M.M.B.C.

[44]Admiralty to Kingcome, 18 December 1863, *ibid.*

[45]Kingcome to Sec. of Adm., 5 December 1863, *ibid.*

[46]Rear-Admiral the Hon. J. Denman to Sec. of Adm., 21 November 1864, *ibid.*

This formative period in Esquimalt's history in the years between 1858 and 1864 occurred at a time when Admiralty policy, in reflecting British government attitudes, opposed spending large sums on shore establishments anywhere in the world. Accordingly, facilities at Esquimalt developed somewhat haphazardly and with great difficulty in view of the high costs of land brought about by the gold rush of 1858-1859 and the erection of mercantile establishments on the harbour shores. Even after plans for the naval and victualling stores depot were approved in 1865, the Commander-in-Chief considered stationing a storeship in Esquimalt Harbour as a cheaper measure than purchasing property ashore. When figures were cited to show that the storeship *Naiad* at Callao cost over £6,000 yearly to operate and required the services of thirty-five men, the Admiralty dismissed the idea of stationing a storeship at Vancouver Island. The Board believed it better to spend money on shore establishments.[47]

What their Lordships had in mind in 1865, when they authorized a small "naval and victualling" depot at Esquimalt, was creating facilities to hold provisions and stores. Among other things, they felt that the increasing importance of the Colony of Vancouver Island made Esquimalt the best choice for such a depot for the Pacific squadron.[48] Actually, however, the Admiralty was merely authorizing the administration of an establishment that already existed.[49]

In 1866 other structures were erected to hold machinery for re-venting guns, to store spars and to house ordnance supplies. During the winter of 1866-1867, St. Paul's Anglican Church was built just south of Signal Hill.[50] A dry-dock was in the planning stage.

Commander Richard C. Mayne had deplored the fact that five British warships stationed at Vancouver Island were reliant on an American dry-dock at Mare Island in San Francisco Bay, the only facility of its kind in the North Pacific. In 1861, the surveying vessel *Hecate*, 6-guns, ran aground and after provisional repairs were made at Esquimalt, she was convoyed by another British warship to Mare Island. Referring to the charged atmosphere in Anglo-American relations at the time of the *Trent* Affair, Mayne complained that this accident occurred when war with the Americans seemed imminent. "Had it broken out," he con-

[47]Denman to Sec. of Adm., 17 August 1865, Adm. 1/5969.
[48]Order-in-Council, 29 June 1865. See note 2 of this chapter.
[49]*Ibid.*
[50]That position proved too exposed, for in 1875 a severe storm nearly blew the wooden structure down and the vibrations of gunfire broke numerous windows. In 1904, the church was moved to its present position at the corner of Esquimalt Road and Grafton Street.

cluded, "the 'Hecate' must have been trapped, and the services of a powerful steamer would have been lost to the country."[51]

Retrenchment

With the planning of the much-needed dry-dock it appeared that Esquimalt soon would be a naval establishment fully capable of serving a squadron of twelve to fifteen ships, ranging in size from the ironclad *Zealous* to the gunboat *Forward*. However, the necessity for economy led the Admiralty to shelve all plans for expansion of the naval base in 1869.

This is not the place to examine fully the implications of drastic economy measures on the efficiency of the fleet. Suffice it to say that as early as the seventeenth century, men such as Samuel Pepys, that diligent historian of maritime affairs, realized that large economies could not be made without some decline in the condition of the naval service. Pepys wrote:

> The ordinary way in all times in England, upon want of money and disquiets in government, [is] to find faults with the management of expensefulness of the Navy, determining generally in some insignificant retrenchments of charge for the better rectifying their complaints; but to the real disservice of the State, the retrenchments having [been] always such as have been afterwards found necessary to be revoked, with increase.[52]

Nonetheless, in Gladstone's first ministry, formed in 1868, H. G. C. Childers, the First Lord of the Admiralty, willingly supported his Prime Minister's ideas for retrenchment in armaments spending. Under Childers, the Admiralty opposed increasing the facilities at Esquimalt to meet all possible emergencies on the station and opposed keeping more than "ordinary stores."[53] The latter policy in limiting naval stores was adopted against the advice of the Storekeeper General of the Admiralty, the Honourable Robert Dundas. He complained vehemently that as long as ships were on duty in the North Pacific a port there for refit and replenishment was essential. He went even further, saying that any economy which might result from reverting to Valparaiso would reproduce the inconvenient system which the Order-in-Council of 1865 had tried to eliminate.[54] But his words went unheeded; in the interests of

---

[51]Richard C. Mayne, *Four Years in British Columbia and Vancouver Island* (London: John Murray, 1862), pp. 24-25.

[52]J. R. Tanner, ed., *Samuel Pepys's Naval Minutes* (London: Navy Records Society, Vol. LX, 1926), pp. 39-40.

[53]Admiralty Minute, 18 March 1869, Adm. 1/6137.

[54]R. Dundas to Sec. of Adm., 9 March 1869, *ibid.*

"economy," the station headquarters reverted to Valparaiso in 1869.[55] In addition, the naval force maintained in the Pacific was reduced to ten ships (one iron-clad as flagship, five corvettes or sloops, three smaller vessels and one stationary storeship) and about two thousand men.[56]

Esquimalt was not alone in suffering from government frugality in 1869. China, East Indies, Cape, West Coast of Africa and South East Coast of South America stations were also reduced by a total of about 14 ships and 2,600 to 2,700 men.[57] To compensate for this reduction, as well as for other reasons, the Admiralty created a training or "Flying Squadron," as it became generally known, consisting of six screw-warships.[58] It made a round-the-world voyage in 1869-1870, calling briefly at various naval bases and coaling stations including Esquimalt.[59] Rival powers may have been impressed with Britain's ability to spare so many ships for this purpose. But they must also have been aware of the decrease in naval strength abroad in subsequent years, as illustrated by the reduction of Pacific station from thirteen ships and 2,968 men in 1869 to nine ships and 1,595 men by 1874.[60]

The development of Esquimalt as a naval base had been halted by 1869. However, the existing facilities continued to be useful to ships of the Pacific squadron, particularly those assigned to duties on the North-west Coast. At that time, there was always one frigate as "post ship" at Esquimalt, plus the gun-vessel *Sparrowhawk* and the gunboat *Boxer* on permanent service for visiting coastal settlements, policing the Indians, and checking illicit whisky traffic.[61]

Esquimalt's buildings still held half of all stores kept on the station. Its coal sheds, timber yards and hospital remained in operation. Its heavy machinery in the factory was still in use: a large screw-cutting lathe, a

---

[55]Admiralty instructions to Rear-Admiral Hastings, 26 January 1869, Adm. 13/40.
[56]Admiralty Minute, 25 January 1869, Adm. 1/6127.
[57]Admiralty Minute, 23 January 1869, *ibid.* There was no reduction on the Australian station at this time.
[58]According to Admiralty draft instructions to Rear-Admiral G. Phipps Hornby, dated 10 June 1869 (Adm. 1/6108) , the cruiser squadron was being sent ". . . with the two-fold purpose of effecting reliefs to Ships and Crews on distant Foreign Stations, the force on which has been somewhat reduced—and also of improving the efficiency of officers and men, especially in handling Ships in Squadrons, upon which so much depends. . . ." Final instructions to this effect were sent to Hornby on 25 November 1869 (Adm. 1/6113) .
[59]For this cruise and the visit to Esquimalt (15-27 May 1870) , see J.B., *The Cruise Round the World of the Flying Squadron, 1869-1870, under the Command of Rear-Admiral G. T. Phipps Hornby* (London: J. D. Potter, 1871) and William Haynes, *My Log: A Journal of the Proceedings of the Flying Squadron* (Devonport: Clarke & Son, 1871) .
[60]See Appendix C for sources and further details on the distribution of the Royal Navy, 1861-1874.
[61]Hastings to Rear-Admiral A. Farquhar, 18 January 1870, Y 28, Adm. 1/6151.

drilling machine, a forge, and a furnace for casting metal were the only equipment of the kind available exclusively to ships of the Pacific squadron. In spite of demands for economy from within or without the Cabinet, circumstances made Esquimalt for strategic reasons the naval base—although not the declared headquarters—of the Royal Navy's ships in the Pacific.[62]

[62]See, for example, Hastings to Sec. of Adm., 22 February 1870, *ibid.*, and Longstaff, *Esquimalt Naval Base*, pp. 27-28.

Chapter 9

A DECADE OF ANGLO-AMERICAN ANTAGONISM
1861-1871

THE GREATEST STIMULUS to development of British territories in North
America during the nineteenth century was fear—whether real or imaginary—of American expansionist tendencies. This was a century of
rivalry between Britain and the United States in continental aspirations
and, increasingly, in maritime enterprise. Long-standing grievances were
involved, some of which originated west of the Rocky Mountains. These
conflicts remained unresolved through the War of 1812 and nearly
resulted in hostilities during the Oregon crisis and the Crimean War. In
the course of the American Civil War, several incidents involving Britain
endangered the peace. But an Anglo-American war was averted by adroit
diplomacy on both sides. The Civil War was barely over when the American government purchased Alaska from Russia, thus increasing the
danger of American expansion into the Canadian Northwest and British
Columbia.

The policies of Britain and the activities of the Royal Navy in the
decade of Anglo-American antagonism extending from the beginning
of the Civil War in 1861 to the entry of British Columbia into the
Canadian confederation in 1871 were designed to safeguard British
sovereignty on the Northwest Coast. In view of plans for a Canadian
trans-continental railway, the headquarters of the Royal Navy's Pacific
squadron at Esquimalt assumed a new position in Imperial defence.
British planners regarded Esquimalt as the eventual terminus of a railway considered vital to the defence of the Empire. They saw it also as a

gateway to British possessions and trade in the Orient. The Canadian Pacific Railway was not completed until 1885, however; until then British Columbia remained isolated from Canada. Because problems of military defence remained unresolved, the Royal Navy continued to safeguard British Columbia.

"Naval Security" During the American Civil War

The period between 1861 and 1871 found British politicians and public alike opposed to building costly fortifications abroad, manned by British troops, invariably at the expense of the taxpayer at home.[1] Self-government implied self-defence; or as Gladstone put it so aptly in 1864, it was "impossible to separate the blessings and benefits of freedom from its burdens."[2] Under successive Secretaries of State for War and the Colonies, the "burdens" were shifted in the main to the self-governing parts of the Empire.[3] But in the case of Vancouver Island and British Columbia, the Select Committee of the House of Commons, appointed in 1861 to consider the apportionment of colonial military expenditure, reported that considerable contributions could not be expected from them to defray costs for the Royal Engineers stationed there since 1859. The reason for this was that these colonies had only just been settled.[4] Although they were not self-governing, as "Colonies Proper" they were classified, perhaps optimistically, as largely responsible for the costs of their own military defence. In March 1862, the Commons, on the basis of this report, adopted a resolution that self-governing colonies should be mainly responsible for their internal order and defence and ought to assist in their own "external defence."[5] Such were the government's intentions.

In point of fact, the colonies of Vancouver Island and British Columbia were unable and unwilling to undertake their own defence. With

---

[1]See C. P. Stacey, *Canada and the British Army, 1846-1871,* rev. ed. (Toronto: University of Toronto Press, 1963), pp. 43ff., and Robert L. Schuyler, "The Recall of the Legions: A Phase in the Decentralization of the British Empire," *American Historical Review,* XXVI (October 1920), 18-36.
[2]Lord John Morley, *The Life of William Ewart Gladstone,* 3 vols. (London: Macmillan, 1903), I, 573.
[3]A separate War Office was established in 1854.
[4]Resolution of Lord Stanley, 21 June 1861, "Report . . . Colonial Military Expenditure," *Parliamentary Papers,* 1861, XXI (423), p. xiv. At that time, British Columbia's contribution (£11,000) to support 138 Royal Engineers (165 were originally sent) engaged on "colonial" not "imperial duties" remained unpaid. Actually, the engineers had been sent at the time of the gold rush in keeping with the policy that "wherever England extended the sway of her sceptre, there she pledged the defence of her sword. . . ." Minutes of Evidence, 18 April 1861, *ibid.,* p. 4.
[5]Great Britain, *Hansard's Parliamentary Debates,* 3rd Series, CLXV, col. 1060. On the labours of the Committee, see Donald C. Gordon. *The Dominion Partnership in Imperial Defense, 1870-1914* (Baltimore: John Hopkins Press, 1965), pp. 12-23.

a population of only about fourteen thousand in 1861, they could ill-afford the detatchment of Royal Engineers—which was disbanded subsequently in November 1863. The defence of the Pacific colonies remained the responsibility of the Navy. As long as warships continued to visit settlements on Vancouver Island and British Columbia a colonial naval force—although permitted by the Colonial Naval Defence Act of 1856—was not required.[6] The colonists knew that the two gunboats, the *Forward* and *Grappler,* assigned permanently for coastal duties and assisted when necessary by steam frigates and corvettes that called at Esquimalt, would usually suffice. The costs of maintaining these ships for the defence of these distant dependencies, however, did little to reduce burdens on the English taxpayer, as the government's reforms had intended.

In the American Civil War, which began in April 1861, Britain occupied the position of observer of a conflict eventually to cripple her trade with both the Union and the Confederacy. In order to avoid becoming involved in the struggle she pursued a policy of neutrality. To this end, Governor James Douglas, previously censured by the Secretary of State for the Colonies for his belligerent plans in response to the American military occupation of San Juan Island in 1859, received carefully-worded instructions dated 11 May 1861 that in the event of an Anglo-American war, ships of the Royal Navy in the North Pacific were to show preference to neither Union nor Confederate forces.[7] By 7 August, the Commander-in-Chief, Pacific, possessed the Queen's Proclamation of 15 May ordering that neutrality was to be observed in all British dealings with the Union and Confederate governments.[8]

British warships, including the flagship and five others, concentrated near the southern tip of Vancouver Island at the outbreak of the Civil War. Danger existed that the unresolved San Juan boundary dispute might lead to something more serious; a few American officials even considered provoking quarrels with Britain, with the conquest of British North America in view.[9] Certainly, the colonies of Vancouver Island and

---

[6]28 *Vic.,* c. 14; under this statute, self-governing colonies could commission their own naval forces. See B. A. Knox, "Colonial Influence on Imperial Policy, 1858-1866: Victoria and the Colonial Defence Act, 1865," *Historical Studies: Australia and New Zealand,* XI (November 1963) , 66-67.

[7]The Duke of Newcastle to Governor James Douglas, 11 May 1861, confid., encl. in A. G. Young to Ozzard, 23 Sept. 1861, R.G. 8, IIIB, Vol. 35, P.A.C.

[8]Queen's Proclamation, 15 May 1861, encl. in C. Paget (Adm.) to Rear-Admiral Sir T. Maitland, 16 May 1861, *ibid.*

[9]Robin W. Winks, *Canada and the United States: The Civil War Years* (Baltimore: John Hopkins Press, 1960) , pp. 35-36, and Kenneth Bourne, *Britain and the Balance of Power in North America, 1815-1908* (London: Longmans, Green & Co., 1967) , pp. 210-211.

British Columbia were likely fields of American conquest. Realizing this, Lord Palmerston, the Prime Minister, suggested sending an infantry battalion from China to British Columbia and increasing the British squadrons in American waters.[10] The Colonial Office supported his view. But the First Lord of the Admiralty, the Duke of Somerset, who was shamefully ignorant of American naval strength in the Pacific, considered the British squadron of twelve ships adequate for the protection of the colonies on the Northwest Coast.[11] Thus, no troops were dispatched; the government recognized in effect that the security of these territories rested with so-called "naval security."[12]

On 8 November 1861 the British packet *Trent* was boarded in Bahama Channel by an armed party of Americans from the U.S.S. *San Jacinto*. Two Confederate commissioners were taken forcibly from the British ship. To the British ministry this incident constituted a flagrant violation of neutral rights at sea; from the British public it elicited some demands for war. The ensuing controversy was perhaps the most alarming development in Anglo-American relations since 1815. Immediately, the Foreign Office sought redress from the American government and instructed the Admiralty to issue orders that the Royal Navy should commence hostilities with United States forces only in self-defence.[13]

The serious nature of the *Trent* crisis is indicated by the fact that the British government took military precautions which resulted in more than eleven thousand fully-equipped troops being sent between 12

[10]Lord Palmerston (Prime Minister) to the Duke of Somerset (Adm.), 26 May 1861, Palmerston Papers, Add. MSS. 48, 582, B.M.
[11]*Ibid.* Somerset thought the United States Navy had only one small vessel in the Pacific. See Bourne, *Britain and the Balance of Power*, p. 215. He evidently failed to check the quarterly returns of commanders-in-chief on foreign stations giving strengths of foreign navies. For the period under review, the annual composition of United States naval forces in the Pacific, as given in Robert E. Johnson, *Thence Round Cape Horn: The Story of United States Naval Forces on Pacific Station, 1818-1923* (Annapolis, Md.: United States Naval Institute, 1963), App. 3, was:

Year	Ships	Year	Ships
1861	9	1867	16
1862	7	1868	15
1863	5	1869	11
1864	8	1870	12
1865	8	1871	12
1866	11		

Statistics on the British naval strength for the Pacific for this period are given in Appendix B.
[12]This strange phrase was used often in the 1860's. See W. C. B. Tunstall, "Imperial Defence, 1815-1870," in *Cambridge History of the British Empire*, II (Cambridge: Cambridge University Press, 1961), 831.
[13]Lord John Russell (F.O.) to Lord Lyons (Br. Minister, Washington), and Russell to Adm., 30 Nov. 1861, in *Official Records of the Union and Confederate Navies in the War of Rebellion*, 30 vols. (Washington, 1894-1922), ser. I, Vol. I, 158ff.

December 1861 and 4 January 1862 to fortify the exposed Canadian frontier.[14]

By the spring of 1862, some eighteen thousand regulars were stationed in British North America. While these figures seem impressive, it should not be overlooked that the British ministry recognized that superiority at sea—particularly on the Atlantic seaboard and the Great Lakes, the chief areas of contention and blockade—would be fundamental to British victory. In consequence, the North American and West Indies station was increased from twenty-two ships to about thirty, the additions comprising mainly battleships and frigates; the Pacific squadron gained a corvette and sloop to bring the total to fourteen vessels. The average number of warships on the Pacific station increased to its highest since the Oregon crisis—needing an average of twelve to sixteen warships—during the years 1860-1867.[15]

Throughout the Civil War, the possibility existed that if Britain were to become involved, American shipping in the Pacific bearing letters-of-marque might prey on British interests scattered throughout the far reaches of that ocean. Thus Rear-Admiral Sir Thomas Maitland, the Commander-in-Chief, Pacific, feared that fifteen American clipper ships at San Francisco might be converted into corvettes carrying twenty to twenty-four guns. He also feared that steamers plying the routes to Panama and Mexico could be similarly armed, not to mention numerous American ships in the guano trade and whaling industry.[16] To meet this contingency, he planned that in the event of war the British Pacific squadron would blockade San Francisco, thereby controlling the centre of American maritime activity on the Pacific coast. Further, at Panama the flagship *Bacchante*, 51 guns, would protect British mail services, Pacific Steam Navigation Company establishments and vessels, and watch ship movements. But because the station headquarters at Esquimalt possessed neither a garrison nor a battery, Maitland did not plan to withdraw the four ships there—the steam frigate *Topaze,* the surveying paddle-sloop *Hecate,* and the gunboats *Forward* and *Grappler*— for service elsewhere on the North Pacific Coast.[17]

With full awareness of the critical state of affairs and of the strength of the United States Navy in the Pacific, Maitland emphasized to the Admiralty the urgency of *"largely increasing without delay"* the Pacific squadron in order to protect British interests from Valparaiso to Van-

---

[14]Bourne, *Britain and the Balance of Power,* p. 229; Stacey, *Canada and the British Army,* p. 118.
[15]See Appendix B.
[16]Rear-Admiral Maitland to Sec. of Adm., 13 January 1862, Adm. 1/5790.
[17]*Ibid.*

couver Island.[18] By the time his plea reached the Admiralty, the Ministry, as noted above, had already strengthened the squadrons in American waters.

Ironically, American naval officers were similarly afraid of Britain's naval strength in the Pacific. Reports of "many" warships joining the British Pacific squadron from the China and East Indies station soon after the *Trent* affair duped the United States Commander-in-Chief, Pacific, into believing that the British were preparing for war with the United States.[19]

Actually, the British Pacific squadron was increased by only two ships, one of which came from the Far East. But in another matter, the apprehensions of the American Commander-in-Chief were well founded. He feared that half the British squadron would suffice to "command" the city of San Francisco and take possession of the dockyard at nearby Mare Island owing to inadequate defences.[20] Certainly, he was right in concluding that these would be a British object of war. Because the British lacked docking facilities at Esquimalt and were dependent on the use of the Mare Island dock, British warships had no sure place to repair defects unless they seized and held San Francisco Bay and its environs.[21]

By contrast, neither the strange activities nor the numerical strength of the Russian Imperial Navy in the Pacific offered a threat to the British, although the more-than-friendly relations between Russia and the United States at this time must have concerned British naval commanders. Much has been written on the purpose of the visits in 1863 of six Russian corvettes to San Francisco Bay and a similar number to New York.[22] There can be little doubt, however, that this was a defensive

[18]*Ibid.*

[19]Report of Flag Officer Charles H. Bell to Gideon Welles (Sec. of the Navy), 29 May 1862; *Official Records of the Union and Confederate Navies,* Ser. I, Vol. I, p. 391.

[20]*Ibid.* The British consul at San Francisco urged Rear-Admiral Maitland to station a British warship there for the protection of British interests; C. Brooker to Maitland, 28 September 1861, Adm. 1/5761.

[21]Incidentally, about this time, Lieutenant Edmund Verney, commanding the gunboat *Grappler*, wrote privately to Arthur Mills, M.P., influential in discussions on colonial defence in London, to ask the Secretary of the Admiralty "what dock accommodation would be available for H.M. fleet in the Pacific, in the event of war with America, and whether H.M. Government contemplates the establishment of a dockyard in Vancouver Island." He added "everybody knows that Nature intended there should be a dockyard at Esquimalt." Verney to Mills, 30 August 1862, BF1214, B.C.A. See also the views of R. C. Mayne, given in the previous chapter, on the necessity of a dockyard at this time.

[22]For a review of this question, see Thomas A. Bailey, *A Diplomatic History of the American People,* 6th ed. (New York: Appleton-Century-Crofts, 1958), pp. 364-65. The Russians were willing to aid in the defence of San Francisco against Confederate ships rumoured to be found there. F. A. Golder, "The Russian Fleet and the Civil War," *American Historical Review,* XX (July 1915), 801-14.

measure on the part of the Russians. Probably they were in American ports seeking shelter from British and French forces, whose governments had opposed Russia's repression of the Poles in the preceding winter of 1862-1863. The inferiority of the Russian Navy in numbers and condition, as well as in supply and leadership meant that rather than face the separate or combined British and French navies at sea, Russian warships preferred to seek refuge as they had during the Crimean War.[23] They represented a danger to the Royal Navy only in alliance with Lincoln's Union government.

Difficulties of Maintaining British Neutrality

Throughout the Civil War, the Union Navy, which from the very outset demonstrated its command of the open seas, effectively blockaded Confederate ports on the Atlantic Ocean and Gulf of Mexico. Because the blockade undermined the strength of the South, the Secretary of the Confederate Navy believed that it could be broken by Confederate raiders preying on Northern commerce, which would compel the North to divert warships to protect her trade.[24] The South thus entered into contract with Liverpool shipbuilders for construction of iron-clads such as the *Alabama*. These were to be equipped with rams and, later, with heavy guns. As a result, relations between Washington and London became severely strained, for the North thought that the supposedly neutral British were assisting the Confederacy. Their resentment was understandable. In July 1862, the *Alabama* sailed from Liverpool from under the watch of British officials, to prey on Union shipping.

New York merchants, bankers and shipping interests feared that English-built Confederate ships and other Confederate privateers would prey on Pacific Mail Steamship Company vessels that carried some $40 million annually from California to Panama, for trans-shipment to New York.[25] The Union Navy, in consequence, was given orders to watch the Panama route.[26] The American consul at Panama knew that the task

---

[23]Rear-Admiral A. A. Popov instructed the Pacific squadron "to make the acquaintance of the colonies of the European sea powers, to seek out their valuable points, and constantly to be on guard. . . ." A. Belomer, "The Second Pacific Squadron," *Morskoy Sbornik*, CCLXXXIII (1914) , 54-55; in E. A. Adamov, "Russian and the United States at the time of the Civil War," *Journal of Modern History*, II (1930) , 598. These do not necessarily imply aggressive tactics on the part of Russia, however.
[24]On the naval objectives of the South, see James D. Bulloch, *The Secret Service of the Confederate States in Europe*, 2 vols. (London: R. Bentley & Son, 1883; reprint, New York and London: T. Yoseloff, 1959) , I, 46.
[25]Brainerd Dyer, "Confederate Naval and Privateering Activities in the Pacific," *Pacific Historical Review*, III (1934) , 433.
[26]Sec. of Navy to Flag Officer J. B. Montgomery, commanding United States Pacific squadron, 27 April 1861; *Official Records of the Union and Confederate Navies*, Ser. I, Vol. I, p. 15.

of the Union Navy would be easier if British warships on the Pacific station captured prizes taken by Confederate privateers. He endeavoured to solicit the support of the British counterpart at Panama by arguing that these prizes were a danger to British as well as to Union shipping, but without success.[27] British policy would not allow collaboration of this sort and the Royal Navy adhered to strict neutrality.

On the question of the use of British ports, the Northern States realized that Victoria and Esquimalt were likely places for parties sympathetic to the Confederacy to equip privateers, because of the proximity of these harbours to the Pacific states. As a matter of fact, a large portion of the population of Vancouver Island favoured the Confederate cause although the exact numbers cannot be known.[28] Consequently, the American consul at Victoria and captains of visiting Union warships watched for Confederate activity, although early rumours that Confederates were outfitting privateers on the Pacific Coast proved groundless.[29]

Simultaneously, United States government officials searched the Great Lakes area for enemy vessels. When it was rumoured in 1861 that the British ship *Peerless*, at Toronto, was a Confederate privateer, this aggravated the charged atmosphere in Anglo-American relations.[30] At this time, British naval commanders were under orders to prohibit the entry of belligerent warships and their prizes into the neutral waters of the British colonies on the Northwest Coast.[31] This measure was designed to prevent warships from converting prizes into privateers in British ports. Moreover, the Foreign Office had instructed the Admiralty to carry out the Queen's Proclamation of Strict Neutrality, dated 31 January 1862, to prevent either side from using British territorial waters and ports.[32] By these steps, the British government demonstrated a willingness to cooperate with the Union to ensure that Confederate privateers were not outfitted in British ports. Failure to do this might have led to war, for the United States was outraged that the Foreign Office did nothing to stop the Confederate raider *Alabama* from sailing out of Liverpool in July of 1862.

[27]Amos Corwine to Charles Henderson, 29 May 1861, encl. in Henderson to Capt. Wm. Graham, Senior Officer at Panama, 31 May 1861, R.G. 8, IIIB, Vol. 35, P.A.C.
[28]Estimating the amount of sympathy for the Confederacy is a difficult matter. However, support for both sides existed in Britain and the Pacific colonies. See the views of Lord Lyons expressed in his letter to Lord John Russell, 6 May 1861, Russell Papers, P.R.O.; in E. D. Adams, *Great Britain and the American Civil War*, 2 vols. (reprint; Gloucester, Mass: Peter Smith, 1957), I, 88, n.2.
[29]Maitland to Sec. of Adm., 14 July 1861, Adm. 1/5761.
[30]Copies of correspondence between the two governments were sent to the Commander-in-Chief, Pacific. See R.G. 8, IIIB, Vol. 35, P.A.C.
[31]Maitland to Douglas, 2 August 1861, *ibid.*
[32]Russell to Adm., 31 January 1862, *ibid.*

Early in 1863, when the American Secretary of State, William Seward, received information that a Confederate commodore was planning to purchase and man the British steamer *Thames* in Victoria, he asked Lord Lyons, the British Minister in Washington, to stop the project. Lyons was able to pacify Seward with a promise that everything would be done by Governor Douglas at Vancouver Island to halt such attempts.[33] But when the ill-informed Collector of Customs for Puget Sound, Victor Smith, reported that Confederate privateers were fitting out at Vancouver Island, that secessionists were active there and that official authorities would not act to stop them, Seward's fears were reinforced. The U.S.S. *Saginaw* was sent to investigate.[34] She found that no privateer had been fitted out at Victoria or elsewhere on the Pacific Coast.[35]

The Union undertook another search of Esquimalt and Victoria in the following year, 1864. This occurred after the American consulate at Victoria had informed the Military Department of Oregon that a Confederate privateer was preparing for sea with the purpose of capturing Union steamers carrying treasure on the Mexican Coast.[36] The U.S.S. *Narragansett*, sent from San Francisco to reconnoitre, found no activity. However, her use of Esquimalt Harbour for days at a time—ostensibly to get in touch with a mail steamer from California and to coal, but actually to gain intelligence of Confederate activity—led the Senior Naval Officer at Esquimalt, Captain Edward Hardinge, to complain to her commander that his action contravened the British policy of strict neutrality.[37] The Admiralty then forwarded instructions that the 48-hour limit for belligerent ships' visits was to be "strictly enforced at Vancouver Island."[38]

In the Pacific, the only real cause for alarm arose from the activities of the Confederate raider *Shenandoah*. After leaving London in October 1864 and receiving armament and ammunition at Madeira, she sailed

---

[33]Copies of this correspondence were sent to the Commander-in-Chief, Pacific, encl. in Paget to Kingcome, 11 May 1863, *ibid*. Governor Douglas, incidentally, had his own plan for conquering American territory as far south as the Columbia River by means of the Royal Navy. See Benjamin F. Gilbert, "Rumours of Confederate Privateers operating in Victoria, Vancouver Island," *British Columbia Historical Quarterly*, XVIII (1954), 240-41.

[34]Wm. Seward to Lyons, 15 April 1863, enclosing telegram from Collector of Customs, San Francisco, 14 April 1863, R.G. 8, IIIB, Vol. 35, P.A.C. Instructions to Lt.-Cdr. W. D. Hopkins of the *Saginaw*, 23 April 1863, *Official Records of the Union and Confederate Navies*, ser. I, Vol. II, pp. 165-66.

[35]Selfridge (Commandant, Mare Island) to Welles, 3 June 1863, *ibid*., pp. 259-60.

[36]Bell to Welles, 9 January 1864, *ibid*., p. 583.

[37]In Rear-Admiral Kingcome to Sec. of Adm., 5 March 1864, copy, R.G. 8, IIIB, Vol. 35, P.A.C.

[38]W. G. Romaine (Adm.) to Kingcome, 27 April 1864, *ibid*.

for Australia by way of the Cape of Good Hope. She made her way into the Pacific in early 1865. During June she destroyed the American whaling fleet in Arctic seas before turning south in search of American merchantmen bound for California from the Orient. When her captain learned on 2 August that the Confederacy had capitulated, he decided to surrender his ship in England. After capturing thirty-eight vessels in her brilliant career, the *Shenandoah*, in the guise of a merchantman, rounded Cape Horn and reached Liverpool on 6 November.[39]

But until United States and British officials on the North Pacific Coast learned of the surrender of the *Shenandoah*, they were forced to consider her still at large. Indeed, in July 1865, she was rumoured to be near Vancouver Island. American warships searched for her at the neutral port of Esquimalt, a likely place to dispose of her armament. The Royal Navy in the Pacific searched for her also, fearing that she would be a danger to neutral shipping should she decide not to surrender. The Commander-in-Chief, Rear-Admiral the Honourable Joseph Denman, wisely instructed his squadron that in case the *Shenandoah* entered Esquimalt Harbour she was not to leave without being disarmed.[40] In doing so, he anticipated the Foreign Office policy of detaining her by force in any British port she entered so that her case could be brought before courts of international law.[41]

Defence Measures at Esquimalt

The possibility that Britain would become embroiled in the Civil War resulted in the first meagre steps being taken to fortify Esquimalt. An opportunity to erect fortifications occurred in 1862 when 110-pounder Armstrong breech-loading guns were ordered for the *Bacchante* and *Topaze* and as replacements for the 68-pounder 95 cwt. guns in the *Clio* and *Tartar*.[42] Rear-Admiral Sir Thomas Maitland decided to use the guns replaced from the *Clio* and the *Tartar*, plus some old 32-pounders, to fortify Esquimalt.[43] The Admiralty, supporting this initiative, sanc-

---

[39]Documents relating to her cruise are in *Official Records of the Union and Confederate Navies*, Ser. 1, Vol. III, pp. 749-838.

[40]Rear-Admiral Denman to Gov. A. G. Kennedy, 9 August 1865, F 1223, B.C.A., and Denman to Sec. of Adm., 7 September 1865, Adm. 1/5924.

[41]Circular of Sec. of State for the Colonies, 7 September 1865, encl. in Kennedy to Denman, 15 November 1865, R.G. 8, IIIB, Vol. 35, P.A.C.

[42]The Armstrong gun, which made its appearance in the 1850's, incorporated striking advances. It was a built-up, wrought iron, rifled, breech-loading gun, but had an unhappy history because its breech was by no means fool-proof, and the Admiralty reverted in the 1860's and 1870's to muzzle-loading rifled guns until technological problems were overcome.

[43]Maitland to Sec. of Adm., 1 February 1862, Adm. 1/5790.

tioned the building of a temporary powder magazine for the battery.[44] By September, work on emplacements for sixteen guns—two 68- and fourteen 32-pounders—had begun on Duntze Head, the best position for commanding the narrow harbour entrance.[45]

These steps appeared to be timely. Within a few months of Maitland's proposal, reports reached him that three iron-plated ships of the Monitor class were being built, one each for the use of the United States Navy at San Francisco, at the Columbia River mouth, and in the waters of the Pacific Northwest. These vessels, with their revolving turrets and heavy armour, were useful in coastal and harbour operations during the Civil War.[46] Maitland thought that if one of them were actually stationed at Port Angeles, fifteen miles distant from Esquimalt and Victoria, it would be proof that in the event of war it surely was intended "for no other purpose than to act against us."[47] He thus urged the Admiralty, without success, to send a vessel of the same type to defend the colony of Vancouver Island.[48] In 1864, his successor, Rear-Admiral Denman, found Americans at San Francisco assembling an iron-cased turret vessel sent out in sections from the eastern United States. Like Maitland, he argued—again without success—that this necessitated a similar vessel to protect Vancouver Island which was "defenceless except by the Squadron."[49]

If the colony of Vancouver Island had been drawn into the American Civil War, in all probability its defensive capabilities would have proved inadequate, particularly if the three British warships usually there (one corvette and two gunboats) had been overpowered. As already mentioned, the disbanding of the detachment of Royal Engineers in 1863, a critical moment, left the island and mainland colonies "deprived of their Sole Military Force and altogether dependent for protection on the Naval Force stationed there," as Governor Douglas complained to Rear-Admiral John Kingcome.[50] Small militia units using arms sent from England were formed at Victoria in 1860, Nanaimo in 1861 and New Westminster in 1863, but apparently nothing was done to organize a volunteer force to man the fortifications on Duntze Head, Esquimalt. By 1865 all of the guns there had yet to be placed in position; the 32-

---

[44]Admiralty Minute, 11 March 1862, *ibid.*

[45]Maitland to Douglas, 8 September 1862, F. 1206, 36, B.C.A. Two days earlier, the *British Colonist* misreported the number of guns to be mounted as fifty.

[46]Their fighting value on the high seas was doubtful. See Harold and Margaret Sprout, *The Rise of American Naval Power, 1776-1918* (Princeton: Princeton University Press, 1939), pp. 171-72.

[47]Maitland to Sec. of Adm., 9 August 1862, Adm. 1/5790.

[48]*Ibid.*

[49]Rear-Admiral Denman to Sec. of Adm., 22 August 1864, Adm. 1/5878.

[50]Douglas to Kingcome, 15 September 1863, Adm. Corr. III, B.C.A.

pounders had carriages but the 68-pounders lacked garrison slides.[51]

The defences of the naval base, however, were put on a more than temporary footing by Rear-Admiral Denman. He was at Valparaiso in early 1865 when he learned of the fall of Richmond and the collapse of the Confederate cause. Well aware of the possibility that when the Union had defeated the Confederacy it would turn on the British territories in North America, he sailed for Vancouver Island in the *Sutlej*, 35 guns, to defend British interests on the Northwest Coast from a possible American attack.[52] After he found that the Royal Navy was the sole defender of the remote British colonies, he recommended to the Admiralty that he be provided with forces adequate to combat those of the United States Navy in time of war. So urgent was the situation that he also recommended that reinforcements should be sent from China or England "the first moment that hostilities appear probable."[53]

Frankness was Denman's characteristic quality. He spoke out sharply on what should be done; British interests on the Northwest Coast should be defended adequately or else abandoned.[54] He was fully cognizant of anti-imperial views then prevailing—that is, that England would be better off without colonies which were expensive to defend and difficult to govern—and he informed the Admiralty that it was not in Britain's interests "to maintain Colonies so remote" which could "only be secured to her by strong fortifications and a very considerable military force."[55] The British Pacific Colonies, so sparsely populated, were not worth the costs of adequate defence; and "looking to the proximity of the American possessions on the Pacific Coast," he reasoned, "I do not consider that it would be possible at any expense, to preserve them to Great Britain for a prolonged period."[56] Either England should rid herself of these colonies or undertake to fortify them adequately.

In a second letter to the Admiralty, Denman re-emphasized his views on colonial defence. Foremost in his mind was the interdependence of the naval depot and the colonies of Vancouver Island and British Columbia. His cogent views on this matter deserved quoting. In reference to the colonies he remarked:

> . . . it appears to me that their value principally consists in the facility they might afford for maintaining our Naval forces in these Seas, and also for the means of repair and supply to the Squadrons

---

51Denman to Sec. of Adm., 24 January 1865, Adm. 1/5924.
52Denman to Sec. of Adm., 3 June 1865, *ibid.*
53*Ibid.*
54*Ibid.*
55*Ibid.*
56*Ibid.*

on the North China Station and in Japan; but in every point of
view it appears to me indispensable either to take immediate measures for securing the possession of them in case of hostilities for rendering them effective for these purposes; or on the other hand, to
lose no time in relieving the Country of the responsibilities involved
in continuing to hold them without making due provision for their
defence.[57]

This frank statement gained the Admiralty's acceptance of a plan
submitted by Denman for "a very formidable defence" of Esquimalt.[58]
Its object was to release the Pacific squadron from merely guarding the
naval base so that it could protect Victoria and the southern tip of
Vancouver Island. Denman made several suggestions for local defence
including moving the shore establishments from Duntze Head to less-
exposed positions within Esquimalt Harbour and mounting guns in
strategic places.[59] His proposal was adopted by the Admiralty, and steps
were taken for its implementation.[60]

For the Commander-in-Chief the question of the security of the naval
base became a matter of even greater importance when he learned that
the United States Navy had decided to establish a depot at Port Angeles
across the Strait of Juan de Fuca from Esquimalt. As already mentioned,
the possibility existed that a Monitor similar to the *Monadnock,* which
had called at San Francisco after the Civil War, would be stationed at
Port Angeles. To defend Esquimalt against an attack by such a vessel,
Denman believed mines would be best.[61] He asked the Admiralty to send
him the necessary plans so that these new instruments of war could be
built in the Esquimalt machine shop.[62] The request caught the Admir-

---

57Denman to Sec. of Adm., 5 September 1865, Adm. 1/5924.
58Denman to Sec. of Adm., 15 June 1865, *ibid.*
59He proposed mounting one 110-pounder Armstrong gun (pivot) at Signal Hill to
bear on approaching vessels, one 40-pounder Armstrong gun (pivot) at Duntze
Head to "command the approach to the harbour," two 68-pounder Armstrong guns
(pivot) on Duntze Head to face the entrance and the harbour, three 32-pounder guns
on Aske Head, and one 40-pounder Armstrong gun on Inskip Island, within the
harbour. *Ibid.*
60Captain G. H. Richards, at this time Hydrographer of the Admiralty and a frequent
promoter of Esquimalt's development in London, supported Denman's plan. He
raised the awkward question of who would man the guns. He concluded that artillery-
men would be required as it would be impossible for the naval force there to
garrison the guns. Memo by Richards, 24 August 1865, appended to *ibid.* The
Secretary of State for the Colonies, Edward Cardwell, concurred with Denman on
the need for defence. F. Rogers (C.O.) to Sec. of Adm., 19 September 1865, Adm.
1/5951.
61He actually used the term "torpedo." Mines were originally called torpedoes. Only
in this same year (1866) was Whitehead perfecting his "locomotive" or "fish"
torpedo with its secret deep-keeping mechanism. See note 63 of this chapter.
62Denman to Sec. of Adm., 14 July 1866, Adm. 1/5969.

alty unprepared, for they had yet to reach a decision on the use of these weapons.[63]

In 1866, the proposed union of the two colonies under the name of British Columbia raised the important question of their protection in the event of war with the United States. Vancouver Island, with its magnificent harbours and rich coal fields, was coveted by American expansionists, Denman advised the Admiralty and because it was the "key" to the defence of the united colony, it should have the aid of Britain both in colonization and defence.[64] He had come to realize that its importance in time of peace was "very small compared with what it would become in time of war."[65]

In order to strengthen British interests at Vancouver Island, he suggested various proposals of a maritime nature including first, making Esquimalt a port of call for trans-Pacific steamers plying the route between Australia and Panama, thereby removing the mail service from American hands; second, building a dock; third, extending the depot; and fourth, defending the chief harbours of the island.[66] Like commanders-in-chief before and after him, Denman had seen little if any value in these colonies initially. But he had been obliged to revise his thinking when he realized the growing importance of the Pacific and the value of the British possessions on the Northwest Coast.

The Fenian Problem

The danger of an American attack passed in 1866 with the restoration of sound Anglo-American relations, but it was replaced by a new fear that engaged the attention of the Royal Navy: possible invasions by the "Fenian Brotherhood," a militant society of Irish-Americans who believed that Irish independence could be won by involving Britain and the United States in war. Fear of the Fenians caused colonial legislatures from Nova Scotia to Vancouver Island to make hurried preparations.[67] In June 1866, some forty thousand Fenians were reported ready to sail from San Francisco for the Northwest Coast. Accordingly, at the request

---

[63]Admiralty Minute, 29 August 1866, *ibid.* Probably no actual torpedoes reached the Pacific until 1876 when H.M.S. *Shah* brought her Whitehead outfit. This was used without success against the Peruvian iron-clad *Huascar*. See Admiral G. A. Ballard, "British Frigates of 1875; the 'Shah'," *Mariner's Mirror*, XX (July 1936), 305-15, and F. G. H. Bedford, *The Life and Letters of Admiral Sir Frederick George Denham Bedford, G.C.B., G.C.M.G.* (printed for private circulation; Newcastle-Upon-Tyne, [1960]) , pp. 52-59.
[64]Denman to Sec. of Adm., 26 August 1866, Adm. 1/5969.
[65]*Ibid.*
[66]*Ibid.*
[67]W. L. Morton, *The Critical Years: The Union of British North America, 1857-1873* (Toronto: McClelland and Stewart, 1964) , p. 169.

of the colonial governments of Vancouver Island and British Columbia, the Commander-in-Chief ordered the steam-sloop *Alert,* 17 guns, to the entrance of Victoria Harbour, the *Forward* to Cadboro Bay (facing San Juan Island from where the Fenians might attack), and the gun-vessel *Sparrowhawk* to New Westminster.[68] The *British Colonist* maintained that the residents of Vancouver Island should be prepared, Fenians or not, saying: "While the naval force stationed in our waters is always ready to maintain British supremacy on the seas, the inhabitants of Vancouver Island will be found equally willing to do their duty on the land."[69] This Victoria newspaper correctly interpreted the times, for during 1866 the ranks of the militia swelled to their greatest numbers for the colonial period, and an artillery company was formed at New Westminster.[70] The numbers were so few, however, that in an emergency, the chief means of defence doubtless would be the naval gunboats assisted by whatever warships were then present at Esquimalt.

The Royal Navy was kept on the alert constantly by the Fenians, who were nothing short of a nuisance. They were most effective in convincing British officials, more often on the local scene than in London, of their strength. A case in point is that of Rear-Admiral George F. Hastings, Commander-in-Chief, Pacific. En route to the Northwest Coast from England, his flagship, the *Zealous,* the first British ironclad in the Pacific, called at San Francisco on a good-will mission.[71] It was 4 July 1867, and in recognition of American independence, as was the custom, the ship was dressed for the occasion and salutes were fired. Hastings received an invitation to take part in the official celebrations on shore, but when he learned that Fenians were to take prominent positions in the ceremonies he concluded that no British officers should attend.[72] As will be seen, his knowledge of the numerical strength of Fenians at San Francisco came to dominate his attitudes about the use of the Royal Navy on the Northwest Coast.

[68]Denman to Sec. of Adm., 25 June and 14 July 1866, Adm. 1/5969.
[69]*British Colonist,* 13 June 1866; in Willard E. Ireland, "Pre-Confederation Defence Problems of the Pacific Colonies," *Canadian Historical Association Annual Report, 1941* (Toronto, 1941), pp. 52-53.
[70]Reginald H. Roy, "The Early Militia and Defence of British Columbia, 1871-1885," *British Columbia Historical Quarterly,* XVIII (1954), 1.
[71]Britain's first iron-hulled battleship, the *Warrior,* was laid down in 1860, but during the Civil War, several wooden ships under construction, such as the *Zealous,* were modified to carry armour. The displacement tonnage of the *Zealous* was 6,096. She was 252 ft. long and carried 3 to $4\frac{1}{2}$ inches of armour amidships, tapering to $2\frac{1}{2}$ inches forward and aft. Her 800 nominal horsepower engine with boiler pressure of 22 lbs. per sq. in. gave her a speed of 12.5 knots on trial. She was capable of 10.5 knots under sail. Her armament consisted of twenty 7-inch $6\frac{1}{2}$ ton muzzle-loading rifled Armstrong guns in the battery, plus two bow and two stern chasers.
[72]The U.S. commandant supported Hastings in this decision. Rear-Admiral Hastings to Sec. of Adm., 5 July 1867, Adm. 1/6008.

At San Francisco, Hastings had also found a large number of American warships; his report, remarkable for its tone of alarm, convinced at least one lord of the Admiralty that the American Navy in the Pacific was "so superior to our small squadron that it would be overlooked" in a war with the United States and thus the colony of British Columbia would be captured.[73] Although suggestions were made to strengthen the British squadron or fortify Esquimalt and Victoria, little was done to remedy the situation, partially because of an easing of Anglo-American tensions. The scarcity of ships at the Commander-in-Chief's disposal, however, forced him to keep the *Zealous* at Esquimalt for almost two years. When the Admiralty objected to this unusual and restrictive manner of using the iron-clad, Hastings countered, on 16 April 1869, that he was awaiting reinforcements and that the Fenian danger made the presence of the *Zealous* at Esquimalt "a matter of imperative necessity."[74]

An examination of the circumstances shows that Hastings had good reason for remaining on the Northwest Coast, because there were several alarms in 1868 and 1869. One incident occurred in March 1868, when an unknown number of Fenians were reported bound from San Francisco in a steamer; the *Forward* was sent to patrol the entrance to Victoria Harbour and warships at Esquimalt, including the *Zealous*, made preparations to act on short notice.[75] Although St. Patrick's Day passed quietly the fears of the British factions at Vancouver Island and British Columbia were increased when Colonel Walsh, fresh from disturbances in Ireland, arrived at San Francisco to a joyous reception from the Fenian Brotherhood.[76] At Victoria and New Westminster, police and militia men were placed at the ready, warships were alerted and a marine guard patrolled the Esquimalt naval establishment day and night.[77]

Throughout the summer of 1868 the situation remained tense. In late October, as the *Zealous* was preparing to leave Esquimalt for Honolulu, San Francisco and Mexico, Hastings received a copy of a telegram sent from the Colonial Office to the Governor of British Columbia warning that the Foreign Office had information on good authority that a Fenian attack might be made on Vancouver Island.[78] This disturbing information seemed to be substantiated by a report from the British Consul in

---

[73]Rear-Admiral Sir Alexander Milne to Henry Corry (Adm.), 17 August 1867, appended to "Return of Foreign Ships of War to 30th June 1867," encl. in Hastings to Sec. of Adm., 5 July 1867, *ibid.*
[74]Hastings to Sec. of Adm., 16 April 1869, Adm. 1/6092.
[75]Hastings to Sec. of Adm., 12 March 1868, Adm. 1/6056.
[76]Hastings to Sec. of Adm., 7 May 1868, *ibid.*
[77]Hastings to Sec. of Adm., 7 July and 9 November 1868, *ibid.*
[78]Hastings to Sec. of Adm., 30 October 1868, *ibid.*

San Francisco that the Fenians had called for an attack on British Columbia, as well as on Nova Scotia and New Brunswick.[79]

The Commander-in-Chief's decisive steps during this "emergency" reveal his deep concern for British territory on the Northwest Coast. Militia and police units were readied and all vessels arriving were examined for suspects. Again the Royal Navy was to act as the main deterrent. To aid the *Sparrowhawk* and *Forward* in defending the Imperial establishments and stores in a colony that was "entirely defenceless and unprepared to meet any attack,"[80] Hastings again decided that the *Zealous* should remain at Esquimalt, this time until the arrival of the two steam-corvettes *Charybdis* and *Satellite*. Later, he sent Captain R. Dawkins and Lieutenant L. Cling as private persons on a passenger steamer to make reconnaissance of various American harbours and settlements on Puget Sound such as Townsend, Ludlow, Seattle and Olympia.[81] These officers found no cause for alarm which seemed to reinforce the Admiralty's views that the Fenian danger was more imaginary than real and that Hastings was obsessed with keeping the *Zealous* on the Northwest Coast for the protection of British Columbia.[82]

The general preparations made during the scare of 1868-1869 were repeated on at least one other occasion. On 29 December 1871 the Lieutenant-Governor of British Columbia, Joseph Trutch, received a warning that Fenians were about to act against the colony. He asked the Senior Naval Officer at Esquimalt, Captain R. P. Cator of the 17-gun corvette *Scout* to station the gunboat *Boxer* inside Victoria Harbour.[83] This was done, and the *Sparrowhawk* took up a position outside of the harbour, checking the movements of shipping while the *Scout* stood by in Esquimalt Harbour.

An ingenious signalling system was invented to warn of a Fenian attack from within or without. In the event of a raid, Victoria police would signal the *Sparrowhawk* by rockets from the government buildings. She then would fire three guns in rapid succession, thereby notifying the *Boxer*—with steam up and guns ready—to land fifty Royal Marines near Government House. After this the *Boxer* would be employed in the harbour as required. This peculiar plan of defence, based on a communications system that now seems antiquated, would probably have been sufficient to face any challenge by armed but disorganized Irishmen.

---

[79]The consul was hampered by lack of funds for getting information in San Francisco about Fenian movements. Such intelligence might have been vital for protecting the colony.
[80]Hastings to Sec. of Adm., 30 October 1868, *ibid.*
[81]Hastings to Sec. of Adm., 26 December 1868, *ibid.*
[82]Noted in Hastings to Sec. of Adm., 16 April 1869, Adm. 1/6092.
[83]The account which follows is based heavily on Roy, "Early Militia," pp. 2-6.

British Columbia had been a Canadian province since 20 July 1871. Yet it still lacked an adequate militia and continued to rely almost solely on the Royal Navy for defence. Consequently, the Executive Council of the province appealed to the Dominion government, on whom the responsibility for the defence of this new part of Canada depended, to press the British government to restore the headquarters of the Pacific station to Esquimalt; it had been removed from there to Valparaiso in 1869. The British government also was asked to station at least one heavy frigate in addition to the gunboats already on the coast, to make proper arrangements for militia organization and to assign one hundred regular troops to British Columbia.[84]

To Captain Cator, however, the whole Fenian "crisis" appeared to be without foundation. To his suggestion that the *Sparrowhawk* be withdrawn from the harbour entrance the Lieutenant-Governor countered that this could not be done without risk to life and property in Victoria.[85] The crisis subsided but the *Sparrowhawk* remained at her station in support of the civil power.

The duty undertaken by the *Sparrowhawk* was perhaps typical of the Royal Navy's vigilance over British territory on the Northwest Coast— particularly during the period after the establishment of the Colony of Vancouver Island in 1849 and of British Columbia in 1858 to the time of inclusion of these united colonies within the Dominion of Canada in 1871. This service continued at least until 1910. Without this presence of British warships on the Pacific Coast, it is conceivable that the orderly development of the Province of British Columbia would not have taken place.

Changing Times in British Columbia

Several influences contributed to the growing importance of Esquimalt as a British naval base in the 1860's: the activities of Confederate and Union vessels along the Pacific seaboard, news of the intention of the United States to establish a naval station at Port Angeles and fear of invasion by Fenians as the Civil War ended. Three additional influences deserve mention: the purchase of Alaska by the United States in 1867; proposals to construct a telegraph line and railroad across British North America to consolidate the Empire in matters of communication and defence and finally the federation of British Columbia with the Dominion of Canada—consummated in 1871 after four years of negotiation.

---

[84]*Ibid.*, p. 5.
[85]J. Trutch to Capt. Cator, 31 January 1872, Papers of the Deputy Minister of Militia and Defence, Canada, No. 6322, P.A.C.; in *ibid.*, p. 6.

In 1867, people in the new United Colony of British Columbia had
good reason to be concerned about possible interference with their
sovereignty. As previously mentioned a large number of Fenians and a
superior American naval force had been found by Rear-Admiral Hastings at San Francisco in July of that year. Three months later, the
administration of Alaska was placed under the War Department of the
United States government, which had purchased this Russian territory
on 30 March 1867.

Negotiations for the acquisition of Alaska had been in progress since
1859, but the Civil War delayed their completion. These negotiations
had prompted John A. Macdonald, later the Prime Minister of Canada,
to declare that a railway to the Pacific would protect British Columbia
from American designs. "I would be quite willing, personally," he wrote
in 1865, "to leave that whole country a wilderness for the next half-
century, but I fear if Englishmen do not go there, Yankees will. . . ."[86] An
expansionist himself, Macdonald knew all too well the views of Americans such as William Seward, Secretary of State and an adroit promoter
of Manifest Destiny, who boasted that the purchase of Alaska made "the
permanent political separation of British Columbia from Alaska and
Washington territory impossible."[87]

The purchase of Alaska brought little reaction in British government
circles. Lord Stanley at the Foreign Office believed that the United States
had bought "a large amount of worthless territory" and, in any case, on
no grounds could the Foreign Office object to the Americans establishing
a military post across the inlet from Port Simpson.[88] Accordingly, the
Royal Navy at Esquimalt remained an observer to the United States
military occupation of Alaska, while at Victoria the *British Colonist* of
16 May 1867 warned that British Columbia, situated between Alaska and
Washington territory, might now be "devoured at a single bite" by the
Americans.[89]

The British position can be explained by the seeming uselessness of
Alaska and also by the fact that limits existed as to how much Britain

---

[86]John A. Macdonald to Edward Watkin, 27 March 1865, private, Macdonald Papers,
P.A.C.; in P. B. Waite, *The Life and Times of Confederation, 1864-1867* (Toronto:
University of Toronto Press, 1962) , p. 307.
[87]Quoted in Charles Vevier, "American Continentalism: An Idea of Expansion, 1845-
1910," *American Historical Review*, LXV (January 1960) , 332. Similar views are given
in Alvin C. Gluek, Jr., *Minnesota and the Manifest Destiny of the Canadian Northwest: A Study in Canadian-American Relations* (Toronto: University of Toronto
Press, 1965) , p. 215.
[88]Quoted in Bourne, *Britain and the Balance of Power*, p. 302. E. H. Hammond
(F.O.) to Under-Secretary of State, Colonial Office, 9 December 1867, C.O. 60/30.
[89]Quoted in Winks, *Canada and the United States*, p. 165.

could now influence the course of events in North America. As one authority has explained:

> The Northern victory in the Civil War destroyed any remaining possibility of a restoration of the balance of power in North America. Thereafter, Canadian-American relations and British policy with respect to the New World were posited upon the assumption that the United States had the preponderance of power on the continent. The provinces became a hostage to a subjective American judgement on the 'good behavior' of the British throughout the world.[90]

At the time of the Alaska purchase, American expansion into the British North American west and far west could still be checked by the building of a Canadian railway, the transfer of Rupert's Land from Hudson's Bay Company to Canadian control, which was completed in 1869, and the confederation of British Columbia with Canada. Seward and his supporters for United States continental dominion were unaware of the speed with which certain Canadians and British were acting to thwart Manifest Destiny.

The tool of Canadian expansion was the railroad with its two-fold purpose of consolidating the British-American territories and facilitating the defence of the British Empire. Macdonald was not the first to imagine the day when British North America would serve as a vital part of an all-British route to link England with her possessions in the Far East.[91] As early as 1852, Captain M. F. Synge, R.E., had been promoting the idea of a "great water route" to the Pacific.[92] His view was refuted by the British travellers, Milton and Cheadle, who wrote in 1865 that "the North-West Passage by land" constituted "the real highway to the Pacific."[93] In referring to the fact that the Americans were spanning the continent with a rail to San Francisco, they asked why the same could not be undertaken through British territory to British Columbia.[94] They held the belief—increasingly popular in the 1860's and afterward—that Vancouver Island with its valuable coal mines constituted an asset to the

---

90Ibid., p. 375.
91See, for example, Sandford Fleming's, *Observations and Practical Suggestions on the Subject of a Railway through British North America, submitted to the Province of Canada, 1863;* in *C.O.* 807/7, No. 74, p. 39, and his first publication on the matter, *A Railway to the Pacific through British Territory* (Port Hope, Ont., 1858) .
92Capt. M. F. Synge, "Proposal for a Rapid Communication with the Pacific and the East, via British North America," *Journal of the Royal Geographical Society,* XXII (1852) , 174-200.
93Viscount Milton and W. B. Cheadle, *The Northwest Passage by Land* (London: Ritter and Galpin, Belle Sauvage Works, 1865) , pp. 395-96.
94The first trans-continental railroad was completed to San Francisco in 1868.

Royal Navy and should be the terminus of a Canadian trans-continental railway.[95]

In numerous current writings on the subject, the related strategic matters of the projected railway and the presence of the Royal Navy in the Pacific overshadowed considerations of settlement and even commerce. For example, one strategist argued in 1861 that the existence of great gold and coal deposits on the Northwest Coast necessitated a strong British military and naval establishment at what he called "this half-way station between Halifax and India."[96] Such precautions would counteract Russian naval development and guard against American filibusters. A Pacific railway, he concluded, would be an economy measure because it "would dispense to a great extent with a standing army in time of peace on the Pacific coast, and facilitate its movements in time of war."[97]

Similar opinions were voiced by Sir Edward Watkin who proposed to the Imperial government that the Grand Trunk Railway be extended to Pacific shores.[98] He raised the question of whether or not the Admiralty intended to establish a naval station at Esquimalt.[99] And he was evidently satisfied with the Admiralty's answer that the small naval base there would gradually increase in importance.[100] With backing from the British ministry, London financial interests and the Canadian government, his "scheme for telegraphic, postal and passenger communications" from Lake Superior to British Columbia promised to end the isolation of the British colonies on the Northwest Coast and add to their security. It would, moreover, increase the importance of Esquimalt in an all-British route to the East.[101]

The entrance of the United Colony of British Columbia into the Canadian federation on 20 July 1871 affected the roles played by Esquimalt and the Royal Navy in the defence of Canada's West Coast. It will be recalled that the influences which led to this federation with other

[95]See R. I. Murchison's presidential address to the Royal Geographical Society, 1861, in the Society's *Proceedings*, V (1860-61), 203.
[96]T. T. Vernon Smith, "Pacific Railway," *Nautical Magazine*, XXXI (1861), 251.
[97]*Ibid.*
[98]For Watkin's activities, see E. E. Rich, *The History of the Hudson's Bay Company, 1670-1870*, 2 vols. (London: Hudson's Bay Record Society, 1958-59), II, 822, 825-33, 843-44.
[99]Watkin to Newcastle, 29 December 1862, encl. in C.O. to Adm., 22 January 1863, Adm. 1/5948.
[100]Minute of C. P[aget], 23 January 1863, *ibid.*
[101]Similarly, the Duke of Newcastle, the Secretary of State for the Colonies, favoured Esquimalt as the terminus of the cable, for obvious strategic reasons. C.O. to Adm., 22 January 1863, *ibid.* Later that year he supported Collins's proposed America-Asia-Europe telegraph on the same grounds. See John S. Galbraith, "Perry McDonough Collins at the Colonial Office," *British Columbia Historical Quarterly*, XVII (1953), 212.

provinces of Canada resulted mainly from the exposed geographical location of British Columbia. Only five years earlier, in 1866, American expansionist tendencies along the exposed British frontier between Lake Superior and the Pacific had induced Governor Frederick Seymour to propose the union of the colonies of Vancouver Island and British Columbia in order to strengthen "British authority, British influence, and British power in the Pacific." From the point of view of the Royal Navy, union would eliminate difficulties faced by the Commander-in-Chief, Pacific, in dealing with two colonies instead of one.[102]

The choice of Victoria as the capital was based partially on its proximity to the naval base at Esquimalt and its communication links with San Francisco and Alaska.[103] In that era of optimism it was easy to imagine that with Imperial aid in defence, British Columbia could become the centre of a great maritime power in the North Pacific.[104]

If the British Columbia government was motivated to seek a place in Confederation by a desire for protection from the United States, it was also lured by promises of prosperity and security. The final terms of entry—important here for their great attention to naval matters—called for the Dominion to assume the colonial debt, to begin a public works program, to guarantee a loan for a dry-dock at Esquimalt, to exert influence on the Imperial government to maintain Esquimalt as a British naval station, and, above all, to begin building a railway to the Pacific.[105]

British Columbia joined Confederation in 1871, but because of political controversy, financial problems and geographic difficulties, fourteen years were to elapse before the Canadian Pacific Railway reached Pacific tidewater at Port Moody on Burrard Inlet to become an instrument of Imperial defence.

The need for common defence by the British North American colonies had already resulted in the union of four of these colonies in 1867. The British North America Act allowed for the organizing of military security and a standardized militia scheme.[106] But the security of British Columbia in 1871 and afterward continued to depend on protection afforded by the Royal Navy.

[102]Seymour to E. Cardwell (C.O.), 17 February 1866, C.O. 880/5, Confidential Print, No. 37, p. 38.

[103]Seymour to the Duke of Buckingham and Chandos (C.O.), 10 December 1867, "Correspondence . . . Capital of British Columbia," *Parliamentary Papers,* 1867-1868, XLVIII (H. of C. 483), p. 8.

[104]J. L. Sinclair to Buckingham and Chandos, 2 September 1867, C.O. 60/31.

[105]Margaret A. Ormsby, *British Columbia: A History* (Toronto: Macmillan, 1958), pp. 245-57.

[106]Richard A. Preston, *Canada and "Imperial Defense"* (Durham, N.C.: Duke University Press), pp. 56-57.

Years of Transition

The decade beginning in 1861 constituted a most difficult period in the history of Anglo-American relations. Residents of the colonies of Vancouver Island and British Columbia, before and after their union in 1866, feared invasion and suffered anxiety for their personal security, a state of mind only partially eased on joining Confederation in 1871. The danger of becoming involved in the American Civil War, threats of Fenian raids, and the purchase of Alaska by the United States contributed to the difficulties of this decade.

The Imperial government was not apathetic to the precarious position of British Columbians, as demonstrated by the actions of successive commanders-in-chief to fortify Esquimalt Harbour. In spite of demands for economy after 1868—and not a few statements in public and parliamentary circles that Britain should rid herself of her burdensome colonies in North America—no change occurred in the policy pursued after 1846; ships of the Royal Navy remained on the coast for the preservation of British interests.

By 1871, Esquimalt had assumed greater prominence in Imperial defence. Strategists began to view the base as the eventual terminus of the projected trans-continental Canadian railroad—a Northwest Passage by rail, so to speak—as well as a link in a telegraphic system to stretch eventually across British North America and the Pacific Ocean, thus reducing the remoteness of the Northwest Coast and enhancing the value of Esquimalt.

Chapter 10

THE FINAL PHASE
1871-1914

AFTER BRITISH COLUMBIA joined the Canadian federation in 1871, the Royal Navy continued to use Esquimalt as a base in the Pacific for almost forty years. Not until 1910, when the Parliament at Ottawa passed the Canadian Naval Service Act, did the British government relinquish the operation and maintenance of Esquimalt to Canadian authorities. During the intervening years, Canadian statesmen were satisfied with arrangements made at the time of Confederation for Britain to look after the sea defences and Canada gradually to assume those of the land. They constantly refused to provide monetary contributions toward the costs of Imperial defence as advocated, for example, by the Imperial Federation League at the first Colonial Conference in London in 1887. By 1910, however, a necessary policy of Imperial-Dominion naval defence had been established, under which a small Canadian navy and a reluctant Canadian government began to assume the duties formerly carried out by the Royal Navy.

Railways, Submarine Cables and Sea Power

At the Colonial Conference of 1887, Canadian spokesmen declared that the Canadian Pacific Railway, completed in 1885, constituted a valuable contribution to the Empire's security. Although it was built primarily to consolidate the new nation, it enabled Britain to assist in the defence of her base at Esquimalt. Furthermore, it enabled her to supply the

Pacific squadron with munitions, provisions and men and to transport troops and stores through the Queen's North American territories to Pacific shores and beyond.[1] Indeed, certain urgent and perishable stores could be sent from Halifax to Esquimalt in seven days in contrast to the previous three months or more on the long sea route around Cape Horn. Moreover, mail and telegrams could be dispatched across Canada to colonial authorities and to naval and military officers in British Columbia rather than over the American-dominated Panama route or through the United States, thus eliminating a situation that was potentially dangerous in case of war. Further—and of vital importance to Britain—the new railway reduced her dependence on two traditional water routes for conveying troops to the East and importing foodstuffs—one by the Cape of Good Hope and the other through the Mediterranean, particularly after the opening of the Suez Canal in 1869. By the 1880's, men in Cabinet offices in Whitehall had come to realize that the Suez route could be blocked in wartime by a European belligerent regardless of International Law which provided for its being open in war as in peace.[2]

The naval base at Esquimalt had been named the terminus of the railroad by an Order-in-Council of 7 June 1873, but because of the cost and because of difficulties in crossing the Strait of Georgia, that decision proved to be a hasty one which led to dispute between the governments of Canada and British Columbia.[3] Burrard Inlet, Howe Sound and Bute Inlet were considered less expensive alternatives. Finally, Burrard Inlet was chosen as the end of the line, against the formidable opposition of the Commander-in-Chief, Pacific, Rear-Admiral Algernon de Horsey.[4] He favoured Esquimalt because he believed that Burrard Inlet occupied a location with questionable security from an attack, especially overland from the United States.[5]

Ultimately, however, the naval base was also served by a railroad—the Esquimalt and Nanaimo Railway—which upon its completion in 1886 constituted an extension of the Canadian Pacific Railway when steamer

[1]"Proceedings of the Colonial Conference," *Parliamentary Papers*, 1887, LVI (Cmd. 5091), pp. 275-76.

[2]Gerald S. Graham, *Empire of the North Atlantic: The Maritime Struggle for North America*, 2nd ed. (Toronto: University of Toronto Press, 1958), p. 282.

[3]In 1874, Prime Minister Mackenzie sent J. D. Edgar to pacify British Columbia on the railway terms with instructions that the railway to Esquimalt was to be "wholly and purely a concession" to the Province. Mackenzie to Edgar, 19 February 1874, C.O. 807/7, no. 74, p. 4. Edgar viewed the east coast of Vancouver Island from H.M.S. *Myrmidon,* and concluded that an island railway would link the Nanaimo coal mines with Esquimalt, "said to be the finest harbour upon the shores of the North Pacific." Edgar to Sec. of State for Canada, 17 June 1874, *ibid.,* p. 109.

[4]See Rear-Admiral A. de Horsey to Sec. of Adm., 26 October 1877, Adm. 1/6414.

[5]D. M. Schurman, "Esquimalt: Defence Problem, 1865-1887," *British Columbia Historical Quarterly,* XIX (1955), 57, n.1. Compare the views of Gen. R. C. Moody in L. J. Burpee, *Sandford Fleming, Empire Builder* (London: H. Milford, 1915), p. 155.

service began from Burrard Inlet to Nanaimo.[6] Together, the railroad and steamer service answered the needs for an ocean terminus at Esquimalt, for a railroad on Burrard Inlet and for a transportation link for the settlements of the Fraser River Valley. Although slight navigational hazards on the inland waters between the open Pacific and the infant town of Vancouver on Burrard Inlet were not yet overcome, this network of railways and steamers allowed Vancouver Island and the so-called Lower Mainland of British Columbia to develop apace. These improved transportation facilities greatly increased the strategic value of the Esquimalt naval base, which the Governor-General of Canada, the Marquis of Landsdowne and others then considered to be the foundation of an Imperial "stronghold" on the shores of the North Pacific. On 10 October 1885 Lord Landsdowne addressed a Civic Banquet in Victoria as follows:

> You have here a naval station likely, I think, in time to become one of the greatest and most important strongholds of the empire. You have a coal supply sufficient for all the navies of the world. You have a line of railway . . . which is ready to bring that coal up to the harbor of Esquimalt. You will shortly have a graving dock, capable of accommodating all but one or two of Her Majesty's ships. You have, in short, all the conditions requisite for the creation of what I believe is spoken of as a *place d'armes*.[7]

The subsequent extensions of the Canadian Pacific Railway by steamers and telegraph systems beyond tidewater by means of trans-Pacific steamers and a submarine cable achieved in effect the objective for which British mariners had long sought—a Northwest Passage from England to the East. In 1887, the Canadian Pacific Railway Company initiated a regular steamer service between Vancouver and Hong Kong via Yokohama. The three vessels in service—which eventually became five—were steamers with a maximum speed of fifteen knots, faster than any others in those seas. They could be converted rapidly into armed merchant cruisers to strengthen the British Pacific squadron and give it a wider grasp in the Pacific, if required. This service—as the Chairman of the Colonial Defence Committee predicted in 1886—linked the Empire together in a "chain of communications between British stations" which did "literally girdle the globe."[8]

In addition to steamships and railways, telegraph and submarine

---

[6]Margaret A. Ormsby, *British Columbia: A History* (Toronto: Macmillan, 1958), pp. 265-69, 304. J. Michael Jones, "The Railroad Healed the Breach," *Canadian Geographical Journal*, LXXIII (1966), 98-101.

[7]*Canadian North-west and British Columbia: Two Speeches by His Excellency the Marquis of Landsdowne* (Ottawa: Department of Agriculture, 1886), p. 13.

[8]Memo. by Maj.-Gen. Andrew Clarke, 16 April 1886, in "Report of the Committee on the Proposals of the C.P.R. for the Establishment of a Line of Steamers in the Pacific," June 1886, C.O. 880/9, Vol. 116, p. 21.

cable installations promised to reduce the time required to communicate between London and distant colonial possessions from months to minutes. Already the Atlantic and Australian cables, completed in 1858 and 1872 respectively, were serving British strategic and commercial interests. In any discussion on a proposed trans-Pacific cable, consideration had to be given the Royal Navy on whose force the defence of the cable stations depended. The positions of these cable terminals determined, in large measure, the centre or centres of operations of the squadron. In other words, the Navy would defend and act from these points. Thus, Esquimalt, Hong Kong and Melbourne, functioning as communications "nerve centres," would enable the Admiralty to better control ship movements and at the same time greatly reduce the decision-making powers required of the commanders-in-chief on the various foreign stations.

Among those who saw the strategic value of a communications link from Britain to Australia via Canada and the Pacific was Sandford Fleming. This Canadian engineer with geopolitical vision was an early promoter of the trans-Canada railway. Even before the Canadian Pacific Railway reached tidewater, he was expounding the opinion that a Pacific cable would play a vital part in the defence of the Empire. Sea power could be made more effective, he contended, by the cable which would facilitate naval operations. In terms of economy, he estimated that its total cost actually would be less than a single iron-clad. Optimistically, Fleming envisaged that a private company, with a small amount of Imperial financial assistance, could establish "a work which would add incalculable strength to Great Britain as a great naval power."[9]

But implementing the project proved to be an expensive and difficult matter. Not until 1902 was the cable laid from Bamfield on Vancouver Island to Auckland, Brisbane, and ultimately Hong Kong by way of Fanning Island, Suva and Norfolk Island. Henceforth Imperial power was strengthened by the almost instant contact between Britain and her colonies within the Pacific rim. These advances in communications technology did not reduce the importance of admirals and their fleets as instruments of diplomacy and force; in fact, they made more effective the deployment of British warships.

Esquimalt Naval Base in the Ascendant

During the last phase of British naval operations in the North Pacific, the sinews of power resided as much in the naval base at Esquimalt as

[9]*Memorandum in Reference to a Scheme for Completing a Great Inter-Colonial and Inter-Continental Telegraph System by Establishing an Electric Cable Across the Pacific Ocean by Sandford Fleming, 20 November 1882* (London, 1882) , p. 9.

in the ships operating from there. "Sea-power does not consist entirely of men-of-war," Admiral Sir Cyprian Bridge wrote in 1907. He added that among other things, "There must be docks, refitting establishments, magazines, and depots of stores."[10] Esquimalt was essentially the supply and repair depot for the Pacific station, yet, because supplies such as Welsh coal came from overseas, control of the sea in wartime was vital: "Thus the primary defence of the out-lying base is the active, sea-going fleet." Bridge explained, "Moderate local defence, chiefly of the human kind in the shape of a garrison, will certainly be needed."[11] In the case of Esquimalt, then, strategists were concerned with the interrelated questions of the need for a dock and the defence of the shore establishment.

The necessity of a dock at Vancouver Island was long apparent both to naval commanders in the Pacific and to the Admiralty. The only dock in the North Pacific to which the Royal Navy had access was the floating dock at Mare Island, near San Francisco, opened in 1854.[12] But this stood in American—and therefore potentially enemy—territory. Moreover, it was inadequate for vessels larger than two thousand tons burthen such as the flagship *Sutlej*. And it had not always proved safe for Her Majesty's ships, such as the *Termagant*, 1,547 tons burthen, which nearly met with disaster in 1861 when she fell from the blocks.[13] Although a larger dock was opened there in 1868, it could not hold the British flagship *Zealous*, 3,716 tons burthen.[14] Other docks existed at Callao, Valparaiso, Hong Kong and Singapore, but the only facility in the Pacific capable of receiving the *Zealous* was at Melbourne, far across the ocean from her place of employment. As the Commander-in-Chief correctly understood this situation in 1868, if a ship her size were to be kept on the Pacific station, a dock at Vancouver Island was a necessity.[15]

Projects to overcome this deficiency date from 1864, but early ones proved abortive because of prohibitive costs. The danger of a war between Britain and Russia in 1877-1878—over Russia's designs in the Balkans—made British strategists more aware of the unprotected state of British Columbia. Because that province was dependent on the Royal

---

[10]Admiral Sir Cyprian Bridge, *Sea-Power and Other Studies* (London: Smith, Elder & Co., 1910), p. 253. Sea power is also based on a strong national economy and on manpower.

[11]*Ibid.*, p. 251.

[12]With a floating dock, the dock floods its tanks, and sinks, allowing the ship to steam or be warped into the dock. It then pumps out and rises, bringing the ship up.

[13]Richard C. Mayne, *Four Years in British Columbia and Vancouver Island* (London: John Murray, 1862), pp. 159-60; also *British Colonist*, 7 December 1861, in Major F. V. Longstaff, *Esquimalt Naval Base: A History of Its Work and Its Defences* (Victoria: Victoria Book and Stationery Ltd., 1941), pp. 24-25.

[14]She drew more than 22 feet, the depth over the sill at Mare Island Dock.

[15]Rear-Admiral G. F. Hastings to Sec. of Adm., 3 December 1868, Adm. 1/6056.

N

Cole I.
Naval Magazines
⅓ ½ 1¼
¾
3 3½
Paterson's Point
Dyke Pt.
Smart I.   Richards I.
5
Macarthy I.   *Plumper Bay*
4¾
5 5
3½   E. & N. Railway Jetty *Indian*
4¼ 5¼ 5½   *Village*
Inskip I.
1½ 4½ 5¼ 6 6 5
6 6
Dunn's Nook   Ashe Head
6 6 6 6
6 6 6 6 *Maple Bank*
Yew Pt.   6 6 6
6 7 7 6   *Munroe*
Head
ESQUIMALT   *HARBOUR* *Pilgrim Cove*
6   5¼ 5¼
8   *Constance Cove*
Fresh water flume 7 5½ 5¾ 6 6   5½ 5½
9   *Grant Knoll*   *Naval Coal*
Wharf
Duntze Hd. R.N. Yard   3¾
Fisgard I.   *Submarine*
Light fixed 70 ft.   *Mining Pier*
Vis. 10 miles   *Signal*
8   *Hill*

Esquimalt Railway Station

Limit of Man of War Anchorage Order in Council (23 April 1894)

Esquimalt and Nanaimo Railway

Military Cemetery
R.N. Cemetery

Admiral's Road   *Level Crossing*

Hudson's Bay Co.
Property   *R.N. Hospital*
Skinner Cove

Lang Cove

Old Road to Victoria

R.N. Recreation Ground   *To Victoria*

Rodd Hill
War Dept. Property

Rifle Range
(Partly Admiralty Property)

Brothers Is.

Soundings in fathoms

100 50 0   500   1000   1500   1760 Yards

From Adm. 116/993

ESQUIMALT NAVAL BASE, 1910

Navy for protection, it was of "paramount importance," a Provincial Executive Council committee reported in 1877, that facilities such as a dock should exist to maintain its very means of defence.[16] From the point of view of naval operations, Rear-Admiral de Horsey considered a dockyard to be an Imperial need and, further, a "mercantile necessity," because Esquimalt would become the terminus of the railroad to the Pacific and steamers would soon be plying the ocean between British Columbia and the Far East. As he saw it, the real question was not one of funds but of Imperial needs—"first for the necessities of the Navy—and secondly for the prosperity of this portion of the Empire."[17]

Although the Commander-in-Chief and the Provincial executive committee shared the view that building a dock and defending the base were imperial rather than colonial responsibilities, the task of building the dock fell to British Columbia, which lacked the necessary financial resources even taking into consideration promises of Admiralty support under terms of the Colonial Docks Loan Act (1865).[18] Construction began in 1880 but was soon suspended for lack of funds. Then, in 1883, to pacify British Columbians who claimed that the federal authority had not fulfilled the terms of union, the Canadian government undertook the responsibility. Thereafter development went ahead steadily.

The long-overdue Esquimalt graving or dry-dock was officially opened and used for the first time on 20 July 1887.[19] It was 400 feet long and 90 feet wide at the coping on top, and it could hold ships of 7,322 tons burthen.[20] The economies and advantages it made possible were soon apparent. By November, the *Cormorant* and *Caroline* had been repaired for about half what would have been charged at San Francisco.[21] As further proof of its value, twenty-four merchant and seventy British

---

[16]"Copy of a Report of a Committee of the Honourable the Executive Council, approved . . . 11th day of June, 1877"; copy in Adm. 116/744, fols. 241-43.

[17]de Horsey to Sec. of Adm., 9 October 1877, fols. 171-78. His proposals reached the British ministry. See "Memorandum Respecting the Canadian Pacific Railway and the Esquimalt Graving Dock," printed for the Cabinet, August 1878, C.O. 880/8, Vol. 98.

[18]28 & 29 *Vic.*, c. 56: "to secure Accommodation for Vessels of the Royal Navy in *British* Possessions abroad."

[19]This type of dock is usually excavated, and made of concrete, masonry lined. After the gates are closed, water is pumped out, leaving the ship dry and on blocks.

[20]Longstaff, *Esquimalt Naval Base*, p. 37, n. 7. The Admiralty report on *Graving Docks, Floating Docks and Patent Slips in the British Empire, 1922* (London: H.M.S.O., 1923), p. 91, describes the length of the dock to be 450 feet, 8 inches. Presumably at some time the dock had been extended from its original length in order to hold the ships of the Canadian Pacific Railway's Empress service. Full descriptions of this and other docks in British Columbia in 1922 are given in *ibid.* pp. 91, 103, 111.

[21]Rear-Admiral M. Culme-Seymour to Sec. of Adm., 9 November 1887, Adm. 116/744, fol. 62.

warships used the facility during the first seven years.[22] In 1891, H.M.S. *Warspite*, a first-class armoured cruiser of 8,400 tons displacement, was in the dry-dock for three months. She was probably the largest British warship to enter it. The dockyard greatly increased the importance of the naval base at Esquimalt. Not only did it furnish a vital service for the Royal Navy, but it led to the rapid expansion of mercantile shipping in the Pacific and to maritime development on the Northwest Coast.

At the time of the war scare of 1877-1878 over differences with Russia, Esquimalt was listed with eleven other Imperial coaling stations and naval establishments as virtually unprotected.[23] In an era when it was argued that Britain's strength depended on her world trade, secure bases from which the Royal Navy could operate to guard this commerce were prime requisites; thus it was contended that these "outposts of the United Kingdom" should be fortified and defended.[24] Although Esquimalt ranked eighth in importance among twelve such establishments— its value to the Royal Navy remained high: "The necessity of a Naval Station in the Pacific is obvious, and Esquimalt is the only British place at present available."[25] But in fact no further precautions had been taken at Esquimalt to keep pace with the great advances in armaments after Rear-Admiral Denman made improvements to its defences in 1866.

The Russian "Bombardment Bogies"

The inadequate state of these defences was evident to Rear-Admiral de Horsey. He knew that the declaration of war between Russia and Turkey in April 1877 would force Britain to take strong measures to strengthen Turkey, her ally in the Middle East, in order to check Russia's drive to the Mediterranean where British strategic and other interests were considerable.[26] Although Britain considered her Mediterranean interests paramount and thus tended to concentrate her forces there, Russia's reply could be to attack elsewhere, such as at British Columbia and the naval base at Esquimalt.[27] Safeguarding these places was given high priority by the Pacific squadron; de Horsey's flagship, the iron-hulled *Shah*, steamed from South American waters to Esquimalt where, on

---

[22]Arthur H. Ives, "First Graving Dock" (typescript, n.d.) , M.M.B.C.
[23]"Memorandum by Colonel Sir W. F. D. Jervois . . . [on] the defenceless condition of our Coaling Stations and Naval Establishments Abroad," 7 January 1875, confidential, Carnarvon Papers, PRO 30/6/122, pp. 44-46.
[24]*Ibid.*
[25]C. H. Nugent, "Memorandum on the Relative Importance of Coaling Stations," 1 April 1877, confidential, *ibid.*, pp. 19-21. The bases were ranked as follows: Cape of Good Hope, Hong Kong, Singapore, Jamaica, King George's Sound, Mauritius, Esquimalt, St. Lucia, Falkland Islands, Ascension and Fiji.
[26]de Horsey to Sec. of Adm., 13 May 1877, Adm. 1/6416.
[27]See A. T. Mahan, *The Influence of Sea Power Upon History, 1660-1783* (London: Sampson Low & Co., 1890) , p. 14.

4 August, she joined four other ships of the squadron, the *Opal, Fantome, Darling* and *Rocket*. [28]

The *Opal* and *Darling* were sent to San Francisco to report on the Russian warships.[29] Actually, the nine Russian ships reported at San Francisco turned out to represent no great threat, the largest being a corvette of two thousand tons displacement; the rest were sloops and gun-vessels. Yet by their number they could provide considerable nuisance value in seizing shipping and threatening the British Columbia Coast.[30]

On 18 February 1878—nine days after Victoria newspapers reported a second visit by a Russian squadron to San Francisco—an excited lookout on Race Rocks flashed a telegraphic message to Esquimalt warning that a Russian warship was bearing down on Victoria.[31] The corvette *Kreyzer*, 11 guns, steamed right into Esquimalt Harbour and as might be imagined, caused considerable concern on shore.[32] Her commander, amazingly ignorant of the dispute between his government and that of Britain, had entered Esquimalt—or so he said—because of bad weather and the need for repairs. But these were merely pretexts in the opinion of the Senior Naval Officer at Esquimalt, who believed that the object of the visit clearly was to determine the defences of the British naval base.[33]

---

[28]On 29 May 1877, the *Shah* and the corvette *Amethyst* fought an inconclusive action with a very small but actual iron-clad, the turret ship *Huascar*, broken away from the Peruvian fleet to turn pirate. The British ships made hits on the *Huascar* but to no immediate purpose; the *Shah* fired the first Whitehead torpedo without a hit; de Horsey became a political sacrifice, the *Shah* was relieved by the battleship *Triumph*, and thereafter, the flagship was a battleship until cruisers were greatly improved. See Admiral G. A. Ballard, "British Frigates of 1875; the 'Shah'," *Mariner's Mirror*, XX (1936), 305-15.

[29]See de Horsey to the Admiralty, 17 March 1877, Adm. 1/6414. The *Opal* found the Russian vessels *Ernack, Tonngouss, Vostock* and *Japonetz* of the Siberian detachment, and the *Bayan, Vasdnick, Abrek* and *Gornoski* on commission in the Pacific. Some of these ships had "fish" torpedoes, fired through bow tubes under water; see Harris to de Horsey, 10 May 1877, encl. in de Horsey to Sec. of Adm., 25 June 1877, *ibid.* When these vessels sailed from San Francisco under sealed orders on 17 May, the *Opal* sailed immediately for Esquimalt.

[30]In London, the crisis prompted a discussion at the Royal United Service Institution in which most participants claimed that Britain should strengthen Esquimalt's defences greatly. See J. C. R. Colomb, "Russian Development and Our Naval and Military Position in the North Pacific," *Journal of the Royal United Service Institution*, XXI (1877), 657-80, and discussion, 680-707. Reginald H. Roy, "The Early Militia and Defence of British Columbia, 1871-1885." *British Columbia Historical Society Quarterly*, XVIII (1954), 13.

[31]*Victoria Colonist*, 9 February 1878.

[32]Not until 1893 were Russian and British warships in the Pacific instructed to give previous notice before visiting a port of the other power. E. MacGregor to Rear-Admiral Hotham, 13 March 1893, R.G. 8 IIIB, Vol. I, fols. 86-88, P.A.C.

[33]From report of Captain F. C. B. Robinson, H.M.S. *Opal*, at Esquimalt, 20 February 1878, described in de Horsey to Sec. of Adm. 4 April 1878, Adm. 1/6454.

In the crisis, the Canadian government and local militia units understandably were anxious to assist the Royal Navy in protecting British Columbia against an expected cruiser raid. Some steps had been taken to improve the defences at the southern tip of Vancouver Island after the 1877 alarm. In 1878, a volunteer artillery corps was raised to man obsolete navy guns placed to guard the entrances to Victoria and Esquimalt harbours.[34]

But these meagre preparations were insufficient according to both the Commander-in-Chief, Pacific, and the Admiralty. On 28 June, de Horsey sent the following confidential report to the Admiralty, revealing his concern:

> The Dockyard [at Esquimalt] is Imperial property, and bears the same relative position to our Squadron in the Pacific as Halifax does to the Squadron in the North Atlantic, but with three fold force, as there is no Bermuda or Jamaica in these waters—no British possession within possible reach for supplies and repairs. It is lamentable to think that in the present defenceless condition of this harbour, and viewing the trifling number of Volunteer Militia, any fairly organized enemy's expedition should suffice to destroy the Dockyard and be masters of the position, until again ejected by hard fighting. This is assuming the absence of Her Majesty's Ships, which, in case of War, must be counted upon. They could not remain here as mere floating batteries, and even if used for that purpose, it is easy to conceive their being enticed away by a feint, or even by false information.[35]

The Commander-in-Chief thus had raised the awkward issue of the extent to which the Navy should be held responsible for securing the naval base. He believed that Esquimalt ought to be defended by "Imperial resources" under "Naval Control".[36] In this the Lords Commissioners of the Admiralty agreed. But in their opinion, the responsibility for shore defence rested with the War Office, to which they recommended strongly that Esquimalt should be made secure from attack "as it is probably the only harbour to which Her Majesty's Ships would have access in time of War on the entire Pacific Coast of America."[37]

The crisis—ended by the Congress of Berlin—did bring some results in that reports were made by military officers on the defences of British Columbia.[38] Generally speaking, however, confusing divisions of author-

---

[34]See Roy, "Early Militia," pp. 13-19.
[35]de Horsey to Sec. of Adm., 28 June 1878, confidential, Adm. 1/6460.
[36]*Ibid.*
[37]Adm. to Under-Secretary of State for War, 1 June 1878, confidential, *ibid.*
[38]By Lt. Col. J. W. Lovell, R.E., Lt.-Col. T. B. Strange, R.A., and Col. Crossman, R.E. See Roy, "Early Militia", pp. 19-22; Richard A. Preston, *Canada and "Imperial Defense"* (Durham, N.C.: Duke University Press, 1967), pp. 130-31, 164-65, and Schurman, "Esquimalt," pp. 62-64.

ity existed between the Imperial and Dominion governments. Canada was not much interested in contributing funds for permanent works at Victoria and Esquimalt, and the number of men available for militia was insufficient for local defence. Therefore, it was not surprising that when a similar although less serious crisis occurred in 1885—this time over Afghanistan—the meagre precautions taken at Esquimalt after 1878 against a potential hit-and-run attack by Russian cruisers were considered inadequate. To increase the deterrent against such a raid, the Admiralty bought two Yarrow first-class torpedo boats from Chile; these boats, ordered to Esquimalt, remained there until early in the twentieth century.[39] As a further precaution, especially for the protection of trade in the Pacific, the Admiralty commissioned the *Britannia* and *Coptic* as mercantile cruisers.[40]

The Russian war scares led to several effects that were auspicious for the development of Esquimalt. Among these were detailed examinations of naval defence protection and, in the case of Esquimalt, eventual cooperation between the British and Canadian governments. On the recommendation of the Colonial Defence Committee, some emergency measures, including the construction of four earth batteries, were taken to fortify Esquimalt in the summer of 1878.[41] About the same time a Royal Commission was appointed "to enquire into the Defence of British Possessions and Commerce Abroad." The Carnarvon Commission, as it was generally called, stated in its Third Report (1882) that Esquimalt must be fortified if the British squadron were kept on the West Coast of North America. At the same time, the Commission questioned the importance of Esquimalt as a naval base because of the insignificance of

[39]Torpedo Boats No. 39, the *Swift,* and No. 40, the *Sure,* were purchased from Chile and sailed 6,000 miles to Esquimalt. Culme-Seymour to Sec. of Adm., 8 September 1885, Adm. 1/6762. They were 100 feet long and 40 tons displacement. Originally they seem to have had spar torpedoes only, but later were fitted with dropping gear. They were escorted on their coasting hop by the *Pelican* as far as Acapulco, then by the *Satellite* to Esquimalt where they were overhauled, commissioned from time to time, taken on cruises and exercised. Finally placed in reserve at the end of 1903, they were sold, probably in 1905.

[40]The Admiralty also decided on two armed mercantile cruisers for the Australian station (*Lusitania* and *Massilia*) and one for the China station (*Pembroke Castle*). The *Britannia* was armed at Coquimbo, but the success of peace negotiations with Russia meant that none of these ships had to be employed. Rear-Admiral J. K. E. Baird to Sec. of Adm., 25 June 1885, and enclosures, Y 121, Adm. 1/6762.

[41]Report of Colonial Defence Committee, encl. in Admiral Sir Alexander Milne to C.O., 1 April 1878, Adm. 1/6460. The Admiralty strongly supported this report, and advised the Colonial Office that the general duties of the Pacific station "make it often impossible to keep H.M. Ships in Ports, and local batteries are therefore indispensable." Hall to Under-Sec. of State for the Colonies, 20 April 1878, *ibid.* Lieut.-Col. D. T. Irwin, Inspector of Artillery, was sent to British Columbia to supervise the erection of the coastal batteries.

British trade on the North Pacific Coast in comparison to other areas. Moreover, the report stated, the Navy would be better able to protect British interests in China and deal with Russian warships in the North-western Pacific more effectively if the Pacific station headquarters were at Hong Kong rather than Esquimalt.[42]

The war scare of 1885 forced a reappraisal of the Carnarvon Commission's arguments, and both the Colonial Defence Committee and the Committee on Colonial Garrisons pressed for cooperation between the Imperial and Dominion governments on the defence of Esquimalt. The Colonial Defence Committee contended that the Canadian government should participate in harbour security, for if Esquimalt and Victoria possessed adequate shore defences this would aid the Royal Navy in guarding "the whole seaboard of British Columbia," including the coal port of Nanaimo and the railway terminus at Burrard Inlet.[43] The Committee on Colonial Garrisons recommended that the British supply the armament and an officer-in-charge and that the Dominion government construct the works and man the garrison.[44] In other words, the major result of the war-scare period was the reawakening of Imperial and Dominion interest in the necessity of defending the naval base.[45]

Shifting Strategy for the Pacific

In addition to its naval base and dockyard at Esquimalt, the Navy required coaling stations at places throughout the Pacific islands and along Pacific shores. However, between Esquimalt and the Falkland Islands no coaling stations existed on British soil. The "Foreign Coaling Stations" used by the Pacific squadron were, from north to south: San Francisco, San Diego, Mazatlan, Acapulco, Panama, Guayaquil, Payta, Callao, Coptapo, Coquimbo, Valparaiso and Ancud.

The Hawaiian Islands lay at the cross-roads of the Pacific—on the direct routes between Panama and Japan, Vancouver and Australia. Thus the possible establishment of a coal depot on this mid-Pacific

---

[42]"Third and Final Report of the Royal Commission appointed to inquire into the Defence of British Possessions Abroad . . . 1882," Carnarvon Papers, PRO 30/6/126. A summary of the Commission's findings as they relate to Esquimalt is in Preston, *Canada and "Imperial Defence,"* pp. 131-33. For their relation to the Empire as a whole, see Donald C. Gordon, *Dominion Partnership in Imperial Defense, 1870-1914* (Baltimore: John Hopkins Press, 1965) , pp. 63-71.

[43]"Defence of Vancouver Island," by H. Jekyll, Sec. of C.D.C., 1 May 1885, printed for the Cabinet, Cab. 11/27, 2M, p. 2.

[44]Report of the Committee on Colonial Garrisons, 1886, confidential, C.O. 323/366, No. 23204, p. 11.

[45]Roy, "Early Militia," p. 28.

position was important to British maritime interests.[46] The advantage
that would accrue to Britain in having a coaling depot there was evident
in 1886 when Rear-Admiral Sir Michael Culme-Seymour informed the
Hawaiian King that unofficially Britain "could not approve of any
other nation having a coaling station or other establishment in the
Sandwich Islands."[47]

Having at last awakened to the strategic value of the Hawaiian Islands,
the British ministry favoured establishing a depot somewhere in the
islands, but it was too late. When news reached London in November
1887 of the cession of Pearl Harbour to the United States as a coaling
and repairing station, all the Foreign Office could do was remind the
Hawaiians and the United States that British warships were free by
treaty to "enter into all harbours, rivers, and places within those Islands
to which the Ships of War of other nations are or may be permitted
to come to anchor there and to remain and refit."[48] In effect, however,
Britain was excluded from the Islands. The cession of Pearl Harbour
gave the United States a foothold that led finally to the annexation
of the Hawaiian Islands in 1898. By that time, in the new period of
Anglo-American *rapprochement,* capped by the Hay-Pauncefote Treaty
of 1901, British protests had all but died away.[49]

As a result of exclusion from Hawaii, the Admiralty immediately
considered other positions in the Eastern Pacific for a coaling station.
In 1881 and 1883, surveys had been made of the Galapagos Islands off
Ecuador; although Tagus Cove was found to be the best site there, it
did not meet with Admiralty approval.[50] The Admiralty realized in
1893 that, although a depot midway between Esquimalt and the Falklands was required, the growth of American interests in Hawaii and
naval power in the Pacific—coupled with the likelihood that Panama
would cede a canal zone to the United States—made the Galapagos a

[46]The Colonial Secretary, Sir Henry Holland, for example, considered that the route
from Esquimalt across the Pacific would develop so that a British coaling station at
Hawaii would become "a necessity." J. Bramston (C.O.) to Sec. of State, F.O., 11 June
1887, confidential, Adm. 1/6865. A short review of British opposition to the "cession"
of Pearl Harbour is given in Merze Tate, *Hawaii: Reciprocity or Annexation* (East
Lansing: Michigan State University Press, 1968), pp. 200-210.
[47]Culme-Seymour to Sec. of Adm., 20 July 1886, Adm. 1/6813.
[48]J. Pauncefote (F.O.) to Under-Sec. of State, C.O., 10 December 1887, confidential,
Adm. 1/6865.
[49]See Merze Tate, "Hawaii: A Symbol of Anglo-American Rapprochement," *Political
Science Quarterly,* LXXIX (1964), 574. On the naval ramifications see Alfred T.
Mahan and Lord Charles Beresford, "Possibilities of an Anglo-American Reunion,"
North American Review, CLIX (1894), 551-73.
[50]Rear-Admiral F. H. Stirling to Sec. of Adm., 24 June 1881, confidential, Adm.
1/6581, and Rear-Admiral A. M. Lyons to Sec. of Adm., 7 February 1883, confidential,
Adm. 1/6666.

questionable location for a British depot. The Admiralty reasoned soundly that in an Anglo-American war a coaling station there would have to be defended by the squadron, while in a war with any other power its necessity would diminish.[51]

As late as 1897-1898, the British government was still considering the Galapagos and it had once more added the Revillagigedo group off Mexico to the list of possibilities.[52] But again the Admiralty and Foreign Office took no action. Aware that the United States government would complain vehemently if the Galapagos Islands became a British coaling station, the Senior Naval Lord bemoaned, "A naval base at the Galapagos is what we have long wanted and might have had without difficulty thirty years ago, but times have changed."[53] In brief, the proximity of American interests in Panama coupled with the necessity of defending the position determined the decision to do without a coaling station in these latitudes. The implication seems clear. In order to uphold her interests in the Pacific, Britain was becoming more and more dependent on good relations with the United States.

While American influence in the Pacific increased, the centre of gravity of British activity continued to shift from the Pacific shores of Latin America to British Columbia, even though the station headquarters had reverted, for reasons of alleged economy, from Esquimalt to Valparaiso in 1869. The relocation of the headquarters at Valparaiso prompted the Canadian government on behalf of British Columbia to urge Britain to maintain a naval base at Esquimalt as part of the terms under which the Pacific province entered Confederation in 1871. Accordingly, Esquimalt was not closed.

By 1882, an anomalous situation had developed at Valparaiso. It was almost deserted by Royal Navy ships and was visited only on annual cruises by the squadron, whose main duties lay in the North Pacific.[54] Consequently, in 1883, Coquimbo and Esquimalt became headquarters of the Southern and Northern Divisions respectively.[55] But by 1900, the Northern Division, for all intents and purposes developed as the

---

[51]See the views of Cyprian Bridge (Director of Naval Intelligence) and Sir A. Hoskins (a Lord of the Admiralty) of 10 April 1893, on Rear-Admiral C. F. Hotham to Sec. of Adm., 20 February 1893, Adm. 1/7142.
[52]"Coaling Station off Central America," 1898. Cab. 11/27, 135M.
[53]Minute of Sir Frederick Richards, 7 December 1897, Adm. 1/7334B.
[54]Lyons to Sec. of Adm., 13 May 1882, Adm. 1/6617. In point of fact, four years before, Valparaiso—the haven of British warships since early in the century—was abandoned because of the dangers of strong winds (or "Northers") during winter months. Coquimbo, farther north, became the depot for consumable and replaceable stores until the storeship *Liffey* was sold in 1903.
[55]Pacific Station Standing Orders, 1888, p. 52; in Y65, Adm. 1/6914.

sole operational region of the Pacific squadron, except for the annual
patrol of the Pacific islands.[56]

During the 1890's, some doubt existed as to whether or not Esquimalt
was the best site in British Columbia for the northern headquarters of
the squadron. The major objection was that it faced Port Angeles across
the Strait of Juan de Fuca, a common resort of American warships. It
was also within easy steaming of the United States naval base at Bremerton.[57] The growth of American naval forces in the Pacific forced
the Admiralty to be as hesitant about maintaining and expanding
Esquimalt as it had been in discussions on the suitability of the Galapagos for a coaling station. Not surprisingly, and for some time, they
contemplated removing the dockyard and naval establishments from
Esquimalt to a position farther from the border of the United States
where they could be better defended against attack.[58] Alternates considered in 1891 were Burrard Inlet, Torquart Harbour on Barclay
Sound, Port Simpson which was proposed as continental railway ter-
minal, and even Naden Harbour in the Queen Charolette Islands,
which could be used to shelter armed cruisers protecting British shipping on the Great Circle route between British Columbia and Asia.

In 1892, the Admiralty reviewed several questions relating to retention of Esquimalt as a naval base and its proper defence against
a raid by American cruisers. Quite simply, Esquimalt provided the
best site available and thus would have to be protected. But to what
degree and in what fashion? The defence of Esquimalt lay not so much
in shore fortifications as in naval power. According to one Lord of
the Admiralty, so long as the Royal Navy had command of the sea
and patrolled the Strait of Juan de Fuca, Esquimalt would be "prac-
tically secure."[59] This was a reassertion of the doctrine that the security
of the Empire depended on sea power. After the Crimean War,
British naval thinking had assumed a questionable defensive attitude,
relying largely on fortifications and coastal craft for naval defence
throughout the Empire. The cobwebs were swept away with the so-
called "Blue Water School" which by the 1890's claimed that the

---

[56]See Rear-Admiral L. A. Beaumont to Sec. of Adm., 27 March 1900, Y144, Adm.
1/7374. Esquimalt again developed into the headquarters of the station, but was
strangely never officially declared as such.

[57]In 1891, Bremerton was established as the Puget Sound Naval Station. Robert E.
Johnson, *Thence Round Cape Horn: The Story of United States Naval Forces on
Pacific Station, 1818-1923* (Annapolis, Md., United States Naval Institute, 1963) , p. 152.

[58]Minute of Major H. Pilkington, Director of Works, 2 February 1891, Adm. 116/820,
fol. 150. Admirals Bedford, Fairfax, and Bridge supported Rear-Admiral Hotham
in the view that Esquimalt should be retained. See *ibid.*, fols. 54, 124-28b.

[59]Minute of E. A. B[arlett, M.P.], 26 February 1892, *ibid.*, fols. 128-28b.

strength of the nation at sea would best secure Britain against invasion and at the same time protect the communications and trade of a widely extended empire.

But such thinking did not eliminate the necessity of shore defences, either at home or abroad. Once the Admiralty knew with certainty that Esquimalt was to be maintained, it became the responsibility of the British and Canadian governments to reach a decision on how the base could be made secure. This was resolved in April 1893.[60] The two governments reached agreement whereby the War Office would defray half the cost of extensive new works and the whole of the cost of armaments while Canada would contribute the other half of the cost of the new works, supply the sites for batteries, and provide £10,000 toward the cost of the barracks for the Canadian troops and Royal Marines who were to garrison the fortress.[61] When completed in 1895, these minimal preparations were adequate to defend Esquimalt and Victoria against a raid by one or two enemy cruisers. At last one of the most difficult problems in imperial defence cooperation had been solved.[62]

Britain at a Disadvantage

British naval policy underwent a revolution between 1896 and 1905 to deal with the rising strength of foreign naval powers. The United States Navy, for example, made the eight ships of the Royal Navy in the Pacific appear small by contrast. When the Commander-in-Chief, Pacific, Rear-Admiral A. K. Bickford, complained bitterly to the Admiralty in 1901 of the disparity between British and American naval forces in the Pacific and of the "dangerously weak state" of the squadron under his command, the Admiralty could do nothing; the necessities of maintaining large forces in European and Chinese

[60]*Memorandum on the Standard of Defence at Esquimalt; Printed for the Committee on Imperial Defence,* May 1903, Cab. 5/1/2c, p. 3.
[61]"The most powerful battery was to be that of Signal Hill, whose two 9.2-inch B[reach] L[oading] guns would reach some 10 miles to counter-bombard any ships attempting to shell the harbour installations from long range. The Fort Rodd Hill and Macaulay Point 6-inch BL gun batteries were for medium-range work of up to 10,000 yards and the three other batteries—Belmont, Duntze Head and Black Rock— were each equipped with two 12-pounder Q[uick] F[iring] guns with fighting ranges of 400 yards and maximum ranges of 8000 yards. Search-lights also were mounted at the quick-firing batteries so covering fire could be brought to bear, by night as well as by day, over the shore-controlled submarine minefield that would be laid to protect the approaches to Esquimalt Harbour in time of war." *Fort Rodd Hill and Fisgard Lighthouse* (National Historic Park Pamphlet, n.d.).
[62]Preston, *Canada and "Imperial Defense,"* p. 198.

waters prohibited an increase in the Pacific squadron.[63] As the First
Naval Lord concluded in a noteworthy document, "The very fact of the
great superiority of the U.S. Squadron in the Pacific should shew us how
impossible it is for us in view of the requirements elsewhere to maintain a Squadron in the Pacific capable of coping with it. It is impossible
for this country in view of the greater development of foreign navies
to be a superior force everywhere."[64] As Rear-Admiral Bickford knew,
in a possible diplomatic crisis over the Alaska boundary or the inter-
ocean canal across Panama, the Pacific squadron would be unable
to support British diplomacy and would have to acquiesce to American
demands.[65]

As early as 1897, the simultaneous rise of American naval power
and hemispheric interests—particularly in the Pacific—had made the
question of the defence of Esquimalt purely academic, for in that year
the Committee on Colonial Defence reported that the cost of defending the base against a full-scale attack by United States cruisers would
be out of all proportion to Canada's resources.[66] The Board of Admiralty, however, was not in agreement. Considering the gold discoveries in the Yukon, the long-standing dispute over the Alaska
panhandle, and the contentious matter of sealing in the Bering Sea,[67]

---

[63]Rear-Admiral A. K. Bickford to Sec. of Adm., 17 September 1901, confidential,
Minute of R. N. Custance (Director of Naval Intelligence), 11 October 1901, Adm.
1/7513 and B. MacGregor to Commander-in-Chief, Pacific, 17 October 1901, R.G. 8,
IIIB, Vol. 15, fol. 134, P.A.C.
[64]Minute of Admiral Walter T. Kerr, 14 October 1901, Adm. 1/7513.
[65]Bickford to Sec. of Adm. 17 September 1901, *ibid.*
[66]W.O. to C.O., 27 October 1897, in *Memorandum on the Standard of Defence at
Esquimalt; Printed for the Committee on Imperial Defence, May 1903*, Cab. 5/1/2c,
p. 4. The estimate for adequate defence was a garrison of 4000 men costing £250,000
per annum. On the American naval implications of territorial expansion in the
Pacific, see Harold and Margaret Sprout, *The Rise of American Naval Power, 1776-
1918* (Princeton: Princeton University Press, 1939), pp. 241-45.
[67]In 1886, Canadian schooners were seized by an American revenue cutter in the
Bering Sea, which the United States claimed was *mare clausum*. Britain protested
that the Bering Sea was open and the captures flagrant violations of International Law.
The ensuing dispute nearly led to war in 1888 when Rear-Admiral Heneage planned
to halt these "unjustifiable acts" by ordering the retaking of some Canadian schooners
that American vessels were convoying through British waters from Sitka to Port
Townsend on Puget Sound. The Foreign Office intervened and Heneage's orders
were cancelled. Heneage to Adm., 9 June 1888, and other correspondence, Adm. 1/6914.
This was but one incident that endangered the peace. During 1891-1893 British and
American warships patrolled the sea, from which sealers had been excluded by a *modus
vivendi*. In 1903, a Paris tribunal upheld the case of Britain, and Canadian sealing
interests received compensation for damages. The duties of the Royal Navy in these
northern waters constituted their principal operations during 1890-1903, involving
two or three vessels for the patrol and the concentration of the remainder of the
Pacific squadron (usually six or seven) at Esquimalt during the critical periods of
Anglo-American disagreement. Rear-Admiral Hotham to Adm., 21 June 1890,
Adm. 1/7023.

the Admiralty wisely refused to discount the possibility of an American attack on British Columbia.[68] In a fiery dispatch to the Colonial Office dated 8 March 1898, the Admiralty Board strongly advocated that Esquimalt be provided with defences beyond the 1893 standard so that it could contribute more adequately to the protection of Canada and the Empire and serve as a base of operations for the Royal Navy in wartime.[69] As their Lordships explained, ". . . deprived of their base and coaling station, Her Majesty's ships could not be maintained in those waters, and without naval defence, the trade and ports of British Columbia would become prey to every enemy, and the province be at mercy of the United States."[70] At all costs British Columbia must be saved from Manifest Destiny.

The plea of the Admiralty Board for "adequate" defences elicited only a partial response. Together, the Admiralty, Colonial Office, War Office, and Treasury reached a decision for what now can be considered the final step toward Imperial protection of Esquimalt. This decision acknowledged that although Esquimalt's defence was primarily a Canadian obligation, the responsibility for maintenance of the garrison of some 323 troops at the base should be assumed jointly by the War Office and Canada because of the inadequate strength and organization of the Dominion's permanent forces.[71]

The growth of American military and sea power caused British policy increasingly to centre on avoiding war with the United States, so that by 1905 it was fully recognized in Whitehall that the best defence of Canada, and thus of Halifax and Esquimalt, rested in a cordial Anglo-American understanding.[72]

The development of the Anglo-American *rapprochement*, however, did not eliminate the necessity of protection from other powers— notably Germany, France, Russia and Japan—all of whom at the turn of the century were making remarkable increases in their naval forces in the Pacific as well as advances in matériel.[73] Under the influence of these circumstances, the British ministry sought and gained

---

[68]Adm. to C.O., 8 March 1898, in *Memorandum on the Standard of Defence at Esquimalt . . . 1903*, Cab. 571/2c, p. 5.

[69]*Ibid.*

[70]*Ibid.*

[71]*Ibid.* This was approved valid to 1909.

[72]See Samuel F. Wells, Jr., "British Strategic Withdrawal from the Western Hemisphere, 1904-1906," *Canadian Historical Review*, XLIX (Dec. 1968), 335-56; especially noteworthy in this article is the description of Admiral Fisher's success in overcoming much opposition to the withdrawal of nearly all British naval forces from Canada and the West Indies.

[73]See Arthur J. Marder, *British Naval Policy, 1880-1905: The Anatomy of British Sea Power* (London: Putnam & Co., 1940), chapter 21, especially p. 432 n. 10, on the naval strengths of the great powers.

an ally that strengthened her sagging naval power in the Pacific. The Anglo-Japanese Alliance of 1902 brought together two powerful "island empires" with overwhelming naval superiority in the Atlantic and Pacific oceans respectively.[74] The agreement was really an insurance policy, effective only if the other partner was attacked by, or at war with two or more powers. For Britain, the alliance had implications of economy for it meant that more warships could be withdrawn from the Pacific and China stations and stationed in or near the North Sea to guard against the growing German menace.[75]

The Anglo-Japanese Alliance, along with the signing of the *Entente* with France in 1904, marked the end of Britain's "splendid isolation." The system of distributing warships among nine foreign stations had been rendered obsolete by changes in strategy and in instruments of war. Technological advances in wireless telegraphy, torpedoes, torpedo boat destroyers, mines, submarines, guns, armour, steel hulls and steam propulsion—in short, a great advance over the naval equipment of 1856—made sea power potentially more effective provided that ships and especially bases were available. Because her strength at sea remained as essential to Britain's survival as ever—and could serve as a restraining influence on her probable enemies—the "new conditions" that Admiral Sir John Fisher, the First Sea Lord, mentioned in his famous recommendation to the Cabinet of October 1904 necessitated a concentration of naval strength in home waters and a reorganization of the squadrons overseas.[76]

In the sweeping fleet reorganizations of 1905, the Pacific, South East Coast of America and North American stations were abolished.[77] Only the Channel, Atlantic, Mediterranean and Eastern commands remained,

---

[74]See Ian H. Nish, *The Anglo-Japanese Alliance: The Diplomacy of Two Island Empires, 1894-1907* (London: Athlone Press, 1966).

[75]Had the German East Asiatic squadron under Admiral Graf von Spey steamed north from the Chilean coast after defeating the British squadron at Coronel in November 1914, Japanese rather than British or Canadian warships would have protected British Columbia, a fact which alarmed many British Columbians at a time when Oriental immigration was a hotly-debated issue. From the commencement of hostilities until the United States entered the conflict in 1917, Japan supplied the main naval protection for British Columbia. Charles J. Woodsworth, *Canada and the Orient: A Study in International Relations* (Toronto: Macmillan, 1941), pp. 102-103, 168-70; P. C. Lowe, "The British Empire and the Anglo-Japanese Alliance, 1911-1915," *History,* LIV (June 1969), 212-25; and Geoffrey Bennett, *Coronel and Falklands* (London: Pan Books, 1967), pp. 53-55, 57, 86-87.

[76]This policy was made public in the celebrated memorandum of the Earl of Selborne, the First Lord of the Admiralty, 6 December 1905: "Distribution and Mobilization of the Fleet," *Parliamentary Papers,* 1905, LXVIII (Cmd. 2335).

[77]Arthur J. Marder, *From the Dreadnought to Scapa Flow: The Royal Navy in the Fisher Era, 1904-1919,* Vol. I, *The Road to War, 1904-1914* (London: Oxford University Press, 1961), pp. 40-43.

the last of these comprising the old China, East Indies, Australian and Pacific squadrons. Naval establishments such as Bermuda, Halifax and Trincomalee which had served the needs of the Navy handsomely under the former distribution system were drastically reduced. This permitted savings of £192,000 from an annual total of £1,292,000[78]—funds vital to the building of new capital ships such as the revolutionary *Dreadnought*.

The Pacific station was closed at sunset on 1 March 1905, when Commodore J. E. C. Goodrich lowered his broad pendant on the *Bonaventure* at Esquimalt[79] and sailed for Hong Kong, leaving Commander A. T. Hunt of H.M.S. *Shearwater* as Commander-in-Charge for Station Duties on the West Coast of America. The victualling depot and hospital at Esquimalt were closed and the munitions and stores transferred to Hong Kong. Only the dockyard and certain bunkering facilities remained in operation at Esquimalt.

The closure of the station did not mean that the Pacific, in particular British Columbia, was ignored by the Royal Navy and the Imperial government. Instead of one unarmoured cruiser, first-class, and two unarmoured cruisers, second-class, the Pacific Ocean was allotted four unarmoured cruisers, second-class. These were all placed under the charge of the Commander-in-Chief of the Eastern Fleet.[80] However, in 1908, the only ships of the Royal Navy actually on the Northwest Coast—the sloops *Algerine* and *Shearwater* and the survey ship *Egeria*—were scarcely sufficient for coastal defence. Yet the advantages of the telegraph, wireless telegraphy, crack cruisers, the trans-Pacific cable and the Canadian Pacific Railway now were such that even if assistance were not available immediately at Esquimalt or Vancouver, troops could be sent from eastern Canada in six days or from England in twenty-six days (including seven for preparation), while warships could be sent from Hong Kong in twenty days. These technological advances actually made British Columbia less remote and probably provided her with more potential military defence than ever before.

Canada Reluctant to Assume Her Defence

The successor to the Royal Navy on the Northwest Coast was, symbolically, the Royal Canadian Navy.[81] Initially in 1907, a scheme invit-

[78]"Financial Effects of Fleet Re-Organization," confidential, Selborne Papers, 1904-1905, pp. 2-3, N.L.

[79]J. Goodrich to Sec. of Adm. 1 March 1905, Adm. 1/7806.

[80]"Naval Necessities," Selborne Papers, pp. 10-11, N.L. and Lt.-Cdr. P. K. Kemp, ed., *The Papers of Admiral Sir John Fisher*, Vol. I (London: Navy Records Society, Vol. III, 1960), pp. 100, 130, 161, 193.

[81]See Gilbert N. Tucker, *The Naval Service of Canada: Its Official History*, 2 vols., (Ottawa, 1952), I, 104-211.

ing Canada and the other self-governing Dominions to contribute finan-
cially to Imperial defence had received strong opposition from Canadian
delegates to the Imperial Conference in London. They maintained
that Canada was already doing her share by protecting the Great Lakes,
policing her fishing grounds, providing trans-continental railways and
assuming the upkeep of Esquimalt and Halifax.

Under Sir Wilfred Laurier, the Prime Minister, the Canadian government determined to create a separate Canadian navy; in 1910 it passed
the Canadian Naval Service Act which established the organizational
structure of the force. At the same time, pre-war cooperation with
Britain and Australia in the naval defence of the Empire was reaching
its zenith.[82] But in terms of units all that the Royal Canadian Navy could
boast were two obsolete cruisers bought from the Admiralty as training
ships—the *Niobe* in the Atlantic and the *Rainbow* in the Pacific.[83]
Not until Britain and Germany declared war in 1914 was the Canadian
force in the Pacific augmented by the hurried purchase of two submarines to protect British Columbia from a seemingly imminent attack
by the German light cruiser *Leipzig*.[84]

Nonetheless, Canada did acquire, somewhat reluctantly, the foundations of two great shore establishments. The transfer of garrisons at
Halifax and Esquimalt from Imperial to Dominion control was completed in 1906.[85] When British troops left Esquimalt on 22 May, a
milestone in Canadian self-defence had been reached. It now remained
to transfer the two dockyards; this was done at Halifax in 1906 and at
Esquimalt on 9 November 1910. It was only a matter of necessary paper-
work before these bases were formally relinquished by the Admiralty
and this was done at Halifax on 13 October 1910, and at Esquimalt on
4 May 1911. The terms of transfer, briefly stated, stipulated that Canada
would maintain the existing facilities of supply and repair and they

[82]Gordon, *Dominion Partnership*, p. 287; see also his "The Admiralty and Dominion
Navies, 1902-1914," *Journal of Modern History*, XXXIII (1961), 407-22.
[83]Gilbert N. Tucker, "The Career of H.M.C.S. 'Rainbow'," *British Columbia Historical Quarterly*, VII (January 1943), 1-30.
[84]As the submarines were purchased by the Premier of the Province, British Columbia
can be said to have been the only province to have had its own navy. For a fascinating
account of these ships, see Gilbert N. Tucker, "Canada's First Submarines, CC 1 and
CC 2: An Episode of the Naval War in the Pacific," *ibid.*, pp. 147-70.
[85]For full details of the conditions of transfer, see Adm. to C.O., October 1907, C.O.
42/914. See also Gordon, *Dominion Partnership*, pp. 185-86, and C. S. MacKinnon,
"The Imperial Fortresses in Canada: Halifax and Esquimalt, 1871-1906," 2 vols.
(Ph.D. thesis, University of Toronto, 1965).

would be available to the Royal Navy should they be needed at any time.[86]

When the Pacific station at Esquimalt was formally closed by the Admiralty and the naval base and dockyard were transferred to the Canadian government, the responsibility the Royal Navy had fulfilled for nearly a century in patrolling and protecting British territory on the Northwest Coast of North America virtually terminated. But the benefits of the long service rendered by successive commanders-in-chief and ships under their command since early in the nineteenth century endured. Under the protection of the Royal Navy, the infant Pacific colonies had grown into a province comprising a part of a dominion. It is no less significant that the Royal Navy contributed to the permanent establishment of British traditions in British Columbia.

Ships of the Royal Navy were among the first belonging to any European nation to penetrate the vast waters of the Pacific. Through the activities of these vessels between 1810 and 1914, Britain could expand her overseas trade and, when necessary, acquire numerous territories within the Pacific rim. That Britain was able to extend her frontiers beyond her own immediate shores to include a section of the Pacific Northwest can be attributed, at least partially, to her strength at sea.

British warships constituted a shield behind which the fur-trading posts of the North West Company and the Hudson's Bay Company and the colonial settlements of Vancouver Island and British Columbia could prosper and mature. These vessels provided protection from attacks by Indians. They stopped lawless gold miners and foreign encroachments. When assaults by Russians in the North Pacific seemed imminent during the Crimean War and during the war scares of 1877-1878 and 1885, the Royal Navy's presence served to allay the fears of British settlers on the Northwest Coast. When difficulties with the United States arose over the Oregon Boundary and the ownership of the San Juan Islands, again the Navy stood by and helped to resolve the disputes. When American Manifest Destiny threatened to absorb the greater part of British North America into the United States, the Royal Navy supplied the deterrent. And when the new Dominion of Canada showed economic inability and even a strong disinclination to undertake the defence of her own coasts, the Royal Navy provided the principal means of protection for forty years after British Columbia entered Confederation.

[86]"Canadian Naval Establishments (Esquimalt Dockyard) Order, 1911," Adm. 116/993, 246ff. For a summary of the Imperial withdrawal from Esquimalt, 1905-1910, see C. P. Stacey, *The Military Problems of Canada* (Toronto: Ryerson, 1940), pp. 69-70.

The influence of the Royal Navy in the history of British Columbia was therefore decisive. Ships of war, as instruments of British policy, played a role that has not yet been sufficiently appreciated. In histories of British Columbia and the Pacific Northwest, attention is frequently given to the impact of explorers, fur traders, settlers and railway builders with little reference to the importance of British ships and seamen.

Yet the division of the greater part of the North American continent between the United States on the one hand and Britain and Canada on the other is due in part to British naval supremacy. Britain's national strategy was based on primacy at sea. Her rivals in the nineteenth century, including Russia and the United States, could never afford to ignore this. Both in the Atlantic and Pacific oceans maritime factors decided the course of empires, and the exercise of sea power by the Royal Navy constituted a determining influence in Canada's possession of a Pacific shore: a fact of certain significance to Canada, to North America, and, ultimately, to the Commonwealth and to the Pacific rim.

Appendix A

CHANGING BOUNDARIES OF THE
PACIFIC STATION

In 1808, THE SOUTH AMERICAN STATION was created. It included within its limits the entire eastern Pacific.[1] From this command evolved the Pacific station, created in 1837, which assumed the duties of the old South America station west of Cape Horn.[2] This development represented a further recognition of British political influence and maritime activity in the Pacific.

The extension of the Royal Navy's influence beyond the Horn paralleled that in the seas east of the Cape of Good Hope. After the Napoleonic Wars, the Indian Ocean, the China Seas and the waters of the Antipodes were visited more frequently by British men-of-war than

[1]The South American station's limits, as defined in 1816, were "to the southward of the line and to the westward of the 30th meridian of west longitude." Admiralty Minute, 18 December 1816, Adm. 3/88; Gerald S. Graham and R. A. Humphreys, eds., *The Navy and South America, 1807-1823: Correspondence of the Commanders-in-Chief on the South American Station* (London: Navy Records Society, vol. CIV, 1962), p. xii.

[2]Although Rear-Admiral C. B. H. Ross was appointed to the command on 4 September 1837, he did not assume "command of Her Majesty's ships and vessels employed on the Western Coast of America, and in the Pacific" until he entered the station limits in early March 1838; Ross to Wood, 19 March 1838, Adm. 1/51. The genesis of the station is explained in John Bach, "The Royal Navy in the South Pacific, 1826-1876" (Ph.D. thesis; University of New South Wales, 1964), chapter 2.

before. The task of ensuring that British traders, missionaries and consular agents would be free from attack or interference in these vast tracts of water rested initially with the East Indies and China station.[3] After 1820, that command extended to the meridian 170° West longitude where it met the western extremity of the South American station. Several subdivisions of the East Indies and China station followed but, by 1859, the increasing importance of Australia, New Zealand and the islands of the western Pacific led to the creation of an independent command: the Australian station.[4] Five years later, the China station became a separate entity charged with halting piracy and protecting British trade and colonial dependencies in those seas.[5] Thus by 1864, the waters within the Pacific rim had been divided into three naval districts: the Pacific, the Australian and the China stations.

Britain's largest naval station was the Pacific, bounded on the north by Bering Strait; on the south by the Antarctic Circle; on the east by the longitude of Cape Horn; and on the west by 170° West longitude.[6] As such, this command encompassed all the American shores west of the Horn and all the islands westward to Samoa. The Navy gave special attention to Pacific South America and to the Galapagos, Hawaiian, Marquesas, Society and Cook Islands. Pitcairn Island, the landing place of the *Bounty* mutineers in 1790, also was closely watched. So, too, were the guano-clad Chincha Islands off the Peruvian Coast, where the horrors of coolie labour never ceased to shock naval commanders who called to guard British ships engaged in transporting this fertilizer to Europe and elsewhere.

At other places along the coasts of the Americas, as developments warranted, the Pacific command undertook various tasks: encouraging Spanish colonies to win their independence; watching British spheres of influence and communications in Central America; guarding British fur traders on the Northwest Coast; securing the British colonies there from Indians, American gold seekers, and from Britain's two North Pacific rivals, Russia and the United States; and protecting Canadian sealing schooners out of Victoria from American interference.

As for the Pacific islands, the western limit of the station receded with the expanding influence in Pacific affairs of the Antipodes and, after 1878, the Western Pacific High Commission. From 1837 to 1866, the

---

[3]For the boundaries of this and the Cape of Good Hope command, see Gerald S. Graham, *Great Britain in the Indian Ocean: A Study of Maritime Enterprise, 1810-1850* (Oxford: Clarendon Press, 1967), Appendix, pp. 455-59.
[4]Admiralty Minute of 25 March 1859, Adm. 1/5716.
[5]Grace Fox, *British Admirals and Chinese Pirates, 1832-1869* (London: Kegan Paul, Trench, Trubner & Co., 1940), p. 51.
[6]S. Herbert (Adm.) to Rear-Admiral Sir George Seymour, 25 July 1844, Adm. 172/4.

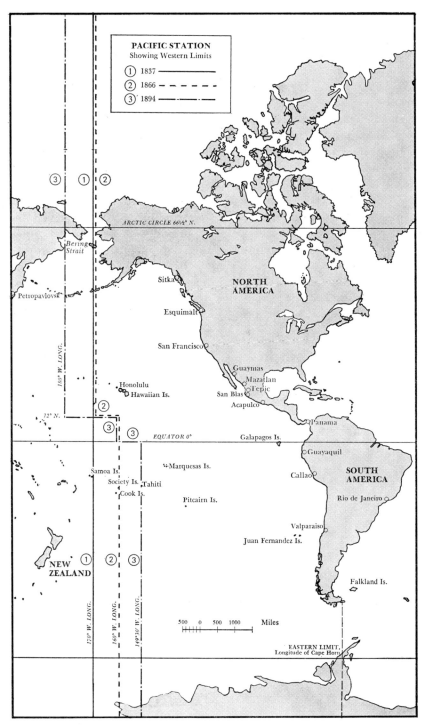

PACIFIC STATION SHOWING WESTERN LIMITS

meridian of 170° West longitude constituted the western boundary; then the Admiralty redefined it as "On the west by the Meridian of 160° West longitude to 12° North latitude thence along the Meridian Northward to Behring Strait."[7] This change established that the Phoenix, Samoan, and Friendly Islands were clearly under the control of the Australian station. In 1894, there was a further limitation of the Pacific station, along with a subsequent expansion of its Australian counterpart to include the Cook Islands and others brought under the jurisdiction of the Pacific Order-in-Council of 1893. At that time all major groups, exclusive of the Hawaiian, Tuamotu and Marquesas Islands, and Fanning and Christmas Island, were to be served by the Australian station. Consequently, the intricate western periphery of the Pacific station became "the meridian of 149°30' West longitude [Tahiti], from the Antarctic circle to the equator; thence along that line west to the meridian of 160° West longitude; thence on that meridian northward to 12° North latitude, along that parallel to the meridian of 180°; thence on that meridian north to the shores of Asia."[8] Such was the complex western limit until closure of this station in 1905.

[7]In Revised Standing Orders to Rear-Admiral C. F. Hillyar, 13 September 1872, Adm. 1/6236, pt. 2.
[8]Evan MacGregor to Rear-Admiral H. F. Stephenson, 1 January 1894, R.G. 8, IIIB, Vol. 3, fol. 2, P.A.C.

Appendix B

PACIFIC STATION: SHIPS AND COMPLEMENTS
1847-1867

Year	Ships	Complements	Year	Ships	Complements
1847	16	3,864	1858	11	2,764
1848	12	3,495	1859	12	2,845
1849	12	2,709	1860	15	3,625
1850	13	2,558	1861	15	3,805
1851	13	2,767	1862	12	2,760
1852	12	2,058	1863	15	3,615
1853	10	1,893	1864	14	3,178
1854	9	1,764	1865	14	2,928
1855	10	2,602	1866	16	3,861
1856	11	2,562	1867	14	3,321
1857	12	2,794			

SOURCE: "Return showing the Number of Her Majesty's ships and vessels on the different Stations on the 1st day of March of each Year from 1847-1867 . . .," *Parliamentary Papers*, 1867-1868, XLV (H. of C. 167), pp. 2-3.

Appendix C

DISTRIBUTION OF THE ROYAL NAVY, 1861-1874, Showing Naval Estimates, Number of Ships and Men By Area and Date

AREA	1861* SHIPS	1861* MEN	1865* SHIPS	1865* MEN	1869* SHIPS	1869* MEN	1874* SHIPS	1874* MEN
China	66	7,970	39	5,153	35	4,118	20	2,428
East Indies			8	1,590	9	2,063	9	1,499
Australia	7	1,325	8	1,566	4	775	9	924
Pacific	15	3,805	14	2,928	13	2,968	9	1,595
South East Coast of America	9	1,772	9	930	11	1,727	5	542
Cape of Good Hope	11	1,775	3	456	16	1,769	11	1,656
West Coast of Africa	15	1,868	22	1,901				
North America & West Indies	23	3,616	29	6,522	21	3,724	16	2,313
Mediterranean	40	17,474	25	7,642	18	3,901	16	2,733
Squadron of Evolution (Home Waters)	14	9,485	8	4,381	10	4,504	7	3,654
Total Seamen, Boys and Marines Voted		77,000		69,000		63,000		60,000
Total Naval Estimates		£12,640,588		£10,392,224		£9,996,641		£10,440,105

*As of 1 April.

SOURCE: *Parliamentary Papers*, 1867-1868 (167), XLV, 638-39; 1868-1869 (422), XXXVIII, 480, and 1876 (225), XLV, 522-23; in C. J. Bartlett, "The Mid-Victorian Reappraisal of Naval Policy," K. Bourne and D. C. Watt, eds., *Studies in International History: Essays Presented to W. Norton Medlicott*, (London: Longmans, Green & Co., 1967), p. 208.

Appendix D

COMMANDERS-IN-CHIEF AND
SENIOR NAVAL OFFICERS
Pacific Station 1837-1914[1]

1. Rear-Admiral of the White Charles Bayne Hodgson Ross, C.B., appointed Commander-in-Chief, Her Majesty's ships and vessels employed and to be employed on the Pacific Station, 4 September 1837; flag in H.M.S. *President,* 50 guns, sail.

2. Rear-Admiral of the White Richard Thomas, appointed 5 May 1841; flag in H.M.S. *Dublin,* 50 guns, sail.

3. Rear-Admiral of the White Sir George Francis Seymour, Kt., C.B., appointed 14 May 1844; flag in H.M.S. *Collingwood,* 80 guns, sail.

4. Rear-Admiral of the White Phipps Hornby, C.B., appointed 25 August 1847; flag in H.M.S. *Asia,* 84 guns, sail.

5. Rear-Admiral of the Blue Fairfax Moresby, C.B., appointed 21 August 1850; flag in H.M.S. *Portland,* 50 guns, sail.

6. Rear-Admiral of the White David Price, appointed 17 August 1853; flag in H.M.S. *President,* 50 guns, sail.

---

[1]From NS 1440-102/2, Canadian Forces Headquarters, Department of National Defence, Ottawa, and published through the courtesy of S. F. Wise of the Directorate of History. This list was compiled by E. C. Russell to whom credit is given; it corrects a number of errors in J. F. Parry, "Sketch of the History of the Naval Establishments at Esquimalt" (typescript, 1906) , pp. 34-35.

7. Rear-Admiral of the White Henry William Bruce, appointed 25 November 1854; flag in H.M.S. *Monarch,* 84 guns, sail.

8. Rear-Admiral of the Red Robert Lambert Baynes, C.B., appointed 8 July 1857; flag in H.M.S. *Ganges,* 84 guns, sail.

NOTE: Each flagship after H.M.S. *Ganges* was steam-screw powered.

9. Rear-Admiral of the White Sir Thomas Maitland, Kt., C.B., appointed 5 May 1860; flag in H.M.S. *Bacchante,* 51 guns, screw.

10. Rear-Admiral of the White John Kingcome, appointed 31 October 1862, promoted Vice-Admiral of the Blue whilst holding appointment, 5 March 1864; flag in H.M.S. *Sutlej,* 35 guns, screw.

11. Rear-Admiral of the White the Honourable Joseph Denman, appointed 10 May 1864; flag in H.M.S. *Sutlej,* 35 guns, screw.

NOTE: Ranks such as "Admiral of the Red" were abolished by Order-in-Council dated 9 July 1864.[2]

12. Rear-Admiral the Honourable George Fowler Hastings, C.B., appointed 21 November 1866; promoted Vice-Admiral whilst holding appointment 10 September 1869; flag in H.M.S. *Zealous,* 20-gun armoured frigate.

13. Rear-Admiral Arthur Farquhar, appointed 1 November 1869; flag in H.M.S. *Zealous,* 20-gun armoured frigate.

14. Rear-Admiral Charles Farrel Hillyar, C.B., appointed 9 July 1872; promoted Vice-Admiral whilst holding appointment, 29 May 1873; flag in H.M.S. *Repulse,* 12-gun armoured frigate.

15. Rear-Admiral the Honourable Arthur Auckland Leopold Pedro Cochrane, C.B., appointed 6 June 1873; flag in H.M.S. *Repulse,* 12-gun armoured frigate.

16. Rear-Admiral George Hancock, appointed 15 April 1876; flag in H.M.S. *Repulse,* 12-gun armoured frigate.

17. Rear-Admiral Algernon Frederick Rous de Horsey, appointed 6 August 1876; flag in H.M.S. *Shah,* 26-gun iron screw/sailing ship.

18. Rear-Admiral Frederick Henry Stirling, appointed 21 July 1879; flag in H.M.S. *Triumph,* iron screw/sailing ship.

---

[2]Before 1864, flag-officers were appointed to fleets which had their own "squadron colours"—"the Red," "the White," or "the Blue." After this date they were called Admiral, Vice-Admiral or Rear-Admiral without the colour designation, although Admiral of the Fleet was retained. In fact, after the Napoleonic Wars, only the White squadron's colours were flown and the White Ensign became the symbol of the Royal Navy, the Red Ensign that of the Merchant Navy, and the Blue Ensign that of the Reserve. Michael Lewis, *The Navy in Transition, 1814-1864: A Social History* (London: Hodder and Stoughton, 1965) , pp. 126-27.

19. Rear-Admiral Algernon McLennan Lyons, appointed 10 December 1881; flag in H.M.S. *Triumph,* iron screw/sailing ship.

20. Rear-Admiral John Kennedy Erskine Baird, appointed 13 September 1884; flag in H.M.S. *Swiftsure,* iron screw/sailing ship.

21. Rear-Admiral Sir Michael Culme-Seymour, Bart., appointed 4 July 1885; flag in H.M.S. *Triumph,* iron screw/sailing ship.

22. Rear-Admiral Algernon Charles Fieschi Heneage, appointed 20 September 1887; promoted Vice-Admiral whilst holding appointment 29 November 1889; flag in H.M. Ships *Triumph* and *Swiftsure.*

23. Rear-Admiral Charles Frederick Hotham, C.B., appointed 4 February 1890; flag in H.M.S. *Warspite,* armoured cruiser.

24. Rear-Admiral Henry Frederick Stephenson, C.B., appointed 2 March 1893; flag in H.M.S. *Royal Arthur,* armoured cruiser.

25. Rear-Admiral Henry St. Leger Bury Palliser, appointed 5 March 1896; flag in H.M.S. *Imperieuse,* armoured cruiser.

26. Rear-Admiral Lewis Anthony Beaumont, appointed 20 March 1899; flag in H.M.S. *Warspite,* armoured cruiser.

27. Rear-Admiral Andrew Kennedy Bickford, C.M.G., appointed 15 October 1900; flag in H.M. Ships *Warspite,* armoured cruiser, and *Grafton,* protected cruiser.

28. Commodore James Edward Clifford Goodrich, M.V.O., R.N., appointed 15 October 1903; broad pendant in H.M. Ships *Grafton,* protected cruiser, and *Bonaventure,* cruiser second class (until 28 February 1905).

29. Commander Allen Thomas Hunt, R.N., appointed Commander-in-Charge for Station Duties on the West Coast of America, succeeding Commodore Goodrich, 1 March 1905; pendant in H.M.S. *Shearwater,* screw-powered sailing sloop.

30. Commander Adrian George Allgood, R.N., appointed 1 August 1906; pendant in H.M.S. *Shearwater.*

31. Commander Charles Wispington Glover Crawford, R.N., appointed 31 December 1907; pendant in H.M.S. *Shearwater.*

32. Commander Gerald William Vivian, R.N., appointed 1 April 1910; pendant in H.M.S. *Shearwater.*

33. Commander Frederic Henry Walter, R.N., appointed 24 April 1912; pendant in H.M.S. *Shearwater.*

34. Captain Robert Gwynne Corbett, R.N., appointed Senior Naval Officer West Coast of America, 10 December 1913; pendant in H.M.S. *Algerine,* screw-powered sailing sloop.

34. (a) *Captain Frederick A. Powlett, R.N., H.M.S. *Newcastle,* 30 August 1914, Senior Naval Officer West Coast of America.

35. Commander Walter Hose, R.C.N., succeeded Captain Corbett 15 August 1914; pendant in H.M.C.S. *Rainbow,* cruiser.

36. Rear-Admiral William Oswald Story, R.N. (Retired), appointed 12 October 1914; Admiral Superintendent Esquimalt Dockyard.

*NOTE: If there appears to be confusion with respect to the identities of Senior Naval Officers at Esquimalt in 1914, such represents quite accurately the confused state of affairs at Esquimalt at the outbreak of war. Even after the transfer of the dockyard to the Canadian Government, there was still a Royal Navy officer responsible to the Admiralty for the West Coast of America. At the same time, the infant Royal Canadian Navy had Commander Hose as the Senior Canadian Naval Officer on the coast. With the outbreak of war, Captain Powlett of H.M.S. *Newcastle* arrived from the Far East and was by seniority the Senior Naval Officer. Meanwhile Cdr. Hose in the *Rainbow* was trying to cope with his sea responsibilities as well as the dockyard. Mostly owing to intransigence on the part of Captain Powlett, there were frictions with the Canadian Government. The problem was resolved by the Canadian Government, sending Rear Admiral Story, a retired RN Officer resident in Canada, to take over the dockyard but not the operational control of ships.

Appendix E

CHANGING TECHNOLOGY IN BRITISH WARSHIPS
1810-1914

THE BRITISH WARSHIP *Racoon,* on the Northwest Coast of America in 1813, had little in common with H.M.S. *Algerine,* stationed at Esquimalt from 1908 to 1919. Both were "sloops," it is true, but they were markedly dissimilar in a number of respects. The following note is an attempt, within limited space, to explain some of the technological changes that occurred in the British fleet in the nineteenth and early twentieth centuries. For this purpose, a few ships that served in the Pacific or called at Esquimalt have been chosen to illustrate the various innovations in propulsion, basic material, armament and hull design.

Naval architects of the eighteenth century continued to perfect the wooden fighting ship, and by the end of the Napoleonic Wars the limits of improvement had probably been reached. Issues of *The Navy List* show that in 1813 there were about 900 ships in the fleet available for service and of these some 650 were in commission at sea. It is not surprising, therefore, that with British naval supremacy solidly established and with great reductions in the naval estimates occurring over approximately the next twenty years, nothing was done to modify ship design. Britain's strength at sea was based on the wooden fighting ship, it was argued, and any deviation from this would undermine the *Pax Britannica,* which was in any case more illusory than real. Hence Viscount Melville, the First Lord of the Admiralty could write in 1828, in words which have been much-quoted, "Their Lordships feel it their bounden duty to discourage to the utmost of their ability the employment of steam vessels, as they consider that the introduction of steam is calculated to strike a fatal blow at the naval supremacy of the empire." This observation is not as ridiculous as it appears at first glance.

British warships of this time were classified into six "rates" according to their number and weight of guns, which of course indicated the number of seamen necessary to man them. The rates were approximately as follows:

SHIPS OF THE LINE (or fit to stand in line of battle):

1st Rates   3-deckers, usually 90 guns or more.
2nd Rates   3-deckers and later 2-deckers large enough to carry up to 90 guns.
3rd Rates   2-deckers, usually carrying 74 guns.

SHIPS BELOW THE LINE (or not fit to be in the line):

4th Rates   Single-deckers (frigates) with 50 to 56 guns on one complete gun deck and some guns on the forecastle and quarter deck.
5th Rates   Frigates of 32 to 44 guns.
6th Rates   Small frigates (and later large sloops).

SHIPS BELOW THE RATES:

Sloops, bomb vessels, gun brigs, cutters and others.

The larger the ship the higher the command. Flagships were invariably ships of the line, that is 1st, 2nd and 3rd rates, and had Captains. But all of the six rates were "post ships" in the early nineteenth century. A post ship was a ship sufficiently large or important to justify the appointment of a "Post Captain," who was so-called to distinguish him from a Commander (originally Master and Commander). The latter had the courtesy title of "Captain," a practice that survived socially until after World War I. Sloops were Commander's commands. In this context "sloop" had nothing to do with the rig: the larger sloops were generally ship-rigged; the smaller ones were brig sloops. Bomb vessels, gun brigs, gun vessels, gunboats, fireships and others were Lieutenant's commands.

Shortly after 1815 the French term "corvette" began to be used in the Royal Navy to indicate a new class of post ship below the 6th rates and above the sloops. They were of two varieties. The first were old 5th rates cut down to one deck. The *Trincomalee* and *Amphitrite* on the

Pacific station at the time of the Crimean War were of this type—38 to 44-gun frigates reduced to 24-gun corvettes. (This practice was also followed with line-of-battleships such as the *America*, 74 guns, which was cut down to a frigate of 50 guns in 1835.) The second variety of corvette was the new large sloop designed by Sir William Symonds, Survey of the Navy and an opponent of steam. The *Dido* and *Daphne* of 18 guns and the *Calypso* (originally 20 and later 18 guns) were in this category. Sometimes they were referred to as sloops but were usually commanded by a Post Captain.

Beginning in the 1840's, the introduction of steam—first paddle-wheel then screw—new and heavier guns, which accordingly meant fewer of them, and armour made any classification based simply on number of guns meaningless. In this transitional period, chaos reigned in describing ships. The frigate *Sutlej*, flagship in 1863-1867, was classified as 35 guns. She was launched in 1855 as a wooden sailing ship of the 4th rate, was converted to steam with screw propulsion in 1859-1860, and carried Armstrong breech-loading guns of varying sizes, her armament making her far superior in this category to a 36- or 42-gun frigate of a decade earlier mounting the standard 32-pound guns and carronades.

Gradually the old terminology, in use since the reign of Charles I, gave way to a new nomenclature. For instance, the *Zealous*, on the Pacific station 1867-1872, was a battleship but not of the first order. She was an ironclad classified as a "screw-ship, armour plated." Her displacement tonnage was 6,096, indicating that she was a large ship for her day, on a "foreign station" at least. H.M.S. *Triumph*, flagship for 1878-1882 and 1885-1888, was a "third class battleship" of 6,650 tons displacement. Another flagship, the *Grafton*, on the station 1902-1904, was a "first-class cruiser" and by that time the classification of the ship itself as a "first-class cruiser" would provide a good indication of its tonnage, armament, range and speed. These ships were made obsolete by the building of the *Dreadnought*, the first all-big-gun turbine battleship, in 1905-1906.

By 1914, the fleet had witnessed great changes in matériel—in propulsion (from sail to steam), in basic materials (from wood to iron and steel), in offence (armament changes, particularly the revolution in the gun and the introduction of shell) and in defence (the bringing in of armour). These technological changes reflected the changing industrialism and gradual mechanization of the age and coincided with advances in communications (railways, telegraphs, cables, and wireless telegraphy), reforms in naval administration, modifications in tactics and improvements in the methods of officer selection and recruitment of seamen. Britain's security now rested on something quite different from the wooden fighting ship of Nelson's day; but the objectives and discipline of the Royal Navy remained the same.

Appendix F

LIST OF BRITISH WARSHIPS ON THE NORTHWEST COAST OF NORTH AMERICA OR IN BRITISH COLUMBIA WATERS, 1778-1908, With Date of Launch or Purchase*

THE LIST OF SHIPS and date of visit which follows had its origins in that of Captain (later Rear-Admiral Sir) John Parry, K.C.B., Hydrographer of the Navy, 1914-1919, as given in his "Sketch of Pacific Naval Establishments from Commencement to 1905" (typescript, 1906). A number of errors have been corrected, and several additions and deletions have been made. The list is essentially confined to ships which visited Esquimalt and also includes ships on the Northwest Coast, 1778-1845, but omits ships that completed full commissions in the Pacific without calling at Esquimalt. It excludes ships of the Flying Squadron (*Liverpool, Liffey, Endymion, Phoebe, Scylla* and *Pearl*) that visited Esquimalt in 1870 except the *Scylla*, which remained on station.

Further information on a particular ship's movements can be found in the ship's log, kept in the Public Records Office, London. Beginning in 1837 with the establishment of the Pacific station and ending in 1854, there are also manuscript volumes in the Adm. 8 series (in the P.R.O.) giving the list of ships on the station for each month. From 1855, these monthly lists are printed and a set is available in the Naval Library, Ministry of Defence, Earl's Court, London. There is an index under ships' names at the end of each annual volume. The *Navy List,* a

---

*Date of launch or purchase given in parenthesis.

periodic publication, gives some information on the ship in question, its officers, size of complement and place of service. Further information on various ships that were in the Pacific and are related to the maritime history of British Columbia will be found in the excellent dossiers compiled by Rear-Admiral P. W. Brock, C.B., D.S.O. Copies of these are in the Maritime Museum of British Columbia, Victoria, while resumes of the design and history of a number of these ships are to be found in the *Bulletin* of this same institution.

Acorn (1884) 1889

Alert (1856) 1860, 1861, 1867

Algerine (1895) 1908 - to R.C.N.

America (1810) 1845

Amethyst I (1844) 1858

Amethyst II (1873) 1875, 1877, 1878

Amphion (1883) 1879-1880, 1889-1890, 1901-1904

Arethusa (1882) 1900

Bacchante (1859) 1861-1863

Blossom (1806) 1818

Bonaventure (1892) 1904-1905

Boxer (1868) 1869-1874

Brisk (1851) 1855

Calypso (1845) 1858-1859

Cameleon (1860) 1868, 1870-1873

Caroline (1882) 1886-1889

Champion I (1824) 1849

Champion II (1878) 1881-1882, 1889-1895

Chanticleer (1861) 1868-1871

Charybdis (1859) 1862-1865, 1869-1871

Chatham (1788) 1791-1794

Clio (1858) 1864-1868

Cockatrice (1832) 1854

Colombine (1862) 1864-1866

Comus (1878) 1882-1883, 1896-1897

Condor (1898) 1900-1901

Conquest (1878) 1886-1889

Constance I (1846) 1848

Constance II (1880) 1883-1885

Cormorant I (1842) 1846

Cormorant II (1877) 1886-1889

Daedalus I (1790) 1791-1794

Daedalus II (1826) 1850-1853

Daphne I (1838) 1851

Daphne II (1888) 1889-1892

Daring (1874) 1875-1878

Devastation (1841) 1861-1864

Dido (1836) 1855

Discovery I (1776) 1778-1779

Discovery II (1789) 1791-1794

Driver (1840) 1850

Egeria (1873) 1898-1905

Espiègle (1881) 1888-1891

Fantome (1873) 1875-1878

Fawn (1856) 1871-1874

Fisgard (1819) 1871-1874

Flora (1893) 1903-1905

Forward (1855) 1860-1869

Ganges (1821) 1858-1860

Gannet (1878) 1879-1883

Garnet (1877) 1891-1894

Grafton (1892) 1902-1904

Grappler (1856) 1860-1868

Havannah (1811) 1858

Hecate (1839) 1861-1863

Herald (1823) 1846, 1847

Heroine (1881) 1883-1886

Hyacinth (1881) 1886-1888, 1893-1895

Icarus (1885) 1889, 1896-1902

Imperieuse (1883) 1896-1899

Inconstant (1836) 1849

Kingfisher (1879) 1881-1884

Leander (1882) 1897-1900
Magicienne (1849) 1857
Malacca (1853) 1866-1867
Melpomene (1883) 1890-1893
Modeste (1837) 1844-1847
Monarch (1822) 1855-1856
Mutine I (1859) 1861-1862
Mutine II (1880) 1882-1885
Myrmidon (1867) 1873-1876
Nymphe (1888) 1890-1895
Opal (1875) 1876-1878
Osprey (1876) 1877-1880
Pandora (1833) 1846, 1848
Pelican (1877) 1879-1881,
   1884-1887
Penguin (1876) 1877-1880
Peterel (1860) 1872-1876
Phaeton (1833) 1897-1903
Pheasant (1888) 1890-1901
Pique (1834) 1854
Plumper (1848) 1857-1861
Portland (1822) 1851-1853
President (1829) 1854-1855
Providence (1791) 1796-1797
Pylades (1854) 1859-1861,
   1869-1871
Racoon (1808) 1813
Reindeer (1866) 1868-1875
Repulse (1868) 1873-1876
Resolution (1771) 1778-1779
Ringdove (1867) 1870
Rocket (1868) 1875-1882
Royal Arthur (1891) 1893-1896
Sappho (1873) 1882-1886
Satellite I (1855) 1856-1860, 1869
Satellite II (1881) 1884-1885,
   1894-1897
Scout (1856) 1866-1867, 1871-1873

Scylla (1856) 1871-1873
Shah (1873) 1876-1879
Shannon (1875) 1870-1880
Shearwater I (1861) 1867
Shearwater II (1901) 1902 - to
   R.C.N.
Sparrowhawk I (1856) 1866-1872
Sparrowhawk II (1897) 1898-1903
Starling (1829) 1837, 1839
Sulphur (1826) 1837, 1839
Sutlej (1855) 1863-1867
Swift (1835) 1852
Swiftsure (1870) 1882-1885,
   1888-1889
Tartar (1854) 1861-1862
T[orpedo]. B[oat]. 39 (1885)
   1885-1904
T.B. 40 (1885) 1885-1904
Tenedos (1870) 1872-1876
Termagent (1847) 1860
Thetis I (1846) 1852-1857
Thetis II (1871) 1870-1882
Topaze (1858) 1860-1863,
   1867-1869
Tribune (1853) 1859-1860,
   1864-1865
Trincomalee (1817) 1853,
   1885-1888
Triumph (1870) 1879-1882,
   1885-1888
Turquoise (1876) 1878-1880
Virago I (1842) 1854
Virago II (1896) 1897-1903
Warspite (1884) 1890-1893,
   1899-1902
Wild Swan (1876) 1885-1888,
   1895-1897
Zealous (1866) 1867-1872

Appendix G

LIST BY TYPES AND CLASSES OF BRITISH WARSHIPS ON THE NORTHWEST COAST OF NORTH AMERICA OR IN BRITISH COLUMBIA WATERS, 1778-1914, AND GIVING DATE OF LAUNCH OR PURCHASE*

1. SAILING SHIPS

SHIPS OF THE LINE

2ND RATE

Canopus Class

> *Asia,* 84 guns, 1824
> *Ganges,* 84 guns, 1821
> *Monarch,* 84 guns, 1832

Superb Class

> *Collingwood,* 80 guns, 1841

*Adapted from a list compiled by Rear-Admiral P. W. Brock, C.B., D.S.O., and published by courtesy of the Maritime Museum of British Columbia.

FRIGATES

4TH RATE

Razée (cut down) 3rd Rate

America, 50 guns, 1810
Portland, 52 guns, 1822
President, 50 guns, 1829

5TH RATE

Fisgard, 46 guns, 1819
Inconstant, 36 guns, 1836
Pique, 36 guns, 1834
Thetis, 36 guns, 1846

6TH RATE

Amethyst, 26 guns, 1844
Imogene, 28 guns, 1831
Samarang, 28 guns, 1822

OTHERS

DISCOVERY SHIPS

Blossom, 26 guns, 1806 (6th rate)
Chatham, 1788 (armed tender)
Daedalus I, 1790 (hired store ship)
Discovery I, 1776 (Cook's ship)
Discovery II, 1789 (Vancouver's ship)
Resolution, 1771
Providence, 1791

SURVEYING SHIPS

Herald, 1823 (ex-*Termagant,* ex-5th rate)
Pandora, 10 guns, 1833
Starling, 4 guns, 1829
Sulphur, 8 guns, 1826 (ex-bomb vessel)

CORVETTES

Designed as Corvettes
Calypso, 18 guns, 1845

Dido, 18 guns, 1836
Daphne, 18 guns, 1838

Razée (cut down) Frigates

Havannah, 19 guns (launched 1811 and cut down 1844)
Daedalus, 20 guns (launched 1826 and cut down 1844)
Amphritite, 24 guns (launched 1816 and cut down 1846)
Trincomalee, 26 guns (launched 1817 and cut down 1847)

SLOOPS

Champion, 18 guns, 1824
Modeste, 18 guns, 1837
Racoon, 24 guns, 1808

BRIG

Swift, 8 guns, 1835

SCHOONER

Cockatrice, 6 guns, 1832

2. STEAM ASSISTED

PADDLE-WHEEL VESSELS

SLOOPS

Driver Class

Cormorant, 6 guns, 1842
Devastation, 6 guns, 1841
Driver, 6 guns, 1840
Virago, 6 guns, 1842
Vixen, 6 guns, 1841

SURVEYING SHIPS

(ex-Sloop)

Hydra Class

Hecate, 1839

Magicienne, 16 guns, 1849

SCREW-FRIGATES

Shannon Class

> *Bacchante,* 51 guns, 1859
> *Liffey,* 51 guns, 1856
> *Topaze,* 51 guns, 1858
> *Liverpool,* 51 guns, 1860
> *Phoebe,* 51 guns, 1854 (converted to screw 1860)
> *Constance,* 50 guns, 1846
> *Sutlej,* 1855

Large Iron Teak-Sheathed Frigate

> *Shah,* 1873

Last Wooden Frigate

> *Endymion,* 51 guns, 1865

Other Classes

> *Termagant,* 31 guns, 1847
> *Tribune,* 31 guns, 1853

SCREW-CORVETTES, SLOOPS, GUN VESSELS and GUN BOATS

CORVETTES

Pearl Class

> *Pearl,* 21 guns, 1855
> *Satellite,* 21 guns, 1855
> *Scout,* 21 guns, 1856
> *Scylla,* 21 guns, 1856
> *Charybdis,* 21 guns, 1859

Covered Deck

> *Clio,* 22 guns, 1858

Wooden Ram-bowed Class

> *Tenedos,* 1870, smaller type
> *Thetis,* 1871, larger type

Last Wooden Class

> *Amethyst,* 1873

"Gem" Class, Composite

> *Opal,* 1875
> *Turquoise,* 1876
> *Garnet,* 1877

Other Classes

> *Brisk,* 16 guns, 1851
> *Pylades,* 21 guns, 1854
> *Malacca,* 13 guns, 1853
> *Tartar,* 20 guns, 1854

SLOOPS

3rd Class (later Surveying Vessel)

> *Plumper,* 1848

Cruiser Class

> *Alert,* 17 guns, 1856
> *Fawn,* 17 guns, 1856

Greyhound Class

> *Mutine,* 17 guns, 1859

Cameleon Class

> *Cameleon,* 17 guns, 1860
> *Chanticleer,* 17 guns, 1861
> *Reindeer,* 17 guns, 1866

Rosario Class

> *Peterel,* 11 guns, 1860
> *Shearwater,* 11 guns, 1861
> *Columbine,* 1862

Daring Class

>*Daring,* 1874
>*Albatross,* 1873
>*Egeria,* 1873
>*Fantome,* 1873
>*Sappho,* 1873

Wild Swan Class

>*Wild Swan,* 1876
>*Osprey,* 1876
>*Penguin,* 1876
>*Cormorant,* 1877
>*Pelican,* 1877
>*Gannet,* 1878
>*Kingfisher,* 1879
>*Mutine,* 1880
>*Espiegle,* 1880

Reindeer Class

>*Acorn,* 1884
>*Icarus,* 1885

Buzzard Class

>*Nymphe,* 1888
>*Daphne,* 1888

GUN VESSELS

Wanderer Class

>*Sparrowhawk,* 4 guns, 1856

Cormorant Class

>*Myrmidon,* 4 guns, 1867

Plover Class

>*Ringdove,* 6 guns, 1867

Beacon Class

> *Boxer,* 4 guns, 1868
> *Rocket,* 4 guns, 1868

GUN BOATS

Forward Class

> *Forward,* 2 guns, 1855
> *Grappler,* 2 guns, 1856

Pheasant Class

> *Pheasant,* 1888

3. ADVANCED STEAM ASSISTED/POWERED

IRONCLADS

> *Zealous,* 1866
> *Repulse,* 1868
> *Swiftsure,* 1870
> *Triumph,* 1870

ARMOURED CRUISERS

> *Shannon,* 1875
> *Imperieuse,* 1883
> *Warspite,* 1884

PROTECTED CRUISERS

1st Class

> *Royal Arthur,* 1891
> *Grafton,* 1892

2nd Class

> *Arethusa,* 1882
> *Leander,* 1882
> *Amphion,* 1883
> *Phaeton,* 1883
> *Melpomene,* 1888 (later 3rd Class)

Rainbow, 1891
Bonaventure, 1892
Flora, 1893

3rd Class (ex-Corvettes)

Champion, 1878
Comus, 1878
Conquest, 1878
Constance, 1880

Satellite Class

Satellite, 1881
Heroine, 1881
Hyacinth, 1881
Caroline, 1882

SLOOPS, STEEL

Algerine, 1895
Condor, 1898
Shearwater, 1901

TORPEDO CRAFT

Torpedo Boats

T.B. 39, 1885
T.B. 40, 1885

Torpedo Boat Destroyers

Virago, 1896
Sparrowhawk, 1897

SELECTED BIBLIOGRAPHY

I. PUBLIC RECORD OFFICE: OFFICIAL CORRESPONDENCE AND RECORDS

Adm. 1. (In-letters from Admirals, Captains and Departments) .
Adm. 2. Continued as Adm. 13 (Out-letters) .
Adm. 3. Rough Minutes.
Adm. 7. Miscellaneous; various reports on foreign navies.
Adm. 12. [IND 4761]. List of Admirals' dispatches, 1813-1847.
Adm. 50. Admirals' Journals, 1855-.
Adm. 53. Ships' Logs.
Adm. 116. Various reports on Esquimalt.
Adm. 128. Naval Stores.
Adm. 155/1. [IND 24473]. Index to first 22 volumes of Pacific Station Records in Ottawa.
Adm. 172/1-4. Pacific Station Records, 1843-1853.
B.T. 1/470/2506. Draft of Vancouver Island Grant, 1848-1849.
Cab. 5 and 11. Various reports on Esquimalt and Halifax.
F.O. 5. America.
F.O. 50. Mexico.
F.O. 58. Pacific Islands.
C.O. 6. Boundaries between British North America and the United States.
C.O. 42. Original Correspondence, Canada.
C.O. 60. Original Correspondence, British Columbia.
C.O. 62. Sessional Papers, British Columbia.
C.O. 63. Government Gazettes, British Columbia.
C.O. 64. Blue Books, British Columbia.
C.O. 338. Register of Correspondence, British Columbia.

C.O. 305. Original Correspondence, Vancouver Island.
C.O. 323/366 No. 23204. Report of the Committee on Colonial Garrisons, 1886.
C.O. 880/9, 10. Strategic uses of the C.P.R.
W.O. 1/552-3. Warre and Vavasour's reports.
W.O. 32, 33. Various reports on Warre and Vavasour, defences of Esquimalt, telegraphic communication, military uses of C.P.R.

II. Public Record Office: "Private" Papers

PRO 30/6 Carnarvon Papers.
PRO 30/9 Colchester Papers.
PRO 30/12 Ellenborough Papers.

III. British Museum: Additional Manuscripts, Various Volumes

Aberdeen Papers.
Barrow Bequest.
Byam Martin Papers.
Gladstone Papers.
Halifax Papers.
Peel Papers.
Add. MSS. 35, 141. Lt. George Peard, Journal of H.M.S. *Blossom*, 1825-1828.

IV. National Maritime Museum

BAY/- Baynes Papers.
BED/- Bedford Papers.
HAM/- Hamond Papers.
JON/- Jenkin Jones Papers.
PHI/- Phipps Hornby Papers.
JOD/21. John Cunningham, "Voyage to the Pacific, 1823-5."
JOD/42. Thomas Dawes, "Journal of H.M.S. 'America'."
LOG/N/P/1. Journal of A. V. Maccall, 1854-1856.

V. Royal Commonwealth Society Library, London

North West Company Documents including William McGillivray [?]. "Some Account of the Trade Carried on by the North-West Company." [1809].

VI. British Library of Political and Economic Science,
London School of Economics

Radcliffe Quine Letters, in Letters of Emigrants to America.

VII. Warwickshire Record Office, Warwick

CR 114A. Seymour of Ragley Collection, 20 vols. (papers of Admiral Sir George Seymour) .

VIII. Hudson's Bay Company Archives, London

A. 8/6-9, 14, 17-20. Correspondence with Adm., F.O., C.O., Ordnance.
A. 11/61-3. Correspondence, Sandwich Islands.
A. 11/64. Correspondence, San Francisco.

B. 191/- Correspondence, Accounts, Sandwich Islands.
B. 223/6/35-42. Letters, Fort Vancouver.
B. 226/6/1-20. Letters, Fort Victoria.
G. 1, 3. Maps and Views.

IX. NAVAL LIBRARY, MINISTRY OF DEFENCE, LONDON

Selborne Papers.
Photo albums of Esquimalt.

X. HYDROGRAPHER'S OFFICE, TAUNTON, SOMERSET

Various papers (indexed) dealing with the Northwest Coast of America, particularly the Parry Papers, vol. I.

XI. PUBLIC ARCHIVES OF CANADA

R.G.8, IIIB. Pacific Station Records, 39 vols.
R.G.9, various reports on the defences of Esquimalt and British Columbia.
R.G.24, F. 71. Henry J. Warre Papers, including Warre's "Travel and Sport in North America, 1839-1846."

XII. PROVINCIAL ARCHIVES, VICTORIA, B.C.

F series; Ships' Letters.
"Admiralty Correspondence," 6 vols.
Journal of R. C. Mayne, 1859-60.

XIII. MARITIME MUSEUM OF BRITISH COLUMBIA, VICTORIA, B.C.

Esquimalt Naval Establishment Records, 3 vols.

XIV. NEW YORK PUBLIC LIBRARY, MANUSCRIPTS DIVISION

F. Ross, "Journal and Water Color Sketches . . . of H.M.S. *Tagus* . . . 1813 . . . 1814."

XV. PRINTED SOURCES

Parliamentary Papers, Hansard and the *Navy List* were used periodically.
The following volumes of *Parliamentary Papers* are of particular value:
"Correspondence Relative to . . . Oregon . . ., 9 Aug. 1842," 1846, LII (Cmd. 695) .
"Treaty between Her Majesty and the United States . . . Oregon Boundary . . . 1846," 1846, LII (722).
"Labuan Papers," 1847-1848, LXII (460) .
"Correspondence between the Hudson's Bay Company and the Secretary of State for the Colonies relative to the Colonization of Vancouver's Island," 1847-1848, XLII (619) .
"Papers relative to the Grant of Vancouver's Island to the Hudson's Bay Company," 1849, XXXV (H. of C. 103) .
"Papers relative to the Discovery of Gold on Fraser's River," 1859 (cmd. 2398, 1st ser.) .
"Papers relative to the Affairs of British Columbia," 1859-60, Part I, XVII (Cmd. 2476) ; Part II, session II (Cmd. 2578) ; Part III, XLIV (Cmd. 2724) ; Part IV, XXXVI (Cmd. 2952) .

"Report from the Select Committee on Colonial Military Expenditure," 1861, XIII (H. of C. 423).

"Papers re: Union of British Columbia and Vancouver Island," 1866, XLIX (3667, 3694).

"Further Papers re: Union of British Columbia and Vancouver Island," 1867, XLVIII (3852).

"Return showing the number of Her Majesty's Ships and Vessels on the Different Stations . . . 1847-1867 . . ." 1867-68, XLV (H. of C. 167).

"Proceedings of the Colonial Conference," 1887, LVI (Cmd. 5091).

"Distribution and Mobilization of the Fleet," and "Arrangements Consequent on the Redistribution of the Fleet, 1905, LXVIII (Cmd. 2335 and 2430).

XVI. OTHER PRINTED CORRESPONDENCE AND PAPERS

British Columbia, Archives. *Report of the Provincial Archives Department of the Province of British Columbia for the Year ended December 31st, 1913.* Victoria, B.C., 1914.

[Carnarvon, Earl of]. *Royal Commission to Enquire into the Defence of British Possessions and Provinces Abroad.* 3 vols.; London: War Office, 1880-1883.

Graham, Gerald S. and Humphreys, R. A., eds. *The Navy and South America, 1807-1823: Correspondence of the Commanders-in-Chief on the South American Station.* London, 1962; Navy Records Society, vol. CIV.

Historical Manuscripts Commission. *Report on the Manuscripts of Earl Bathurst, at Cirencester Park.* London: H.M.S.O., 1923.

Kemp, P. K. ed. *The Papers of Admiral Sir John Fisher, Vol. I.* London, 1960; Navy Records Society, vol. CII.

Miller, Hunter, ed. *Treaties and Other International Acts of the U.S.A.* 8 vols.; Washington, 1931-1948.

Oliver, Edmund H. ed. *The Canadian North-West: Early Development and Legislative Records.* Publication No. 9 of the Public Archives of Canada, 2 vols.; Ottawa, 1914-1915.

"Report of Lieutenant Neil M. Howison on Oregon," *House Miscellaneous Documents*, 30th Congress, 1st Sessions, no. 29.

Tanner, J. R., ed. *Samuel Pepys's Naval Minutes.* London, 1926; Navy Records Society, vol. LX.

United States. *Alaskan Boundary Tribunal Proceedings.* Senate Documents, Fifty-eighth Congress, Second Session. Washington, 1904, 7 vols.

United States. *American State Papers, Foreign Relations.* 6 vols.; Washington, 1833-1859.

United States. *Official Records of the Union and Confederate Navies in the War of the Rebellion.* 30 vols.; Washington, 1894-1922.

United States. *Pig War National Historical Park . . . 1965.* Washington, 1965.

XVII. UNPUBLISHED WORKS

Anderson, Alexander Caulfield. "History of the Northwest Coast." Typescript in Provincial Archives, Victoria, B.C., from original in Academy of Pacific Coast History, University of California, Berkeley, 1878.

Bach, J. P. S. "The Royal Navy in the South Pacific, 1826-1876." Ph.D. thesis, University of New South Wales, 1964.

Brock, Rear-Admiral P. W. "H.M.S. *President*." Typescript in Maritime Museum of British Columbia, Victoria, n.d.

Farrington, Lt.-Cdr. L. "The Versatile Beaver: Her Majesty's Ship Beaver Charts the Seas, 1863-1870." Typescript in Provincial Archives, Victoria, B.C., 1958.

Finlayson, Roderick. "History of Vancouver Island and the Northwest Coast." Transcript in Provincial Archives, Victoria, B.C., n.d.

Hacking, Norman. "Early Maritime History of British Columbia." M.A. thesis, University of British Columbia, 1934.

Ives, Arthur. "First Graving Dock." Typescript in Maritime Museum of British Columbia, Victoria, B.C., n.d.

Levirs, F. P. "The British Attitude to the Oregon Question, 1846." M.A. thesis, University of British Columbia, 1931.

Mackinnon, C. S. "The Imperial Fortresses in Canada: Halifax and Esquimalt, 1871-1906." 2 vols.; Ph.D. thesis, University of Toronto, 1965.

Parry, John Franklin. "Sketch of the History of the Naval Establishments at Esquimalt from their Commencement until the Abolition of the Pacific Squadron in 1905 and Miscellaneous Matters Connecting British Columbia with His Majesty's Navy." Read before the Natural History Society of B.C., 19 February 1906; from *Victoria Daily Times*, 20 and 21 February 1906.

Roberts, Joseph. "The Origins of the Esquimalt and Nanaimo Railway: a Problem in British Columbia Politics." M.A. thesis, University of British Columbia, 1937.

Russell, E. C. "The Royal Navy on the North-West Coast of America, 1837-1860." B.A. thesis, University of British Columbia, 1951.

Sandilands, R. W. "The History of Hydrographic Surveying in British Columbia." Typescript; Canadian Hydrographic Service, 1965.

Troubetzkoy, A. S. "Extracts from the Esquimalt Naval Establishment Records, 1862-1881." Typescript, n.d.

XVIII. PUBLISHED CONTEMPORARY ACCOUNTS, VOYAGES, MEMOIRS AND CORRESPONDENCE

"Appeal of the North West Company to the British Government to Forestall John Jacob Astor's Columbian Enterprise," *Canadian Historical Review*, XVII (September 1936), 304-11.

Aylmer, Capt. Fenton, ed. *A Cruise in the Pacific. From the Log of a Naval Officer.* 2 vols. London: Hurst and Blackett, 1860.

B., J. *The Cruise Round the World of the Flying Squadron, 1869-1870, under the Command of Rear-Admiral G. T. Phipps Hornby.* London: J. D. Potter, 1871.

Barry, J. Neilson, ed. "Broughton's Log of a Reconnaissance of the San Juan Islands in 1792," *Washington Historical Quarterly*, XXI (Jan. 1930), 55-60.

Beaglehole, J. C., ed. *The Journals of Captain Cook on His Voyages of Discovery: The Voyage of the "Resolution" and " Discovery," 1776-1780.* 2 parts. Cambridge: Hakluyt Society, 1967.

Beechey, Frederick W. *Narrative of a Voyage to the Pacific and Beering's Strait, to co-operate with the Polar Expeditions, 1825-28.* 2 vols. London: Colburn and Bentley, 1831.

Belcher, Sir Edward. *Narrative of a Voyage round the World performed in Her Majesty's Ship "Sulphur," during the years 1836-1842.* 2 vols. London: Henry Colburn, 1843.

Brown, Robert. *On the Geographical Distribution and Physical Characteristics of the Coal-Fields of the North Pacific.* Edinburgh: Neill and Co., 1867.

Bruce, Capt. H. W. "A Winter Passage round Cape Horn," *Nautical Magazine*, VII (1838), 577-87.

Byron, Lord G. A. *Voyage of the "Blonde" to the Sandwich Islands, 1824-5.* London: John Murray, 1826.

Coues, Elliot, ed. *New Light on the Early History of the Greater Northwest: The Manuscript Journals of Alexander Henry . . . and of David Thompson.* 3 vols. London: Suckling & Co., 1897.

Corney, Peter. *Voyages in the North Pacific. Narrative of several trading voyages from 1813 to 1818, between the North West Coast of America, the Hawaiian Islands and China, with a Description of the Russian Establishments on the North-West Coast.* Honolulu: Thom. G. Thrum, 1896. Reprinted from *London Literary Gazette* of 1821.

Cox, Ross. *Adventures on the Columbia River, including the Narrative of a Residence of Six Years on the Western Side of the Rocky Mountains.* 2 vols. London: H. Colburn and R. Bentley, 1831.

Crowe, George. *The Commission of H.M.S. "Terrible," 1898-1902.* London: George Newnes, 1903.

Denman, Rear-Admiral, and others. *The Bombardment of Valparaiso.* Liverpool, 1866.

Douglas, George, ed. "Royal Navy Ships on the Columbia River in 1839," *The Beaver,* Outfit 285 (Autumn 1954), 38-41.

Eardley-Wilmot, Lieutenant S. *Our Journal in the Pacific by the Officers of H.M.S. Zealous.* London: Longmans, Green & Co., 1873.

Elliot, T. C., ed. "The Sale of Astoria, 1813," *Oregon Historical Quarterly,* XXXIII (March 1932), 43-50.

Evans, Robley D. *A Sailor's Log: Recollections of Forty Years of Naval Life.* New York: D. Appleton & Co., 1901.

[Finlayson, Roderick]. *Biography,* Victoria, B.C. [1891].

FitzRoy, Robert. *Narrative of the Surveying Voyages of Her Majesty's Ships "Adventure" and "Beagle" Between the Years 1826 and 1836.* 3 vols. London: Henry Colburn, 1839.

Fleming, Sandford. *Memorandum in Reference to a Scheme for Completing a Great Inter-Colonial and Inter-Continental Telegraph System by Establishing an Electric Cable Across the Pacific . . . .* London, 1882.

———. *A Railway to the Pacific Through British Territory.* Port Hope, Ont., 1858.

Forbes, Charles. *Vancouver Island, its Resources and Capabilities, as a Colony.* Victoria: The Colonial Government, 1862.

Fremantle, Admiral Sir E. R. *The Navy as I Have Known It, 1849-99.* London, 1904.

"A Glance at Vancouver and Queen Charlotte Islands—By the Officers of H.M.S. "Virago"—in the Summer of 1853," *Nautical Magazine,* XXIII (March 1854), 113-23.

Glazebrook, G. P. DeT., ed. *The Hargrave Correspondence, 1821-1842.* Toronto: Champlain Society, 1938, vol. XXIV.

Glover, Richard, ed. *David Thompson's Narrative, 1784-1812.* Toronto: Champlain Society, 1962, vol. XL.

Grant, W. C. "Description of Vancouver Island," *Journal of the Royal Geographical Society,* XXVII (1857), 268-320.

Grey, Earl. *The Colonial Policy of Lord John Russell's Administration.* 2 vols. London: R. Bentley, 1853.

Gunns, G. H. *The Log of H.M.S. "Sutlej," Pacific and China Stations, 1904-1906.* London: Westminster Press, 1906.

Hall, Basil. *Extracts from a Journal, written on the Coasts of Chili, Peru, and Mexico, in the Years 1820, 1821, 1822.* 2nd ed.; 2 vols. Edinburgh: Archibald Constable & Co., 1824.

Hathaway, R. W. *The Logs of H.M.S. "Arethusa" 1899-1903.* London: Westminster Press, 1903.

Hawgood, John A., ed. *First and Last Consul: Thomas Oliver Larkin and the Ameri-*

canization of California—a Selection of Letters. San Marino, Calif.: Huntington Library, 1962.

Haynes, William. *My Log: A Journal of the Proceedings of the Flying Squadron*. Devonport: Clarke and Son, 1871.

Hazlitt, William C. *British Columbia and Vancouver Island*. London: G. Routledge & Co., 1858.

"HMS *Modeste* on the Pacific Coast 1843-47: Log and Letters," *Oregon Historical Quarterly*, LXI (December 1960) , 408-36.

Howay, F. W. and others, eds. "Angus McDonald: A Few Items of the West," *Washington Historical Quarterly*, VIII (July 1917) , 188-229.

——, ed. *The Early History of the Fraser River Mines*. Victoria, B.C.: Provincial Archives, Memoir VI, 1926.

Howison, Neil M. "Report of Lieutenant Neil M. Howison on Oregon, 1846," *Oregon Historical Quarterly*, XIV (March 1913) , 1-60.

Hussey, John A., ed. *The Voyage of the "Racoon": A "Secret" Journal of a Visit to Oregon, California and Hawaii, 1813-1814* [by Francis Phillips]. San Francisco: Book Club of California, 1958.

Ireland, Willard E., ed. "James Douglas and the Russian American Company, 1840," *British Columbia Historical Quarterly*, V (January 1941) , 53-66.

Journal of the Journey of His Excellency the Governor-General of Canada [Lord Dufferin] *from Government House, Ottawa, to British Columbia and Back*. London: Webster & Larkin, 1877.

Kemble, Parker H., ed. "The U.S. *Essex* versus H.M.S. *Phoebe*," United States Naval Institute *Proceedings*, LVII (1931) , 199-202.

Kennedy, Capt. W. R., R.N. *Sporting Adventures in the Pacific, whilst in command of the "Reindeer."* London: Sampson Low, Marston, Searle & Rivington, 1876.

Lamb, W. Kaye, ed. "Correspondence Relating to the Establishment of a Naval Base at Esquimalt, 1851-57," *British Columbia Historical Quarterly*, VI (October 1942) , 277-94.

——, ed. "Four Letters Relating to the Cruise of the 'Thetis,' 1852-53," *British Columbia Historical Quarterly*, VI (1942) , 189-206.

——, ed. *Journal of a Voyage to the North West Coast of North America during the Years 1811, 1812, 1813 and 1814*, by Gabriel Franchère. Toronto: Champlain Society, 1969, vol. XLV.

Landsdowne, Marquis of. *Canadian North-West and British Columbia: Two Speeches by His Excellency the Marquis of Lorne*. Ottawa: Department of Agriculture, 1886.

MacDonald, Duncan G. F. *British Columbia and Vancouver's Island*. London: Longman, Green, Longman, Roberts & Green, 1862.

Macfie, Matthew. *Vancouver Island and British Columbia*. London: Longman, Green, Longman, Roberts & Green, 1865.

Martin, Robert M. *The Hudson's Bay Territories and Vancouver's Island with an Exposition of the chartered Rights, Conduct, and Policy of the Honourable Hudson's Bay Corporation*. London: T. Brettell, 1849.

Mayne, Richard C. *Four Years in British Columbia and Vancouver Island: An Account of their Forests, Rivers, Coasts, Gold Fields, and Resources for Colonization*. London: John Murray, 1862.

——. "Report on a Journey in British Columbia in the Districts Bordering on the Thompson, Fraser and Harrison Rivers," *Journal of the Royal Geographical Society*, XXXI (1861) , 213-23 (being the text of a report to the Admiralty, 7 July 1859) .

Meany, Edmond S., ed. *Vancouver's Discovery of Puget Sound*. Portland, Ore.: Binfords-Mort, 1942.

Melrose, Robert. "Royal Emigrant's Almanack concerning Five Years Servitude under the Hudson's Bay Company on Vancouver's Island." Ms. B.C. Archives. Published in Vol. VII (1943) of *British Columbia Historical Quarterly*, nos. 2, 3 and 4.

Milton, Viscount and Cheadle, W. B. *The North-west Passage by Land . . . . An Expedition from the Atlantic to the Pacific, undertaken with the view of exploring a route across the continent through British Territory, by one of the northern passes in the Rocky Mountains.* London: Petter and Galpin, Belle Sauvage Works, 1865.

Moresby, Admiral John. *Two Admirals.* 1st ed. London: John Murray, 1909; revised ed. London: Methuen & Co., 1913.

Norman, Francis M. *"Martello Tower" in China and the Pacific in H.M.S. "Tribune," 1856-60.* London: George Allen, 1902.

"Notes on Vancouver Island," *Nautical Magazine*, XVIII (June 1849) , 299-302.

"Oregon and Vancouver Island," *The Nautical Magazine*, XVII (October 1848) , 517-23.

Osborne, Lt. Sherard. "Notes Made on a Passage to the Ports of San Blas and Mazatlan, on the Coast of America," *Nautical Magazine*, XVIII (March 1849) , 139-45.

Palmer, William H. *Pages from a Seaman's Log: Being the First Eighteen Months of the Cruise of H.M.S. Warspite in the Pacific.* Victoria: Munroe Miller, 1891.

Payette, B. C., ed. *The Oregon Country Under the Union Jack.* Montreal: privately printed, 1961.

Pemberton, J. D. *Vancouver Island and British Columbia.* London: Longman, Green, Longman, and Roberts, 1860.

Porter, David. *Journal of a Cruise Made to the Pacific Ocean . . . in the United States Frigate "Essex" . . . 1812, 1813, and 1814,* 2 vols. Philadelphia, 1815.

"Port Clarence to San Francisco [1854]—by Captain Henry Trollope, H.M.S. 'Rattlesnake'," *Nautical Magazine*, XXXII (September 1863) , 449-54.

"Proceedings of H.M.S. *Sulphur* in the Pacific Ocean," *Nautical Magazine*, VII (1838) , 611-22.

Rattray, Alex. *Vancouver Island and British Columbia; where they are, what they are, and what they may become.* London: Smith, Elder & Co., 1862.

Rich, E. E., ed. *The Letters of John McLoughlin from Fort Vancouver to the Governor and Committee, First Series, 1825-38.* London: Hudson's Bay Record Society. 1941, vol. IV.

——, ed. *The Letters of John McLoughlin from Fort Vancouver to the Governor and Committee, Second Series, 1839-44.* London: Hudson's Bay Record Society, 1943, vol. VI.

——, ed. *The Letters of John McLoughlin from Fort Vancouver to the Governor and Committee, Third Series, 1844-46.* London: Hudson's Bay Record Society, 1944, vol. VII.

Richards, Capt. George Henry, R.N. *Vancouver Island Pilot: Sailing Directions for the Coasts of Vancouver Island and British Columbia.* London: Hydrographic Office, Admiralty, 1861.

Schafer, Joseph, ed. "Documents relative to Warre and Vavasour's Military Reconnoissance [sic] in Oregon, 1845-6," *Quarterly of the Oregon Historical Society*, X (March 1909) , 1-99, with maps of defences attached.

——, ed. "Letters of Sir George Simpson, 1841-1843," *American Historical Review*, XIV (October 1908) , 70-94.

"Secret Mission of Warre and Vavasour," *Washington Historical Quarterly*, III (April 1912) , 131-53. [Reports of Warre and Vavasour from F.O. 5/440, 442, 457.]

Seemann, Berthold C. *Narrative of the Voyage of H.M.S. "Herald," 1845-51.* 2 vols. London: Reeve & Co., 1853.

Simpson, Sir George. *Narrative of a Journey round the World During the Years 1841 and 1842.* 2 vols. London: H. Colburn, 1847.

Slacum, William A. "Report on Oregon, 1836-7," *Oregon Historical Quarterly*, XIII (1912) , 175-224.

Smith, Dorothy Blakey, ed. "The Journal of Arthur Thomas Bushby, 1858-1859," *British Columbia Historical Quarterly*, XXI (January-October 1957-1958) , 83-198.

Stapleton, Edward J., ed. *Some Official Correspondence of George Canning.* 2 vols. London: Longmans, Green and Co., 1887.

Tate, Vernon D., ed. "Spanish Documents Relating to the Voyage of the *Racoon* to Astoria and San Francisco," *Hispanic American Historical Review*, XVIII (May 1938) , 183-91.

Tronson, J. M. *Personal Narrative of a Voyage . . . in H.M.S. Barracouta.* London: Smith, Elder & Co., 1859.

Twiss, Travers. *The Oregon Question Examined in Respect to Facts and the Law of Nations.* London: Longman, Brown, Green and Longmans, 1846.

Van Alstyne, Richard W., ed. "Anglo-American Relations, 1853-57," *American Historical Review*, XLII (April 1937) , 491-500.

Walpole, Lieut. Frederick. *Four Years in the Pacific in Her Majesty's Ship "Collingwood" from 1844 to 1848.* 2 vols. London: R. Bentley, 1849.

Watson, G. C. *The Commission of H.M.S. "Amphion," Pacific Station, 1900-1904.* London: Westminster Press, 1904.

Whittingham, Paul Bernard. *Notes on the Late Expedition against the Russian Settlements in Eastern Siberia; and of a Visit to Japan and the Shores of Tartary, and of the Sea of Okhotsk.* London: Longman, Brown, Green and Longmans, 1856.

Wilkes, Charles. *Narrative of the United States Exploring Expedition During the Years 1838, 1839, 1840, 1841, 1842.* Philadelphia: Lea and Blanchard, 1845.

——. "Report on the Territory of Oregon by Charles Wilkes, Commander of the United States Exploring Expedition, 1838-1842," *Quarterly of the Oregon Historical Society*, XII (1911) , 269-99.

Wilson, George T. *The Log of H.M.S. "Phaeton," 1900-1903.* London: Westminster Press, 1903.

Wood, Commander James. "Vancouver Island,—British Columbia," *Nautical Magazine*, XXVII (December, 1858) , 663-66.

XIX. SELECT BOOKS

Adams, E. D. *Great Britain and the American Civil War.* 2 vols. London: Longmans, Green, & Co., 1925; reprint, London: Peter Smith, 1957.

Admiralty, *Graving Docks, Floating Docks and Patent Slips in the British Empire, 1922.* London: His Majesty's Stationery Office, 1923.

Albion, Robert G. *Forests and Sea Power: The Timber Problem of the Royal Navy, 1652-1862.* Cambridge, Mass.: Harvard University Press, 1926.

Allen, H. C. *Great Britain and the United States, A History of Anglo-American Relations (1783-1952).* New York: St. Martin's Press, 1955.

Anderson, Bern. *Surveyor of the Sea; the Life and Voyages of Captain George Vancouver.* Toronto: University of Toronto Press, 1960.

Audain, James. *From Coalmine to Castle; the Story of the Dunsmuirs of Vancouver Island*, New York: Pageant Press, 1955.

Bancroft, Hubert H. *British Columbia, 1792-1887.* (vol. XXVII, *History of the Pacific States of North America*) . San Francisco: History Company, 1887.

——. *The Northwest Coast* (vols. XXII and XXIII, History of the Pacific States of North America) , 2 vols. San Francisco: A. L. Bancroft & Co., 1884.

Barrow, Sir John. *Voyages of Discovery and Research within the Arctic Regions, from the Year 1818 to the Present Time.* London: John Murray, 1846.

Bartlett, C. J. *Great Britain and Sea Power, 1815-1853.* Oxford: Clarendon Press, 1963.

Baxter, James P. *The Introduction of the Ironclad Warship.* Cambridge, Mass.: Harvard University Press, 1923.

Bedford, F. G. H. *The Life and Letters of Admiral Sir Frederick George Denham Bedford, G.C.B., G.C.M.G.* Printed privately, Newcastle upon Tyne, [1960].

Bennett, Geoffrey. *Coronel and Falklands.* Paperback ed., London: Pan, 1967.

Bourne, Kenneth, *Britain and the Balance of Power in North America, 1815-1908.* London: Longmans, Green, & Co.,1967.

Bradley, H. W. *The American Frontier in Hawaii, 1789-1843.* Palo Alto: Stanford University Press, 1942.

Bridge, Admiral Sir Cyprian. *Sea-Power and Other Studies.* London: Smith, Elder & Co., 1910.

Briggs, Sir John Henry. *Naval Administrations, 1827-1892.* London: Sampson Low & Co., 1897.

Brodie, Bernard. *Sea Power in the Machine Age.* Princeton: Princeton University Press, 1941.

Brookes, Jean I. *International Rivalry in the Pacific Islands, 1800-1875.* Berkeley and Los Angeles: University of California Press, 1941.

Bulloch, James D. *The Secret Service of the Confederate States in Europe or How the Confederate Cruisers Were Equipped.* 2 vols. London: R. Bentley & Son, 1883; reprint, New York and London: T. Yoseloff, 1959.

Burt, Alfred C. *The United States, Great Britain and British North America, from the Revolution to the Establishment of Peace after the War of 1812.* New Haven: Yale University Press, 1940.

Campbell, Charles S. *Anglo-American Understanding, 1898-1903.* Baltimore: John Hopkins Press, 1957.

Chevigny, Hector: *Russian America: the Great Alaskan Venture, 1741-1867.* New York: Viking Press, 1965.

Clark, Robert C. *History of the Willamette Valley, Oregon.* 2 vols. Chicago: S. J. Clarke, 1927.

Clowes, William Laird, and others. *The Royal Navy.* 7 vols. London: Sampson Low & Co., 1897-1913.

Dawson, Commander L. S., comp. *Memoirs of Hydrography . . . 1750-1885.* 2 vols. Eastbourne: Henry W. Keay, 1885.

Davidson, G. C. *The North West Company.* Berkeley: University of California Press, 1918.

Day, Vice-Admiral Sir Archibald. *The Admiralty Hydrographic Service, 1795-1919.* London: H.M.S.O., 1967.

de Kiewiet, C. W. and Underhill, F. W., eds. *The Dufferin-Carnarvon Correspondence, 1874-1878.* Toronto: Champlain Society, 1955, vol. XXXIII.

Duff, Wilson. *The Indian History of British Columbia: Volume I, the Impact of the White Man.* Victoria, B.C.; Provincial Museum, 1964.

Egerton, Mrs. Fred (Mary Augusta) . *Admiral of the Fleet Sir Geoffrey Phipps Hornby, G. C. B. A Biography.* Edinburgh: Wm. Blackwood and Sons, 1896.

England, Meteorological Office. *Monthly Meteorological Charts of the Eastern Pacific Ocean.* London, 1950.

——. *Weather in the China Seas and in the Western Part of the North Pacific Ocean.* 3 vols. London, 1945.

Findlay, Alexander G. *A Directory for the Navigation of the Pacific.* 2 parts. London: R. H. Laurie, 1851.

Galbraith, John S. *The Hudson's Bay Company as an Imperial Factor, 1821-1869.* Berkeley and Los Angeles: University of California Press, 1957.

Gluek, Alvin C., Jr. *Minnesota and the Manifest Destiny of the Canadian Northwest: A Study in Canadian-American Relations.* Toronto: University of Toronto Press, 1965.

Golder, Frank A. *Russian Expansion in the Pacific, 1641-1850.* Cleveland: Arthur H. Clark Co., 1914.

Gordon, Donald C. *The Dominion Partnership in Imperial Defense, 1870-1914.* Baltimore: John Hopkins Press, 1965.

Graebner, Norman A. *Empire on the Pacific.* New York: Ronald Press Company, 1955.

Graham, Gerald S. *Empire of the North Atlantic: The Maritime Struggle for North America.* 2nd ed.; Toronto: University of Toronto Press, 1958.

——. *The Politics of Naval Supremacy: Studies in British Maritime Ascendancy.* Cambridge: Cambridge University Press, 1965.

Greenhow, Robert. *History of Oregon and California and the Other Territories on the North-West Coast of North America.* London: John Murray, 1844.

——. *Memoir on the North West Coast of North America.* Washington: Blair & Rives, 1840.

Harlow, Neil. *The Maps of San Francisco Bay.* San Francisco: Book Club of California, 1950.

Henry, Joseph Kaye. *Flora of Southern British Columbia and Vancouver Island.* Toronto: W. J. Gage & Co. [1915].

Howay, F. W. *The Work of the Royal Engineers in British Columbia 1858 to 1863.* Victoria, B.C.: Printed by Richard Wolfenden, 1910.

——, Sage, W. N. and Angus, H. F. *British Columbia and the United States.* New Haven: Yale University Press, 1942.

——, and Scholefield, E.O.S. *British Columbia. From the Earliest Times to the Present.* 4 vols. Vancouver: S. J. Clarke, 1914.

Hussey, John A. *The History of Fort Vancouver.* Tacoma: Washington State Historical Society, 1957.

Imlah, Albert H. *Lord Ellenborough: A Biography of Edward Law, Earl of Ellenborough, Governor-General of India.* Cambridge, Mass.: Harvard Historical Studies, 1939. Vol. 43.

Innis, Harold A. *The Fur Trade in Canada.* Rev. ed., New Haven: Yale University Press, 1962.

Irving, Washington. *Astoria, or Anecdotes of an Enterprise Beyond the Rocky Mountains.* 3 vols. London: R. Bentley, 1836.

Irwin, Leonard B. *Pacific Railways and Nationalism in the Canadian-American Northwest, 1845-73.* Reprint; New York: Greenwood Press, 1968.

Jevons, W. S. *The Coal Question.* 3rd ed., rev. London: Macmillan & Co., 1906.

Johnson, Robert E. *Thence Round Cape Horn: The Story of United States Naval Forces on Pacific Station, 1818-1923.* Annapolis, Md.: United States Naval Institute, 1963.

Jones, Wilbur D. *Lord Aberdeen and the Americas.* Athens, Georgia: University of Georgia Press, 1958.

Kuykendall, R. S. *The Hawaiian Kingdom, 1778-1854.* Honolulu: University of Hawaii Press, 1938.

Lewis, Michael A. *The Navy in Transition, 1814-1864: A Social History*. London: George Allen & Unwin, 1965.

Longstaff, F. V. *Esquimalt Naval Base: A History of Its Work and Its Defences*. Victoria, B.C.: Victoria Book & Stationery Co., 1941.

——. *H.M.C.S. Naden Naval Barracks, A History of Its Work, Senior Officers, and Ships*. 2nd ed., Victoria, B.C.: Published by the Author, 1957.

Mackinder, Halford J. *Democratic Ideas and Reality: A Study in the Politics of Reconstruction*. London: Constable and Co., 1919.

McCabe, James O. *The San Juan Boundary Question*. Toronto: University of Toronto Press, 1964.

MacCain, Charles W. *History of S.S. "Beaver."* Vancouver, B.C.: 1894.

McKay, Corday. *Queen Charlotte Islands*. Victoria, B.C.: Province of British Columbia, Department of Education, 1953.

Mahan, A. T. *The Influence of Sea Power Upon History, 1660-1783*. London: Sampson Low & Co., 1890.

——. *Sea Power in its Relations to the War of 1812*. 2 vols. Boston: Little, Brown & Co., 1905.

Marder, Arthur J. *British Naval Policy, 1880-1905: The Anatomy of British Sea Power*. London: Putnam & Co., 1940.

——. *From the Dreadnought to Scapa Flow: the Royal Navy in the Fisher Era, 1904-1919*. Vol. I, *The Road to War, 1904-1914*. London: Oxford University Press, 1961.

Markham, Admiral Sir Albert H. *The Life of Sir Clements R. Markham*. London: John Murray, 1917.

Merk, Frederick. *Manifest Destiny and Mission in American History: A Reinterpretation*. New York: Knopf, 1963.

——. *The Monroe Doctrine and American Expansionism, 1843-1849*. New York: Knopf, 1966.

——. *The Oregon Question: Essays in Anglo-American Diplomacy and Politics*. Cambridge, Mass.: Belknap Press, 1967.

Miller, Hunter. *San Juan Archipelago: Study of the Joint Occupation of San Juan Island*. Bellows Falls, Vt.: Printed at the Wyndham Press, 1943.

Milton, Viscount. *History of the San Juan Water Boundary Question*. London: Cassell, Petter, and Galpin, 1869.

Morley, Lord John. *The Life of William Ewart Gladstone*. 3 vols. London: Macmillan, 1903.

Morrell, W. P. *Britain in the Pacific Islands*. Oxford: Clarendon Press, 1960.

——. *Britain Colonial Policy in the Age of Peel and Russell*. Oxford: Clarendon Press, 1930.

Morton, A. S. *A History of the Canadian West to 1870-71*. London, T. Nelson & Sons, [1939].

Morton, W. L. *The Critical Years: The Union of British North America, 1857-1873*. Toronto: McClelland & Stewart, 1964.

Murray, Keith A. *The Pig War*. Tacoma: Washington State Historical Society, 1968.

Nicholson, George. *Vancouver Island's West Coast, 1762-1962*. Victoria, B.C.: Morriss Printing Company, 1962.

Nish, Ian H. *The Anglo-Japanese Alliance: The Diplomacy of Two Island Empires, 1894-1907*. London: Athlone Press, 1966.

O'Byrne, William. *A Naval Biographical Dictionary*. London: J. Murray, 1849.

Ollivier, Maurice, ed. *The Colonial and Imperial Conferences from 1887 to 1937*. 3 vols. Ottawa, 1954.

Ormsby, Margaret A. *British Columbia: A History*. Toronto: Macmillan, 1958.

Parizeau, Henri D. *The Development of Hydrography on the Coast of Canada since the Earliest Discoveries.* Toronto: University of Toronto Press, 1934. Reprint from Pacific Science Association, *Proceedings of the Fifth Science Congress,* vol. II.

Penn, Geoffrey. *"Up Funnel, Down Screw!" The Story of the Naval Engineer.* London: Hollis & Carter, 1955.

Perkins, Dexter. *The Monroe Doctrine, 1823-1826.* Cambridge, Mass.: Harvard University Press, 1932.

———. *The Monroe Doctrine, 1826-1867.* Baltimore: The John Hopkins Press, 1933.

Platt, D. C. M. *Finance, Trade, and Politics in British Foreign Policy, 1815-1914.* Oxford: Clarendon Press, 1968.

Porter, Kenneth W. *John Jacob Astor, Business Man.* 2 vols. Cambridge, Mass.: Harvard University Press, 1931.

Preston, Richard A. *Canada and "Imperial Defense."* Durham, N.C.: Duke University Press, 1967.

Ravenstein, Ernest G. *The Russians on the Amur: its Discovery, Conquest and Colonization.* London: Trubner & Co., 1861.

Rich, E. E. *The Fur Trade and the Northwest to 1857.* Toronto: McClelland & Stewart, 1967.

———. *The History of the Hudson's Bay Company, 1670-1870.* 2 vols. London: Hudson's Bay Record Society, 1958-1959.

Ritchie, G. S. *The Admiralty Chart.* New York: American Elsevier Publishing Company, 1967.

Robinson, Leigh Burpee. *Esquimalt: "Place of Shoaling Waters."* Victoria, B.C.: Quality Press, 1947.

Roskill, Capt. S. W. *The Strategy of Sea Power: Its Development and Application.* London: Collins, 1962.

Rydell, Raymond A. *Cape Horn to the Pacific, the Rise and Decline of an Ocean Highway.* Berkeley and Los Angeles: University of California Press, 1952.

Sage, Walter N. *Sir James Douglas and British Columbia.* Toronto: University of Toronto Press, 1930.

Scholefield, Guy H. *The Pacific: its Past and Future and the Policy of the Great Powers from the 18th Century.* London: John Murray, 1919.

Seattle Historical Society. *The H. W. McCurdy Marine History of the Pacific Northwest.* Seattle, 1966.

Sellers, Charles. *James K. Polk: Continentalist, 1843-1846.* Princeton: Princeton University Press, 1966.

Sherman, Edwin A. *The Life of the Late Rear-Admiral John Drake Sloat.* Oakland, Calif.: Carruth & Carruth, 1902.

Shelton, W. George, ed. *British Columbia and Confederation.* Victoria, B.C.: Morriss Printing for the University of Victoria, 1967.

Shiels, Archie W. *San Juan Islands: The Cronstadt of the Pacific.* Juneau: Empire Printing Company, 1938.

Sprout, Harold and Margaret. *The Rise of American Naval Power, 1776-1918.* Princeton: Princeton University Press, 1939.

Spry, Irene M. *The Palliser Expedition. An Account of John Palliser's British North American Expedition, 1857-1860.* London: Macmillan, 1964.

Stacey, C. P. *Canada and the British Army, 1846-1871.* Rev. ed., Toronto: University of Toronto Press, 1963.

———. *The Military Problems of Canada: A Survey of Defence Policies and Strategic Conditions Past and Present.* Toronto: Ryerson Press, 1940.

Tansill, Charles C. *Canadian-American Relations, 1875-1911.* New Haven: Yale University Press, 1943.

Tate, Merze. *Hawaii: Reciprocity or Annexation*. East Lansing: Michigan State University Press, 1968.

Temperley, Harold W. V. *England and the Near East, The Crimea*. London: Longmans Green & Co., 1936.

——. *The Foreign Policy of Canning, 1822-1827*. London, 1925.

Tucker, Gilbert N. *The Naval Service of Canada: Its Official History*. 2 vols. Ottawa, 1952.

Van Alstyne, R. W. *The Rising American Empire*. Oxford: Basil Blackwell. 1960.

Walbran, Capt. John T. *British Columbia Coast Names, 1592-1906*. Ottawa: Government Printing Bureau, 1909.

Ward, John M. *British Policy in the South Pacific, 1783-1893: A Study in British Policy towards the South Pacific Islands prior to the Establishment of Governments by Great Powers*. Sydney: Australasian Publishing Co., 1948.

Williams, Glyndwr. *The British Search for the North West Passage in the Eighteenth Century*. London: Longmans, Green and Company, 1962.

Wilson, H. W. *Ironclads in Action*. London: Sampson Low & Co., 1896.

Winks, Robin W. *Canada and the United States: The Civil War Years*. Baltimore: The John Hopkins Press, 1960.

Woodsworth, Charles J. *Canada and the Orient: A Study in International Relations*. Toronto: Macmillan, 1941.

Wright, E. W., ed. *Lewis and Dryden's Marine History of the Pacific North-West*. Portland, Ore.: Lewis & Dryden Printing Company, 1895.

Yonge, C. D. *The History of the British Navy*. 3 vols. London: R. Bentley, 1866.

XX. Articles in Books and Periodicals

Adamov, E. A. "Russia and the United States at the Time of the Civil War," *Journal of Modern History*, II (1930), 586-602.

Adams, Ephraim D. "English Interest in the Annexation of California," *American Historical Review*, XIV (July 1909), 744-63.

Bach, John, "The Maintenance of Royal Navy Vessels in the Pacific Ocean, 1825-1875," *Mariner's Mirror*, LVI (August 1970), 259-736.

Bailey, Thomas A. "The North Pacific Sealing Convention of 1911," *Pacific Historical Review*, IV (1935), 1-14.

Ballard, Admiral G. A. "British Frigates of 1875; the 'Shah'," *Mariner's Mirror*, XX (July 1936), 305-15.

——. "The Fighting Ship from 1860-1890," *Mariner's Mirror*, XXXVIII (February 1952), 23-33.

Bartlett, C. V. "The Mid-Victorian Reappraisal of Naval Policy," in K. Bourne and D. C. Watt, eds., *Studies in International History: Essays Presented to W. Norton Medlicott* (London: Longmans, Green & Co., 1967), pp. 189-208.

Barry, J. Neilson. "San Juan Island in the Civil War," *Washington Historical Quarterly*, XX (April 1929), 134-36.

Basalla, George. "The Voyage of the *Beagle* without Darwin," *Mariner's Mirror*, XLIX (1963), 42-8.

Blue, George Vern. "France and the Oregon Question," *Oregon Historical Quarterly*, XXXIV (1933), 39-59 and 144-63.

——. "The Policy of France towards the Hawaiian Islands from the Earliest Times to the Treaty of 1846," *"Publications of the Archives of Hawaii*, no. 5, 51-93.

Bradley, Harold W. "Hawaii and the American Penetration of the Northeastern Pacific, 1800-1845," *Pacific Historical Review*, XII (September 1943), 277.

Brooke, George M., Jr. "The Vest Pocket War of Commodore Jones," *Pacific Historical Review*, XXXI (1962), 217-33.

Burns, Flora H. "The Exploits of Lieut. Mayne," *The Beaver*, Outfit 289 (Autumn 1958) , 12-17.

Campbell, Charles S., Jr. "The Bering Sea Settlements of 1892," *Pacific Historical Review*, XXXII (1963) , 347-38.

Colomb, Capt. J. C. R. "Russian Development and Our Naval and Military Position in the North Pacific," *Royal United Service Institution Journal*, XXI (1878) , 659-707.

Coughlin, Sister Magdalen. "California Ports: A Key to Diplomacy for the West Coast." *Journal of the West*, V (April 1966) , 153-71.

Davidson, D. C. "Relation of the Hudson's Bay Company with the Russian American Company on the Northwest Coast, 1829-1867," *British Columbia Historical Quarterly*, V (January 1941) , 33-51.

——. "The War Scare of 1854: The Pacific Coast and the Crimean War," *"British Columbia Historical Quarterly*, V (October 1941) , 243-54.

de Thierry, C. "Naval Bases of the Empire: Esquimalt and Halifax," *Windsor Magazine*, 1907, 593-600.

Dyer, Brainerd. "Confederate Naval and Privateering Activities in the Pacific," *Pacific Historical Review*, III (1934) , 433-443.

Elliot, T. C. "British Values in Oregon, 1847," *Oregon Historical Quarterly*, XXXII (March 1931) , 27-45.

Fish, Andrew. "The Last Phase of the Oregon Boundary Question: The Struggle for San Juan Island," *Quarterly of the Oregon Historical Society*, XXII (September 1921) , 161-224.

Galbraith, John S. "The Early History of the Puget's Sound Agricultural Company, 1838-1843," *Oregon Historical Quarterly*, LV (1954) , 234-59.

——. "Fitzgerald versus the Hudson's Bay Company: the Founding of Vancouver Island," *British Columbia Historical Quarterly*, XVI (1952) , 191-207.

——. "France as a Factor in the Oregon Negotiations," *Pacific Northwest Quarterly*, XLIV (April 1953) , 69-73.

——. "A Note on the British Fur Trade in California, 1821-1846," *Pacific Historical Review*, XXIV (1955) , 253-60.

——. "Perry McDonough Collins at the Colonial Office," *British Columbia Historical Quarterly*, XVII (1953) , 207-14.

Gates, Charles M. "The West in American Diplomacy, 1812-15," *Mississippi Valley Historical Review*, XXVI (1939-40) , 499-510.

Gilbert, Benjamin F. "Rumours of Confederate Privateers Operating in Victoria, Vancouver Island," *British Columbia Historical Quarterly*, XVIII (1954) , 239-55.

Golder, Frank A. "Proposals for Russian Occupation of the Hawaiian Islands," *Publications of the Archives of Hawaii*, no. 5, 39-50.

——. "Russian-American Relations during the Crimean War," *American Historical Review*, XXXI (1926) , 462-76.

——. "The Russian Fleet and the Civil War," *American Historical Review*, XX (July 1915) , 801-14.

Gordon, Donald C. "The Admiralty and Dominion Navies, 1902-1914," *Journal of Modern History*, XXXIII (1961) , 407-22.

Gosnell, R. E. "Pacific Province: Colonial History, 1849-1871," in *Canada and Its Provinces*. 23 vols. (Toronto, 1914) , XXI, 75-178.

Gough, Barry M. "H.M.S. *America* on the North Pacific Coast," *Oregon Historical Quarterly*, LXX (December 1969) , 292-311.

——. "The Records of the Royal Navy's Pacific Station," *Journal of Pacific History*, IV (1969) , 146-53.

Graebner, Norman A. "American Interest in California, 1845," *Pacific Historical Review,* XX (1953) , 13-28.

——. "Maritime Factors in the Oregon Compromise," *Pacific Historical Review,* XX (November 1951) , 331-46.

Graham, Gerald S. "The Transition from Paddle-Wheel to Screw Propeller," *Mariner's Mirror,* XLIV (1958) , 35-48.

"H.M.C.S. 'Rainbow'," *British Columbia Magazine,* VI (November 1910) , 1005-1010.

Hacking, Norman. "Paddlewheels and British Oak on the North Pacific," *The Beaver,* Outfit 265 (March 1935) , 25-8.

Howay, F. W. "An Outline Sketch of the Maritime Fur Trade," *Canadian Historical Association, Annual Report, 1932* (Toronto, 1932) , 5-14.

Ireland, Willard E. "The Evolution of the Boundaries of British Columbia," *British Columbia Historical Quarterly,* III (October 1939) , 263-82.

——. "Pre-Confederation Defence Problems of the Pacific Colonies," *Canadian Historical Association Annual Report, 1941* (Toronto, 1941) , 41-54.

Jackson, C. Ian. "The Stikine Territory Lease and Its Relevance to the Alaska Purchase," *Pacific Historical Review,* XXXVI (August 1967) , 289-306.

Jones, J. Michael. "The Railroad Healed the Breach," *Canadian Geographical Journal,* LXXIII (September 1966) , 98-101.

Jones, Jr., Oakah L. "The [U.S.] Pacific Squadron and the Conquest of California, 1846-1847," *Journal of the West,* V (April 1966) , 187-202.

Jones, Wilbur D. and J. C. Vison. "British Preparedness and the Oregon Settlement," *Pacific Historical Review,* XX (November 1953) , 353-63.

Jordon, Mabel E. "H.M.C. Dockyard, Esquimalt," *Canadian Geographical Journal,* L (April 1955) , 124-32.

Judson, Katherine. "British Side of the Restoration of Oregon," *Oregon Historical Quarterly,* XX (1919) , 243-60 and 305-30.

Kemble, John H. "Coal from the Northwest Coast, 1848-1850," *British Columbia Historical Quarterly,* II (April 1938) , 123-30.

Knaplund, Paul. "James Stephen on Granting Vancouver Island to the Hudson's Bay Company, 1846-1848," *British Columbia Historical Quarterly,* IX (October 1945) , 259-71.

——. "Letters from James Edward Fitzgerald to W. E. Gladstone Concerning Vancouver Island and the Hudson's Bay Company," *British Columbia Historical Quarterly* XIII (January 1949) , 1-21.

Knox, B. A. "Colonial Influence on Imperial Policy, 1858-1866; Victoria and the Colonial Naval Defence Act, 1865," *Historical Studies: Australia and New Zealand,* XI (November 1963) , 61-79.

Laing, Lionel H. "An Unauthorized Admiralty Court in British Columbia," *Washington Historical Quarterly,* XXVI (1935) , 10-15.

Lamb, W. Kaye. "Early Lumbering on Vancouver Island," *British Columbia Historical Quarterly,* II (1938) , 31-53 and 95-121.

——. "The Founding of Fort Victoria," *British Columbia Historical Quarterly,* VII (April 1943) , 71-92.

——. "The Governorship of Richard Blanshard," *British Columbia Historical Quarterly,* XIV (1950) , 1-40.

Laurie, Maj.-Gen. J. W. "The Protection of our Naval Base in the North Pacific," *Journal of the Royal United Service Institution,* XXVIII (1883) , 357-81.

Leader, H. A. "McLoughlin's Answer to the Warre Report," *Oregon Historical Quarterly,* XXXIII (September 1932) , 214-29.

Lewis, Michael. "An Eye-Witness at Petropaulovski, 1854," *Mariner's Mirror,* XLIX (November 1963) , 265-72.

Lincoln, A. "The Beechey Expedition Visits San Francisco, *Pacific Discovery*, XXII (1969), 1-8.

Long, John W., Jr. "The Origin and Development of the San Juan Island Water Boundary Controversy," *Pacific Northwest Quarterly*, XLIII (July 1952), 187-213.

Longstaff, F. V. "The Centenary of the Pacific Station, 1837-1937," *British Columbia Historical Quarterly*, III (1939), 221-23.

——. "H.M.S. Ganges, 1821 to 1929," *Canadian Defence Quarterly* (July 1929), 487-92.

——. "Notes on the Early History of the Pacific Station and the Inception of the Esquimalt Royal Naval Establishment," *Canadian Defence Quarterly*, III (April 1926), 309-18.

——. "Notes on the History of the Pacific Station from the Colonial Period and the Early Period of Confederation until the Regular Service Across Canada of the C.P.R. in 1887," *Canadian Defence Quarterly*, IV (April 1927), 292-309.

——. "Spanish Naval Bases and Ports on the Pacific Coast of Mexico, 1513-1883," *British Columbia Historical Quarterly*, XVI (1952), 181-9.

——. and Lamb, W. Kaye. "The Royal Navy on the Northwest Coast, 1813-1850," *British Columbia Historical Quarterly*, IX (1945), 1-24 and 113-28.

McKelvie, B. A. "The Founding of Nanaimo," *British Columbia Historical Quarterly*, VIII (July 1944), 169-88.

Maxwell, J. A. "Lord Dufferin and the Difficulties with British Columbia, 1874-77," *Canadian Historical Review*, XII (December 1931), 364-87.

Merk, Frederick. "British Government Propaganda and the Oregon Treaty," *American Historical Review*, XL (October 1934), 38-62.

——. "British Party Politics and the Oregon Treaty," *American Historical Review*, XXXVII (July 1932), 653-77.

——. "The Genesis of the Oregon Question," *Mississippi Valley Historical Review*, XXXVI (1950), 583-612.

——. "The Oregon Pioneers and the Boundary," *American Historical Review*, XXIX (July 1924), 681-99.

Miller, Hunter. "Russian Opinion on the Cession of Alaska," *American Historical Review*, XLVIII (April 1943), 521-32.

Morton, Arthur S. "The North West Company's Columbian Enterprise and David Thompson," *Canadian Historical Review*, XVII (September 1936), 266-88.

Nasatir, A. P. "International Rivalry for California and the Establishment of the British Consulate," *California Historical Society Quarterly*, XLVI (March 1967), 53-70.

Nichols, Irby C., Jr. "The Russian Ukase and the Monroe Doctrine: A Re-evaluation," *Pacific Historical Review*, XXXVI (February 1967), 13-26.

O'Neil, Marion. "The Maritime Activities of the North West Company, 1813-1821," *Washington Historical Quarterly*, XXI (October 1930), 243-67.

Paul, Rodman W. "'Old Californians' in British Gold Fields," *Huntington Library Quarterly*, XVII (1954), 161-72.

Porter, Kenneth W. "The Cruise of the *Forester*," *Washington Historical Quarterly*, XXIII (1932), 261-85.

Ramm, Agatha. "The Crimean War," in *The Zenith of European Power, 1830-1870*, vol. X of *The New Cambridge Modern History* (Cambridge: Cambridge University Press, 1967), 487-92.

Reddaway, W. F. "The Crimean War and the French Alliance, 1853-1858," in A. W. Ward and G. P. Gooch, eds., *The Cambridge History of British Foreign Policy*. 3 vols. (Cambridge: Cambridge University Press, 1923), II, 357-402.

Rose, J. Holland. "Sea Power and the Winning of British Columbia," *Mariner's Mirror*, VII (March 1921), 74-79.

Ross, Frank E. "The Retreat of the Hudson's Bay Company in the Pacific North-west," *Canadian Historical Review,* XVIII (September 1937), 262-80.

Roy, Reginald H. "The Early Militia and Defence of British Columbia, 1871-1885," *British Columbia Historical Quarterly,* XVIII (1954), 1-28.

Sage, Walter N. "Canada on the Pacific: 1866-1925," *Washington Historical Quarterly,* XVII (April 1926), 91-104.

——. "The Gold Colony of British Columbia," *Canadian Historical Review,* II (1921), 340-59.

Schafer, Joseph. "The British Attitude toward the Oregon Question, 1815-1846," *American Historical Review,* XVI (January 1911), 273-299.

Schurman, Donald M. "Esquimalt: Defence Problem, 1865-1887," *British Columbia Historical Quarterly,* XIX (1955), 57-69.

Senior, W. "The Treasure Frigate 'Thetis'," *Mariner's Mirror,* II (February 1912), 33-37.

Smith, Goldwin. "Notes on the Problems of San Juan," *Pacific Northwest Quarterly,* XXXI (1940), 181-86.

Stacey, C. P. "The Hudson's Bay Company and Anglo-American Military Rivalries during the Oregon Dispute," *Canadian Historical Review,* XVIII (September 1937), 281-300.

——. "The Myth of the Unguarded Frontier, 1815-1871," *American Historical Review,* LVI (October 1950), 1-18.

Stewart, Alice R. "Sir John A. Macdonald and the Imperial Defence Commission of 1879," *Canadian Historical Review,* XXXV (June 1954), 119-39.

Story, D. A. "H.M. Naval Yard, Halifax in the Early Sixties," *Collections of the Nova Scotia Historical Society,* XXII (1933), 43-71.

Tate, Merze. "British Opposition to the Cession of Pearl Harbour," *Pacific Historical Review,* XXIX (November 1960), 380-94.

——. "Hawaii: A Symbol of Anglo-American Rapprochement," *Political Science Quar-terly,* LXXIX (December 1964), 555-75.

——. "Great Britain and the Sovereignty of Hawaii," *Pacific Historical Review,* XXXI (1962), 327-48.

——. "Twisting the Lion's Tail over Hawaii," *Pacific Historical Review,* XXXVI (February 1967), 27-46.

"The Transfer of Esquimalt," *British Columbia Magazine,* VI (November 1910), 1011-14.

Tunen, Alfred. "The Dispute over the San Juan Island Water Boundary," *Washing-ton Historical Quarterly,* XXIII (1932), 38-46, 133-37, 196-204, and 286-300.

Tyler, David B. "The Wilkes Expedition: The First United States Exploring Expedi-tion, 1838-1842," *Memoirs of the American Philosophical Society,* vol. LXXIII (1968).

Van Alstyne, Richard W. "Great Britain, the United States, and Hawaiian Indepen-dence, 1850-1855," *Pacific Historical Review,* IV (1935), 15-24.

——. "International Rivalries in the Pacific Northwest," *Oregon Historical Quarterly,* XLVI (1945), 185-218.

Vevier, Charles. "American Continentalism: An Idea of Expansion, 1845-1910," *Ameri-can Historical Review,* LXV (January 1960), 323-35.

Wells, Samuel F., Jr. "British Strategic Withdrawal from the Western Hemisphere, 1904-1906," *Canadian Historical Review,* XLIX (December 1968), 335-56.

Wolfenden, Madge. "Esquimalt Dockyard's First Buildings," *British Columbia His-torical Quarterly,* X (July 1946), 235-40.

INDEX